RACE, ETHNICITY, AND AMERICAN DECLINE

This book explores the deterioration of the promise of the American dream, particularly for Black Americans. Cal Jillson traces the source and cause of that decline to race prejudice, first in the stark form of human slavery and later in various forms of racial and ethnic discrimination, that has distorted American progress over the past four centuries and now portends American decline. Employing historical analysis of race and ethnicity in American life from colonial to modern times, the chapters examine the various understandings of race and ethnicity in American public life and politics and ask what those understandings imply for political and policy approaches to addressing injustice and restoring the American dream. Drawing on sources from political science, history, sociology, and economics, this book will supplement a main text in upper division courses on race and ethnicity, political sociology, public opinion, demography, and public policy.

Cal Jillson is Professor of Political Science at Southern Methodist University. He is the author or editor of 14 books including *American Government: Political Development and Institutional Change* (12th ed., 2023), *Texas Politics: Governing the Lone Star State* (9th ed., 2024), *Lone Star Tarnished: A Critical Look at Texas Politics and Public Policy* (4th ed., 2021), and *The American Dream in History, Politics, and Fiction* (2016).

RACE, ETHNICITY, AND AMERICAN DECLINE

Cal Jillson

Southern Methodist University

NEW YORK AND LONDON

Designed cover image: Getty/ ANDREY DENISYUK

First published 2024
by Routledge
605 Third Avenue, New York, NY 10158

and by Routledge
4 Park Square, Milton Park, Abingdon, Oxon, OX14 4RN

Routledge is an imprint of the Taylor & Francis Group, an informa business

© 2024 Cal Jillson

The right of Cal Jillson to be identified as author of this work has been asserted in accordance with sections 77 and 78 of the Copyright, Designs and Patents Act 1988.

All rights reserved. No part of this book may be reprinted or reproduced or utilised in any form or by any electronic, mechanical, or other means, now known or hereafter invented, including photocopying and recording, or in any information storage or retrieval system, without permission in writing from the publishers.

Trademark notice: Product or corporate names may be trademarks or registered trademarks, and are used only for identification and explanation without intent to infringe.

Library of Congress Cataloging-in-Publication Data
Names: Jillson, Calvin C., 1949– author.
Title: Race, ethnicity, and American decline / Cal Jillson.
Description: New York, NY : Routledge, 2024. | Includes bibliographical
  references and index. | Summary: "Historical overview of racial
  discrimination in the United States"—Provided by publisher.
Identifiers: LCCN 2023037785 (print) | LCCN 2023037786 (ebook) |
  ISBN 9781032582399 (hardback) | ISBN 9781032582382 (paperback) |
  ISBN 9781003449188 (ebook)
Subjects: LCSH: Racism—United States—History. | Racism—United States—
  Political aspects. | Political culture—United States. | African Americans—
  United States—Social conditions—History. | United States—Politics and
  government. | Race relations—United States—Political aspects.
Classification: LCC E184.A1 J447 2024 (print) | LCC E184.A1 (ebook) |
  DDC 305.800973—dc23/eng/20231002
LC record available at https://lccn.loc.gov/2023037785
LC ebook record available at https://lccn.loc.gov/2023037786

ISBN: 978-1-032-58239-9 (hbk)
ISBN: 978-1-032-58238-2 (pbk)
ISBN: 978-1-003-44918-8 (ebk)

DOI: 10.4324/9781003449188

Typeset in Sabon
by Apex CoVantage, LLC

"There is no room for injustice anywhere in the American mansion. But there is always room for understanding toward those who see the old ways crumbling. And to them today I say simply this: It must come. It is right that it should come."

President Lyndon Baines Johnson at the signing
of the Voting Rights Act August 6, 1965

CONTENTS

List of Figures	*ix*
List of Tables	*xi*
About the Author	*xii*
Other Books by Cal Jillson	*xiii*
Acknowledgments	*xiv*
Preface	*xv*

1 Racial Orders and the Structure of American Life	1
2 Demographic Stability and Change in American History	29
3 Citizenship, Suffrage, and Race in America	65
4 Race, Ethnicity, and the American Mind	100
5 Race, Education, and Social Competition	132
6 Income, Wealth, and Race in America	161
7 Race and Health in America	195
8 Housing, Neighborhoods, and Opportunity's Environmental Context	226

9 Race, Ethnicity, and the Criminal Justice System   255

10 Social Justice and the Modern American Promise:
    The Way Forward   282

Index   *303*

FIGURES

2.1	Percent of U.S. Population by Decade, Race, and Ethnicity, 1610–2060	47
2.2	Percent of U.S. Black Population Living in the South, 1900–2021	51
3.1	Percent Reported Registered in Presidential Elections by Race and Ethnicity, 1968–2020	81
3.2	Percent Reported Voting in Presidential Elections by Race and Ethnicity, 1964–2020	82
3.3	Percent of Votes Cast in Presidential Elections by Race and Ethnicity, 1948–2020	83
3.4	Percent Voting Democrat in Presidential Elections by Race and Ethnicity, 1948–2020	84
3.5	Number of Black, Hispanic, and Asian Members of Congress, 1953–2023	90
3.6	Would You Vote for a Black Man for President, 1958–2020	91
4.1	American Opinion on Interracial Marriage (Approve), 1958–2021	106
4.2	Public Officials Don't Care What People Think (Percent Responding Agree), 1952–2020	109
4.3	Race Relations Will Always Be a Problem, 1963–2021	110
4.4	How Satisfied with How Blacks Are Treated, 2001–2021	111
4.5	Are New Civil Rights Laws Needed?, 1993–2020	113
4.6	Do Blacks Have Equal Access to Jobs with Whites?, 1963–2021	116

Figures

5.1	Illiteracy Among Blacks and Whites in the U.S., 1870–1979	138
5.2	High School Completion by Age (25–29), Race, and Ethnicity, 1920–2022	143
6.1	Regional Per Capita Income as a Percentage of U.S. Per Capita Income, 1840–1950	171
6.2	Median Income of Families by Race and Ethnicity, 1947–2021 (in 2021 dollars)	175
6.3	Black and Hispanic Male Income as a Proportion of White Male Income, 1948–2021 (in 2021 dollars)	176
6.4	Civilian Labor Force Participation by Race, Ethnicity, and Gender, 1948–2021	180
6.5	Unemployment Rate by Race and Ethnicity, 1948–2021	182
6.6	Poverty Status of People in Families by Race and Ethnicity, 1959–2021	183
6.7	Family Median Net Worth by Race and Ethnicity, 1983–2019 (in thousands of 2019 dollars)	187
7.1	Life Expectancy by Race and Gender, 1900–2021	208
7.2	U.S. Infant Mortality Per 1,000 Live Births by Race, 1915–2020	211
7.3	Age-Adjusted Death Rates by Race and Gender, 1900–2020	213
7.4	Percent of Americans Without Health Insurance by Race and Ethnicity, 1987–2021	214
8.1	Dissimilarity Index and Isolation Index, 1890–2000	232
8.2	Home Ownership Rates by Race and Ethnicity, 1870–2021	242
8.3	Median Price of Houses as a Multiple of Median Income by Race, 1963–2021	245
9.1	U.S. State and Federal Prison Population by Race and Ethnicity, 1923–2021	264
9.2	Incarceration Rates by Race and Ethnicity, 1923–2021	266

TABLES

2.1 U.S. Population Growth by Decade, Race, and Ethnicity, 1610–2060   44
2.2 Immigration and Black Migration by Decade, 1820–2020   50
2.3 U.S. Total Fertility Rate by Race and Ethnicity, 1940–2021   55
2.4 Components of Population Change in the U.S., 1950–2020, with Projections to 2060   56
5.1 Enrollment in Elementary, Secondary, and Post-Secondary Schools, 1869–2023 (in thousands)   136
5.2 Percent of Black Elementary and Secondary School Students Going to School with Any White Students in Eleven Southern States, 1954–1973   146
5.3 Percent of Persons 25 to 29 with B.A. or Higher by Race and Ethnicity, 1940–2022   151
7.1 Infant Deaths Among Enslaved Women as a Percent of Total Population and Deaths, 1850   201
8.1 Indices of Racial Dissimilarity in Selected Northern and Southern Cities, 1860–2020   234
9.1 Lynchings in the United States, 1882–1962   261
9.2 Lynchings by U.S. Region, 1882–1962   261
9.3 Persons Executed in the U.S. by Race and Ethnicity, 1608–2022   271
9.4 Executions Per Decade under Civil Authority, 1890–2020   272
9.5 Executions by Region, 1976–2022   272

ABOUT THE AUTHOR

Cal Jillson received his Ph.D. in Government and Politics from the University of Maryland, College Park, in 1979. He taught at Louisiana State University (1980–1987) and the University of Colorado (1987–1995). Professor Jillson chaired the Department of Political Science at the University of Colorado, Boulder, from 1989 to 1993, before joining the faculty of Southern Methodist University in July 1995, where he served as Chair in the Department of Political Science and Director of the John G. Tower Center for Political Studies from 1995 to 2001. He is the author of eight books and editor of six more. His recent books are *American Government: Political Development and Institutional Change* (12th ed., 2023), *Texas Politics: Governing the Lone Star State* (9th ed., 2024), *Lone Star Tarnished: A Critical Look at Texas Politics and Public Policy* (4th ed., 2021), and *The American Dream in History, Politics, and Fiction* (2016). He speaks frequently to civic, corporate, and professional groups and is interviewed by the media hundreds of times each year.

OTHER BOOKS BY CAL JILLSON

Authored:
- *Constitution-Making: Conflict and Consensus in the Federal Convention of 1787* (1988)
- *Congressional Dynamics: Structure, Coordination, and Choice in the First American Congress, 1744-1789*, with Rick K. Wilson (1994)
- *American Government: Political Change and Institutional Development* (1999, 12th ed. 2023)
- *Pursuing the American Dream: Opportunity and Exclusion over Four Centuries* (2004)
- *Texas Politics: Governing the Lone Star State* (2007, 9th ed. 2024)
- *Lone Star Tarnished: A Critical Look at Texas Politics and Public Policy* (2012, 4th ed. 2021)
- *The American Dream in History, Politics, and Fiction* (2016)
- *American Government: Constitutional Democracy under Pressure* (2018, 2nd ed. 2021)

Edited:
- *The Dynamics of American Politics: Approaches and Interpretations*, with Lawrence C. Dodd (1994)
- *New Perspectives on American Politics*, with Lawrence C. Dodd (1994)
- *Pathways to Democracy: The Political Economy of Democratic Transitions*, with James F. Hollifield (2000)
- *Taiwan's National Security: Dilemmas and Opportunities*, with Alexander C. Tan and Steve Chan (2001)
- *Perspectives on American Government: Readings in Political Development and Institutional Change*, with David Brian Robertson (2010, 2nd ed. 2014)

ACKNOWLEDGMENTS

As always, many people and institutions play critical roles in the completion of a book. My wife Jane held the world at bay while I focused, often selfishly, on the tasks at hand. The team at Routledge, led by Leanne Hinves, Jacqueline Dorsey, and Alex Landucci, improved the book and ran a smooth and orderly review and production process. Lusana Taylor-Khan handled the delicate editorial work with light but steady hand. Southern Methodist University, through its Political Science Department and Dedman College of Arts and Sciences, provided a sabbatical during the spring 2022 semester that was very well-timed. Chris Carberry of the Political Science Department provided great help with manuscript preparation and with the presentation of tables and figures. Perhaps the broadest debt owed at the end of a process like this is to all of those scholars that went before, honored in the footnotes, who offered evidence, ideas, and interpretations that I was able to puzzle over as I looked for my own way through the thicket.

PREFACE

> "Now this brings us to two things. . . . the American Negro's experience of life, and . . . the American dream. . . . It would be hard to find any two things more absolutely opposed."
> James Baldwin, 1964, "The Uses of the Blues"

Most Americans are concerned and many are deeply worried that the health and stability of our democracy and the standing and role of our nation in the world are compromised.[1] Old assumptions and comfortable certainties about the fundamental fairness of our society and the essential goodness of its actions in the world have been shaken. These doubts and concerns are justified, but their origins are not fully appreciated. They derive, I will argue, from long-standing and deep racial and ethnic rifts in our society that have sapped our cohesion, purpose, and direction. Half a century ago, the historian Donald Robinson declared that "the basic issue" facing the Founding generation and their successors in the early national period "was relations between the races, and it is because of reluctance to confront this issue squarely that American democracy has been unable to solve its greatest and continuing crisis by political means."[2] It is time to take this insight seriously and to explore its implications for our nation's history and future.

To make Robinson's point somewhat more broadly, we might simply say that despite tremendous changes in our nation over the course of its history, we remain divided, hobbled, and increasingly enervated by racial and ethnic tensions and inequalities. While White supremacy had, until recently, been driven underground in America, inequalities of opportunity and result in incomes, wealth, education, health, housing, and justice by race and ethnicity have remained glaring. Even if we are willing to absolve the Founders of their reluctance to confront racism, seeing them as good men from another time, what are we to say of ourselves?

The historic conflict between our principles – liberty, equality, opportunity, and the rule of law – and our practices – slavery, segregation, and ongoing discrimination – is too stark to deny. That the promise of the country has been offered to some and withheld from others also is undeniable. These public facts explain why the American dream, the claim that opportunity was open to all willing to prepare well and work hard, has always been touted by political, social, and economic elites, and either demanded as a promise unfulfilled or scorned as a lie by the excluded and the oppressed. As James Baldwin noted in the headnote to this Preface, few elements of American life are more "absolutely opposed" than the promise of the American dream and the reality of Black life. Black people, of course, have not been alone in their exclusion and estrangement from the American dream. Native Americans joined them in misery from the earliest days and in this book we add Hispanics, Asians, and others as they enter our national story.

Race, Ethnicity, and American Decline explores the extent to which race prejudice, first in the stark forms of native displacement and human slavery and later in various manifestations of racial and ethnic discrimination, has distorted American growth and development over the past four centuries and now portends American decline. We feel the gathering danger in our collective bones. While the challenges we face are both foreign and domestic, American leaders from George Washington to Abraham Lincoln, Franklin D. Roosevelt, Ronald Reagan, and many others have argued that foreign threats could be managed as long as our common commitment to the Constitution and to democratic principles and norms remained strong. Few would argue today that our domestic ideals and institutions do remain strong. In fact, Ken Hersh, President of the George W. Bush Presidential Center, at the center's tenth anniversary in 2023, warned that: "we find ourselves in a two-front war. We have dangerous external adversaries at a time when those inside our country begin to doubt . . . the very institutions that are designed to support our democracy here at home."[3] So we focus in this book on how racial and ethnic tensions have weakened our senses of national meaning and purpose and how resolving, or at least ameliorating, them might repair our doubts and reduce our vulnerabilities.

Race as an Architectural Flaw in the American Republic

The Founders well knew that great nations fail and fall. With Rome always in mind, they did what they could within the republican tradition to balance and protect liberty and security for White men and their families. But in compromises they felt compelled to make by political, economic, and social realities, they built human slavery into the constitutional and legal design of the new nation. In the oft-told story of Benjamin Franklin leaving the Constitutional Convention of 1787 on its final day, a concerned citizen asked what kind of government had been given them. Franklin replied cryptically, "A republic, if you can keep it." Franklin could afford to be cryptic because he was confident that the citizen knew that he was referring to collapse of the Roman republic into Caesar's imperium. The citizen likely nodded knowingly and somewhat ruefully. Both the great Dr. Franklin and the anonymous citizen knew that founding a republic was a mere prelude to the struggle to maintain it in peace and prosperity.

Later generations of Americans, including our own, also have been unsettled by Franklin's sobering admonition. The challenge, even warning, in the phrase "A republic, if you can keep it" has darkened American minds in many periods of international threat and domestic instability. Recently, the historian Edward J. Watts' *Mortal Republic: How Rome Fell into Tyranny* again sounded this old alarm. Watts wrote: "Roman history could not more clearly show that, when citizens look away as their leaders engage in . . . corrosive behaviors, . . . condoning political obstruction and courting political violence, . . . their republic is in mortal danger."[4] Rome fascinated the Founding generation and many today because it rose so high and fell so far. Are we Rome? Perhaps! The insurrection at the Capitol on January 6, 2021 suggested to many that we stand on the precipice, but we are not yet fallen.

The great lesson of Roman history is that nations remain strong and confident when they maintain a level of cohesion, a broad agreement on principles, traditions, and goals that most, even if never all, citizens share. Shared values do not preclude disagreement and division, sometimes deep and protracted, but they are the glue that limit divisions and pull the nation back together when they abate. David Brooks, the *New York Times* opinion columnist, wrote in a piece entitled, "This Is How Truth Dies," that "Great nations thrive by constantly refreshing" a reservoir of shared history, ideals, and stories of challenges met and matched. In our case, those shared commitments and convictions refresh "knowledge of who we are as a people, how we got here, . . . what we find admirable and dishonorable, what kind of world we hope to build together." If the reservoir runs dry, shared convictions and commitments weaken and divisions widen. Brooks concluded by observing that, "Today many of us feel that America is suffering an epistemic crisis. We don't see the same reality."[5] This loss of shared purpose, direction, and mission disrupts efforts in domestic politics, blocking solutions to issues like rising inequality, poor schools, and an ineffectual pandemic response; and leadership in international politics, blocking solutions to issues like climate change, global poverty, and the spread of autocracy.[6]

Our own leaders and public, to say nothing of world leaders and their publics, sense U.S. confusion and decline.[7] Joe Biden told reporters during the first news conference of his presidency that he saw "a battle between the utility of democracies in the twenty-first century and autocracies," that we must win in order to "prove that democracy works."[8] Ominously, in late 2023, the leaders of thirteen presidential centers, foundations, or libraries, all but one from Hoover through Obama, felt the need to call for a "commitment to the principles of democracy."[9] Long-held presumptions, even articles of faith, now need to be proven again. Friends are worried too. The scuttled U.S. withdrawal from Afghanistan in summer 2021 led to questions of American commitment and competence, but it has been domestic instability that has caused the greatest concern. In November 2021, the American delegation to the annual Halifax International Security Forum, got an earful from worried allies about the strength of our democracy. With the January 6 Capitol insurrection clearly in mind, former Australian prime minister Malcolm Turnbull said: "When you see the absolute essential foundations of the democracy being challenged from within, and where you see a political party, the Republican Party – not all of them, but many of them – actually challenging the constitutional institutions on which this great democracy of well over two centuries depends, that's what really undermines public international faith in American democracy."[10]

Some of the damage to our international reputation and standing was repaired when the Russians invaded Ukraine, sparking a remarkable Ukrainian resistance and opening the door to U.S. leadership of NATO's dramatic resurgence. But as the Ukrainian military and people stood their ground, absorbing the initial Russian advance and then pushing it back on several fronts, a disturbing question arose in many minds – could we, would we, fight like that if pressed? Or are the big lie of a stolen election and the scenes of the January 6 invasion of the Capitol wounds too deep to allow us to pull together even in an emergency? Many Americans worry that they are, and our leaders seem, at best, uncertain.[11] In the wake of another senseless mass shooting in May 2022, this time by a White supremacist targeting Black shoppers in a Buffalo supermarket, President Biden visited the city to console the bereaved and to warn the nation that: "The American experiment in democracy is in danger. . . . Hate and fear are being given too much oxygen by those . . . who don't understand America."[12] Sadly, and maybe ominously, those who Biden said don't understand America are themselves Americans.

While Biden sees a fight to vindicate democracy and stabilize America's place in a changing world, "China is increasingly sure that America is in long-term, irreversible, decline, . . . that 'the East is rising, and the West is in decline,' as Chinese leaders put it."[13] In one early meeting between senior Biden administration diplomats and Chinese diplomats, the Chinese argued that the U.S. "had no right to lecture others on human rights abuses or the preservation of democracy. They talked about Black Lives Matter, and the contradictions in an American democratic system that leaves so many behind."[14] Like Russia and much of the developing world, China sees domestic racial tensions and divisions as America's key domestic weakness. Our first instinct, of course, is to reject any criticism that authoritarians may offer, but the fact that opponents point to a weakness does not mean that it is not a weakness. We know that racial and ethnic divisions have long plagued our nation and so we should act decisively to address them for our own sake as well as to disappoint gleeful predictions of our decline.

Race in the American Mind

Throughout American history, whether in the long eras of slavery and Jim Crow, or in our own day, many White Americans have seen the status and place of Black Americans as natural and appropriate, as earned, rather than as wrongly imposed and unjust. Black leaders have always been uncertain about how to attack the smug complacency of White supremacy. In 1785, Thomas Jefferson famously declared his suspicion that Black people were intellectually inferior to White people. In 1791, Benjamin Banneker, a Black mathematician and author, sent Jefferson a long plea, fifteen-paragraphs, urging his fair assessment of Black potential; saying "we are a race of Beings . . . considered rather as brutish than human, and scarcely capable of mental endowments." Banneker asked Jefferson to "embrace every opportunity to eradicate that train of absurd and false opinions." Jefferson replied, almost unintelligibly, with a single paragraph, praising Banneker's accomplishments, but offering little solace and only the most ambiguous aid; saying, "I can add with truth that nobody wishes more ardently to see a good system commenced for raising the condition both of their body and mind to what it ought to be, as fast as the imbecility of their present existence, and other circumstances which cannot be neglected, will admit."[15]

Subsequent Black leaders have been equally dismayed by White perceptions of their people's nature and capacities. Before the Civil War, speaking to the Colored National Convention at Rochester in July 1853, Frederick Douglass lamented the fact that: "Our white fellow-countrymen do not know us. They are strangers to our character, ignorant of our capacity, oblivious to our history and progress, and are misinformed as to the principles and ideas that control and guide us as a people."[16] In 1897, W.E.B. Du Bois delivered an address before the Negro Academy entitled, "The Conservation of Races," in which he asked, and not just for himself: "Am I an American or am I a Negro? Can I be both? Or is it my duty to cease to be a Negro as soon as possible and be an American?"[17] Du Bois knew that ceasing to be a Negro was not possible, that America would not allow it; so did that mean that Negroes could not be Americans? The Black activist and author James Baldwin also despaired of the enveloping Black experience of rejection; writing, "I'm talking about what happens to you if . . . you watch your children growing up and no matter what you do, no matter *what* you do, you are powerless, you are really powerless, against the force of the world that is out to tell your child that he has no right to be alive. . . . I don't know what 'the Negro problem' means to white people, but this is what it means to Negroes."[18]

As if in answer to the cries of Black leaders from Banneker to Baldwin, Martin Luther King declared: "White America must recognize that justice for black people cannot be achieved without radical changes in the structure of our society. The comfortable, the entrenched, the privileged cannot continue to tremble at the prospect of change in the status quo."[19] But support for change has been thin and resistance common because many White people do not tremble; they steel themselves for defense of what they believe they have earned and they look at others, especially Black people, as already having what they have earned.

Not surprisingly, some Black leaders have concluded that the wall of White denial that has long met their pleas and demands is simply unbreachable. Derrick Bell, Harvard law professor and one of the founders of the now famous analytical perspective called "critical race theory," declared that "*Black people will never gain full equality in this country.*" Bell made the critical point that the full effect even of great civil rights advances like the end of slavery and the dismantling of Jim Crow have tended to slip away as the old presumptions of White supremacy reasserted themselves and traditional patterns of privilege adapt and return in new shapes and forms. Looking forward, he predicted that: "*Even those herculean efforts we hail as successful will produce no more than temporary 'peaks of progress,' short-lived victories that slide into irrelevance as racial patterns adapt in ways that maintain white dominance.*"[20]

Is There a Path Forward?

Social change in America has always been two steps forward, one back, and where race has been concerned, sometimes one step forward and two back. After the social and political advances of the American Revolution, the Civil War, and the end of Jim Crow segregation, conservative backlashes have checked many of the early gains and limited further progress.[21] For example, the revolution, with its expansive rhetoric of freedom and equality, led to new civil rights for Black people, including voting and militia service, not only in New England but in less likely places like Delaware and North Carolina, but during the early decades of the new century, these rights were rolled back everywhere but in New England. In the wake of the Civil War, new constitutional amendments and laws promised an end to slavery as well as guaranteeing equal rights, including suffrage for Black men, but within just a few decades, all those promises had been broken and the deep discrimination of Jim Crow had settled across the land. In the middle decades of the twentieth century, President Lyndon B. Johnson's Great Society programs, including major civil rights, voting rights, education, and open housing initiatives, were intended to usher Black people into the American mainstream; nonetheless, the tide soon began to turn again. The promise of integration, permitting Black people and other minorities to benefit from the full range of federal government programs, quickly drained White support from many of those programs and spending cuts soon followed.[22] Despite the halting progress of many decades, even centuries, the yawning gaps between the opportunities and achievements of White, Black, and Hispanic people remain wide to this day.

The crux of the political problem involved in closing those gaps lies in three interrelated realities. The first reality, uncomfortable as it is, is that during most of American history public and private authorities sanctioned the seizure and destruction of Black wealth, often by deliberate and malicious acts of violence, including during broad historical periods like slavery and Jim Crow and specific assaults like the bombing, burning, and killing in the Greenwood section, also called the Black Wall Street, of Tulsa, Oklahoma, in 1921.[23] Just as importantly, modern exclusions and denials continue to limit minority opportunity, income, and wealth. White appropriation of the value of Black and minority labor during most of American history left Black people and others poorer and White people, at least some White people, richer than they otherwise would have been.

The second reality, literally axiomatic in its implications, was expressed by California Supreme Court Justice Mathew Tobriner early in the famous affirmative action case, *Regents of the University of California v. Bakke* (1978). Tobriner made the undeniable point that, "Whenever there is a limited pool of resources from which minorities have been disproportionately excluded, equalization of opportunity can only be accomplished by a reallocation of such resources; those who have previously enjoyed a disproportionate advantage must give up some of that advantage if those who have historically had less are to be afforded an equal share."[24] Ideally, a growing economy might allow a larger share to those formerly denied a fair share without delivering a visibly thinner slice to the formerly advantaged, but even this would be unlikely to go unnoticed and uncontested. A net transfer of opportunities and assets from White people to Black people and others is unknown to American history and is only dimly in prospect now.

The third reality is that many White people, particularly wealthy White people, deny that they have any responsibility for what happened to Black people and other minorities long ago and they assert that minorities today enjoy all the rights and opportunities that White people enjoy. Yale psychologist Michael W. Kraus and his colleagues explain that most Americans, but especially White "Americans hold an unyielding belief in a specific, optimistic narrative regarding racial progress" which says "that society has come a very long way already and is moving rapidly and perhaps naturally toward full racial equality."[25] Many White people then reason that if racial and ethnic inequalities largely are a thing of the past, then everyone today is on an equal footing and fair competition explains social and economic results. "High-income White Americans," comfortable in the results of this competition, "may be particularly motivated to perceive society as fair and just and thus believe that their elevated social status is based solely on individual merit rather than the persistence of racial or class-based discrimination."[26]

The facts of Black life in America and their widespread denial by White Americans, has produced deep concern for the social and political health of the nation.[27] Professor Eddie Glaude, Jr., Chair of the African American Studies Department at Princeton, warned that, "A moral reckoning is upon us, and we have to decide, once and for all, whether or not we are truly to be a multiracial democracy."[28] Are we ready as a people to look at these questions anew? If so, perhaps – just maybe – the best information available about race and racial divisions in our country will facilitate a tense but meaningful conversation on the issues – so here we go.

The Line of March

Race, Ethnicity, and American Decline will unfold in ten chapters. Chapter 1 opens with a brief discussion of race, slavery, and the slave trade in the Western tradition to provide context for the discussion of these topics in our history. We then explore the academic literature on the social structure of race, often called "racial orders," "racial regimes," "racial frames," or "racial scripts," in American history and in contemporary American life. Racial orders and racial regimes constitute the deep structural presumptions of precedence and superiority, subservience and inferiority, that underpin society's distribution of access, opportunity, and benefits. Racial orders are stable, characterizing eras, but not unchanging. Racial frames and racial scripts structure and guide how race is seen, interpreted, and acted in America. Chapter 1 concludes by describing the dominant racial orders in American history from colonization, through slavery and Jim Crow, to the mid-twentieth century Civil Rights Revolution and its challenge by the ideology of a colorblind society.

Chapter 2 begins with a discussion of two demographic tragedies that followed from early European contact with the Americas; the "great dying" in which native populations were effectively swept away by violence and disease, and the Atlantic slave trade that brought millions of captive Africans to the Americas. We then deploy census and other data to describe demographic change over the course of American history. Throughout the seventeenth, eighteenth, and nineteenth centuries a White majority over or very near 80 percent of the total population dominated a Black minority in slavery and segregation. During the twentieth century, America's biracial society became more complex as the Hispanic and Asian populations increased, but the White/Black tension in American life has always been most profound. Even more recently, a blooming diversity has threatened White dominance and tensions have escalated. Demographic change engenders a great deal of angst and anger, especially among White people, who fear diminishment if not displacement.

Chapter 3 deals with the slowly changing American sense of citizenship – full social and civil rights – over the course of our history. These constitutional provisions, laws, and norms operationalized the demographic fact of White dominance from the colonial period, disrupted only briefly by the Civil War and Reconstruction, well into the twentieth century. Later in U.S. history, when appropriate data becomes available, we present and discuss voter registration, turnout, and partisanship by race and ethnicity. This chapter traces the fight for civil recognition for American racial and ethnic minorities, including Black, Hispanic, and Asian people, and demonstrates how politics has by turns both hastened and slowed full social and political inclusion.

Chapter 4, entitled "Race, Ethnicity, and the American Mind," highlights the broad evolution of political ideology and public opinion on issues touching race and ethnicity. How are the racial frames discussed in Chapter 1 reflected in the public's views on race and ethnicity? How do Americans' conceptions of race and ethnicity affect their views on politics and public policy? The arrival of modern survey research in the twentieth century provides fascinating detail. Some key questions, such as those on interracial marriage, school desegregation, and willingness to vote for a

Black or other minority person for president, have been asked for many decades. Other questions have been asked more recently, but all will show a pervasive but not immobile division between the attitudes and opinions of White people and minorities on issues of race and ethnicity.

Five chapters then lay out differences of access and outcome by race and ethnicity on major dimensions of public life and policy including education, income and wealth, health, housing, and policing, courts, and incarceration. Each draws on the best available data, usually back to about 1950, but sometimes much further. Each chapter begins with a historical discussion of the topic and then moves to demonstrate that while discrimination may be less intense than it once was, the distributions of opportunities, benefits, and exclusions in American life were set early, during the worst of times, and have changed very little over the past half century and more.

Chapter 5 deals with educational access, opportunity, and results by race and ethnicity from the nation's beginning to the present. During the colonial period and throughout the nineteenth century, before and after the end of slavery, education developed more rapidly in the North than in the South, with slavery, Jim Crow segregation, and racial animus driving the regional differences. Public primary schools rose early in the North, while the South generally depended on private academies until after the Civil War. When public schools did come to the South segregation reigned and rural and Black schools received about half the per pupil funding of urban and White schools. While segregation was at least partially dismantled during the middle decades of the twentieth century and funding gaps were narrowed, segregation and funding discrimination have grown again. Similar gaps are evident at the college and university levels. Today, as we will see in some detail, minority educational opportunity and attainment from elementary school through college continue to lag White opportunity and attainment.

In Chapter 6, we analyze patterns of income and wealth by race and ethnicity over the course of the nation's history, with excellent data since the mid-twentieth century. Since education is the principal credential for employment, no one should be surprised that income and wealth also vary by race and ethnicity. Scholars have long sought to estimate the share of the value created by slaves that they were allowed to consume in food, shelter, medical care, and other expenses – usually concluding that it was between a fifth and half. Free Black wages in the nineteenth century were about half those of White wages, and over the course of the first two-thirds of the twentieth century that proportion rose to about 70 percent but it has fallen more recently. As we shall see, Black and minority workers, male and female, make less than their White peers at every educational level. Not surprisingly, Black and Hispanic wealth as a proportion of White wealth varies year-to-year with economic fluctuations, but it usually averages 10 to 15 percent of White wealth.

In Chapter 7, we explore health disparities by race and ethnicity over the course of American history. Life expectancy in the nation's early years for White people was about forty years and for Black people about twenty-five. As medical science slowly advanced, especially in the late nineteenth and early twentieth century, life expectancies rose, but Black life expectancy always trailed White life expectancy and does to this day. In slavery, Black persons received enough medical care to keep them healthy enough to work, but in freedom, especially during Jim Crow, Black persons were denied medical care or care was delivered in second-class segregated settings. Moreover, the White medical community, during slavery and later, experimented on Black patients, and not just in the Tuskegee syphilis experiments, in ways that ignored their very humanity. These historical memories slowed Black acceptance of the COVID-19 vaccines when they became available early in 2021. In addition, we show that Black people and other minorities are less likely to have health insurance, receive less and less timely care, and have worse medical outcomes than White people.

In Chapter 8, we review the broader context of community life in America. All of us grew up in neighborhoods and homes that were conducive to our development and future thriving or detrimental to them. For most of American history, Black and minority legal status, income, and wealth did not permit free choice of where to live or whether to buy a home. After the Civil War, and even more so as the Great Migration of Black people out of the South got underway, the lines of racial residential segregation hardened. Public and private forces limited Black and minority housing options to ghettos and then within the ghettos constructed wealth-destroying systems, like redlining and high interest mortgages. Ghettos concentrate joblessness, poverty, poor schools, and crime. Moreover, poor minority neighborhoods are much less able to defend themselves against adverse zoning and siting decisions, resulting in chemical plants, dumps, waste incinerators, sewage treatment plants, and other noxious, neighborhood-unfriendly sites.

In Chapter 9, we review the much discussed relationship between minority people and communities and the criminal justice system – police, courts, and jails and prisons. All aspects of the criminal justice system, throughout the nation's history, have been created by White authorities to limit and control threats from the poor and marginalized. Plantation justice, chains and whips, were replaced by police, courts, and prisons in the late-nineteenth and twentieth centuries. Prisoner leasing preserved slavery's control of many Black men into the twentieth century and in the second half of the century the "carceral" state arose to control Black people, Hispanic people, and others. Today, we have the largest system of jails and prisons in the world, we cling to execution as a punishment for some crimes, and the victims of both incarceration and execution in the U.S. are disproportionately Black and minority.

The final chapter presents political arguments and policy recommendations designed to advance social, political, and economic equality in America. However, this chapter also discusses, in light of the roles that race and ethnicity have played in American history and the fraught moment at which we have arrived, how likely effective reforms are to be made. Does the current moment have greater potential to change U.S. race relations than other major turning points, such as the American Revolution, the Civil War and Reconstruction, the Civil Rights Revolution of the mid-twentieth century? It would seem not, but even when gains have been made, it is sobering to recall that they have been hard to hold. Earlier gains have all been met, checked, and at least partially rolled back by racial orders and regimes that buttressed White privilege. Many hoped that the interracial uprising that followed the murder of George Floyd would open the door to racial reform, but the moment passed quickly. If justice remains elusive, can America thrive and prosper or will the nation's historic inability to resolve its racial tensions lead to its decline, perhaps its demise?

Notes

1 Gary Gerstle, *The Rise and Fall of the Neoliberal Order: America and the World in the Free Market Era* (New York: Oxford University Press, 2022), 289. See also Martin Wolf, *The Crisis of Democratic Capitalism* (New York: Penguin Press, 2023), 360, 379.
2 Donald Robinson, *Slavery in the Structure of American Politics, 1765–1820* (New York: Harcourt, Brace, Jovanovich, 1970), 438. See also, more recently, Jon Meacham, *The Soul of America: The Battle for Our Better Angels* (New York: Random House, 2018), 15, 24; Theodore R. Johnson, *When the Stars Begin to Fall: Overcoming Racism and Renewing the Promise of* America (New York: Grove Press, 2021), 6, 29–30, 46; David Hackett Fischer, *African Founders: How Enslaved People Expanded American Ideals* (New York: Simon & Schuster, 2022), 179; Thomas E. Ricks, *First Principles: What America's Founders Learned From the Greeks and Romans and How That Shaped Our Country* (New York: HarperCollins, 2020), 12, 267, 291; Kermit Roosevelt III, *The Nation That Never Was: Reconstructing America's Story* (Chicago, IL: University of Chicago Press, 2022), 92–93; Edward J. Larson, *American*

Inheritance: Liberty and Slavery in the Birth of a Nation, 1765–1795 (New York: Norton, 2023), 148, 268.
3 Michael Williams, "Domestic Doubts Amid 'Two Front War,'" *Dallas Morning News*, April 21, 2023, 1B, 2B.
4 Edward J. Watts, *Mortal Republic: How Rome Fell into Tyranny* (New York: Basic Books, 2018), 10. See also Ricks, *First Principles*, 6–8, 237–238; Francis Fukuyama, *The Origins of Political Order: From Prehistoric Times to the French Revolution* (New York: Farrar, Straus, and Giroux, 2011), 7, 23, 44; David Lauter, "As Right-Wing Violence Spreads, Republicans Duck Responsibility," *Los Angeles Times*, May 20, 2022.
5 David Brooks, "This Is How Truth Dies," *New York Times*, July 21, 2021, A21. See also Danielle S. Allen, *Talking to Strangers: Anxieties of Citizenship Since Brown v. Board of Education* (Chicago, IL: University of Chicago Press, 2004), xvi; Jill Lepore, *This America: The Case for the Nation* (New York: Liveright, 2019), 15, 18–20; David W. Blight, "The Irrepressible Conflict: Was the Civil War Inevitable? As America Struggles Through Another Era of Deep Division, The Old Question Takes on New Urgency," *New York Times Magazine*, December 25, 2022, 30; Johnson, *When the Stars Begin to Fall*, 55, 63, 103; Thomas Bryne Edsall, *The Point of No Return: American Democracy at the Crossroads* (Princeton, NJ: Princeton University Press, 2023), 57; Joe Biden, "Howard University Class of 2023 Commencement Address," May 13, 2023. Biden said, "We're living through one of the most consequential moments in our history with fundamental questions at stake for our nation. Who are we? What do we stand for? What do we believe? Who will we be?"
6 Richard Haass, The *Bill of Obligations: Ten Habits of Good Citizens* (New York: Penguin Press, 2023). See also Michael Wayne Santos, *Rediscovering a Nation: Will the Real America Please Stand Up* (Lanham, MD: Rowman and Littlefield, 2022), x, xii.
7 George Packer, *Last Best Hope: America in Crisis and Renewal* (New York: Farrar, Straus, and Giroux, 2021), 10, 42, 48, 147–151. See also Lepore, *This America*, 17.
8 David E. Sanger, "Biden Stakes Out His Challenge with China: 'Prove Democracy Works'," *New York Times*, March 27, 2021, A10. See also Paul Mozur, Amy Chang Chien, John Liu, and Chris Buckley, "Pelosi Prods China, Stoking Simmering Tensions," *New York Times*, August 4, 2022, A1, A19; Donald Judd and Maegan Vazquez, "Efforts to Strengthen the World's Democracies Working, Biden Says," *CNN*, March 29, 2023. But American leaders have frequently seen our democratic institutions as embattled; see Harry V. Jaffa, *Crisis of the House Divided: An Interpretation of the Issues in the Lincoln-Douglas Debates* (Chicago, IL: University of Chicago Press, 1959, 1982), 83–90.
9 George W. Bush Presidential Center, "Presidential Centers Affirm that Democracy Holds Us Together," September 8, 2023.
10 Andrew Desiderio, Alexander Ward, and Paul McLeary, "'No Grounds for Cockiness': Tough Love for U.S. at Pro-Democracy Conference," *Politico*, November 21, 2021. See also Sarah Repucci, "From Freedom to Reform: A Call to Strengthen America's Battered Democracy," Freedom House Special Report, March 2021; Damien Cave, "Allies Wonder Why America Can't Fix Itself," *New York Times*, November 9, 2022, A1, A11.
11 Rogan Kersh, *Dreams of a More Perfect Union* (Ithaca, NY: Cornell University Press, 2001), 193, 277–280.

12 Chris Megerian and Zeke Miller, "Biden Urges Nation to 'Reject the Lie'," *The Associated Press*, May 17, 2022. See also Michael D. Shear, "Ahead of Midterms, Biden Shifts from Compromise to Combat," *New York Times*, September 1, 2022, A1, A12.
13 Chaguan, "China Sees Its Moment," *The Economist*, April 3, 2021, 36. See also Natal Toosi, "Biden's Summit for Democracy Gets Under Autocrat's Skin," *Politico*, December 7, 2021.
14 David E. Sanger, "Defying U.S., China and Russia Set the Tone for a Cold, New Era," *New York Times*, March 31, 2021, A1, A17.
15 Benjamin Banneker to Thomas Jefferson, August 19, 1791, *Papers of Thomas Jefferson* (Princeton, NJ: Princeton University Press, 1986), 22:49, Jefferson's response, 97–98.
16 Michelle Alexander, *The New Jim Crow: Mass Incarceration in the Age of Colorblindness* (New York: The New Press, 2010; 10th anniversary ed., 2020), 175; Proceedings of the Colored National Convention, held in Rochester, July 6–8, 1853, Rochester, NY: printed at the office of Frederick Douglass's Papers, 1853, 16, https://www.omeka.coloredconventions.org/items/show/458/.
17 Herbert Aptheker, ed., *Pamphlets and Leaflets by W.E.B. Du Bois* (White Plains, NY: Kraus-Thompson Organization Limited, 1986), 5.
18 James Baldwin, "The Uses of the Blues," in Randall Kenan, ed., *The Cross of Redemption: Uncollected Writings* (New York: Pantheon Books, 2010), 60. Originally published in *Playboy*, January 1964.
19 James Melvin Washington, *A Testament of Hope: The Essential Writings and Speeches of Martin Luther King, Jr.* (San Francisco: HarperCollins, 1986), 314.
20 Derrick Bell, *Faces at the Bottom of the Well* (New York: Basic Books, 1992), 12; italics in the original.
21 Michael C. Steiner, *Horace Kallen in the Heartland: The Midwestern Roots of American Pluralism* (Lawrence, KS: University Press of Kansas, 2020), 2.
22 Douglas S. Massey and Nancy A. Denton, *American Apartheid: Segregation and the Making of the Underclass* (Cambridge, MA: Harvard University Press, 1993), 2. See also Desmond S. King and Rogers M. Smith, *Still a House Divided: Race and Politics in Obama's America* (Princeton, NJ: Princeton University Press, 2011); William A. Darity and A. Kirsten Mullen, *From Here to Equality: Reparations for Black Americans in the Twenty-First Century* (Chapel Hill, NC: University of North Carolina Press, 2020), 6; Michael Omi and Howard Winant, *Racial Formation in the United States*, 3rd ed. (New York: Routledge, 2015), 58; Sheryll Cashin, *White Space, Black Hood: Opportunity Hoarding and Segregation in the Age of Inequality* (Boston, MA: Beacon Press, 2021), 5.
23 Jim Mitchell, "Opinion: Black Wealth Gap Is 300 Years in the Making," *Dallas Morning News*, June 7, 2021, 8A. See also Victor Luckerson, *Built from the Fire: The Epic Story of Tulsa's Greenwood District, America's Black Wall Street* (New York: Random House, 2023).
24 Ellen Messer-Davidow, *The Making of Reverse Discrimination: How DeFunis and Bakke Bleached Racism from Equal Protection* (Lawrence, KS: University Press of Kansas, 2021), 230.
25 Michael W. Kraus, Ivuoma N. Onyeador, Natalie M. Daumeyer, Julian M. Rucker, and Jennifer A. Richeson, "The Misperception of Racial Economic Inequality," *Perspectives on Psychological Science* 14, no. 6 (2019): 900. See also Jonathan M. Metzl, *Dying of Whiteness: How the Politics of Racial*

Resentment is Killing America's Heartland (New York: Basic Books, 2020), 271–272; Roosevelt, *The Nation That Never Was*, 223.
26 Kraus, et al., "The Misperception of Racial Economic Inequality," 912.
27 Heather McGhee, *The Sum of Us: What Racism Costs Everyone and How We Can Prosper Together* (New York: OneWorld, 2021), 6. See also Robert P. Jones, *White Too Long: The Legacy of White Supremacy in American Christianity* (New York: Simon & Schuster, 2020), 158–163; Johnson, *When the Stars Begin to Fall*, 171–174.
28 Eddie S. Glaude, Jr., *Begin Again: James Baldwin's America and Its Urgent Lessons for Our Own* (New York: Crown Books, 2020), xix.

1
RACIAL ORDERS AND THE STRUCTURE OF AMERICAN LIFE

> "O, yes, I say it plain, America never was America to me, And yet I swear this oath – America will be!"
>
> Langston Hughes, 1935, "Let America Be America Again"

It is frequently said that slavery was and remains America's "original sin." By this it is meant that the adoption and determined maintenance of slavery through the first 250 years of American history produced deep and profound racial injustices and inequalities. Those injustices remained clear in subsequent periods of our history, including the period of Jim Crow segregation, and they remain clear in social and economic inequalities today. In this and subsequent chapters we explore the origins, development, and current status of those inequalities and we conclude by asking how they might effectively be addressed – perhaps even eliminated.

We focus on the historic conflict between White Americans and Black Americans because that is where the template for racial hierarchy was set, but we do not ignore the implications of this conflict for other minority groups, including Native Americans, and more recently, Hispanics and Asians. Initially, White settlers simply marked Native Americans down as "savages" beyond the bounds of civil society, Hispanics were disdained as a "mongrel race" of Native American, African, and European blood, while Asians were excluded as so radically different as to preclude even the possibility of citizenship. While much has changed since the nation's early days, the formal institutions of slavery and Jim Crow are long gone, not everything has changed and so we must confront the fact that racial hierarchy

DOI: 10.4324/9781003449188-1

2 Racial Orders and the Structure of American Life

and White supremacy still haunt our society. Minorities in America know that when the pressure is on, the category not-White still threatens to envelop them all.

We approach the study of race in America both from 30,000 feet, the panoramic view, and from the more granular view at street level. We often begin with the panoramic view, but then usually bracket it, even a little skeptically, and move to street level where the opportunities, limits, and exclusions of real life have always been most visible. Nonetheless, to set the stage, we start with the panoramic view in this and the next chapter before descending to street level for much of the remainder of the book.

The Emergence of Race in the Western Tradition

There are huge literatures on slavery, the slave trade, and race in the history of the Western world that must be at least broadly canvassed to provide background and context for their impact on American history. This broader context is important because slavery in the Americas has been presented, especially recently, as uniquely and unprecedentedly horrifying. It both was and was not.[1] It was, particularly to our modern instincts, because holding another human by force, demanding unremitting labor from them, and then expropriating the value of that labor, to say nothing of the wholesale violations of persons, families, and peoples, is not simply unjust, it is horrifying. But it was not uniquely so because slavery was an integral and pervasive aspect of human society from the earliest times and horrors were always attendant to it.

Scholars of slavery, the slave trade, and race make several broad claims that must be summarized and evaluated before we can turn to race relations in America. The first broad claim, indisputably correct and important to keep in mind, is that slavery and the trade in slaves were an early and constant presence in the history of the world. Slavery can be traced back to the Neolithic transition from hunter-gatherer culture to agriculture, and in the Western world is clearly documented in the Middle East, especially Sumer and Mesopotamia, from 6000 BCE.[2] The first legal reference to slavery is in the Babylonian King Hammurabi's famous Code, 1754 BCE, where slavery was acknowledged and slave stealing was defined as a capital offense. Egypt, of course, was a slave society too. The biblical narrative of Moses leading the Israelites out of slavery in Egypt to the promised land is thought by archaeologists to have occurred around 1450 BCE. In fact, some readers will recall that God gave Moses the Ten Commandments in Exodus 20 of the Bible and then in the very next chapter, Exodus 21:1–11, laid out the terms of buying and selling male and female servants, effectively slaves, among the Hebrews. Leviticus 25:44–46 approved hereditary slavery for those taken or purchased by Hebrews from among the peoples of the surrounding nations. Later, slavery was common in ancient Greece and throughout the Roman world. It permeated the Islamic societies of the Middle East, North Africa, and southern and eastern Europe, with their slave administrators, soldiers, and laborers, but also with their *harems* and castrated eunuchs – all horrifying in their own special way.[3] Though they might have stretched their timeframe back several millennia, the historians Robert Fogel and Stanley Engerman were accurate in writing that: "For nearly three thousand years – from the time of King Solomon [990–931 BCE] to the eve of the American Revolution – virtually every major statesman, philosopher, theologian, writer, and critic accepted the existence and legitimacy of slavery."[4]

While slavery was general in human history into the nineteenth century, it was more common in some times and places, and was variously defined and sometimes limited in law and practice. Almost universally, defeat in wars and lesser conflicts were assumed to legitimate slavery, because if the conqueror could have killed the conquered, enslaving them instead was thought to be a mercy.[5] Intentional slave raiding and kidnapping also brought many to slavery, as did judicial proceedings, debt, and other distress, especially famine.[6] In the Roman world, infanticide through infant exposure assumed that abandoned infants could be and often were salvaged and enslaved.

The Western slave trade, on the other hand, was both general and increasingly focused on Africa and Africans over time. Perhaps the distinction between retail and wholesale trade in slaves might help to clarify the patterns involved. For millennia slaves were bought, sold, inherited, and exchanged inside the relatively narrow geographical confines within which most men, even elite men, traveled, traded, and fought.[7] According to scholars, this local retail trade was supplemented by two wider streams of wholesale trade out of Slavic Eastern Europe, Anatolia, and the Caucasus, and out of sub-Saharan Africa. The military and administrative ranks, as well as the *harems* of the Middle East and Mamluk Egypt, were filled out of what is now Turkey, Georgia, and the regions between the Black and Caspian Seas.[8] A modest stream of enslaved Africans, most out of Sudan into Egypt and beyond, was expanded as Islamic armies spread out of the Arabian Peninsula across the Middle East, North Africa, and southern and eastern Europe. Early work by Ralph Austen, professor of African history at the University of Chicago, Paul Lovejoy, Canada Research Chair in African Diaspora History at York University, and others, concluded that a rising stream of several thousand persons a year between 650 AD and 1600 AD were taken out of East Africa, north via the trans-Saharan overland route, the coastal route, and across the seas to Arabia. The total of about

7.2 million slaves over nearly a thousand years, together with smaller but unknown numbers over earlier millennia, allowed Paul Lovejoy to conclude that 10 to 12 million were taken out of East Africa into the Muslim world before the Atlantic slave trade got well underway.[9] The Atlantic slave trade, to which we will turn in Chapter 2, sent millions more out of West Africa to the Americas beginning late in the fifteenth century.

The second broad claim, more disputed than the first, is that while slavery and the trade in slaves existed throughout history, racism did not. Lerone Bennett, Jr. wrote in *Before the Mayflower* that, "Ancient slavery ... had little or nothing to do with race" and had "no implications of racial inferiority."[10] A similar point, made with more nuance by Boston University historian Ibram X. Kendi, declared that: "All in all, ethnic and religious and color prejudice existed in the ancient world. Constructions of *races* – white Europe, Black Africa, for instance – did not, and therefore racist ideas did not. But crucially, the foundations of race and racist ideas were laid."[11] It is certainly true that Africa was home to storied civilizations, and not just in Egypt and along the North African coast, but also the West African empires of Ghana (ninth to eleventh centuries), Mali (eleventh to fourteenth centuries), and Songhai (fifteenth to sixteenth centuries).[12] But agreeing that Africa had accomplishments that the broader West respected does not entail the assumption that race prejudice was unknown to the ancient world. If "color prejudice" existed and provided the foundation for later race consciousness and racism, the distinction between color prejudice and racism is, as the lawyers say, not dispositive – ultimately settling nothing of consequence.

The reasons are several. First, the ancient world, by which is usually meant the greater Mediterranean, eastern Europe, and the Middle East, knew little – in most cases nothing – of East Asia, Oceania, or the Americas and just a little more of Africa below the Sahara.[13] Second, most people in the ancient world, save only for a thin smattering of traders, adventurers, and warriors, were geographically isolated and mobility was limited, so they knew little of the world beyond their own direct observations and all they saw were people very much like themselves.[14] And third, human difference was conceived less as race than as what today we would call cultural heritage or ethnicity. Among cultural and ethnic groups, distinctions certainly were made and hierarchy adjudged – Greeks versus barbarians, for example.[15] But comparisons and judgments about Europeans versus Asians or Africans were largely unavailable to be made because few people had the broad geographical perspective that would have allowed such generalizations. So, as Kendi said, racism as we might think about it today did not exist, but hierarchical distinctions between and among peoples did, including distinctions of color, and the foundations were laid. Once the peoples of the world began to come into more regular contact with each other, difference struck the eye, and race and racism became ready constructs.

The third broad claim that scholars make about slavery, the slave trade, and race concerns how modernity spawned and then matured conceptions of race and racism. This broad claim is striking indeed and must be unpacked. Sociologists Michael Omi and Howard Winant, among the most influential contemporary students of race, contend that: "The idea of race barely existed before the Enlightenment and the onset of modernity. . . . It is linked to the conquest of the Americas, the rise of capitalism, the circumnavigation of the globe, the Atlantic slave trade, and the rise of European and then American domination."[16] Joe Feagin, another prominent sociologist and student of race, made a very similar point, saying: "Strikingly, colonialism, capitalism, modernity, and global exploitation all have a common genealogy. European colonialism and capitalism were in their early stages of development when they generated the cross-Atlantic slavery system. . . . The rise of Western capitalism is rooted in the global seizing of the land, resources, and labor of people of color by violent means."[17] These are broad, even dramatic, claims. What are we to make of a reading of history that links the birth of race and racism to modernity, to the structure of the modern world, through the rise of capitalism and technological advances in industry, weaponry, and navigation, which promoted contact with human difference at scale and made possible the Atlantic slave trade and European domination and exploitation of the Americas?

As we review and analyze the role of race in American history, we will have to keep the following question in mind. Does the simultaneous rise of capitalism, colonialism, racism, and the Atlantic slave trade mean that they are inexorably intertwined, that the Atlantic slave trade wove racism into the very warp and woof, the very composition and structure of modern life; or might we conclude that racism, while pervasive, is still discrete enough to be subject to serial and ongoing amelioration? Happily, and quite clearly, history suggests that amelioration is more than possible if we have the courage and confidence to work toward it. Modernity, broadly understood, expanded and even worsened slavery through the Atlantic slave trade, before it slowly limited, constrained, and rejected it by the middle of the nineteenth century. While slavery has not been excised from the modern world, it has been driven to the fringes of global society.[18] Racism may follow, but, as with slavery, only if we and other peoples make it a moral, cultural, and political priority.

The Permanence of Race in American History

Even if we agree that there is some meaningful sense in which the ancient world did not know race and racism, because men had not yet seen the world in whole, that world fell before European exploration and colonization. European contact with the Americas was part of a broader exploration, highlighted by Magellan's circumnavigation of the globe, completed in 1521, that tied the world and its peoples together. European domination of the "Age of Discovery" gave rise to a sense of racial hierarchy that permeated the American mind from its earliest days. Race in the seventeenth century, which is when European settlement of North America actually began, was part of the deep structure of the European, and hence the American, mind.

Race is basic and unavoidable; it is a bright thread, easily followed, through a complex social reality. Michael Omi and Howard Winant define race in the U.S. as: "a *master category* – a fundamental concept that has profoundly shaped, and continues to shape, the history, polity, economic structure, and culture of the United States." What makes race, like gender, a master category is that it has a "non-reducible *visual dimension* . . . Bodies are visually read and narrated in ways that draw upon an ensemble of symbolic meanings and associations."[19] The visible nature of race makes it stickier, harder to ignore, more resistant to change. Strikingly, race has always been a matter of first impression; but first impressions and the "symbolic meanings and associations" they conjure change over time and, as they do, society may open to new relationships between the races.

Among scholars of race in American history, all agree that great changes have taken place in race relations from colonial to modern times but that the scars of racial hierarchy remain visible today. Most see history punctuated by periods in which tensions build to a crisis, reforms are achieved, and backlash builds as reformist energies ebb. But some argue that because America has been and remains a racist nation, conservative counter-attacks often undercut and degrade reforms, while others focus on racial reforms that, despite occasional backsliding, sum to ongoing racial progress.[20]

Several influential scholars see race as foundational, resilient, and deeply embedded in our nation's structure and consciousness.[21] Omi and Winant encouraged Americans to grasp "a deep truth: that white supremacy was not an excrescence on the basically egalitarian and democratic 'American creed,' but a fundamental component of U.S. society. . . . The major institutions and social relationships of U.S. society – law, political organization, economic relationships, religion, cultural life, residential patterns – have been structured from the beginning by this system."[22] The Georgetown Law professor Sheryll Cashin wrote that; "Each time the United States seems to dismantle a peculiar Black subordinating institution, it constructs a new one and attendant myths to justify the racial order."[23] Princeton professor of African-American Studies Eddie S. Glaude decried the ongoing commitment of the nation to its racist culture, writing: "Throughout this country's history, from the Revolutionary War period to Reconstruction to the black freedom movement of the mid-twentieth century, the United States has faced moments of crisis. . . . In each instance the country chose to remain exactly what it was: a racist nation that claimed to be democratic. These were and are moments of national betrayal."[24] These bold declarations highlight what Omi and Winant, Cashin, and Glaude take to be the fundamental and continuous impact of race and racism on American history. President Joe Biden also pointed to the resilience of racism in his 2023 Howard University Commencement speech, declaring that "American history has . . . been a constant push and pull for more than 240 years between the best of us, the American ideal that we're all created equal – and the worst of us, the harsh reality that . . . progress towards justice often meets ferocious pushback from the oldest and most sinister of forces."[25] These observers and many others see race as a defining feature of American culture and life.

Other scholars see clearer patterns in American history; sometimes called policy regimes, in which a stable regime is followed by regime disruption and the reconstitution of a related but changed racial regime. Ibram X. Kendi summarized his review of race in American history by writing: "I saw a *dual* and *dueling* history of racial progress and the simultaneous progression of racism. I saw the antiracist force of equality and the racist force of inequality marching forward, progressing in rhetoric, in tactics, in policies."[26] Political scientists Desmond King and Rogers Smith have described the periods of racial policy conflict that they see in American history and politics this way: "American politics has always been shaped by contests between rival policy alliances, from slavery and anti-slavery coalitions, through proponents and opponents of Jim Crow segregation and disfranchisement, to post-1970 debates over color-blind and race-conscious policies."[27] The sociologist Joe Feagin made the same point, though just barely hinting of progress over time, saying: "Historically, periods of dismantling aspects of a racist system have lasted a decade or two, and then been followed by significant backtracking, retrenchment, or slowing down of racial change."[28] While racism remains a deep-seated challenge to American life, institutions, and principles, some historical periods see stasis while others see lurching change, even progress.

Social scientists increasingly have described the great crises of American history as multiple revolutions, constitutions, and reconstructions. These terms are used almost interchangeably, but a broader understanding of the episodic struggle over race in American history has emerged. Each period of revolutionary change experienced a decade or more of rising tensions preceding the years of crisis, revolution, and social turmoil. Progressive forces then sought to implement and enforce a new constitutional and legal order against the inevitable conservative backlash. Once a new equilibrium took hold, somewhere between the gains attained during resolution of the crisis and ground lost to the backlash, a period, often decades long, of tense calm ensued. When legal structures change, especially when they change against a substantial segment of the popular will, traditional social norms, rituals, and practices have an ability to hunker down, to weather the storm, and to survive. Elements of the old order commonly reassert themselves, perhaps in new and revised forms, especially once attention has flagged as it almost always does after a great social battle apparently has been won. The winners relax and the losers sharpen and repair their weapons.[29]

Scholars have identified three peaks in the battle against discrimination and injustice. The American Revolution, the Civil War and Reconstruction, and the Civil Rights movement of the mid-twentieth century produced new policy regimes that did not dismantle but did reconstitute and reorganize existing policy regimes. The First Founding came in the American Revolution and featured the Declaration's call for freedom and independence. The Second Founding highlighted the Civil War era end of slavery, promise of racial equality, and grant of suffrage to Black men.[30] The Third Founding, the modern civil rights revolution, stressed the promise of civil, social, and economic equality.[31] Throughout this book, the periods 1776–1789, 1861–1876, 1954–1968, will be shown to be peaks in the fighting, victories won and then defended, sometimes effectively, sometimes not, against the inevitable backlash.[32]

Race in America Before the First Founding

Most traditional tellings of American origins begin with the storied pilgrim landing in 1620 at Plymouth Rock in the Massachusetts Bay Colony. Sure, there were some early scrapes with local Native Americans, but what has long resonated with subsequent generations of Americans were those same Native Americans saving the starving colonists in that first winter and then, of course, Thanksgiving.[33] Alternatively, many students of race identify the first landing of African captives at Jamestown in 1619 as a, perhaps the, formative event in American history. Almost fifteen months before the Mayflower arrived at Plymouth, the White Lion, an English privateer operating under a Dutch commission, dropped anchor in the harbor at Jamestown, Virginia, with twenty captive Africans on board.[34] The Africans had been taken in the raid of a Spanish slave ship in the Caribbean and the captain, anxious to get back to his piracy, traded the Africans for food and supplies for his ship. While the legal status of these and other Africans was uncertain for a time, the brutal fact is that the first Black people in English North America were traded for supplies. But by the 1660s, Virginia and Maryland, then others, defined the position of Black people in law. First, Black people could be held as servants for life, then sex and marriage between White and Black people was made punishable and children born to Black women were assigned their mother's status, rather than their father's as among White people, and finally slavery became a hereditary legal status. Over the remainder of the seventeenth century slavery spread throughout the colonies and became the defining social structure in the states from Maryland and Virginia south through the Carolinas.[35]

Part of what made Black slavery in America so resilient, so long-lasting, were the range and prestige of its supporters and apologists. The religious and cultural supporters of racism argued that God placed some high and some low – both individuals and races – and that legal distinctions were merely a reflection of the laws of nature and nature's God. Many saw physical, intellectual, and biological differences that they thought fairly shouted hierarchy. Moreover, as the seventeenth century turned into the eighteenth, great men grounded these apparent truths in the leading philosophy, history, and science of the day.[36]

In Europe, Voltaire (1694–1778), Carl Linnaeus (1707–1778), David Hume (1711–1776), and Immanuel Kant (1724–1804), among others, spoke directly about race, and many Americans, certainly including Thomas Jefferson (1743–1826), listened intently. Voltaire opined that: "The Negro race is a species of men as different from ours as the breed of spaniels is from that of greyhounds. . . . If their understanding is not of a different nature from ours it is at least greatly inferior. They are not capable of any great application or association of ideas, and seem formed neither for the advantages nor the abuses of philosophy."[37] For the philosopher Voltaire, this was, of course, a devastating critique. Carl Linnaeus, a founder of what would become anthropology, produced a taxonomy of world races based on color called *Systema Naturae* (1735). Linnaeus found four broad "families of man," among which White Europeans were the most advanced. The renowned Scottish philosopher David Hume announced in 1748 that: "There never was a civilized nation of any other complexion than white, nor even any individual eminent either in action or speculation."[38] Immanuel Kant was similarly convinced that among the world's races, the White European was "more controlled in his passions, more intelligent than any other race of people in the world."[39] Finally, in 1776, a young associate of Kant named Johann Friedrich Blumenbach published a doctoral dissertation entitled

"On the Natural Varieties of Humanity." Over the next quarter century, he systematically made the case for racial hierarchy with Europeans at the apex and Africans at the base.[40]

Leading members of the revolutionary generation in America were avid, if not always close, readers of European history, philosophy, and science. The Founders' survey of history convinced them that every republic in the ancient and the modern world had rested on a class of unfree laborers. So slavery was not in question, it had a long history, and obvious racial differences were understood to warrant slavery. Thomas Jefferson best reflected the crippling presumptions that pervaded the White American mind as it accommodated slavery during the Founding and early national periods. Jefferson believed that the differences between Black people and White people were real and deeply meaningful, but he also thought that the ideals of the Revolution were incompatible with slavery and that the practice should therefore be reassessed. But his own reassessment never reached emancipation; the idea of a peaceful, prosperous, biracial society was inconceivable to him. Jefferson's ultimate rejection of Black freedom and equality, while by no means surprising for his time, would reverberate deep into the future.

Jefferson had a characteristically American fear of the socio-cultural and political implications of racial differences and the conflicts that might flow from them. On the issue of substantive racial differences Jefferson declared of Black people that: "In general, their existence appears to participate more of sensation than reflection. . . . [I]n memory they are equal to the whites; in reason much inferior . . . and, that in imagination they are dull, tasteless, and anomalous. . . . I advance it therefore as a suspicion only, that the blacks, whether originally a distinct race, or made distinct by time and circumstances, are inferior to the whites. . . ."[41]

In Jefferson's view, history had produced such a gulf between White and Black people that it could not be bridged. Again, Jefferson predicted that: "Deep rooted prejudices entertained by whites; ten thousand recollections, by the blacks, of injuries they have sustained; new provocations; the real distinctions which nature has made; and many other circumstances, will divide us into parties; and produce convulsions which will probably never end but in the extermination of the one or the other race."[42] Only a little less ominously, Jefferson suggested that extermination of freed Black people might be avoided by voluntary colonization to Latin America or Africa: "Nothing is more certainly written in the book of fate, than that these people are to be free; nor is it less certain that the two races, equally free, cannot live in the same government. Nature, habit, opinion has drawn indelible lines of distinction between them."[43] So, slavery will someday end, but when it does, the freed slaves must go.

Not surprisingly, Jefferson's fellow Virginian and plantation slaveowner, General George Washington had reservations about Black character and capacity so he sought to prohibit their military service during the Revolutionary War. Over time, the presence of Black soldiers in the New England regiments and militia and, probably more importantly, manpower shortages, forced Washington to relent. By the end of the war, 5,000 Black men had served in the revolutionary army and another 1,000 in the naval forces.[44] In the first American war, as in future wars, Black military service brought some gains, but much disappointment, as the racist presumptions of the broader society changed little.

The crisis of the revolution opened the door to social and political change, but just a crack and not for long. As we will see in more detail in Chapter 3, some progress was made during the revolutionary era, but by half-steps, due to widespread presumptions of White supremacy and Black inferiority and inability. The historian Kate Masur wrote that the nation's first civil rights "movement began in the era of the American Revolution, when demands for citizenship and equal rights for Black Americans were part of broader revolutionary currents that emphasized the dignity and fundamental equality of all humanity."[45] Similarly, the historian Van Gosse has described "a First Reconstruction beginning in the North during the Revolution . . . a nonviolent, slow-moving Reconstruction – defined by emancipation, the birthright citizenship of any man born on the soil, and the enforcement of judicial equality."[46] While many of the racial reforms won outside New England were lost to a postwar conservative counteroffensive, basic citizenship rights held in New England's core. The great Black social scientist and activist W.E.B. Du Bois adjudged that: "the American Revolution of 1776–1781 was only a partial and incomplete anti-imperial transformation, since it was dominated by elites and left slavery intact."[47] This pattern of civil rights advances lost in whole or in part to White resistance and retrenchment has been characteristic of American history.

The Civil War, Reconstruction, and the Second American Founding

Acceptance of racial hierarchy was broad in early nineteenth-century America, loosened only modestly by Enlightenment commitments to natural rights. By mid-century natural rights' convictions were fading before a growing intellectual consensus among natural and social scientists, theologians, and business and social elites, concerning racial hierarchy and, more specifically, White superiority and Black inferiority.[48] The historian John Haller described this White social consensus by writing that: "Almost the whole of scientific thought in both America and Europe in the decades before Darwin accepted race inferiority, irrespective of whether the races sprang from a single original pair or were created separately."[49] Whether God created all of humankind from Adam and Eve as described in Genesis, created separate races from the beginning, or forced mankind's separation only after the flood, segregationists declared that God, nature, and science demanded racial separation in America.

White supremacy was explicit in southern social, political, legal, and economic principles and institutions from its earliest settlement, but the Confederacy grounded its very constitution on them. Less than a month before the rebel guns opened up on Fort Sumter on April 12, 1861, Alexander H. Stephens, formerly a prominent member of the U.S. House, an opponent of secession until Georgia decided upon it, and then Vice President of the Confederacy, elevated White supremacy to constitutional status in his famous/infamous "Cornerstone Speech." Stephens boldly declared that the South rejected the whole idea of human equality, saying: "Our new government is founded upon exactly the opposite idea; its foundations are laid, its corner-stone rests upon the great truth, that the negro is not equal to the white man; that slavery – subordination to the superior race – is his natural and normal condition. This, our new government, is the first, in the history of the world, based on this great physical, philosophical, and moral truth." Stephens charged that the North futilely sought "to make things equal which the Creator had made unequal."[50]

Even in the North, men had always wondered. Abraham Lincoln had long been ambivalent about slavery and even more about Black people themselves. In a speech delivered at Peoria on October 16, 1854, in opposition to Democratic Senator Stephen A. Douglas' Kansas/Nebraska Act and its claim that "popular sovereignty" meant that White people had the right to decide by plebiscite whether they would have slavery or not, Lincoln reasoned that Black people had certain rights as laid out in the Declaration of Independence. But as a politician seeking election in a racist nation, Lincoln knew he could not leave this human rights claim unmodified, so he declared, echoing Jefferson and many others, that once freed Black people would have to be exiled. "My first impulse would be to free all the slaves, and send them to Liberia— to their own native land." But Lincoln recognized that removal to Africa was well-nigh impossible as a simple logistical matter, so he asked rhetorically: "What then? Free them all, and keep them among us as underlings? . . . Free them, and make them politically and socially our equals. My own feelings will not admit of this, and if mine would, we well know that those of the great mass of white people will not." So Lincoln drew what he considered to be the only democratic conclusion, "A universal feeling," even a widely held feeling of racial animus, "whether well or ill founded, cannot be safely disregarded."[51] While the political space between Lincoln and Douglas would widen, in 1854 it was not that great.

Nearly eight years later, Lincoln as president in the second year of the Civil War still sought to calm White fears of Black equality. In an open letter of August 20, 1862, Horace Greeley, abolitionist editor of the influential *New York Tribune*, demanded that Lincoln free the slaves as a moral matter and as a war measure that would stagger the South. Lincoln replied just two days later, announcing again a policy that he thought clear. With ill-disguised impatience, Lincoln wrote: "My paramount object in this struggle is to save the Union, and is not either to save or to destroy slavery. If I could save the Union without freeing any slave, I would do it; and if I could save it by freeing all the slaves, I would do it; . . . What I do about slavery and the colored race, I do because I believe it helps to save the Union."[52]

Within a matter of months, Lincoln's understanding of what best would save the Union evolved. A timely Union victory in the Battle of Antietam and a growing sense in the North that the war was turning in their favor, allowed Lincoln to issue a preliminary Emancipation Proclamation on September 22, 1862, declaring that areas still in rebellion on January 1, 1863, would undergo emancipation as Union forces came into control of their territory.[53] The Emancipation Proclamation also called for the recruitment of Black military units. The response was immediate and sustained: approximately 180,000 Black troops served in the Army and another 19,000 served in the Navy. Once again, war service brought them little, and that little not for long.

Among Lincoln's most frustrated and impatient, but hopeful, supporters was the former slave and increasingly prominent abolitionist spokesman Frederick Douglass (1818–1895). Born Frederick Augustus Washington Bailey, to Harriett Bailey and an anonymous father, suspected to be Harriett's White master, in Talbot County, Maryland, he was a slave for the first twenty years of his life. Douglass escaped North in 1838, eventually settled in New Bedford, Massachusetts, married Anna Murray Douglass, who he had known in Baltimore, and started a family. Douglass was by 1843 increasingly and soon exclusively involved in abolition work. Over the next fifty years, he became the best known Black man in America and in much of Europe. Three versions of this life story, *Narrative of the Life of Frederick Douglass, an American Slave, Written by Himself* (1845), *My Bondage and My Freedom* (1855), and *Life and Times of Frederick Douglass* (1881), revised in 1892, established his literary fame and national presence. David W. Blight, Douglass' most prominent modern biographer, described him as "a proponent of classic nineteenth-century liberalism, . . . [who] loved the Declaration of Independence, the natural-rights tradition, and especially the reinvented U.S. Constitution fashioned in Reconstruction."[54]

Douglass had a distinctive ability to use the nation's symbols and values to his advantage.[55] His love of the Declaration of Independence drove him to demand its promises for himself and his people, most famously in his Fourth of July oration (actually delivered on the fifth) at Rochester, New York, in 1852. Douglass drew his audience in by asking: "Fellow-citizens, . . . why am I called upon to speak here today?" While Douglass was by 1852 a free man, most of his Black brethren were still enslaved, so he proceeded to challenge his listeners by asking: "What, to the American slave, is your fourth of July? I answer: a day that reveals to him, more than all other days in the year, the gross injustice and cruelty to which he is the constant victim. To him, your celebration is a sham; . . . your shouts of liberty and equality, hollow mocking . . . – a thin veil to cover up crimes which would disgrace a nation of savages."[56] In a speech delivered five years later, Douglass reminded, even warned, his listeners, that crisis and tumult, agitation and disruption, would be necessary to bring freedom to the enslaved, saying: "If there is no struggle there is no progress. Those who profess to favor freedom and yet deprecate agitation are men who want crops without plowing up the ground; they want rain without thunder and lightning. They want the ocean without the awful roar of its many waters." He concluded somberly that, "Power concedes nothing without a demand. It never did and never will."[57] Douglass' prewar role was to hurry on the crisis.

As we have seen, Lincoln was ready to demand that the South adhere to the Constitution, but reluctant to demand Black freedom even once the war began. Others in Washington, attuned to the opportunities that crises present, were more willing to seize the moment and drive toward emancipation. On April 7, 1862, Illinois Republican Senator Lyman Trumbull urged his colleagues "not to let pass this opportunity which a wicked rebellion presents, of making it the means of giving freedom to millions of the human race, and thereby destroying to a great extent the source and origin of the rebellion."[58] Pennsylvania Congressman Thaddeus Stevens saw the forces arrayed against radical change quite clearly and was dismayed. Not long before his death on August 11, 1868, with slavery ended but Reconstruction barely underway, violent opposition already evident, Stevens sadly said: "In my youth, in my manhood, in my old age, I had fondly dreamed that when any fortunate chance should have broken up for awhile the foundations of our institutions [we] would have so remodeled all our institutions as to have freed them from every vestige of human oppression, of inequality of rights. . . . This bright dream has vanished 'like the baseless fabric of a vision.'"[59] The crisis had come, progress had been made, the slaves had been freed, but the forces of backlash were raw and powerful.

A Northern newspaperman traveling through the postwar South reported that: "The whites seem wholly unable to comprehend that freedom for the negro means the same thing as freedom for them."[60] While Southern White opinion blamed the North and Black people themselves for the war and its aftermath, it must be said Northern White opinion on race was only marginally more open and accepting of Black racial presence, let alone equality. Though the war was won, as Reconstruction ground on, many others in the North lost their will for the fight and abandoned the cause of Black equality. Freedom yes, equality no. Soon the desire for White regional reconciliation overcame the Northern will to press for Black security let alone equality. Not surprisingly, what struck the modern scholar of race, Henry Louis Gates, Jr. most forcefully about Reconstruction was just "how painfully short it was," just a "decade or so during which Reconstruction policy attempted to redress almost two and a centuries of Anglo-American slavery."[61]

The great mid-twentieth century historian of the South, C. Vann Woodward, wrote in *The Burden of Southern History* that: "Southern whites . . . used craft and guile, force and violence, economic pressure and physical terror, and all the subtle psychological devices of race prejudice and propaganda at their command."[62] The South remained convinced that social and racial hierarchy rightly awarded unchallenged primacy to an elite of White planters and a professional class of merchants, lawyers, doctors, and ministers. These convictions were unshaken by the outcome of the war. Even before the grip of Reconstruction loosened, the South's traditional elite began "an intellectual quest to reaffirm [their] authority as the dominant force in the region's political, social, and economic life."[63]

The "race prejudice" Woodward noted was national and Southern elites knew it and depended upon it. In 1874, as Reconstruction was being dismantled and the South returned to the control of its White citizens, Guy Morrison Bryan, Speaker of the Texas House, wrote reassuringly to Ohio Governor Rutherford B. Hayes, a friend from their days at Kenyon College, that: "There is *no desire on the part of the South to put back the negro into slavery.* . . . All concur that the negroes are *citizens.* . . . But we want *good government*, for their sake as well as our own. *They* do not know how to *govern* . . . it would be far better for the negroe [sic], that the intelligent tax paying citizens should govern."[64] Besides, it was argued, who knew better than Southern White elites how best to manage their states and their people, including their Black people, as they all struggled to recover from the war?[65]

Less than three years after Bryan wrote to Hayes, Hayes became president, but it was a rocky ride. The presidential election of 1876 was contested and finally resolved in the Compromise of 1877, in which Democrats agreed to allow Hayes to assume office in exchange for Republican agreement to withdraw Union troops from the South. Reconstruction unraveled quickly in the wake of this agreement between White regional elites. By 1883 the United States Supreme Court had declared that provisions of law guaranteeing Black citizens equal rights in public spaces such as trains, hotels, and restaurants were unconstitutional constraints on the rights of White private citizens. As the historian David Levering Lewis has written, "by its fateful invalidation of the Civil Rights Act of 1875 in all matters state and local, the Supreme Court of the United States handed 90 percent of the African-American population over to the discretionary mercies of southern legislatures and courts."[66]

That is not to say, of course, that no gains were made in the Second American Revolution. The Thirteenth Amendment affirmed and broadened the Emancipation Proclamation by ending slavery throughout the land; the Fourteenth Amendment promised equal rights and due process to Black people; and the Fifteenth Amendment seemed to award Black men the right to vote.[67] But established traditions, norms, and expectations die hard, even in the face of constitutional and legal change. As with the First Founding, so with the Second Founding; once the shouts, the marches, and the battles for liberty and equality quieted and attention faded, many hard won gains were lost.[68] The Second American Revolution, like the First, brought important reforms, but stopped short of the remorseless root and branch challenge to White supremacy that real equality would have required.

Jim Crow and the Era of Segregation

One of the greatest intellectual supports to the rise of Jim Crow segregation was the work of the naturalist Charles Darwin and, even more explicitly, his acolytes. Charles Darwin (1809–1882) was an English natural scientist, particularly influential in geology and biology, whose observations of change and development in nature underpin important aspects of modern science and culture to this day. The impact of Darwin's work, beginning with *On the Origin of Species* (1859) and culminating in *The Descent of Man* (1871), on thinking about race in America and the world came only over the course of decades. Darwin described a process of biological change called "natural selection." Natural selection was driven by changes in nature and climate, changes in predator populations, and "competition" among individual members of a species, producing the "survival of the fittest" and the dominance over time of their most effective traits in the broader population of the species. Partly by his own pen, but mostly by the work of others, Darwin's ideas produced social Darwinism, the conviction that open competition for advantage – for wealth and status – in society and the economy as in the rest of nature drove positive development and change. *Laissez-faire* capitalism became the order of the day in the late nineteenth century, while scientific racism and eugenics operated powerfully on thinking about social organization and structure.

While Darwin sought to distinguish between human evolution and evolution through natural selection in the plant and animal kingdoms, most interpreters thought he had drawn a fairly straight line from *On the Origin of Species* to *The Descent of Man*. In fact, he did write in *The Descent of Man* that the races of men in the world differed both physically and mentally. Darwin evinced "no doubt that the various races . . . differ much from each other. . . . The American aborigines, Negroes and Europeans are as different from each other in mind as any three races that can be named."[69] The message seemed clear; science had shown White people to occupy the pinnacle of the hierarchy of races, Black people the base.

Not surprisingly, White social and economic elites – led by the Robber Barons of the day – found social Darwinism particularly compelling. They had won the competition among all comers, they were the best and the fittest, and to interfere with their activities on behalf of those less fortunate – less competitive and fit – was not just inefficient, but immoral. The unfit would suffer by such coddling and the dynamism and growth of society and the economy would decline if their most innovative and productive members were constrained. Winners earned their rewards and losers had no basis for complaint and every right to try again. *Laissez-faire*, though it might on occasion seem cruel, was the way in nature and must be in society as well.

As the nineteenth century drew to a close, popular opinion was permeated by "an almost overwhelming presumption that evolutionary science had found laws fixing some races, such as the Negro, outside the possibility of the Caucasian's progress and civilization."[70] Separation of races so different from each other seemed only common sense. But separation was never benign; it was always favorable to White people and prejudicial to Black people. Political scientists Michael Dawson and Megan Francis have described the purpose of Jim Crow institutions as "a comprehensive system of oppression to create two societies, separate and unequal, between blacks and whites. Jim Crow laws mandated segregation in all areas of public life, including schools, work, department stores, courts, marriage, and transportation. . . . aided by the Supreme Court's decision in *Plessy v. Ferguson*."[71] Even more debilitating to opponents of racism was the widespread denial among White people that separation of the races represented inequality in any way, and, because it did not, complaints about schools, restaurants, hospitals – you have yours, too – could be rejected as special pleading. Douglas A. Blackmon noted, with an undercurrent of skeptical amazement, that:

> Never before in American history had so large a portion of the populace adopted such explicitly false and calculated propaganda. Many southern whites actually came to believe claims that black schools were equally funded, . . . and that black citizens were equally defended by the courts – as preposterous as those claims actually were.

Moreover, those who knew better chuckled up their sleeves as they "relished the clever fabrication of this mythology, and how it so effectively stymied the busybody friends of African-Americans in the North."[72] From the era's leading natural scientists, with Darwin on the tallest pedestal, to prominent social scientists, led by Herbert Spencer and William Graham Sumner, to scientific popularizers like Madison Grant and Lothrop Stoddard, to iconic literary creations like Tom Buchanan in F. Scott Fitzgerald's *The Great Gatsby* (1925), social Darwinism seemed to buttress White supremacy. But threats were growing. Madison Grant's *The Passing of the Great Race* (1916) and Lothrop Stoddard's *The Rising Tide of Color Against White World Supremacy* (1920) and *The Revolt Against Civilization: The Menace of the Under Man* (1922) advocated eugenics and immigration control to defend White, Anglo-Saxon, culture.[73] F. Scott Fitzgerald captured this broad cultural concern in a speech he wrote for his character Tom Buchanan in *Gatsby*. Tom Buchanan exemplified the entitled elites of the Roaring '20s. In a discussion of what was wrong with the country, Tom ranted:

> Civilization's going to pieces. . . . I've gotten to be a terrible pessimist about things. Have you read 'The Rise of the Colored Empires' by this man Goddard? . . . Well, it's a fine book, and everybody ought to read it. The idea is if we don't look out the white race will be – will be utterly submerged. It's all scientific stuff; it's been proved. . . . It's up to us, who are the dominant race, to watch out or these other races will have control of things.[74]

As the Roaring '20s, including the famed Harlem Renaissance, collapsed into the Great Depression, Black citizens received another extended and unmistakable lesson in their permanent secondary status. The economic catastrophe of the depression made more urgent the question of where exactly each group fit within the nation's racial hierarchy. Scholars make the point that while the Irish in the nineteenth century and Southern and Eastern Europeans in the late nineteenth and early twentieth centuries experienced searing discrimination, it was not the same as the exclusion faced by Black citizens and, to a somewhat lesser degree, by Native Americans, Hispanics, and Asians. David R. Roediger emphasized that Southern and Eastern European immigrants were "Victimized, but not in the same way as African Americans or immigrants of color, the new immigrant could claim . . . naturalization via whiteness. This tie of race with fitness for naturalized citizenship mattered greatly . . . in giving immigrant groups political power."[75] White immigrants, many initially considered non-White, or at least insufficiently White, became White, often by vehemently rejecting Black people and Blackness. Black Americans remained a sharply excluded group.

Yet, change was afoot and one of the biggest catalysts for that change came from an unlikely source. In 1938, the Carnegie Corporation provided $300,000 to a research team headed by two Swedish scholars, Gunnar Myrdal and Richard Sterner, to produce social science studies of "the Negro problem" in America. With Myrdal increasingly in the lead, a top-flight team of White and Black social scientists, including Ralph Bunche and the Black sociologist E. Franklin Frazier, produced several volumes, most famously Myrdal's *An American Dilemma* (1944).[76] Myrdal explained in the Introduction that: "The American Negro problem is a problem in the heart of the [White][77] American." Myrdal anticipated an ongoing battle, rather than willing White change, noting that "the pro-slavery theory of the *antebellum* South is basic to certain ideas, attitudes, and policies prevalent in all fields of human relations even at the present time." Myrdal bemoaned the fact that these ideas, attitudes, and politics meant that "the great majority of Southern conservative white people do not see the handwriting on the wall. They . . . live again in the pathetic illusion that the [race] matter is settled. . . . They think no adjustments are called for."[78] Albert Einstein, the world-famous physicist, in a 1946 commencement address at Lincoln University, joined his voice with Myrdal's in saying: "separation [of the races] is not a disease of colored people. It is a disease of white people. I do not intend to be quiet about it."[79] Others spoke out as well, but conservatives still knew that cultural inertia was on their side.

From the Third American Revolution to the Color-Blind Society

A third revolution in the nation's racial policy order – the mid-twentieth century civil rights movement – again elicited the hope of lasting change. The assault on segregation began in the 1940s and 1950s, with the desegregation of the military and then of public schools. Nonetheless, much remained to be done after Lyndon B. Johnson prevailed in the 1964 presidential election to win for himself the office he had inherited in the wake of John F. Kennedy's assassination. President Johnson's Assistant Secretary of Labor, Daniel Patrick Moynihan, later a Harvard scholar and three term U.S. Senator, wrote a famous report entitled, "The Negro Family: The Case for National Action." On the opening page of the report, Moynihan wrote, "The racist virus in the American bloodstream still afflicts us. Negroes will encounter serious personal prejudice for at least another generation." Obviously, while Moynihan correctly identified the virus, he underestimated its virulence and tenacity.[80]

Just as Frederick Douglass had pushed a reluctant Abraham Lincoln to the Second American Founding, Martin Luther King, Jr. pushed a similarly reluctant LBJ to the Third American Founding. Like Douglass, King drew on the nation's most sacred political documents and principles; most directly in his "I Have a Dream" speech delivered before the Lincoln Memorial on August 28, 1963. King demanded that the nation's claim that "all men are created equal" finally be realized. LBJ and big Democratic majorities in Congress responded with a bundle of landmark legislation, including the Civil Rights Acts of 1964 and 1965, the Voting Rights Act of 1965, the Immigration Act of 1965, and the Fair Housing Act of 1968. Black Americans were promised real equality in society, the economy, housing markets, and the voting booth. But as Frederick Douglass had predicted 100 years earlier, you cannot expect rain without some thunder and lightning. Johnson was stunned when his accomplishments were met with several summers of urban protests and riots.

Almost before the ink was dry on LBJ's Great Society program, reservations began to mount among the White public. Duke sociologist Eduardo Bonilla-Silva, author of *Racism Without Racists*, noted that, "whites support almost all the goals of the civil rights movement in principle, but object in practice to almost all the policies that have been developed to make those goals a reality."[81] Omi and Winant point out that neither this pattern nor its conservative results are new: "Just as many whites in the nineteenth century had opposed slavery but resisted a comprehensive reorganization of their privileged status vis-à-vis emancipated blacks, so too the neoconservatives opposed overt discrimination, but resisted an in-depth confrontation with the enduring benefits that race conferred on whites."[82] As a result, "instead of being dismantled, Jim Crow economic structures and relations have evolved as the basis for a new neoliberal racial order and continue to perpetuate racial inequality in the modern era."[83]

Nonetheless, Americans have changed the way they talk about race; the old epithets so common to an earlier day are rarely heard today. But is the change deeper than common speech? Scholars disagree about the nature and feel of racism in post-60s America. The overt racism of police dogs and water cannons largely is gone, but did the rise to dominance of the colorblind vision of society mean that racism had been defeated?[84] Some argued that racism had simply been normalized, as with the Republican party's Southern Strategy, where oblique references to states' rights, parental choice, and law and order were intended to reposition "white supremacism as a mainstream political initiative in the aftermath of the civil rights reforms."[85] Robin DiAngelo had a different take on the apparent disappearance of racism, arguing that it had simply been defined away. She wrote that: "After the civil rights movement, to be a good, moral person and to be complicit with racism became mutually exclusive.... To accomplish this adaptation, racism first needed to be reduced to simple, isolated, and extreme acts of prejudice.... based on conscious dislike of someone because of race."[86] Therefore, unless you were screaming epithets at a Black person, fists clenched, eyes bulging, and arteries standing out on your neck, you probably were not a racist.

Again, Desmond King and Rogers Smith see modern American politics, like previous eras of our politics, as "shaped by rival coalitions of political actors and institutions.... One coalition contends that laws and policies should be crafted in as 'color-blind' fashion as possible, treating people as individuals without reference to their racial identities. The other coalition insists that laws and policies should be made with constant, conscious concern to reduce severe racial inequalities in different areas of American life."[87] Not surprisingly, particularly from a historical perspective, King and Smith note, somewhat laconically, that: "color-blind positions are far more popular than race-conscious ones among the nation's still predominantly white electorate."[88] Dawson and Francis add that: "The postracial narrative is persuasive because it plays to the desires of a citizenry with race fatigue – the large majority of white Americans are convinced that blacks have achieved racial equality, and many also believe that blacks are demanding unfair racial advantages."[89] We will explore these beliefs in much greater detail in Chapter 4.

As during the era of the Robber Barons, new science helped challenge the civil rights movement and buttress the call for a colorblind society. The genetic revolution, like social Darwinism, affected how Americans thought about race, society, and politics. While the theory of natural selection reinforced the conviction that racial differences were real and immutable, the genetic revolution challenged the long-held sense of racial difference and hierarchy. Remarkably, both worked to White advantage and Black detriment.

In the early 1950s, James Watson and Francis Crick discovered the three-dimensional structure of DNA, the molecule carrying heredity. By the 1980s, Francis Collins, until recently Director of the U.S. National

Institutes of Health, led efforts to map particular gene sequences critical to the treatment of particular diseases, including cystic fibrosis and Huntington's disease. In 1992, J. Craig Venter, an NIH scientist, left the agency to found the Institute for Genomic Research (TIGR), now the J. Craig Venter Institute, with the goal of mapping the entire human genome. Venter and others accomplished this goal in 2001 to great scientific and social acclaim. Venter and the broader scientific community reported that genomic mapping demonstrated a common humanity, derived from a common ancestry, in which no bright lines between the races were to be found. Hence, they reasoned, race was a social construct with no roots, no meaning, in science.

Social scientists, as they had with Darwin's work a century and a half earlier, adopted and extended the genomic work of Venter and others. Isabel Wilkerson, in a *New York Times Magazine* piece drawn in spirit from her book *Caste*, observed that: "In the American caste system, the signal of rank is what we call race. . . . And yet, in recent decades, we have learned from the human genome that all human beings are 99.9 percent the same."[90] There are important truths here, but one wonders whether the findings of genomic science flow best into the narratives of progressive or conservative social policy advocates. Certainly, Spencer's and Sumner's translation of natural selection into social Darwinism put wind into the sails of small government conservatives for decades. But so far genomic science has had less, even limited, popular impact. Likely Robin DiAngelo's formulation will hold up best; race may be both unreal in science and all too real in society. She writes: "Whiteness, like race, may not be *true* – it's not a biologically heritable characteristic that has roots in physiological structures or in genes or chromosomes. But it is *real*, in the sense that societies and rights and goods and resources and privileges have been built on its foundation."[91] Real or not as a scientific concept, race is powerful enough as a social construct to divide, weaken, and disrupt societies all over the world, none more obviously than the U.S.

Despite the fact that race remains a powerful social signifier in American life, the genomic revolution undercut the ability of Black and other disadvantaged groups to make political claims. If we are all genetically very similar, almost the same, the less notice of race – which does not really exist, right? – the better. Let government prepare general and neutral rules, and then let people compete within the framework of those rules to find their place in the world. This "new neoliberal racial order" was characterized by "a set of policies and ideological tenets that include the privatization of public assets; the deregulation or elimination of state services; . . . and the use of market language to legitimate new norms and neutralize opposition."[92] Just as in the age of *Plessy*, advocates of colorblind public policy argue that market solutions and neutral regulations make discussions of race, ethnicity, and gender seem like pleading for special treatment and unwarranted advantage.[93]

In this chapter, we have seen that White supremacy was a pillar of the American political culture from the earliest colonial times well into the twentieth century and beyond.[94] This conclusion is uncomfortable to the modern American mind and fits poorly with our preferred national story – ever widening access to the American dream – but it is hard to deny. Sheryll Cashin has written provocatively that White supremacy has adapted to survive as "One anti-Black caste system – chattel slavery – was replaced by another [Jim Crow], and then another [colorblindness], down through the generations."[95] In Chapter 2 we describe the demographic turmoil that followed European first contact with the Americas and we deploy demographic data, from the U.S. Census and other sources, to demonstrate and explain why White supremacy has been such a robust part of our national history. For the first 350 years of American history, White people constituted about 80 percent of the total population. Moreover, White people were free, Black people were not. White supremacy seemed evident to the dominant elements of society and no voices to whom they were willing to listen spoke against it. Ideas so well rooted and seemingly obvious are hard to eradicate.

Notes

1. Alan Watson, *Roman Slave Law* (Baltimore, MD: Johns Hopkins University Press, 1887), xviii.
2. David Brion Davis, *Inhuman Bondage* (New York: Oxford University Press, 2006), 32, 40.
3. Jan Hinrich Hagedorn, *Domestic Slavery in Syria and Egypt, 1200–1500* (Gottingen, Germany: Bonn University Press, 2020), 19, 139–144. See also *Slavery and South Asian History*, ed. Indrani Chatterjee and Richard M. Eaton (Bloomington: Indiana University Press, 2006), especially Ramya Sreenivasan, "Drudges, Dancing Girls, and Concubines: Female Slaves in Rajput Polity: 1500–1850," 139; Francis Fukuyama, *The Origins of Political Order: From Prehistoric Times to the French Revolution* (New York: Farrar, Straus, and Giroux, 2011), 101, 206.
4. Robert William Fogel and Stanley L. Engerman, *Time on the Cross: The Economics of American Negro Slavery* (New York: W.W. Norton, 1974, 1989), 29–30. See also Martin Wolf, *The Crisis of Democratic Capitalism* (New York: Penguin Press, 2023), 18.
5. Bernard Lewis, *The Muslim Discovery of Europe* (New York: Norton, originally published in 1982, reissued as Norton paperback, 2001), 65, 188.
6. Kermit Roosevelt III, *The Nation That Never Was: Reconstructing America's Story* (Chicago, IL: University of Chicago Press, 2022), 47, 56.

7 Lewis, *The Muslim Discovery of Europe*, 187.
8 William J. Bernstein, *A Splendid Exchange: How Trade Shaped the World* (New York: Grove Press, 2008), 121–122. See also Vivian Yee, "Dutch Exhibit Links Egypt to Africa. Ire Boils Over in Egypt," *New York Times*, June 19, 2023, A4.
9 Paul E. Lovejoy, *Transformations in Slavery: A History of Slavery in Africa*, 3rd ed. (New York: Cambridge University Press, 2012), 22. See also Davis, *Inhuman Bondage*, 61; Bernstein, *A Splendid Exchange*, 275.
10 Lerone Bennett, Jr., *Before the Mayflower: A History of the Negro in America, 1619–1962* (Chicago, IL: Johnson Publishing Company, 1962; Eastford, CT: Martino Fine Books, 2016), 33, 36.
11 Ibram X. Kendi, *Stamped from the Beginning: The Definitive History of Racist Ideas in America* (New York: Bold Type Books, 2017), 18. See also Tyler Stovall, *White Freedom: The Racial History of an Idea* (Princeton, NJ: Princeton University Press, 2021), 16–17.
12 Howard W. French, *Born in Blackness: Africa, Africans, and the Making of the Modern World, 1471 to the Second World War* (New York: Liveright, 2021). See also Lovejoy, *Transformations in Slavery*, xv.
13 Charles C. Mann, *1493: Uncovering the New World Columbus Created* (New York: Alfred A. Knopf, 2011), 5.
14 Alfred W. Crosby, Jr., *The Columbian Exchange: Biological and Cultural Consequences of First Contact*, 30th anniversary ed. (Westport, CT: Praeger, 2003), 36. See, for example, the Babylonian map of the world, circa 700 to 500 BCE, at digitalmapsoftheancientworld.com/ancient-maps/Babylonian-map-of-the-world/. Note that the cuneiform inscription to the map concludes of the nations beyond Mesopotamia, "their interior no-one knows."
15 George Makari, *Of Fear and Strangers: A History of Xenophobia* (New York: W.W. Norton, 2021). See also "Know Thyself: The African Genome Project," *The Economist*, June 26, 2021, 16.
16 Michael Omi and Howard Winant, *Racial Formation in the United States*, 3rd ed. (New York: Routledge, 2015), 245, see also 112–113. See also Thomas Piketty, *A Brief History of Equality* (Cambridge, MA: Harvard University Press, 2022), 48–49, 66.
17 Joe R. Feagin, *The White Racial Frame: Centuries of Racial Framing and Counter-Framing*, 3rd ed. (New York: Routledge, 2020), 36–37. See also Isabel Wilkerson, *Caste: The Origins of Our Discontents* (New York: Random House, 2020), 64, 29, 40–43.
18 Richard B. Allen, "Human Trafficking in Asia Before 1900: A Preliminary Census," *International Institute for Asian Studies*, Autumn 2020, 32.
19 Omi and Winant, *Racial Formation*, 106, 111. See also Juliet Hooker, *Race and the Politics of Solidarity* (New York: Oxford University Press, 2009), 4, 167–169.
20 Roosevelt, *The Nation That Never Was*, 15–16.
21 Wilkerson, *Caste*, 17, 19, see also 70–71. See also Natalia Molina, *How Race is Made in America: Immigration, Citizenship, and the Historical Power of Racial Scripts* (Berkeley, CA: University of California Press, 2014), 3; Isabel Wilkerson, "America's Enduring Caste System," *The New York Times Magazine*, July 5, 2020, 26–33, 49–52, especially 31.
22 Omi and Winant, *Racial Formation*, 130, 196, 140; see also 76, 214.
23 Sheryll Cashin, *White Space, Black Hood: Opportunity Hoarding and Segregation in the Age of Inequality* (Boston, MA: Beacon Press, 2021), 4.
24 Eddie S. Glaude, Jr., *Begin Again: James Baldwin's America and Its Urgent Lessons for Our Own* (New York: Crown Books, 2020), 23. See also Theodore R.

Johnson, *When the Stars Begin to Fall: Overcoming Racism and Renewing the Promise of America* (New York: Grove Press, 2021), 8.
25 Joe Biden, "Howard University Class of 2023 Commencement Address," May 13, 2023.
26 Kendi, *Stamped from the Beginning*, x. See also Peniel E. Joseph, *The Third Reconstruction: America's Struggle for Racial Justice in the Twenty-First Century* (New York: Basic Books, 2022), 136, 144–145.
27 Rogers M. Smith and Desmond S. King, "White Protectionism in America," *Perspectives on Politics* 19, no. 2 (2020): 2. See also Desmond S. King and Rogers M. Smith, *Still a House Divided: Race and Politics in Obama's America* (Princeton, NJ: Princeton University Press, 2011), 8–9; Gary Gerstle, *American Crucible: Race and Nation in the Twentieth Century* (Princeton, NJ: Princeton University Press, 2001, rev. ed. 2017), xiv, 4–5.
28 Feagin, *The White Racial Frame*, 2, 38, 50–54, 107–108.
29 Richard Haass, *The Bill of Obligations: The Ten Habits of Good Citizens* (New York: Penguin Press, 2023), 65–66.
30 Eric Foner, *The Second Founding: How the Civil War and Reconstruction Remade the Constitution* (New York: W.W. Norton, 2019). See also Harry V. Jaffa, *Crisis of the House Divided: An Interpretation of the Issues in the Lincoln-Douglas Debates* (Chicago, IL: University of Chicago Press, 1959, 1982), 43–44, 241; Noah Feldman, *The Broken Constitution: Lincoln, Slavery and the Refounding of America* (New York: Farrar, Straus, and Giroux, 2021); Roosevelt, *The Nation That Never Was*, 52, 155, 167, 179.
31 George Packer, *Last Best Hope: America in Crisis and Renewal* (New York: Farrar, Straus, and Giroux, 2021), 53, 167, 187. See also Joseph, *The Third Reconstruction*, 13, 33–34.
32 Robert N. Bellah, "Civil Religion in America," *Daedalus* 96, no. 1 (Winter 1967): 16.
33 Adam Dahl, *Empire of the People: Settler Colonialism and the Foundations of Modern Democratic Thought* (Lawrence, KS: University Press of Kansas, 2018), 166, 180.
34 Bennett, *Before the Mayflower*, 29–30. See also Jon Meacham, *American Gospel: God, the Founding Fathers, and the Making of a Nation* (New York: Random House, 2006), 44.
35 Colin Woodard, *American Character: A History of the Epic Struggle Between Individual Liberty and the Common Good* (New York: Penguin Books, 2017), 75, 47. See also Michael Tadman, "The Demographic Cost of Sugar: Debates on Slave Societies and Natural Increase in the Americas," *The American Historical Review* 105, no. 5 (December 2000): 1534–1575; Piketty, *A Brief History of Equality*, 56; Dahl, *Empire of the People*, 12, 128–129.
36 Edward J. Larson, *American Inheritance: Liberty and Slavery in the Birth of a Nation, 1765–1795* (New York: Norton, 2023), 259–260.
37 Voltaire, *Additions to the Essay on General History*, vol. 22, *The Works of M. De Voltaire*, trans. T. Franklin, et al. (London: Crowder, et al., 1763), 227–228, 234.
38 Winthrop D. Jordan, Christopher L. Brown, and Peter H. Wood, *White Over Black: American Attitudes Toward the Negro, 1550–1812* (Chapel Hill: University of North Carolina Press, 1968; 2nd ed., 2012), 253.
39 Emmanuel Chukwudi Eze, ed., *Race and the Enlightenment: A Reader* (Cambridge, MA: Blackwell, 1997), 38–64, see 64. See also Donald Yacovone, *Teaching White Supremacy: America's Democratic Ordeal and the Forging of Our National Identity* (New York: Pantheon Books, 2022), 10.

40 David Hackett Fischer, *African Founders: How Enslaved People Expanded American Ideals* (New York: Simon & Schuster, 2022), 102, 196.
41 Thomas Jefferson, *Notes on the State of Virginia*, ed. William Peden (New York: W.W. Norton, 1972), 139, 143.
42 Jefferson, *Notes on the State of Virginia*, 138.
43 Thomas Jefferson, *The Life and Selected Writings of Thomas Jefferson*, ed. Adrienne Koch and William Peden (New York: The Modern Library, 1944), 51. See also Harry V. Jaffa, *A New Birth of Freedom: Abraham Lincoln and the Coming of the Civil War* (New York: Rowman and Littlefield, 2000), 21–23.
44 Larson, *American Inheritance*, 129–130.
45 Kate Masur, *Until Justice Be Done: America's First Civil Rights Movement, from the Revolution to Reconstruction* (New York: W.W. Norton, 2021), xiii.
46 Van Gosse, *The First Reconstruction: Black Politics in America from the Revolution to the Civil War* (Chapel Hill, NC: University of North Carolina Press, 2021), 2–3.
47 Omi and Winant, *Racial Formation*, 139. See also Christopher Leslie Brown, "The Problems of Slavery," in *The Oxford Handbook of the American Revolution*, ed. Edward G. Gray and Jane Kamensky (New York: Oxford University Press, 2013), 428.
48 Robert P. Jones, *White Too Long: The Legacy of White Supremacy in American Christianity* (New York: Simon & Schuster, 2020), 2–3.
49 John S. Haller, Jr., *Outcasts from Evolution: Scientific Attitudes of Racial Inferiority, 1859–1900* (Carbondale, IL: Southern Illinois University Press, 1971, 1995), 77, see also 132, 166.
50 Henry Cleveland, *Alexander H. Stephens, in Public and Private: With Letters and Speeches, Before, During, and Since the War* (Philadelphia, PA: National Publishing Co., 1866), 717–729, see 721–722. See also King and Smith, *Still a House Divided*, 49; Leon F. Litwack, *Been in the Storm So Long: The Aftermath of Slavery* (New York: Vintage Books, 1980), 16; Jill Lepore, *This America: The Case for the Nation* (New York: Liveright, 2019), 60; Jon Meacham, *The Soul of America: The Battle for Our Better Angels* (New York: Random House, 2018), 54.
51 John G. Nicolay and John Hay, eds., *Complete Works of Abraham Lincoln* (New York: The Lamb Publishing Co., 1905), 2:206–207.
52 Nicolay and Hay, *Complete Works of Abraham Lincoln*, 8:16.
53 David Herbert Donald, *Lincoln* (New York: Simon & Schuster, 1995), 398, 429–431. See also Ian Haney López, *Merge Left: Fusing Race and Class, Winning Elections, and Saving America* (New York: The New Press, 2019), 191.
54 David W. Blight, *Frederick Douglass: Prophet of Freedom* (New York: Simon & Schuster, 2018), xv.
55 Vernon L. Parrington, *Main Currents in American Thought: An Interpretation of American Literature from the Beginnings to 1920* (New York: Harcourt, Brace and Company, 1927, 1930), 3:285.
56 John M. Blassingame, ed., *The Frederick Douglass Papers* (New Haven, CT: Yale University Press, 1982), 2:367, 371.
57 Frederick Douglass, "If There is No Struggle, There is No Progress," https://www.blackpast.org/african-american-history/1857-frederick-douglass-if-there-no-struggle-there-no-progress/.
58 *Congressional Globe*, 37th Cong., 2nd sess., 1562 (1862). See also Paul M. Rego, *Lyman Trumbull and the Second Founding of the United States* (Lawrence, KS: University Press of Kansas, 2022), 48–49.

59 Beverly Wilson Palmer, ed., and Holly Byers Ochoa, assoc. ed., *The Selected Papers of Thaddeus Stevens* (Pittsburgh, PA: University of Pittsburgh Press, 1997), 2:156.
60 Litwack, *Been in the Storm So Long*, 364. See also Sidney Andrews, *The South Since the War* (Boston: Tichnor and Fields, 1866), 398; Roger L. Ransom and Richard Sutch, *One Kind of Freedom: The Economic Consequences of Emancipation* (New York: Cambridge University Press, 1977, 2nd ed., 2001), 23. See also Meacham, *The Soul of America*, 58.
61 Henry Louis Gates, Jr., *Stony the Road: Reconstruction, White Supremacy, and the Rise of Jim Crow* (New York: Penguin Books, 2020), 6, 20.
62 C. Vann Woodward, *The Burden of Southern History*, rev. ed. (Baton Rouge, LA: Louisiana State University Press, 1968), 105. See also Leon F. Litwack, *Trouble in Mind: Black Southerners in the Age of Jim Crow* (New York: Vintage Books, 1998), 218–219.
63 Fred Arthur Bailey, "Free Speech and the 'Lost Cause' in Texas: A Study of Social Control in the New South," *Southern Historical Quarterly* 97, no. 3 (January 1994): 454.
64 Patrick L. Cox and Michael Phillips, *The House Will Come to Order: How the Texas Speaker Became a Power in State and National Politics* (Austin, TX: University of Texas Press, 2010), 14. Emphasis in the original.
65 Douglas A. Blackmon, *Slavery by Another Name: The Re-Enslavement of Black Americans from the Civil War to World War II* (New York: Anchor Books, 2009), 237–241.
66 David Levering Lewis, *W.E.B. Du Bois: A Biography, 1868–1963* (New York: Henry Holt and Company, 2009), 50.
67 Rego, *Lyman Trumbull and the Second Founding of the United States*, 2. See also Richard F. Bensel, *Yankee Leviathan: The Origins of Central State Authority in America, 1859–1877* (New York: Cambridge University Press, 1990), 10.
68 Woodrow Wilson, "The Reconstruction of the Southern States," *Atlantic Monthly*, January 1901, 1.
69 Charles Darwin, *The Origin of Species and The Descent of Man* (New York: The Modern Library, 1936), 530–531, 539. See also King and Smith, *Still a House Divided*, 56; Haller, *Outcasts from Evolution*, 87.
70 Haller, *Outcasts from Evolution*, 138, see also 166.
71 Michael C. Dawson and Megan Ming Francis, "Black Politics and the Neoliberal Racial Order," *Public Culture* 28, no. 1 (2016): 33.
72 Blackmon, *Slavery by Another Name*, 169.
73 Gates, *Stony the Road*, 78–79. See also Lepore, *This America*, 88–95.
74 F. Scott Fitzgerald, *The Great Gatsby* (New York: Charles Scribner's Sons, 1925, 1968), 9.
75 David R. Roediger, *Working Toward Whiteness: How America's Immigrants Became White* (New York: Basic Books, 2005), 121. See also Chad R. Williams, *The Wounded World: W.E.B. Du Bois and the First World War* (New York: Farrar, Straus, and Giroux, 2023).
76 Clare L. Spark, "Race, Caste, or Class? The Bunche-Myrdal Dispute Over an American Dilemma," *International Journal of Politics, Culture, and Society* 14, no. 3 (2001): 465.
77 Added by the author. Myrdal does not say it, but it is clearly what he means.
78 Gunnar Myrdal, *An American Dilemma: The Negro Problem and Modern Democracy* (New York: Harper and Brothers, 1944), xlvii, 86, 519.
79 Fred Jerome and Rodger Taylor, *Einstein on Race and Racism* (New Brunswick, NJ: Rutgers University Press, 2005), 91.

80 Gerstle, *American Crucible*, 268–269. See also Gary Gerstle, *The Rise and Fall of the Neoliberal Order: America and the World in the Free Market Era* (New York: Oxford University Press, 2022), 53–54, 113, 135.
81 Eduardo Bonilla-Silva, *Racism Without Racists: Color-Blind Racism and the Persistence of Racial Inequality in America*, 5th ed. (Lanham, MD: Rowman and Littlefield, 2018), 142.
82 Omi and Winant, *Racial Formation*, 201. See also Richard Johnson, *The End of the Second Reconstruction* (New York: Polity, 2020).
83 Dawson and Francis, "Black Politics and the Neoliberal Racial Order," 30. See also Elizabeth Hinton, *America on Fire: The Untold History of Police Violence and Black Rebellion Since the 1960s* (New York: Liveright, 2021), 13; Nicholas Eubank and Adriane Fresh, "Enfranchisement and Incarceration After the 1965 Voting Rights Act," *American Political Science Review* 116, no. 3 (August 2022): 791–806.
84 Thomas Bryne Edsall, *The Point of No Return: American Democracy at the Crossroads* (Princeton, NJ: Princeton University Press, 2023), 179. See also Michael Wayne Santos, *Rediscovering a Nation: Will the Real America Please Stand Up* (Lanham, MD: Rowman and Littlefield, 2022), 80.
85 Omi and Winant, *Racial Formation*, 191.
86 Robin DiAngelo, *White Fragility: Why It's So Hard for White People to Talk About Racism* (Boston, MA: Beacon Press, 2018), 71. See also Charles M. Blow, "Justices Enshrine Racial Imbalance," *New York Times*, July 6, 2023, A23.
87 King and Smith, *Still a House Divided*, 7.
88 King and Smith, *Still a House Divided*, 8, see also 114.
89 Dawson and Francis, "Black Politics and the Neoliberal Racial Order," 30.
90 Wilkerson, "America's Enduring Caste System," 31.
91 DiAngelo, *White Fragility*, x. See also Yascha Mounk, *The Great Experiment: Why Diverse Democracies Fall Apart and How They Can Endure* (New York: Penguin Press, 2022), 41, 114.
92 Dawson and Francis, "Black Politics and the Neoliberal Racial Order," 27.
93 Jennifer Schuessler, "Scholars See Familiar Twist as King's Speech Is Cited," *New York Times*, March 24, 2022, A11. See also Jared Clemons, "From 'Freedom Now!' to 'Black Lives Matter': Retrieving King and Randolph to Theorize Contemporary White Antiracism," *Perspectives on Politics* 20, no. 4 (December 2022): 1291.
94 Heather McGhee, *The Sum of Us: What Racism Costs Everyone and How We Can Prosper Together* (New York: OneWorld, 2021), 7. See also "Race and Liberal Philosophy," *The Economist*, July 11, 2020, 47.
95 Cashin, *White Space, Black Hood*, 199. See also Leslie Alexander and Michelle Alexander, "Fear," in *The 1619 Project*, ed. Nikole Hannah-Jones, Caitlin Roper, Ilena Silverman, and Jake Silverstein (New York: The New York Times Co., 2021), 102.

2
DEMOGRAPHIC STABILITY AND CHANGE IN AMERICAN HISTORY

"I want a home here not only for the negro, the mulatto and the Latin races, but I want the Asiatic to find a home here in the United States, and to feel at home here, both for his sake and for ours. The outspread wings of the American Eagle are broad enough to shelter all who are likely to come."

Frederick Douglass, 1867, "Composite Nation"

The Americas were among the last broad expanses of the earth to be occupied by humans. Early hominids left Africa hundreds of thousands of years ago and their descendants, Peking Man in the East and Neanderthals in the West, Denisovans, and others, were not displaced until modern man, homo sapiens, began spreading from Africa 70,000 to 100,000 years ago. Not until the last Ice Age began to give way about 30,000 years ago did human populations across Eurasia begin to grow in numbers and expand their ranges of foraging and exploration. Only 17,000 to 20,000 years ago, some say longer, with much of the earth's water yet trapped in ice sheets and the land bridge between Asia and North America at the Bering Straits still open, a very few of the globe's approximately 4 million humans crossed into the New World. After rising sea levels submerged the land bridge from Asia around 14,000 years ago, humans continued to spread throughout the Americas but they were isolated from humans in the rest of the world.[1]

Today we think of the Americas, especially North America, as rich and bountiful. And so it likely appeared to those early adventurers, but the

DOI: 10.4324/9781003449188-2

future would uncover stark limitations. As the environmental historian Alfred Crosby pointed out, "The ancestors of the Indians crossed into the isolation of America probably before agriculture had been invented, . . . [and] before the major domestications of wild animals had been accomplished." Moreover, they crossed into continents that had severely limited prospects for domesticable plants or animals. In Eurasia, suitable grains (wheat, rice, corn, barley, and sorghum) and large mammals (horses, cattle, pigs, sheep and goats) were available to be domesticated to man's benefit and service; in the Americas none of the large mammals and only teosinte, the base of corn, were present. Nonetheless, isolation in the Americas allowed populations to expand, particularly in the central valley of Mexico, which became home to the Aztec Empire, and in Peru and the Andean highlands, where the Inca held sway. In the millennia between first human arrival in the Americas and first contact with Europeans, population growth continued but social development was stunted and slow. Written language was limited and rudimentary, they had no animals that they rode or used as beasts of burden, and they did not have the wheel. "When Columbus arrived, even the most advanced Indians were barely out of the Stone Age."[2] And Native Americans were not just technologically primitive.

Historically, isolated communities have built up immunities over time to local pathogens but been tragically vulnerable to contact with outsiders. The economist Angus Deaton and many others have noted that contact between previously isolated communities "brought new threats of disease. These 'new' diseases, transmitted from previously unconnected civilizations, brought infections against which local populations had no immunity."[3] Across Africa and Eurasia, military campaigns, nomadic wandering, slaving, and trade brought once isolated communities into occasional and then increasingly regular contact with each other. The historian Ian Morris wrote that "as more and more merchants and nomads moved along" trade routes like the silk road, civilizational cores in the West, the East, and South Asia came into more frequent contact and "the disease pools began to merge, setting loose horrors for everyone."[4] Plagues carried away a quarter to a third of the population in parts of China, Mesopotamia, and Egypt early in the first millennia, as did the Black Death in Europe during the sixth and the fourteenth centuries, but over the centuries these epidemics left behind rising levels of immunity. The peoples of the Americas were spared these ravages, but were left unprepared for their collision with the rest of the world when it finally occurred.

The written history of the Americas begins with a demographic implosion of monumental proportions. While there is much that we do not know about the indigenous populations of the Americas at first contact – Christopher Columbus landed in what is now the Bahamas on

October 12, 1492 – there are a few big things we do know. First, most of the indigenous peoples of the Americas were pre-literate, including the Inca of South America, while a few were literate, but heavily pictographic. For example, the Aztec of Mexico had the same word for writing and drawing. There were mathematical and astronomical accomplishments, but no written histories, no censuses, and few records of any kind.[5] Second, devastating decline from invasion, disease, and famine came so quickly that few European records were made, or could have been made, about the societies of the Americas pre-contact. One stunning description left by "A Spanish priest travelling with Cortez conveys the scale of the devastation: 'They died in heaps, like bedbugs. . . . In many places it happened that everyone in a house died, and, as it was impossible to bury the great number of dead, they pulled down the houses over them so that their homes became their tombs.'"[6] Third, Columbus and those who followed soon after brought not only death, disease, and expropriation, they also brought food grains as well as domesticated mammals that did not then exist in the Americas. The world of the Americas pre-contact was lost in a human cataclysm, the Great Dying, and remade by Europeans who perpetrated a second cataclysm, the Atlantic slave trade. These were vast world-shaping dramas that defy understanding and even imagination.

The Great Dying in the Americas

The tragic events unleashed in the Americas were the product of the world's separate continents and civilizations being bound ever closer together by chains of commerce and conquest. Pushed by Portugal's Prince Henry "the navigator" and his Spanish counterparts, followed soon by the Dutch, English, French, and others, explorers seeking a route east to India and China crept down the west coast of Africa during the whole of the fifteenth century. Christopher Columbus, sailing for the Catholic monarchs, King Ferdinand of Aragon and Queen Isabella of Castile, sought India by sailing west across the Atlantic. In October 1492, Columbus sighted India, or at least what he thought was India and later came to be known as the West Indies or Caribbean. After exploring the Caribbean for four months, fruitlessly interrogating the natives about gold, Columbus headed back to Spain. Vasco da Gama, in 1498, sailed around the southern tip of Africa and on to India. But the quest to know, control, and exploit the world had just begun.

Christopher Columbus, the European mariner traditionally credited with "discovering" the Americas in 1492, kept an admiral's log or journal in which he recorded his impressions of the new world.[7] Three things struck Columbus most forcefully about the people he encountered: their color, culture, and capacity for defense. Columbus, at first contact with the Americas and their inhabitants, was struck powerfully by racial difference. A veteran of voyages to the West coast of Africa, Columbus wrote that the hair of the indigenous peoples of the Caribbean was "not kinky, but straight and coarse like horsehair; the whole forehead and head is very broad, moreso than any other race that I have ever seen." He reported several times in his log that, "They themselves are not at all black, but of the color of the Canary Islanders." Upon reaching Hispaniola, modern Cuba, the first crew members ashore reported that "they are whiter than the others, and that among these they saw two wenches as white as they can be in Spain." And a few days later, Columbus himself wrote that, "they are . . . so white that if they went clothed and protected themselves from the sun and air they would be almost as white as in Spain."[8] In the end, the fact that some natives seemed almost White gained them little. Columbus' immediate conclusion was that these people "ought to make good slaves for they are of quick intelligence since I notice that they repeat what is said to them."

Nearly as evident as color to both Europeans and the indigenous peoples of the Indies were differences of culture and the hierarchical implications of those differences. Columbus wrote, "these people were very poor in everything. They all go quite naked as their mothers bore them; . . . They have no iron. . . . I saw neither sheep nor goats nor any other beast . . . except dogs which don't bark."[9] Poor, naked – no horses, cattle, or pigs – and their dogs don't bark. We know what the native islanders thought as they looked back at Columbus, his men, and ships only from what the Europeans recorded. Several of the early parties that Columbus sent to explore returned with the same report. "They think that we have come from the sky," appeared more than half a dozen times in Columbus' log.[10] Two passages from the log tell us a great deal about the presumptions that both sides developed about each other and how they acted on those presumptions. First, the scouts who returned to tell that the islanders thought Columbus' ships "came from the sky," also recounted that when they took leave of the islanders, "500 men and women would have come with them, for they thought they were returning to the sky."[11] Soon thereafter, Columbus recorded this remarkable account, suggesting that some needed a bit more persuasion to accompany the admiral:

> Yesterday came aboard the ship a dugout with six young men, and five came on board; these I ordered to be detained and I am bringing them. And afterwards I sent to a house which is on the western bank of the river, and they brought seven head of women, small and large, and three boys. I did this because the men would behave better in Spain with

women of their country than without them; for already many times I happened to take men of Guinea that they might learn the language in Portugal, and after they had returned and it was expected to make some use of them in their own country, . . . but in reaching home it never proved to be so. . . . But these, having their women, will find it good business to do what they are told.[12]

Finally, Columbus understood his mission to be to explore, claim whatever he found for his employers and sovereigns, survey any riches, especially gold, and assess the islanders' ability to defend themselves and their riches. Columbus reported that, "they bear no arms, nor know thereof; for I showed them swords and they grasped them by the blade and cut themselves through ignorance." Later in the voyage, writing in the third person, he wrote, "And the Admiral assures the Sovereigns that 10 men could put to flight 10,000, so cowardly and timid are they; and neither do they bear arms, except some darts, on the end of which they have a sharpened, fire-hardened" point.[13] Moreover, because the Spaniards, navigating by compass in three-masted ships, with armor, broadswords, muskets, and cannon, confronted native peoples barely beyond a Stone Age culture, without the wheel or writing beyond pictorial glyphs, no weapons beyond clubs, spears, bows, arrows, and slings, and no beasts of burden or domesticated animals beyond dogs, a sense of hierarchy on both sides was immediate.[14] Within weeks of first contact, Columbus had formed critical conclusions that he shared with "the Sovereigns;" these people are not actually White, they are effectively defenseless, and they may have riches. Though the mainland empires of the Aztecs and Incas tried to defend themselves and repel the invaders, Columbus' predictions held up remarkably well.

In sum, Columbus and his men found the natives of the Caribbean surprisingly light complected but not White, culturally and technologically impoverished, and defenseless. The Europeans were surprised by what they found in the Caribbean, but they had seen less advanced societies before, in the Canary Islands, Guinea, and the rest of Africa. The native populations of the Americas, on the other hand, initially had no idea who or what these interlopers were. All the native peoples had to help them make sense of the newcomers were their traditional religious, cultural, and political traditions. Though they studied the newcomers closely, they could not imagine that their whole way of life, whole existence, was under threat so they reacted slowly. Before long, however, the natives knew that something was very wrong; these strangers brought death and disease. For the natives this was doom, for the Europeans it was an open pathway.

One popular telling of the story of early European contact with the Americas has populous, settled, successful societies decimated and dispossessed in mere decades by marauding Europeans.[15] While there is some truth to this perspective, the full story has many elements. The devastation of native populations in the Americas was so complete as to remind one of the biblical references to the "four horsemen of the apocalypse;" often rendered as war, pestilence, famine, and death.[16] War came in two forms, conquest from outside by the conquistadors, and domestic conflicts including unstable alliances, regional competition, and wars of succession. As a result, tiny bands of conquistadors swept away much larger, but looser and poorly armed, native armies. As leaders fell, bloody succession squabbles further weakened native defenses. In fact, leadership contests often found both, or all, sides appealing to the invaders for support.

Moreover, political fragmentation meant that the invaders found ready allies among leaders who believed, almost always wrongly, that the enemy of my enemy is my friend. The historian of Mesoamerica, Caroline Dodds Pennock, noted that "there were hundreds of independent polities in Mexico, all struggling to maintain themselves in the precarious world created by the European invasion." By the time Cortés laid siege to Montezuma's capital in 1521 "he had tens of thousands of Tlaxcalan allies" supplementing his ranks.[17] Such political fragmentation existed throughout the Americas and it vastly increased native vulnerability.

Despite the destruction brought by war, disease took a far greater toll as foreign pathogens tore through native populations.[18] War and sickness interrupted agriculture and trade so starvation and death followed in their wake generation after generation. Population estimates for all of the Americas vary dramatically, from a lower range of about 20 million to an upper range approaching 160 million, with average estimates of 40 to 60 million. The estimates for North America alone (the U.S. and Canada) ranged from 900,000 to 18 million. Whatever the population numbers of the pre-contact Americas, most agree that within little more than a century they had fallen by 80 to 90 percent through a combination of conflict, disease, and starvation.[19]

The journalist Colin Woodard described the stunning consequences of the Americas' early contact with the wider world thusly: "the entire Western Hemisphere. . . . [was] populated by perhaps 100 million people. . . . But by 1630 the population of the Americas had crashed by 80 to 90 percent as epidemics and warfare spread from points of European contact."[20] The social policy advocate Heather McGhee wrote: "The death toll of South and North American Indigenous people in the century after first contact was so massive – an estimated 56 million lives, or 90 percent of all the lands' original inhabitants, through either war or disease – that it changed the amount of carbon in the atmosphere."[21] This striking sentence, based on a scholarly article by the geographer Alexander Koch and his colleagues, seems to directly connect deaths to changing carbon levels in the atmosphere. It neglects to mention that the deaths, and they were massive, led to reduced cultivation, the return of grasslands, forests, and jungles, and it was the increased vegetation that reduced the amount of carbon in the atmosphere.[22] Koch and his colleagues conclude their article as follows: "We conclude that the Great Dying of Indigenous Peoples of the Americas led to the abandonment of enough cleared land . . . that the resulting terrestrial carbon uptake had a detectable impact on both atmospheric CO_2 and global surface air temperatures."[23] Not quite as dramatic, but more accurate.

The Great Dying in the Americas was an unprecedented event in world history, and it was set in motion – caused – by European contact, but how should it be described and evaluated? The sociologist Joe Feagin contended that the traditional literature on first contact and its consequences underappreciated the success of the native societies, writing: "Critical facts, such as the reality that the indigenous peoples were often the successful and established *settlers* of lands stolen from them, are suppressed in these narratives."[24] This framing – successful indigenous societies, unexpectedly fallen upon by rapacious Europeans, with their superior weapons and mysterious diseases – is not quite as uncommon as Feagin suggested, it is the progressive staple. But we must consider that with and behind the soldiers came explorers, priests, and finally settlers. When the image of the invading European is of the bloody Hernán Cortés or the bloodier Francisco Pizarro, the frame holds; less so when the image is of John Winthrop, much less Roger Williams or Anne Hutchinson. After all, the saintly Mr. Williams carried all the same pathogens as the bloody Pizarro. Magellan circumnavigated the globe in a three-year voyage, 1519–1521, conclusively tying the continents together. Tragedy for the indigenous peoples of the Americas followed contact with the broader world, no question, but one struggles to imagine a different, more peaceful – but also historically plausible – outcome.[25]

The indigenous societies in what would become the United States did not produce the great empires that existed in Mexico and South America, meaning that conquistadors searching for gold soon concluded that they were wasting their time, but demographic tragedy came to these natives too. There were no great cities, but there were both hunting tribes and more stable native agricultural communities in their unknown numbers scattered across the continent. But the mere European presence sparked plagues that emptied whole villages. Hernando de Soto's march through the lower Mississippi Valley in 1540 found decimation already well along.[26] As Tiya Miles recounted in *The 1619 Project*, "Disease, political instability, and slaving . . . ravaged Mississippi chiefdoms in the century and a half after

Europeans arrived and led to widespread social collapse that left behind what the anthropologist Robbie Ethridge has termed a 'shatter zone.'"[27]

While the results of these early contacts were certainly brutal, they were not always conceived that way. As the proprietors of the Virginia Company prepared to launch their Jamestown venture in 1606, the instructions written to guide the colonists on first arrival treated the indigenous peoples of the region as curiosities. The native peoples were described variously as "the natural people of the country," "the naturals," and "the country people."[28] They were not to be provoked unnecessarily, certainly not initially, but they were to be nudged out of the way as settler needs dictated. The instructions gave no sense that "the naturals" had established claims that needed to be respected. As settler numbers grew, they became stronger and more bold as "the naturals" became weaker. Alexis de Tocqueville found these events to be puzzling but not of great moment, calling them, "A strange thing! There are peoples who have so completely disappeared from the earth that the very memory of the name has been effaced; their languages are lost, their glory has vanished like a sound without an echo."[29] Native communities throughout the Americas suffered similar fates.

No single example of White settler entitlement to the exclusion of other claims and interests speaks louder than the young Thomas Jefferson's stern reminder to England's King George III that settlers had taken and held their American lands in their own names, not his name. Jefferson, just thirty-one years old in July 1774, declared in his famous "A Summary View of the Rights of British America" that: "America was conquered, and her settlements made and firmly established, at the expense of individuals . . . . Their own blood was spilt in acquiring lands for the settlement, their own fortunes expended in making that settlement effectual. For themselves they fought, for themselves they conquered, and for themselves alone they have right to hold."[30] Jefferson, speaking for the Continental Congress, is stark and clear: we took this land from its previous inhabitants, to be sure, but not for you, for ourselves and intend to hold it and work it for our own benefit.

The African Slave Trade to the Americas

While most of the work of depopulating the Americas of its original inhabitants was done by natural forces that neither the Europeans or their indigenous victims understood, slavery and the African slave trade were strictly man's evil work.[31] But as we noted in Chapter 1, the African slave trade had been underway for thousands of years by the time Columbus bumbled into the Caribbean. Out of a total of about 25 million Africans sold into slavery, about as many were sent north and east out of Africa between 650

AD and the U.S. Civil War as went west out of Africa to the New World, between Columbus' first landing and the Civil War. And the supply never waned; Lovejoy noted "that there were at least as many enslaved people in Africa as there were in the Americas at any time in the past. . . . At the outbreak of the U.S. Civil War, there were probably more slaves in the Muslim states of West Africa than in the Confederacy. . . ."[32]

In Africa, political fragmentation and tribal rivalries fueled domestic slavery and the international slave trade. A thick African infrastructure of slave gathering, control, and transportation to the Atlantic coast where European and American traders waited ensconced in forts, made the slave trade possible. African princes and their agents, called slatees, brought enslaved Africans to them for purchase and later sale in the Americas.[33] The image often promoted of free Africans ripped from their happy families and villages by European and American slave merchants is simply not plausible. Slave vending on this industrial scale simply must be an organized, authorized, and protected domestic industry.[34] European and American blame came in the purchase, transportation, and use of African slaves in the Americas.

Again, the numbers involved in the Atlantic slave trade, while staggeringly large, are estimates, though more clustered estimates than those regarding early Africa or the indigenous populations of the Americas. The historian David Levering Lewis reported that: "For four hundred years, African slave magnates fed several million black men, women, and children to . . . the rapacious Atlantic slave trade. . . . between ten and fifteen million people [are] estimated to have been shipped out of Africa between 1450 and 1860, . . ."[35] The first seven decades of Lewis' timeframe involved the slave trade from West Africa to Europe, mostly Iberia, but it soon swung around to the Americas. The most authoritative numbers for the Atlantic slave trade are from the Trans-Atlantic Slave Trade Database, developed by social and economic historians David Eltis and David Richardson. Eltis and Richardson report that 35,000 slave ship voyages carried 12.5 million people toward the Americas between 1520 and 1866. 10.7 million enslaved people completed the journey while nearly 2 million others died on the horrific "middle passage." The vast majority went to South America and the Caribbean, 4.8 million and 4.7 million respectively, while 800,000 went to Central America and nearly 400,000 to North America.[36] These recent studies place the North American share of the Atlantic slave trade at 3.5 to 5 percent of the total. It seems a small number, but it has shaped and distorted our history.

Famously, in August 1619 the White Lion, an English privateer, traded twenty Africans to Virginia Governor George Yeardley in exchange for resupply.[37] Their status was not immediately settled but their numbers grew and within a few decades the legal definition of slaves and the limits on their interactions with White colonists were set. As early as 1630, the Virginia General Assembly sentenced Hugh Davis to a public whipping "for abusing himself to the dishonor of God and shame of Christians, by defiling his body in lying with a negro."[38] In 1662, the Virginia General Assembly insured intergenerational slavery, even of the offspring of White overseers and owners, by declaring "that all children borne in this country shall be held bond or free only according to the condition of the mother. . . ."[39] By 1700, there were about 16,000 slaves in Virginia and nearly 28,000 in the colonies overall, the majority native-born. Continued importation and natural increase, some aggressively managed, grew these numbers rapidly.[40]

Slavery in the New Nation

By the time the colonies declared independence from England, there were more than half a million Black people in the United States; the vast majority were in the South and more than 90 percent were enslaved. The new nation moved quickly and on multiple fronts to entrench slavery and to define citizenship by race. The nation's primary founding document, the U.S. Constitution, written in 1787 and ratified and implemented by 1789, separated "free persons" from "Indians not taxed, and three fifths of all other persons" for purposes of representation and direct taxes in Article I, section 2. Moreover, one of the first acts of the new Congress, completed on March 26, 1790, was a Naturalization Act. The Naturalization Act limited those eligible to become citizens to "free white persons" of "good character." Aliens who were not free White persons were ineligible for citizenship. These provisions held until after the Civil War ended chattel slavery and Congress in 1870 amended the Naturalization Act to include persons of "African descent." That still left the category of aliens, not White or Black, ineligible for citizenship and the puzzle of who, exactly, counted as White.[41] Congress did not fully remove racial restrictions on eligibility to U.S. citizenship until passage of the Immigration and Nationality Act of 1952.[42]

The Black population, always predominantly in the South and enslaved, grew rapidly before the Civil War. The number of Black people in America rose by 82 percent, from 757,208 to 1,377,808, between 1790 and 1810 and then more than doubled again over the next forty years, reaching 3.6 million by 1850. Both free and enslaved Black people resisted their oppression in myriad ways, sometimes by fleeing the nation entirely. In fact, modest emigration preceded the Civil War; some 13,000 Black Americans emigrated to Liberia between 1820 and 1865 and as many as 20,000 fled, via the Underground Railroad and other paths, to Canada in the 1850s, while others hid nervously in the North.[43] Fewer, mostly Black Texans, splashed across the Rio Grande into Mexico.

In 1860, Black people comprised nearly 40 percent of the population of the South and the value of slaves constituted half of the region's net wealth. Inevitably, the Civil War brought tremendous economic, social, and political upheaval to the plantation South. By the end of 1863, a full year after Lincoln's Emancipation Proclamation had declared slaves in the states still in rebellion to be free, 400,000 former slaves had fled their masters and found relative safety behind the advancing Union lines. The war ended in April 1865, and "with more than a million ex-slaves under some form of Federal custody," almost 200,000 Black men having served in the Union effort, and 80,000 about to serve as occupation troops after the war, Black expectations ran high.[44] Moreover, Black people were a majority of the population in three southern states: South Carolina (61 percent), Mississippi (59 percent), and Louisiana (52 percent), and a near majority in three more, Florida (48 percent), Alabama (47 percent), and Georgia (46 percent).[45] White Southerners, on the other hand, simply could not fathom that they might be expected to treat their former slaves as social and political equals. As it dawned on them that Black numbers threatened traditional White dominance, the bottom rail going to the top in the phrase of the day, disbelief turned to sullen rage, and intimidation, violence, and terror soon followed.

Military occupation and political reconstruction of the South offered some, but only some, protection to the freedmen and their families into the mid-1870s. Once Union troops were withdrawn from the South in the wake of the presidential election of 1876, the freedmen were increasingly exposed and vulnerable.[46] As White supremacy reasserted itself and the earliest Jim Crow laws again restricted Black opportunity, a slowly growing trickle of Black people and families sought security, and perhaps even opportunity, outside the South. Black citizens from Mississippi, Louisiana, Texas, and Tennessee – the numbers are variously stated and range from several thousand to 40,000, still well less than 1 percent of the Southern Black population – left for Kansas in the spring and summer of 1879.[47] Similarly, many Black people sought land in the Oklahoma Indian territory once it was opened to non-Indians in 1890.[48] Overall, nearly 325,000 Blacks left the South, mostly for Northern cities, between 1870 and 1900.[49]

While American politics in the nineteenth century was commonly conceived in Black and White, others were impinging on the Anglo-American mind in puzzling, often irritating, ways. As Anglos began filtering into Mexican Texas in the 1820s, their disdain for local officials and citizens was often barely concealed. By 1836 Anglos outnumbered Mexicans ten-to-one and had had enough of feigning deference and respect. A six-week revolution produced an independent Republic of Texas and Anglos began pushing Mexicans toward and often beyond the southern border. As the historian Neil Foley has explained, the Anglo Texans and their former countrymen in the United States "regarded the Mexicans as little better than Indians and utterly incapable of becoming civilized members of the Anglo-American republic. Of course, Mexicans were principally of indigenous origin, a biological and visible fact that stoked the fears that many Anglos had of racial intermixing."[50]

When the independent Republic of Texas became an American state late in 1845, it sparked a brief war with Mexico – April 1846 to February 1848 – that concluded with the Treaty of Guadalupe Hidalgo. In this treaty, the northern half of Mexico became the American Southwest from Texas to California and north to Utah, Nevada, and Colorado. With the territory came about 117,000 Mexican citizens, which the treaty gave the option of relocating to what remained of Mexico or accepting U.S. citizenship. Three thousand chose to relocate and the rest became American citizens. But as Foley explained, U.S. "Citizenship bestowed about as many rights and privileges on Mexican Americans, Asian Americans, and Native Americans as it . . . [did] on black Americans in the South after the Civil War."[51] Natalia Molina has declared that "Mexicans. . . . were increasingly positioned alongside Indians, Asians, or blacks in immigration discourse" and in the public mind.[52]

Immigrants have always had to fight for a place in the American tapestry. Before the Civil War, nearly 3 million Irish Catholics abandoned oppression and famine at home to look for better in America. Initially not considered fully White, their social and economic options were limited. Options were even more limited for the Chinese, who began arriving in California during the Gold Rush of the late 1840s and stayed to build railroads in the West and Southwest into the 1860s and beyond.[53] When the golden spike was driven at Promontory Point, Utah, on May 10, 1869, completing the first transcontinental railroad, it was the Irish building from the East and the Chinese from the West that had wielded the shovels, picks, and hammers. Political scientists Carol Nackenoff and Julie Novkov reported that "of the more than two hundred thousand [Chinese laborers] who had come by the late 1870s, only about a quarter returned to stay in China" while the rest remained in the U.S. These newcomers, then as now, took the hard, dangerous jobs that no one else wanted.[54] The Chinese, for their pains, got the Chinese Exclusion Act of 1882, not repealed until 1943. Because White Americans have always been very aware of race, as the nation became more diverse, the desire to keep track of racial and ethnic numbers became more pressing. The U.S. Census, and how it defined Americans by race and ethnicity, was the means by which this was done.

The Census: How Americans Have Been Counted

The United States Constitution mandated in Article I, section 2 that an "actual enumeration shall be made within three years after the first meeting of the Congress of the United States, and within every subsequent term of ten years, . . . " The census, as this "actual enumeration" was called in Article I, section 9, was not to be conducted for its own sake, but to facilitate an accurate allocation of seats in the U.S. House of Representatives and direct taxes according to "the whole number of free persons, including those bound to service for a term of years, and excluding Indians not taxed, three fifths of all other persons." Free persons, including indentured servants, were overwhelmingly, though not exclusively, White, and to be counted as full persons, while Indians were excluded from the count as not paying taxes or voting, and all other persons, meaning Black slaves, were to be counted at three fifths.

As Congress and the Washington administration, through Jefferson's State Department, began to prepare for the census, purposes beyond congressional apportionment and direct tax administration began to occur to the nation's leaders. To better gauge the industrial and military capacities of the population, they developed three categories of free White people – free White men over sixteen, free White men under sixteen, and free White women. Two other categories – all other free persons and slaves – covered Black people. White people and free Black people counted as one full person while enslaved Black people were also counted, but their weight for purposes of representation and direct taxation was reduced to three fifths. This basic structure governed administration of the census through 1840, but over time the designation of categories of persons to be enumerated and the purposes to which census results were to be put became more complex.

As with much of U.S. culture, the census initially focused on and distinguished between White and Black people, with others being included later, always warily, and usually as something of an afterthought. In 1850, census enumerators were instructed to separate Black people, slave and free, into two categories: Blacks and mulattos. Mulattos might be a mixture of Black and any other race, but in the antebellum U.S. the mixture was overwhelmingly Black and White, often as the result of relations between enslaved Black women and their owners, overseers, or others with authoritative access. The race scientists of the day were convinced that racial mixing resulted in genetic degradation and they needed the mulatto category broken out to help them prove their point. In 1890, the categories of quadroon (one-quarter Black) and octoroon (one-eighth Black) were added, and in 1930 the infamous "one drop" rule became part of census enumerator instructions – "a person of mixed White and Negro blood was to be returned as Negro, no matter how small the percentage of Negro blood."[55] Interestingly, until 1960, racial identification was assigned by the census enumerator rather than by the respondent him or herself, which given the one drop rule would have been tricky. One assumes that some, maybe even most, enumerators asked respondents about their race if they were unsure, but others might have been unwilling to broach a potentially delicate question.

Hispanics have also been a puzzle to the Census Bureau. While initially the numbers would have been very small, from 1790 through 1920 Hispanics were counted in the census as White. As Hispanic numbers began to rise, particularly as the poverty and instability attendant to the Mexican Revolution of 1910 to 1920 drove Mexicans north into the U.S., the census of 1930 created a separate racial category – Mexican. This experiment was fraught with political danger. Hispanics knew the benefit of being counted as White and the danger of being counted as anything else, but they also knew that White people did not see them as brothers. As the historian Neil Foley has written, "Over time Mexicans came to locate themselves in the ethnoracial middle ground between Anglo Americans and African Americans, not White enough to claim equality with Anglos and yet, in many cases, White enough to escape the worst features of the Jim Crow South."[56]

An extended selection from a *Houston Post* editorial in 1944 showed the paper struggling, unsuccessfully, to urge acceptance of Hispanics and explain what might be the source of their ill-treatment. The editor wrote: "There is some discrimination against Mexicans in Texas, and it is reasonably subject to criticism." OK so far! "But in the main it is not, as in the case of negroes, a racial discrimination, for Texans regard Mexicans as being of the Caucasian race, though they are part Indian – many of them full-blooded. In candid truth, this prejudice is primarily a mere repugnance to the personal uncouthness of the peons [who] are ragged, filthy, ignorant and speak no English; almost as primitive as their savage Indian ancestors."[57] Whether we take this as the common White opinion of the day or a cruel tongue-in-cheek joke at the expense of Mexicans, it says a lot about how White Americans saw Mexicans. Not Black to be sure, but descended from savages nonetheless. Citizens, voters – not hardly.

Hispanics were again broken out in the 1980 census, but by then the Civil Rights Revolution, including the Chicano movement, had increased the benefits and reduced the dangers of being separately identified and accurately counted. Since 1980, Hispanic origin has been queried in the census with several options provided for ethnicity and country of origin, separate from the questions about race. Additional options for expressing race and ethnicity have allowed new insights. For example, in 2022 the Pew Research Center pointed out that there were 6 million Afro-Latinos in the U.S. About 87 percent identified as Latino, most of the rest, but not all, identified as Black.[58]

Even more puzzling for the census, and to some extent for the broader society, were Asians. In 1870, the census sought to account for the Chinese laborers that had arrived in California during the Gold Rush and those that came later to mine, farm, and build the railroads, by adding "Chinese" as a racial category. After 1910, categories including "Other" and "some other race" were added to catch a broader swath of Asians and from 1920 to 1940 "Hindus" was added to catch South Asians. Since 2000 six Asian designations as well as "other Asian" have been added. Boxes that welcome elaboration are also now part of the census.

The census data in Table 2.1 make several fairly straightforward points that together explain the White majority's sense of the nation. First, colonial and early national America were clearly understood and actively constructed as a biracial, White supremacist society. White citizens, almost always 80 percent or more of the total population, dominated, usually owned, a Black population of slaves. Calling the accompanying social ethic "White supremacy" is not hyperbole. The presumption of White supremacy and superiority, even among many who thought themselves "friends of the Negro", was pervasive. As other groups, principally Hispanics and Asians, entered the national consciousness, they were assigned, in law and social usage, to intermediate levels of the racial hierarchy between Whites and Blacks. Second, in the late nineteenth and early twentieth centuries, when "off-White" Southern and Eastern European immigration produced concern, immigration was tightly limited from the early 1920s through the mid-1960s. Only in the second half of the twentieth century did racial and ethnic diversity, beyond the White/Black dichotomy, impinge upon the popular mind except in Texas, the Southwest, and the Far West. And third, only dimly after the 1970s and more starkly in the last couple of decades have White Americans begun to realize that demographic trends will produce a majority-minority society soon.

Finally, the Census Bureau not only counts residents of the U.S. every ten years, the bureau and its related American Community Survey produces annual updates and, disconcertingly for some, projections of total population and population by race and ethnicity forward to 2060. To get a better feel for the demographic trends at work since the mid-twentieth century, look at the White column of data in Table 2.1. In the "Father Knows Best" America of 1950, when the White ascendency still felt totally

44 Demographic Stability and Change in American History

TABLE 2.1 U.S. Population Growth by Decade, Race, and Ethnicity, 1610–2060

Decade	White	Black	Hispanic	American Indian	Asian	Other Race	Total
1610	350						350
1620	2,282	20					2,302
1630	4,586	60					4,646
1640	26,037	597					26,634
1650	48,768	1,600					50,368
1660	72,138	2,920					75,058
1670	107,400	4,535					111,935
1680	144,536	6,971					151,507
1690	193,643	16,729					210,372
1700	223,071	27,817					250,888
1710	286,845	44,866					331,711
1720	397,346	68,839					466,185
1730	538,424	91,021					629,445
1740	755,539	150,024					905,563
1750	934,340	236,420					1,170,760
1760	1,267,819	325,806					1,593,625
1770	1,688,254	459,822					2,148,076
1780	2,204,949	575,420					2,780,369
1790	3,172,006	757,208					3,929,214
1800	4,306,446	1,002,037					5,308,483
1810	5,862,073	1,377,808					7,239,881
1820	7,866,797	1,771,656					9,638,453
1830	10,532,060	2,328,642					12,860,702
1840	14,189,705	2,873,648					17,063,353
1850	19,435,961	3,638,808	117,107				23,191,876

Demographic Stability and Change in American History   45

1860	26,643,583	4,441,830	200,000	44,021		31,364,367
1870	33,200,392	4,880,009	300,000	25,731		38,469,386
1880	42,837,395	6,580,793	393,555	66,407		49,983,763
1890	54,365,570	7,470,040	450,000	58,806		62,453,930
1900	66,809,196	8,833,994	503,189	237,196		76,497,764
1910	80,933,963	9,827,763	797,994	265,683		91,972,266
1920	93,534,761	10,463,131	1,286,154	244,437		105,710,620
1930	108,572,310	11,891,143	1,714,435	332,397		122,775,051
1940	116,356,846	12,685,518	1,858,024	333,969		131,489,275
1950	134,942,028	15,042,286	3,558,761	343,410	48,604	154,256,122
1960	158,454,956	18,860,117	5,814,784	508,675	75,045	184,279,020
1970	169,023,068	22,539,362	9,589,216	795,110	230,064	203,703,221
1980	180,256,366	26,495,025	14,608,673	1,420,400	6,758,319	233,039,222
1990	188,128,296	29,986,060	22,354,059	1,959,234	9,804,847	259,506,158
2000	195,577,000	34,314,000	35,306,000	2,097,000	3,898,000	281,916,000
2010	197,326,000	37,926,000	49,099,000	2,263,000	6,984,000	308,757,000
2020	197,925,000	41,704,000	61,710,000	2,443,000	9,790,000	333,040,000
2030	197,992,000	45,322,000	72,189,000	2,575,000	12,669,000	355,101,000
2040	193,210,000	48,550,000	84,197,000	2,659,000	16,276,000	373,528,000
2050	185,954,000	51,664,000	95,442,000	2,701,000	20,450,000	388,923,000
2060	179,162,000	54,949,000	105,777,000	2,722,000	25,255,000	404,483,000

Note: Missing data for Hispanics in 1860, 1870, 1890, and 1930 has been interpolated from surrounding data.

Sources: U.S. Census Bureau, *Historical Statistics of the United States, Colonial Times to 1970, Part 2*, Chapter 2, "Colonial and Pre-Federal Statistics," Series 21–19, "Estimated Population of the American Colonies, 1610–1780," 1168; Campbell Gibson and Kay Jung, "Historical Census Statistics on Population Totals by Race, 1790 to 1990," Working Paper #56, September 2002, Table 1, "United States – Race and Hispanic Origin: 1790–1990," 29; Brian Gratton and Myron P. Guttman, "Hispanics in the United States, 1850–1990," *Historical Methods* 33, no. 3 (Summer 2000): Table 2, 142; ProQuest, *Statistical Abstract of the United States, 2023 Online Edition*, Table 6, "Resident Population by Sex, Race, and Hispanic Origin, 2000 to 2021," and Table 13, "Resident Population Projections by Race and Hispanic Origin: 2020 to 2060."

secure, nearly 135 million White residents surveyed a society in which 15 million Black people, 3.6 million Hispanics, and a thin scattering of others played delimited roles. By 2000, nearly 196 million White residents nervously surveyed a social landscape in which 34 million Black people, a remarkable 35 million Hispanics, up from 3.6 million in 1950, and 10.7 million Asians, up from 255,000 in 1950, demanded equal opportunity and treatment. And then White numbers crested and began to decline while minority numbers continued to grow. The census projected that between 2020 and 2060 the White population would decline by more than 19 million, while Black numbers would grow by more than 13 million, Hispanic numbers by more than 45 million, and Asian numbers by more than 16 million – unless of course something were done to stem the tide, or the "invasion" as some call it. Border wall anyone! How about Remain in Mexico until we call you?

The rapid growth of the Hispanic population in the U.S. slowed somewhat in recent years, but from an absolutely blistering pace, fed both by high fertility and immigration rates. In 1970, the Hispanic population was under 10 million, by 1990 it had more than doubled to 22.4 million, more than doubled again to 49 million in 2010, and increased to 60.4 million in 2020. In percentage terms, the Hispanic population rose from 4.7 percent in 1970 to 18.5 percent in 2020. Among Hispanics in the U.S., the majority (37 million or 62 percent) are of Mexican origin, just under 10 percent are Puerto Rican, 4 percent Cuban, and smaller numbers hail from virtually every country to the south.[59]

The remarkable growth of the Asian population, unlike the Hispanic population, has only picked up speed in recent years. From just over half a million in 1960, the Asian population rose to 10.7 million in 2000 and to nearly 20 million in 2020. From one-half of 1 percent in 1960, to 4.2 percent in 2000, Asians made up 7 percent of the nation's population in 2020. Among Asians, the Chinese constitute the largest share at 5.4 million, or 23 percent, followed by Indians at 4.6 million, or 20 percent, and Filipinos at 4.2 million, or 18 percent.[60]

The census data presented in Table 2.1 can testify even more clearly when converted to percentage terms and presented graphically, as in Figure 2.1. From first settlement into the early twentieth century, the U.S. was a biracial society, with the White population dominant and Black population enslaved or otherwise oppressed. No other racial or ethnic group reached 1 percent of the total population, and so are not included in Figure 2.1, until Hispanics broke 1 percent in 1920, Asian and Other in 1980. Native Americans, once counted, never broke 1 percent. In every enumeration, colony counts until 1790 and census counts through 1970, White citizens constituted more than 80 percent of all Americans, except for several decades

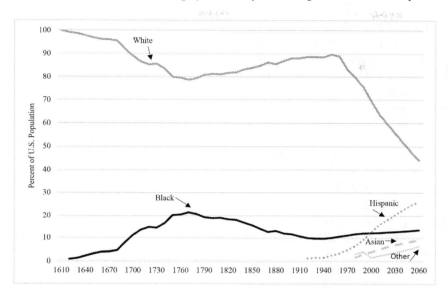

FIGURE 2.1 Percent of U.S. Population by Decade, Race, and Ethnicity, 1610–2060

Note: Hispanic, Asian, and Other not listed until more than 1 percent. Native Americans only recently were included in these surveys and since then, they have not yet reached the 1 percent margin for inclusion on the chart.

Sources: U.S. Census Bureau, *Historical Statistics of the United States, Colonial Times to 1970, Part 2*, Chapter 2, "Colonial and Pre-Federal Statistics," Series 21–19, "Estimated Population of the American Colonies, 1610–1780," 1168; Campbell Gibson and Kay Jung, "Historical Census Statistics on Population Totals by Race, 1790 to 1990," Working Paper #56, September 2002, Table 1, "United States – Race and Hispanic Origin: 1790–1990," 29; Brian Gratton and Myron P. Guttman, "Hispanics in the United States, 1850–1990," *Historical Methods* 33, no. 3 (Summer 2000): Table 2, 142; ProQuest, *Statistical Abstract of the United States, 2023 Online Edition*, Table 6, "Resident Population by Sex, Race, and Hispanic Origin, 2000 to 2021," and Table 13, "Resident Population Projections by Race and Hispanic Origin: 2020 to 2060."

between 1750 and 1790 when a burgeoning slave population broke 20 percent and pushed the White population down into the high 70s. In fact, between 1870 and 1960 White Americans constituted more than 85 percent of the total population – 88.8 percent in 1960. Then, as we shall see shortly, the immigration limits imposed in the 1920s were removed and the new immigration regime adopted in the 1960s encouraged Latin American and Asian immigration. White population numbers slowly plateaued and the White share of the total population, as displayed in Figure 2.1, began a steady decline of about 4 to 6 percent per decade. The non-Hispanic White population was projected to be 44 percent by 2060 – still a plurality, but no longer a majority.[61] It would be foolish not to declare that the data presented in Figure 2.1 are a nearly full explanation of the social and political tensions around immigration in recent decades and today.

One of the most noxious products of these great changes, emanating from the nether reaches of the far right – 8chan, Daily Stormer, and the like – is replacement theory. Several of the worst mass shootings of recent years, including the 2015 shooting at the Charleston, South Carolina, Emanuel AME Church in which nine people, all African-American, died; the 2018 Pittsburgh synagogue shooting in which eleven Jewish worshippers died; the 2019 El Paso Walmart shooting in which twenty-three mostly Hispanic victims died; and the 2022 Buffalo grocery store shooting, in which ten Black people died; as well as the 2017 Charlottesville march, all featured White supremacist killers convinced that "real" Americans were being replaced by "outsiders." The broad claim is that the growing diversity of the U.S. population and society, unquestionably real over the last half century, was a liberal plot, perhaps Jewish, to replace independent, freedom-loving, traditional Americans with more tractable, compliant, replacement non-Whites. A third of American adults claimed to believe some elements or aspects of replacement theory.[62] The act of counting, neutral in itself, highlighted issues of presence, place, and power in America, and many White Americans did not like what they saw. Now we turn to a closer look at demographic changes in the United States since the Civil War and how Black, White, and other Americans have responded to them.

The End of Mass Immigration and the Black Response

The Civil War was barely past when the debate over the racial makeup of the American future was joined anew. In an address entitled "The Fortune of the Republic" (1878), Ralph Waldo Emerson, one of the nineteenth century's most prominent literary figures, declared, "we shall be a multitude of people. . . . doors wide open. . . . to every nation, to every race and skin, white men, red men, yellow men, black men. . . . The land is wide enough, the soil has bread for all."[63] Not everyone agreed. Francis Amasa Walker, Superintendent of the 1870 and 1880 censuses, the longtime President of the Massachusetts Institute of Technology (MIT), warned that rising numbers of immigrants and declining birth rates among the native-born White population promised dangerous demographic changes. Sound familiar? During the 1870s, 94 percent of immigrants still came from Northern and Western Europe, but during the 1880s that share fell to 86 percent and then to 65 percent in the 1890s as the numbers from Southern and Eastern Europe steadily rose. During the first two decades of the twentieth century, the balance continued to shift. The new immigrants were not of the many colors that Emerson envisioned, but they differed from previous immigrants in language and religion and, most American elites thought, in social, intellectual, and democratic capability. So when the new immigrants reached numerical parity with the old in the first decade of the new century, and then to 65 percent of all immigrants in the 1910s, the response was dramatic.[64]

As we see in Table 2.2, between 1880 and 1920, 23.5 million immigrants came to America, more than 8 million in the 1900s and 1.3 million in 1907 alone.[65] Then U.S. elites moved to cut off the flow; in 1917 Congress passed an Immigration Act requiring immigrants to pass a literacy test and pay a fee of $8. Immigration declined but in 1921 and 1924 Congress passed quota acts to limit overall immigration while advantaging the traditional Northern and Western European sources and limiting numbers from Southern and Eastern European sources. Asians, strictly limited since the 1880s, were prohibited as ineligible for naturalization. Immigration fell by 85 percent; only about 3 million immigrants arrived in America from the mid-1920s until the limits began to be loosened in the 1950s.[66]

Internal migration was another source of social change and accompanying angst. A thin trickle of Black Southerners, numbering about 325,000, left for the Midwest and for the major cities of the North between the Civil War's end and 1900. Nonetheless, as the twentieth century opened, the vast majority of Black Americans still lived in the South under increasingly stringent Jim Crow restrictions. W.E.B. Du Bois, the leading Black intellectual of the early twentieth century, asked in a famous 1900 speech, entitled "The Address to the Country," "Cannot the nation that has absorbed ten million foreigners into its political life without catastrophe absorb ten million Negro Americans into that same political life at less cost than their unjust and illegal exclusion will involve?"[67] Many White Americans thought not. While Du Bois was addressing the country, other lesser lights, tired of waiting, had been slipping on their walking shoes. A wonderfully rich colloquy between a Black southern father and son, the father a former slave, highlighted the emotions and calculations that pervaded Black southern life during the first two-thirds of the twentieth century. The son, a Black minister, wrote, "My father was born and brought up a slave. He was taught his place and was content to keep it." The father says, "I know that there are certain things that I must do, and I do them . . . [but my son] has been through the eighth grade; he reads easily. For a year I have been keeping him from going to Chicago; but he tells me . . . that in the fall he's going." The son explains, "When a young white man talks rough to me, I can't talk rough to him. You can stand that; I can't. I have some education, and inside I have the feelin's of a white man. I'm going."[68]

TABLE 2.2 Immigration and Black Migration by Decade, 1820–2020

	Legal Immigration	Black Northern Migration
1820s	128,502	
1830s	538,381	
1840s	1,427,337	20,000
1850s	2,814,554	
1860s	2,081,261	
1870s	2,742,137	70,000
1880s	5,248,568	80,000
1890s	3,694,294	174,000
1900s	8,202,388	197,000
1910s	6,347,380	525,000
1920s	4,295,510	877,000
1930s	699,375	400,000
1940s	856,608	1,400,000
1950s	2,499,268	1,500,000
1960s	3,213,749	1,400,000
1970s	4,248,203	-342,000
1980s	6,244,379	
1990s	9,775,398	
2000s	10,299,430	
2010s	10,633,000	

Sources: Legal immigration: U.S. Department of Homeland Security, *Yearbook of Immigration Statistics*, Table 1, "Persons Obtaining Lawful Permanent Resident Status, Fiscal Years 1820–2019"; Black migration: Douglas S. Massey and Nancy A. Denton, *American Apartheid: Segregation and the Making of the Underclass* (Cambridge, MA: Harvard University Press, 1993), 27–29, 43–45, 60. Estimate for 1820–1865 is from Howard Temperley, ed., *After Slavery: Emancipation and Its Discontents* (Portland, OR: Frank Cass, 2000), 68, and David W. Blight, *Frederick Douglass: Prophet of Freedom* (New York: Simon & Schuster, 2018), 240.

With push factors like economic discrimination, political disenfranchisement, mob violence, legal segregation, and the whole humiliating apparatus of Jim Crow, and the pull factors of the lighter form of Northern discrimination, urban life, and the possibility of factory jobs no longer filled by new immigrants, the Great Migration got underway. As Figure 2.2 shows, 90 percent of Black Americans lived in the South in 1900 and 89 percent still lived there in 1910, but the floodgates were about to open. By 1930, the Black population in the Northeast had tripled, the Black population of Detroit had grown by 611 percent and that of Chicago by 114 percent.[69] Between World War I and 1970, some 6 million Black people and as many White people left the South for better opportunities in the North and West, but it was Black citizens for whom the changes were most

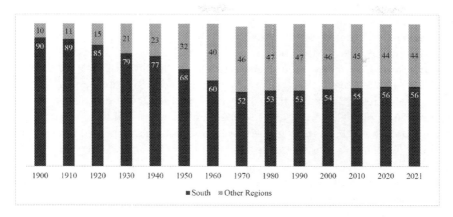

FIGURE 2.2 Percent of U.S. Black Population Living in the South, 1900–2021

Sources: Christine Tamir, "The Growing Diversity of Black America," Pew Research Center, March 25, 2021; Christine Tamir, et al., "Facts About the U.S. Black Population," Pew Research Center, March 2, 2023.

dramatic and, as we shall see, most problematic.[70] After a steady decade-by-decade migration to the North and West, just over half of Black Americans, 52 percent, lived in the South in 1970.

Most scholars of the Great Migration, including Isabel Wilkerson in her book *The Warmth of Other Suns*, agree that the benefits of relocating from the rural South to the urban North and West outweighed the costs – but the costs were real.[71] World War I created a manufacturing boom in the North while it simultaneously, though only temporarily, shut off the immigrant flow, thus drawing Black workers out of the South into factory jobs not previously open to them. However, it also brought Black arrivals for the first time into direct contact and competition with the recent Southern and Eastern European immigrants, themselves suspected of not being fully White. For the new immigrants, "like the earlier Irish, the surest touchstone of citizenship was distance between themselves and Americans of African ancestry. . . . The subtle and not-so-subtle advantages of light skin were a social reality."[72] Immigrants, of course, quickly learned this and determined to benefit from it.

The cumulative pressures of social change, war, and the flight of the South's exploited labor force were explosive. Armed police in the South tried to stem the loss of labor and armed White Northerners soon massed to drive away the new arrivals. David Levering Lewis, pointing to national turmoil from 1917 through 1919, described "a tidal wave of homicides, arson, mayhem, and organized racial combat. . . . Race riots on a national scale, the flight out of the South of hundreds of thousands of

African-Americans, the explosion of labor strikes from coast to coast . . . made race relations far worse than they already were."[73]

While the Great Migration is often described as starting with World War I, and 1.8 million Black people did leave the South by 1940, in that year 77 percent of the Black population remained below the Mason–Dixon line, down just 12 percent from 1910. Migration slowed during the Great Depression of the 1930s, but pressures continued to build. As the depression lifted and the nation geared up industrially and then militarily for World War II, Black Americans were again on the move. Between 1940 and 1970, 4.4 million Black people left the South, two and one-half times as many as had left during the previous thirty years. The great economic historian of the South, Numan V. Bartley, author of *The New South, 1945–1980*, adjudged that World War II had as great an economic and demographic impact on the South as the Civil War.[74]

Postwar America: The Exodus Slows and the Doors Swing Open

As with World War I, World War II drew millions of Black citizens out of the rural South into the military and into the industrial cities of the North and West. As with World War I, patriotism and a way out from behind the plow drew many Black men into the military services. The push factors on the civilian side were racial discrimination and violence in the South, the pull factors were jobs and a less intense and deadly discrimination outside the South. During and after World War II the South remained unsettled. Beyond historic racial tensions, Bartley described a volatile situation, in which: "The wartime social and economic disruptions in the region, the return of some 400,000 African-American veterans, and the voting drives and other black protest activities contributed to the anti-black rampage in the region during late 1945 and through much of 1946 . . . white groups killed blacks who had voted or had participated in civil rights events."[75] The economic historian Gavin Wright explained how counterintuitive and economically – though not socially – irrational this intense regional battle was, saying "Between 1940 and the 1960s, the South thus presents us with an amazing economic spectacle. It was the most rapidly growing region in the country [largely due to war spending]. . . . at the same time that job-hungry workers were leaving the region by the thousands, often to go to cities where they faced hostility, unemployment, and a host of social problems."[76] Despite the powerful forces behind the exodus, the sacrifices of going, especially to family, home, and community were deeply felt by many.[77]

As the Civil Rights Revolution gathered steam during the 1940s and 1950s, before its crescendo in the 1960s, it began to broaden out. Rather than simply demanding better treatment for Black people in America, the civil rights movement and the broader social justice movements demanded change in the nation's exclusionary and racist immigration regime. Not only should Black, Hispanics, and Asian people enjoy equal rights and opportunities in America, but "the colored peoples of the world", as Du Bois had called them, deserved an immigration status equal to that of any European. Finally, in 1965, the same year Congress passed and President Lyndon B. Johnson signed the Civil Rights Act and the Voting Rights Act, the Immigration and Nationality Act of 1965, also known as the Hart-Celler Act, was passed and signed.

The Hart-Celler Act abolished the country immigration quotas put in place in 1924 to favor Northern and Western Europeans over Southern and Eastern Europeans and completely barring many others, especially Asians. Instead, Hart-Celler prioritized immigrants with needed or valuable economic skills, both high-end like engineers and doctors, and low-end like agricultural laborers, including those fleeing violence and political oppression.[78] Moreover, immigrants had the right to bring family members once they were settled. Family unification provisions changed the immigration flows dramatically. Though little recognized at the time, few European residents had family members they wished to bring to America and fewer still had credible asylum claims to press. Latin Americans in the U.S., especially Mexicans, did have family members they wanted to bring and many other Latin Americans did have credible asylum claims. Many Asians, and not just Chinese and Indians, but Vietnamese, Cambodians, Pakistanis, and many others had either skills or asylum claims. The historian Tyler Stovall reported that, "From 1965 to 2000, ninety percent of new immigrants to the United States came from outside Europe."[79] This single piece of legislation and subsequent amendments had a tremendous impact on immigration patterns and, eventually, on the demographic makeup of the nation. A quick glance back at Figure 2.1 will confirm this claim.

As political scientists Chris Garcia and Gabriel Sanchez explained, "Between 1980 and 1990, the Hispanic population in the United States increased by about 55 percent, and between 1990 and 2000, it grew by about 58 percent. . . . About half of the Hispanic increase was due to immigration; the other half to natural increases." Moreover, "the Hispanic population had equaled or surpassed that of African Americans in the year 2000."[80] Growth in the Asian population started later but eventually eclipsed even Hispanic growth rates. In the half century between 1970 and 2020, the immigrant population in America increased from 9.6 million persons in 1970, to 14.1 million in 1980, to 19.8 million in 1990, 31 million in 2000, 40 million in 2010, and 43.8 million in 2020 – a four and a half fold increase over half a century. In percentage terms over this same period, the increase was from 4.7 percent in 1970 to 13.7 percent in 2020 – just short of the 14.7 percent posted in 1910. This increasingly diverse society triggered many old challenges and taboos, some remarkably telling.

Immigration, Intermarriage, and Racial Diversity in America

Immigration increases diversity, so, not surprisingly, Americans have been suspicious of immigrants. From Benjamin Franklin's famous derision of Germans flocking into Pennsylvania in the 1750s, to the Know Nothing party rejection of the Irish in the 1850s, to the tight immigration quotas in place into the 1950s, to, most recently, the demand that a wall be built along the Mexican border, the stranger, particularly the swarthy stranger, has been suspect. The Roper polling organization has asked respondents since 1965 whether immigration should be increased, decreased, or held at present levels; in every instance more respondents have favored limiting immigration than have favored increasing it.[81] As we have seen and shall see more fully below, those deeply worried about immigration had better fasten their seatbelts.

Many factors suggest that the presence and importance of immigrants in the U.S. will continue to rise, but two factors, fertility rates and ongoing immigration, legal and illegal, virtually guarantee it. The census has long gathered and reported fertility rates, defined as the number of children the average woman would have in a lifetime if she experienced the rates occurring in a given year, for two categories of women, White, and "Black and Other." Hispanics and Asians were added in 1990. A national fertility rate of 2.11 children per woman would hold total population steady, fewer and the population would decline, more it would grow.

Table 2.3 shows that White women were well above the replacement rate of 2.11 children per woman between 1940 and 1970, but in most periods since 1970 have been well below that rate. Until 2000, Black women were mixed with others, which might have increased their fertility numbers somewhat, but they remained above replacement levels until 2010, sometimes a full point above White women. Since numbers began to be provided separately in 1990, Hispanic fertility rates have run well above replacement rates and have been the source of much hand-wringing over the decades. But they too have fallen below the replacement rate in just the past few years. While fertility rates have been falling for some groups, especially in the White population, for decades, and for other groups more recently, the COVID-19 pandemic of 2020 and into 2022 pushed fertility and birth rates down further. The 4 percent decline in births in the U.S. in 2020 was the largest decline since 1973, down from 3.8 million in 2018 to 3.75 million in 2019 to just 3.6 million births in 2020.[82] Fertility rates

TABLE 2.3 U.S. Total Fertility Rate by Race and Ethnicity, 1940–2021

Year	White	Black and Other*	Hispanic	Asian/PI	U.S. Average
1940–44	2.46	3.01			2.52
1945–49	2.92	3.49			2.99
1950–54	3.22	4.19			3.34
1955–59	3.55	4.72			3.69
1960–64	3.33	4.33			3.45
1965–69	2.51	3.36			2.62
1970–74	2.01	2.70			2.11
1975–79	1.72	2.33			1.81
1980–84	1.76	2.10		1.95	1.82
1985–89	1.83	2.24			1.90
1990–94	1.99	2.42	2.96	2.00	2.06
1995–99	2.03	2.16			2.05
2000–04	2.05	2.04	2.76	1.86	2.04
2005–09	2.09	2.13	2.94	1.95	2.09
2010–14	1.90	1.91	2.21	1.71	1.89
2015–19	1.70	1.82	2.02	1.60	1.77
2020–21	1.58	1.69	1.89	1.37	1.65

* Black and Other becomes Black alone after 2000.

Sources: U.S. Census, *Statistical Abstract of the United States*, *1981*, "Vital Statistics," #84, "Total Fertility and Intrinsic Rate of Natural Increase, 1940–1979;" *2001*, #73, "1960–1999;" *2015*, #91, "Total Fertility by Race and Hispanic Origin, 1980–2013;" *2023*, #86, "2010–2020."

for all major racial and ethnic populations in the U.S. are now well below replacement rates.

Given declining fertility rates, the U.S. population would be falling without immigrants continuing to add to the nation's numbers. Table 2.4 highlights the fact that U.S. population growth, once driven principally by natural increase, women in the U.S. having babies, is increasingly driven by immigration. In 1950, the early stages of the post-World War II population boom, fully 93 percent of population growth reflected domestic births while just 7 percent reflected international migrants. Fifty years later, in 2000, natural increase still accounted for nearly 80 percent of population growth while migration accounted for the remaining 20 percent. By 2020, as domestic fertility continued its decline, just half of population growth came from natural increase and the other half from migration. U.S. census projections suggest that by 2060, fully 81 percent of population growth will come from migration and just 19 percent from domestic natural increase.

TABLE 2.4 Components of Population Change in the U.S., 1950–2020, with Projections to 2060

Year	Population	Numerical Change	Natural Increase	Net Migration	% from Natural Increase	% from Net Migration
1950	151,325,798					
1960	179,323,175	27,997,377	25,907,377	2,090,000	93	7
1970	203,302,031	23,978,856	21,556,856	2,422,000	90	10
1980	226,542,199	23,240,168	20,017,168	3,223,000	86	14
1990	248,718,302	22,176,103	16,521,103	5,655,000	74	26
2000	281,424,603	32,706,301	25,963,301	6,743,000	79	21
2010	308,746,065	27,321,462	20,060,462	7,261,000	73	27
2020	331,449,281	22,703,743	12,075,360	11,045,760	51	49
2030	359,402,000	24,899,000	12,127,000	13,064,000	48	52
2040	380,219,000	20,817,000	7,350,000	13,890,000	35	65
2050	398,328,000	18,109,000	3,729,000	14,496,000	21	79
2060	416,795,000	18,467,000	3,520,000	14,880,000	19	81

Sources: U.S. Bureau of the Census, *Statistical Abstract of the United States, 2023*, Table 1, "Population and Area, 1790–2020"; U.S. Bureau of the Census, *Statistical Abstract of the United States, 2022*, "Projected Population Size and Births, Deaths, and Migration"; U.S. Bureau of the Census, *Main Projection Series of the United States, 2017–2060*, Table 1; *The Changing Demographic Profile of the United States*, March 31, 2011, https://www.everycrsreport.com/reports/RL32701.html#_Toc29041681.

Future economic growth in the U.S. will depend on a combination of population growth and worker productivity growth.[83] With domestic population growth expected to be less than 1 percent per decade and productivity growth slipping to 2 to 2.5 percent annually, a shrinking workforce and laggard economy will struggle to sustain an aging population. But U.S. immigration policy continues to be stalemated in Washington, D.C. While most Republicans favor strict border controls, particularly on our southern border, most Democrats favor increased immigration. Unfortunately, most Democrats support our current immigration policies favoring family unification and asylum claimants, while too few favor a revised policy advantaging the educated, trained, and talented along with immigrants for agriculture, construction, and other crucial jobs. Why the reluctance about immigration?

Increased diversity threatens White supremacy in many ways, some quite fundamental. As we have seen, sex and marriage across racial lines, and attitudes toward them, have haunted American history. Miscegenation, as racial mixing was commonly called, was long practiced and loudly decried. As Isabel Wilkerson recounted in *Caste*, "Virginia became the first colony to outlaw marriage between blacks and whites. . . . [Eventually,] forty-one of the fifty states passed laws making intermarriage a crime." Other nations limited or banned interracial marriage, but "the United States alone created a system based on . . . the idea that a single drop of African blood, . . . could taint the purity of someone who might otherwise be presumed to be European."[84] The "one drop" rule, often described in state law as "no trace" or "no ascertainable trace" of Black blood in persons expecting to be recognized as White, remained on some state law books into the 1960s and beyond. While anti-miscegenation statutes usually targeted Black people, some targeted Native Americans and Asians as well. In 1905, California passed a law "barring intermarriage between whites and 'Mongolians' [meaning Chinese], although Chinese could presumably marry Blacks and possibly Native Americans."[85]

Critically, these laws did little to limit interracial sex, and by many who pushed them were never intended to, but they did declare any progeny to be Black or at least mixed race and outside any line of social acknowledgement, let alone inheritance. Recent DNA studies have cast new light into this historical dark corner. The geneticist Steven Micheletti calculated that "European men contributed three times more to the modern gene pool of people of African descent than European women did."[86] Let that sink in; historically, White men contributed three times as much to the DNA of today's African-Americans as did White women. Why? Because they could and so they did, all the time abhorring the practice and denying the legitimacy of the progeny.

The response of Black intellectual leaders to the facts of interracial sexual relations and the role of dominance and violence within them was abhorrence mixed with ambivalence. W.E.B. Du Bois, given to ambivalence in almost nothing, described his own genetic mélange at birth this way: "having gotten myself born, with a flood of Negro blood, a strain of French, a bit of Dutch, but, thank God! no 'Anglo-Saxon,' I came to the days of my childhood."[87] Less entertaining, but more practical, E. Franklin Frazier, the first Black President of the American Sociological Association in 1948, wrote: "intermarriage in the future will bring about a fundamental type of assimilation."[88] Similarly, the Howard University classics professor Hera Morgan observed in 1957 that, "The life of a people is not static. It has nothing to fear from the mingling of hearts, minds, and bodies with the different."[89] But change was slow to come. In fact, legal limits on interracial marriage existed in many states until struck down in 1967 by the U.S. Supreme Court in the landmark *Loving v. Virginia*. We will discuss *Loving v. Virginia* in more detail in Chapter 4.

Many decades after Du Bois, Frazier, and Morgan wrote, one has to say that while Du Bois' abhorrence is still shared by some, there is slow movement in the direction that Frazier and Morgan forecast. But even that slow movement reflects the traditional racial and ethnic hierarchy. Political scientist Ashley Jardina recently wrote that: "we continue to organize our political and social world by dividing individuals into different racial groups. . . . the nation today remains marked by an enduring racial hierarchy, one in which whites are at the top, blacks are at the bottom, and other racial and ethnic groups fall somewhere in between."[90] Similarly, Harvard sociologist David R. Williams wrote: "All racial ethnic minority groups are stereotyped more negatively than whites, . . . Blacks are viewed the worst, then Latinos, who are viewed twice as negatively as Asians. There is a hierarchy of rank."[91] In general, that hierarchy runs, top to bottom, from White, to Asian, Hispanic, and Black. Other factors affect marriage choices, love of course, also class (i.e., money), future promise, and physical beauty – but racial hierarchy is a powerful factor in its own right.

One sees the traditional racial hierarchy very clearly in the intermarriage data collected by the U.S. Census, especially in who gets to make this choice and of whom, but one also sees the defenses against interracial marriage beginning to crack and the cracks beginning to widen. The census has reported racial intermarriage rates since 1960 and in more detail since 1980. While what constitutes an interracial marriage, especially for Hispanics as Hispanic is a broad ethnicity rather than a race, is a bit murky; in general terms, marriages across race and ethnic lines in 1960 constituted less than 1 percent of all marriages, 3 percent by 1967, the year the Supreme Court struck down some state prohibitions on such marriages,

15 percent in 2010, and 17 percent in 2015. Out-marriage is least common for White Americans, 9 percent in 2010, and Black Americans, 17 percent, and most common for Hispanics and Asians at 26 and 28 percent respectively. The most common form of interracial or ethnic marriage is White/Latino at 43 percent of all such marriages in 2010.[92]

In 2017, using 2015 data, Pew Research Center reported that White men who married out choose Hispanic partners seven times more frequently and Asian partners four times more frequently than Black partners. Hence, more Hispanic and Asian women married out than did Hispanic and Asian men. And Black men married out twice as frequently as Black women, leaving what is commonly referred to as a "marriage deficit" for Black women.[93] One is reminded of Zora Neale Hurston's most famous literary line, from *Their Eyes Were Watching God* (1937), where the elderly Nanny tells the young and beautiful Janie: "Honey, de white man is de ruler of everything. . . . De nigger woman is de mule uh de world as fur as Ah can see."[94] As Nanny knew, racial hierarchy was, if not permanent, at least resilient, and while interracial marriage might blur some lines, it was unlikely to rub them out anytime soon.

Clearly, the United States and its dominant White majority have been very sensitive to the racial and ethnic composition of the nation and of the roles that various groups may or may not play.[95] Not surprisingly then, the racial politics of citizenship, suffrage, and partisanship have been particularly fraught. Chapter 3, entitled "Citizenship, Suffrage, and Race in America" will explore these issues in our history and in our contemporary politics.

Notes

1 Ian Morris, *Why the West Rules—For Now: The Patterns of History, and What They Reveal About the Future* (New York: Farrar, Straus, and Giroux, 2010), 68, 84–85. See also Jared Diamond, *Guns, Germs, and Steel: The Fates of Human Societies* (New York: W.W. Norton, 2017, first published 1997), 13, 27, 35, 65.
2 Alfred W. Crosby, Jr., *The Columbian Exchange: Biological and Cultural Consequences of First Contact*, 30th anniversary ed. (Westport, CT: Praeger, 2003), 21, 30. See also Diamond, *Guns, Germs, and Steel*, 15; Caroline Dodds Pennock, *On Savage Shores: How Indigenous Americans Discovered Europe* (New York: Alfred A. Knopf, 2023), 95.
3 Angus Deaton, *The Great Escape: Health, Wealth, and the Origins of Inequality* (Princeton, NJ: Princeton University Press, 2013), 80.
4 Morris, *Why the West Rules—For Now*, 296.
5 Pennock, *On Savage Shores*, 4, see also 7.
6 Steven Johnson, *Extra Life: A Short History of Living Longer* (New York: Riverhead Books, 2021), 37.
7 Christopher Columbus, *Journals and Other Documents on the Life and Voyages of Christopher Columbus*, trans. Samuel Eliot Morrison (New York: Heritage Press, 1963), 66, 90. See also Crosby, *The Columbian Exchange*, 4.

60 Demographic Stability and Change in American History

8 Columbus, *Journals*, 66, 119, 122.
9 Columbus, *Journals*, 65, 72, 91.
10 Columbus, *Journals*, 90, 68, 78, 92, 109.
11 Columbus, *Journals*, 90.
12 Columbus, *Journals*, 93.
13 Columbus, *Journals*, 65, 109, see also 122–123.
14 Charles C. Mann, *1491: New Revelations of the Americas Before Columbus* (New York: Alfred A. Knopf, 2005), 78, 84, 172, 273. See also Thomas Piketty, *A Brief History of Equality* (Cambridge, MA: Harvard University Press, 2022), 50–55, 63; Pennock, *On Savage Shores*, 33, 41, 95.
15 Mann, *1491*, 27, 323, 326. See also Charles C. Mann, *1493: Uncovering the New World Columbus Created* (New York: Alfred A. Knopf, 2011), xiv.
16 See Zechariah 1:8–11, Ezekiel 14:21, and Revelation 6:1–8.
17 Pennock, *On Savage Shores*, 21, 89, 108–110.
18 Diamond, *Guns, Germs, and Steel*, 75, 189, 201–203.
19 Mann, *1491*, 55, 93–94.
20 Colin Woodard, *American Nations: A History of the Eleven Rival Regional Cultures of North America* (New York: Viking Penguin, 2011), 24–26.
21 Heather McGhee, *The Sum of Us: What Racism Costs Everyone and How We Can Prosper Together* (New York: OneWorld, 2021), 7.
22 Alexander Koch, Chris Brierly, Mark M. Maslin, and Simon L. Lewis, "Earth System Impacts of the European Arrival and the Great Dying in the Americas after 1492," *Quaternary Science Reviews* 207 (March 2019): 13–36.
23 Koch, et al., "Earth System Impacts," 30.
24 Joe R. Feagin, *The White Racial Frame: Centuries of Racial Framing and Counter-Framing*, 3rd ed. (New York: Routledge, 2020), 22.
25 Mann, *1491*, 106–107.
26 Diamond, *Guns, Germs, and Steel*, 202. See also Michael C. Steiner, *Horace Kallen in the Heartland: The Midwestern Roots of American Pluralism* (Lawrence, KS: University Press of Kansas, 2020), 12.
27 Tiya Miles, "Dispossession," in *The 1619 Project*, ed. Nikole Hannah-Jones, Caitlin Roper, Ilena Silverman, and Jake Silverstein (New York: The New York Times Co., 2021), 142.
28 Philip L. Barbour and Richard Hakluyt, *The Jamestown Voyages Under the First Charter, 1606–1609* (London: Cambridge University Press, 1969), series II, vol. 136, 49–54. See also Benjamin Woolley, *Savage Kingdom: The True Story of Jamestown, 1607, and the Settlement of America* (New York: HarperCollins, 2007), 32.
29 Alexis de Tocqueville, *Democracy in America* (Chicago: University of Chicago Press, 2000), 26. See also Adam Dahl, *Empire of the People: Settler Colonialism and the Foundations of Modern Democratic Thought* (Lawrence, KS: University Press of Kansas, 2018), 80–81.
30 Thomas Jefferson, *The Papers of Thomas Jefferson*, ed. Julian P. Boyd (Princeton, NJ: Princeton University Press, 1950), 1:122.
31 Khalil Gibran Muhammad, "Sugar," in *The 1619 Project*, 75.
32 Paul E. Lovejoy, *Transformations in Slavery: The History of Slavery in Africa*, 3rd ed. (New York: Cambridge University Press, 2011), xxiv.
33 Lovejoy, *Transformations in Slavery*, 45–107, see especially 53.
34 David Brion Davis, *Inhuman Bondage* (New York: Oxford University Press, 2006), 89–90. See also William J. Bernstein, *A Splendid Exchange: How Trade Shaped the World* (New York: Grove Press, 2008), 273–274.
35 David Levering Lewis, *W.E.B. Du Bois: A Biography, 1868–1963* (New York: Henry Holt and Company, 2009), 8. See also Robert William Fogel and Stanley

L. Engerman, *Time on the Cross: The Economics of American Nego Slavery* (New York: W.W. Norton, 1974/1995), 15.
36 David Hackett Fischer, *African Founders: How Enslaved People Expanded American Ideals* (New York: Simon & Schuster, 2022), 4–5, and Tables 1.1 and 1.2, 27–28. See also Christine Kenneally, "DNA Study Shows Legacy of Slavery's Brutality," *New York Times*, July 24, 2020, A14.
37 Ibram X. Kendi, *Stamped from the Beginning: The Definitive History of Racist Ideas in America* (New York: Bold Type Books, 2017), 38.
38 *Hening's Statutes at Large, Laws of Virginia*, 14 vol. (New York: R. W. & G. Bartow, 1823); reprint by University Press of Virginia, 1969, 1:146.
39 *Hening's Statutes at Large*, 2:170. See also Kendi, *Stamped from the Beginning*, 41.
40 Fischer, *African Founders*, 302.
41 Natalia Molina, *How Race is Made in America: Immigration, Citizenship, and the Historical Power of Racial Scripts* (Berkeley, CA: University of California Press, 2014), 24, 72. See also Kendi, *Stamped from the Beginning*, 121, and McGhee, *The Sum of Us*, 13.
42 Ashley Jardina, *White Identity Politics* (New York: Cambridge University Press, 2019), 119.
43 Howard Temperley, ed., *After Slavery: Emancipation and Its Discontents* (Portland, OR: Frank Cass, 2000), 68. See also Rogan Kersh, *Dreams of a More Perfect Union* (Ithaca, NY: Cornell University Press, 2001), 129; David W. Blight, *Frederick Douglass: Prophet of Freedom* (New York: Simon & Schuster, 2018), 240; Richard F. Bensel, *Yankee Leviathan: The Origins of Central State Authority in America, 1859–1877* (New York: Cambridge University Press, 1990), 31.
44 Leon F. Litwack, *Been in the Storm So Long: The Aftermath of Slavery* (New York: Vintage Books, 1979), 134, 268, and Kendi, *Stamped from the Beginning*, 221, 224.
45 Charles M. Blow, "Why We Need a Second Great Migration," *New York Times*, January 10, 2021, SR 4–5. See also Earl Black and Merle Black, *The Rise of Southern Republicans* (Cambridge, MA: Harvard University Press, 2002), 17–20.
46 Bensel, *Yankee Leviathan*, 380, 398.
47 Blight, *Frederick Douglass*, 601. See also Lerone Bennett, Jr., *Before the Mayflower: A History of the Negro in America, 1619–1962* (Chicago, IL: Johnson Publishing Company, 1962; Eastford, CT: Martino Fine Books, 2016), 236; Leon F. Litwack, *Trouble in Mind: Black Southerners in the Age of Jim Crow* (New York: Vintage Books, 1998), 135; Merline Pitre, *Through Many Dangers, Toils and Snares: Black Leadership in Texas, 1868–1898* (College Station, TX: Texas A&M University Press, 2016), 40, 192, 194.
48 Desmond S. King, *The Liberty of Strangers: Making the American Nation* (New York: Oxford University Press, 2005), 56. See also Ralph Ellison, *Going to the Territory* (New York: Random House, 1986), 131–132; Steiner, *Horace Kallen in the Heartland*, 36.
49 Douglas S. Massey and Nancy A. Denton, *American Apartheid: Segregation and the Making of the Underclass* (Cambridge, MA: Harvard University Press, 1993), 27–28.
50 Neil Foley, *Mexicans in the Making of America* (Cambridge, MA: Harvard University Press, 2014), 15. See also Dahl, *Empire of the People*, 115; Harry V. Jaffa, *Crisis of the House Divided: An Interpretation of the Issues in the Lincoln-Douglas Debates* (Chicago, IL: University of Chicago Press, 1959, 1982), 34, 67–69, 76, 95–96, 100–102; David Herbert Donald, *Lincoln* (New York: Simon & Schuster, 1995), 122.

51 Foley, *Mexicans in the Making of America*, 39.
52 Molina, *How Race is Made in America*, 23.
53 Mae Ngai, *The Chinese Question: The Gold Rushes and Global Politics* (New York: W.W. Norton, 2021).
54 Carol Nackenoff and Julie Novkov, *American by Birth: Wong Kim Ark and the Battle for Citizenship* (Lawrence, KS: University Press of Kansas, 2021), 30.
55 Anna Brown, "The Changing Categories the U.S. Census Has Used to Measure Race," Fact Tank, Pew Research Center, February 25, 2020.
56 Neil Foley, *The White Scourge: Mexicans, Blacks, and Poor Whites in Texas Cotton Culture* (Berkeley, CA: University of California Press, 1997), 41.
57 Foley, *Mexicans in the Making of America*, 87.
58 Ana Gonzalez-Barrera, "About 6 Million U.S. Adults Identify as Afro-Latino," Pew Research Center, May 2, 2022.
59 Jens Manuel Krogstad and Luis Noe-Bustamante, "Key Facts About U.S. Latinos for National Hispanic Heritage Month," Pew Research Center, September 10, 2020.
60 Abby Budiman and Neil G. Ruiz, "Key Facts About Asian Americans, A Diverse and Growing Population," Pew Research Center, April 29, 2021.
61 Nackenoff and Novkov, *American by Birth*, 128, 147.
62 Nicholas Confessore and Karen Yourish, "Creeping into the Mainstream, A Theory Turns Hate into Terror," *New York Times*, May 16, 2022, A1, A20.
63 Ralph Waldo Emerson, "The Fortune of the Republic," *Complete Works of Ralph Waldo Emerson* (New York: Houghton Mifflin, 1903–1904), 11: 538, 541. See also Frederick Douglass, "Composite Nation," in Parker Fraternity Course, Boston, 1867, www.loc.gov/item/mss1187900406/, and Martha S. Jones, "Citizenship," in *The 1619 Project*, 236.
64 David R. Roediger, *Working Toward Whiteness: How America's Immigrants Became White* (New York: Basic Books, 2005), 64–65, 146.
65 Jared A. Goldstein, *Real Americans: National Identity, Violence, and the Constitution* (Lawrence, KS: University Press of Kansas, 2022), 47.
66 Gary Gerstle, *American Crucible: Race and Nation in the Twentieth Century* (Princeton, NJ: Princeton University Press, 2001, rev. ed. 2017), 94. See also Richard F. Bensel, *The Political Economy of American Industrialization, 1877–1900* (New York: Cambridge University Press, 2000), 149–152, 207–208.
67 W.E.B Du Bois, "Address to the Nation," https://users.wfu.edu/zulick/341/niagara.html.
68 Robert A. Margo, *Race and Schooling in the South, 1880–1950: An Economic History* (Chicago, IL: University of Chicago Press, 1990), 120. See also Valerie Sweeney Prince, *Burnin' Down the House: Home in African American Literature* (New York: Columbia University Press, 2004), 14.
69 Henry Louis Gates, Jr., *Stony the Road: Reconstruction, White Supremacy, and the Rise of Jim Crow* (New York: Penguin Books, 2020), 203. See also Steiner, *Horace Kallen in the Heartland*, 16.
70 Kendi, *Stamped from the Beginning*, 309. See also Jack Temple Kirby, *Rural Worlds Lost: The American South, 1920–1960* (Baton Rouge, LA: Louisiana State University Press, 1987), 309, 320; Gavin Wright, *Old South, New South: Revolutions in the Southern Economy Since the Civil War* (Baton Rouge, LA: Louisiana State University Press, 1997), 198.
71 Isabel Wilkerson, *The Warmth of Other Suns: The Epic Story of America's Great Migration* (New York: Vintage Books, 2011). See also especially Wright, *Old South, New South*, 237.

72 Lewis, *Du Bois*, 62. See also Litwack, *Trouble in Mind*, 358; Neil Foley, *Quest for Equality: The Failed Promise of Black-Brown Solidarity* (Cambridge, MA: Harvard University Press, 2010), 14; Van Gosse, *The First Reconstruction: Black Politics in America from the Revolution to the Civil War* (Chapel Hill, NC: University of North Carolina Press, 2021), 382.
73 Lewis, *Du Bois*, 381.
74 Numan V. Bartley, *The New South, 1945–1980: The Story of the South's Modernization* (Baton Rouge, LA: Louisiana State University Press, 1996), 11.
75 Bartley, *The New South, 1945–1980*, 76.
76 Wright, *Old South, New South*, 256–257.
77 Wilkerson, *The Warmth of Other Suns*. See also Neil Fligstein, *Going North: The Migration of Blacks and Whites from the South, 1900–1950* (New York: Academic Press, 1981), 18.
78 Desmond S. King and Rogers M. Smith, *Still a House Divided: Race and Politics in Obama's America* (Princeton, NJ: Princeton University Press, 2011), 239.
79 Tyler Stovall, *White Freedom: The Racial History of an Idea* (Princeton, NJ: Princeton University Press, 2021), 287. See also Jardina, *White Identity Politics*, 11, 157. See also Michael Omi and Howard Winant, *Racial Formation in the United States*, 3rd ed. (New York: Routledge, 2015), 8.
80 F. Chris Garcia and Gabriel R. Sanchez, *Hispanics and the U.S. Political System: Moving into the Mainstream* (New York: Routledge, 2008), 1–2, 59.
81 Jardina, *White Identity Politics*, 161.
82 Jacqueline Howard, "U.S. Births Fell During the Pandemic, CDC Data Show," *CNN Health*, June 23, 2021. See also "The 2020 Census: America Is Stagnating," *The Economist*, February 5, 2022, 25–26.
83 Dana Goldstein and Daniel Victor, "Birthrate in the U.S. Increases by 1 Percent After Years of a Steady Decline," *New York Times*, May 25, 2022, A21.
84 Isabel Wilkerson, *Caste: The Origins of Our Discontents* (New York: Random House, 2020), 111, 121.
85 Nackenoff and Novkov, *American by Birth*, 74.
86 Steven Micheletti, et al., "Genetic Consequences of the Transatlantic Slave Trade in the Americas," *American Journal of Human Genetics* 107, no. 2 (August 2020): 265–277, see especially Table 1. See also Christine Kenneally, "DNA Study Shows Legacy of Slavery's Brutality," *New York Times*, July 24, 2020, A14.
87 W.E.B. Du Bois, *Darkwater: Voices from Within the Veil* (New York: Harcourt, Brace and Company, 1920), 9. For alternative views of racial purity see the great Civil War–era abolitionist leader Wendell Phillips in Kersh, *Dreams of a More Perfect Union*, 247, and Associate Justice Henry Billings Brown, author of *Plessy v. Ferguson*, in Donald Yacovone, *Teaching White Supremacy: America's Democratic Ordeal and the Forging of Our National Identity* (New York: Pantheon Books, 2022), 35.
88 E. Franklin Frazier, *The Negro Family in the United States* (Chicago, IL: University of Chicago Press, 1939), 368.
89 Steiner, *Horace Kallen in the Heartland*, 157.
90 Jardina, *White Identity Politics*, 22, see also 33. See also Luis Noe-Bustamante, et al., "Majority of Latinos Say Skin Color Impacts Opportunity in America and Shapes Daily Life," Pew Research Center, November 4, 2021.
91 Wilkerson, *Caste*, 186–187.
92 Foley, *Mexicans in the Making of America*, 236. See also Samuel L. Perry, "Religion and Whites' Attitudes Toward Interracial Marriage with

African-Americans, Asians, and Latinos," *Journal for the Scientific Study of Religion* 52, no. 2 (June 2013): 425–442.
93 Gretchen Livingston and Anna Bowen, "Intermarriage in the U.S. 50 Years After *Loving v. Virginia*," Pew Research Center, May 2017. See also Tayler J. Mathews and Glenn S. Johnson, "Skin Complexion in the Twenty-First Century: The Impact of Colorism on African-American Women," *Race, Gender, and Class*, 22, no. 1–2 (2017): 248–274.
94 Zora Neale Hurston, *Hurston: Novels and Stories* (New York: The Library of America, 1995), 186.
95 Vasiliki Fouka and Marco Tabellini, "Changing In-Group Boundaries: The Effect of Immigration on Race Relations in the United States," *American Political Science Review* 116, no. 3 (August 2022): 968–984.

3
CITIZENSHIP, SUFFRAGE, AND RACE IN AMERICA

> "I appear here . . . having the interest that every true citizen should have in the welfare, the stability, the permanence and the prosperity of our free institutions, and in this spirit I shall criticize our government to-night."
>
> Frederick Douglass, 1867 "Sources of Danger to the Republic"

In Chapter 1, we introduced the concepts of racial orders and racial regimes. Both phrases refer to coherent and integrated sets of institutions, laws, policies, and norms that structure the relations, often hierarchical relations, between races, and later races and ethnicities, in various eras of our nation's history – including slavery, Jim Crow segregation, and the mid-twentieth century civil rights era. In Chapter 2, we traced the demographic history of the nation, highlighting both the centuries-long era of White super-majority domination of an enslaved and oppressed Black minority and the more recent era of a blooming racial and ethnic diversity that has challenged and deeply unsettled at least some part of the traditional White majority. Here we review the constitutional, legal, and electoral provisions and rules that have buttressed the White majority and limited and often excluded Black people and other minorities. Throughout American history, access to citizenship and suffrage, or their denial, have defined inclusion and exclusion.[1] The right to suffrage – to register, to vote, and to have that vote counted – has long been seen to be the necessary antecedent to a broader and more secure Black liberty; Frederick Douglass called suffrage "the keystone to the arch of human liberty."

DOI: 10.4324/9781003449188-3

Much more recently Congressman John Lewis movingly touted voting and active citizenship as key tools for defending the broader role and rights of Black people in America. John Lewis, a civil rights icon who represented Georgia's fifth congressional district from 1987 to 2020, died on July 17, 2020. On July 30, 2020, *The New York Times* ran an op-ed written by Lewis shortly before his death entitled, "Together, You Can Redeem the Soul of Our Nation." Lewis wrote in universal terms but with the nation's Black citizens front of mind, counseling that: "Democracy is not a state. It is an act, . . . The vote is the most powerful non-violent change agent you have in a democratic society. You must use it because it is not guaranteed. You can lose it."[2] Congressman Lewis packed a lot of Black history into his final charge to those to whom he passed the torch. That history has been an ongoing fight for acceptance and inclusion.

The Indiana University of Pennsylvania historian Wang Xi has written extensively about the evolution of citizenship and suffrage in America. Like much of the racial regimes literature, Xi finds familiar periods of regime change, writing that: "The development of American citizenship can roughly be divided in three eras or phases: the Founding era, the Civil War and Reconstruction era, and the New Deal–Great Society era. Each of these eras was centered at a major event or transformation in the state-building process . . ."[3] Elsewhere, Xi evaluated, as we will here, the conservative backlashes that followed transformative expansions of citizenship and suffrage rights in the Revolutionary period, the Civil War and Reconstruction era, and the civil rights era of the mid-twentieth century.

For most of the nation's history, few White Americans were willing to conceive of Black Americans and other persons of color as citizens with the same civil and political rights that they enjoyed. Nonetheless, during the nation's early history, some Black people, always under 10 percent, were free and were allowed, within greater or lesser constraints, to participate in political life during both the colonial and early national periods. But the limits on Black political participation were very real, even in the North, throughout the colonial period and then steadily tightened during the early national and antebellum periods of U.S. history. Moreover, sectional mistrust shaped the constitutional provisions governing citizenship and civil rights, especially suffrage rights, in the states and the nation.[4]

As a result, the nation's electoral playing field tilted to the South.[5] Twelve of the nation's first eighteen presidents, two-thirds of them from George Washington to Ulysses S. Grant, were slaveowners at some point in their lives. Washington and Jefferson held 600+, Zachary Taylor 300, Andrew Jackson 200, Madison 100, Monroe 75, with others ranging down to Martin Van Buren's and U.S. Grant's one each. Remarkably, from Washington's ascension to the presidency in 1789 through the death of the twelfth president, Zachary Taylor, in 1850, only the two Adams', both one-term presidents from Massachusetts, did not own slaves at some point in their lives and only two of the others, Van Buren and William Henry Harrison, owned fewer than a dozen. So, from the nation's founding, the presumptions of America's political leadership class were accepting, even protective, of slavery and of racial hierarchy more broadly.

Black Citizenship and Suffrage in the Early Republic

The American Revolution, like the eras of the Civil War and the Great Society, had prominent civil rights and voting rights dimensions. Each was also followed by a conservative counterrevolution that swept away many newly won civil and voting rights' gains. The American Revolution included multiple struggles, one with the British for national independence, another between North and South to set the constitutional design and distribution of powers between the nation and the states, and still another within each of the states over citizenship and civil rights including voting, jury and militia service, and, in some states, the right to be a resident at all. Finally, another struggle occurred as thousands of Black soldiers joined the fight, mostly though not exclusively on the British side, in the hope of gaining freedom, citizenship, and suffrage.[6]

The American Revolution produced national independence but it could not produce national unity. When the Constitutional Convention met in Philadelphia during the summer of 1787 to strengthen the national government and better address the exigencies of the Union, stark and ultimately insurmountable disagreements quickly surfaced among the delegates. Rather than risk failure, the Convention adopted a series of large state/small state and interregional compromises, including the infamous three-fifths compromise that counted slaves as three-fifths of a person for purposes of representation in Congress. The three-fifths compromise did the slaves no good but it did increase their masters' weight in Congress and the Electoral College. These compromises limited national authority and embedded federalism and states' rights in the service of human chattel slavery in the new Constitution.[7] These bargains and compromises bought time for the new nation to grow and strengthen, but at the cost of building a near fatal flaw into the national moral, cultural, and institutional architecture.[8] Those costs were again, and not for the last time, paid by the nation's Black residents.[9]

Sectional conflict in the Constitutional Convention produced a federal system in which the national government had important enumerated powers, mostly in national security, military affairs, and economic policy, but most day-to-day governing was left to the states.[10] Because the right to vote was more open in the Northern states than in the Southern states, both for White and free Black citizens, no national suffrage rules could be agreed upon in the convention. Instead, Article I, section 4, of the Constitution provided that, "The times, places and manner of holding elections for Senators and Representatives, shall be prescribed in each state by the legislature thereof; but the Congress may at any time by law make or alter such regulations, . . ." State legislatures also set the rules for voting in their own state and local elections. Until after the Civil War, the Congress rarely interfered when states set electoral rules to reflect their state cultures and concerns. As always, regional variation in Black rights was dramatic and few gains, even when they occurred, were secure.

Between 1776 and 1800, seven states – New Hampshire, Vermont, Massachusetts, Rhode Island, Connecticut, New York, and Pennsylvania – abolished slavery or passed gradual emancipation statutes designed to end it by the mid-1820s.[11] Ten thousand free Black people became 200,000 by 1810.[12] They struggled, sometimes successfully, sometimes not, for the right to vote. During the revolutionary era, most state electoral laws did not formally exclude free Black men from voting, and they did vote as a matter of course in New England, regularly in the Middle Atlantic states, but further south social and political pressures excluded most. During the 1790s, most New England states, including Maine, Vermont, New Hampshire, and Massachusetts, and several Middle Atlantic states, including New York, New Jersey, and Delaware, allowed free Black men to vote. Pennsylvania, Maryland, and even North Carolina allowed free Black men to vote for a time. As always, Black freedom and opportunity sparked a sustained backlash.

When revolutionary passions cooled, state after state, from Connecticut and New York through Delaware and Maryland, moved to limit voting to White men or to drastically limit Black men's suffrage through property qualifications to which White citizens were not subject.[13] Maryland disenfranchised free Black men in 1783, Delaware in 1787, New Jersey in 1807, Connecticut in 1818, Rhode Island in 1822, Tennessee and North Carolina in 1835, and Pennsylvania in 1838. In 1821 New York instituted a property qualification for Black men that excluded most. Every state that entered the Union after 1800, with the exception of Maine in 1820, restricted the vote to White men and only Rhode Island in 1842 restored the right to vote to Black men once it had been removed.[14]

Several states served as regional leaders and steered their neighbors in radically different directions. Massachusetts promoted and defended Black citizenship throughout the revolutionary and early national periods. Massachusetts welcomed, or at least did not discourage Black residency, citizenship, voting, and jury participation. Black children attended public schools. Even here, however, Black militia service was denied and Black intermarriage with Whites was forbidden until 1843. All of New England followed Massachusetts' lead toward a biracial, though not thoroughly egalitarian, society.

The Mid-Atlantic states, led by New York and Pennsylvania, produced a more mixed and mottled picture of Black civil liberties. In New York, Black residents enjoyed more social and political freedom upstate, particularly in western New York, than they did in the city. Black men were legally entitled to vote in New York, between 1777 and 1821, though often obstructed. In 1821, Martin Van Buren's Bucktail faction of the Democratic Party controlled a state constitutional convention that effectively disenfranchised most Black men by placing a $250 freehold property requirement on them. No such property qualification existed for White voters and unrestricted Black suffrage was not restored until 1860. Pennsylvania allowed men, White and Black, who paid a very modest county tax to vote from the revolutionary era through Black disenfranchisement in 1838. However, various devices limited actual Black voting. In Philadelphia, White and Black leaders simply agreed that Black social, economic, and personal rights would be protected in exchange for electoral abstention. Moreover, in the city and elsewhere, Black men, whether they paid the required county tax or not, might simply be left off the rolls and therefore remain ineligible to vote. Individual Black citizens had to decide whether to complain or simply let it go; most decided to let it go. New Jersey and Delaware took similar actions to limit Black voting.

Ohio led the new midwestern states into a deeper and rawer racism than existed in most of the northern and Middle Atlantic coastal states. Ohio became a state in 1803 and its first state legislature passed a series of Black laws limiting migration and residency rights, requiring bonds and testaments against indigency, limiting jury service, testimony in courts against Whites, voting, and eventually Black children attending school with White children. Real as these constitutional and legal limits on Black political participation were, they were often applied strategically. For example, the dominant political party in a precinct, city, or region might allow some Black voting if they were confident that they would receive those votes. It is also important to recall that most judgments, as to residency, property requirements, even race were made seat of the pants. In 1823, Ohio courts ruled that mixed race citizens with more than half White blood, say a citizen who had a Black forebearer some generations back, or White father and "mulatto" mother, were legally White and entitled to vote. Election judges effectively had a free hand to wave through those they knew or trusted politically and wave off those they found suspicious. Indiana (1816), Illinois (1818), Michigan (1837), and Iowa (1839) all selected liberally from

Ohio's smorgasbord of racial restrictions and humiliations when they entered the Union. Ohio repealed most of its Black laws in 1849, but some of her neighbors were slower to move toward civil equality.

Black Americans came very early to recognize that the states were volatile and that, therefore, the national government and the party most identified with the national government represented their best chance for order, security, and liberty.[15] Before the Civil War, those free Black men that could vote, always a small minority, supported the Federalists while they remained viable, then briefly the National Republicans, the Whigs, then even more briefly the Free Soil and Know Nothing parties, before they flocked to the Republicans in the 1850s and thereafter. Not surprisingly, Black voters generally spurned the various iterations of the Democratic Party as the party of states' rights, slavery, and the South.[16]

Black Citizenship and Suffrage in Antebellum America

Regional tensions festered as the nation grew and expanded through the second quarter of the nineteenth century. One remarkable story will help make this point. Frederick Douglass escaped slavery in Maryland in September 1838 by fleeing to New York and then on to Massachusetts. Historian David Blight described the remarkable civil transformation that Douglass met: "In Massachusetts in the late 1830s, men, including blacks, registered to vote by paying a small annual tax. . . . [S]till 'illegal' as a fugitive from Southern justice and the property rights of his owner, [Douglass] could instantly become a voter by paying $1.50 and having his name placed on the tax rolls."[17] He did just that. Southern slaveowners, of course, fumed over what they thought to be subversion of their constitutional right to hold and use slaves.

As the South sought to extend slavery into the territories and some Northern states moved to limit and even rescind free Black rights, abolitionists like Douglass became increasingly outraged. In May 1847 he delivered a speech entitled "Country, Conscience, and the Anti-Slavery Cause" before a meeting of the American Anti-Slavery Society that shocked many of his White and some of his Black listeners. Douglass declared, "I have no love for America, as such; I have no patriotism, I have no country. . . . The institutions of this Country do not know me – do not recognize me as a man. . . . I desire to see it overthrown as speedily as possible, and its Constitution shivered in a thousand fragments."[18] Readers will remember that five years later Douglass again shocked an audience by asking what relevance the Fourth of July had for him or those Black citizens he "represented." But more importantly, attentive readers will hear a modern voice, that of the Rev. Jeremiah Wright, the Obama family's Black Chicago preacher, in Douglass' declaration – "I have no love for America." If anything, Wright caught more hell than Douglass did for essentially making the same inflammatory point. Why should we love a nation that does not love us?

Though Black rights, for freemen and slaves, had been receding for decades, the U.S. Supreme Court, behind its Chief Justice, Roger B. Taney of Maryland, sought to sunder once and for all the very idea of Black rights. Taney chose an unlikely case involving a Virginia-born slave named Dred Scott to reject Black rights. Scott was taken from Virginia to Missouri, another slave state, and then to Illinois and Wisconsin, both free states. When the family of Scott's owner returned to Missouri, Scott and his family were taken with them. When Scott's owner died, Scott sued, arguing that his residence in a free state made him free.[19]

The Court's infamous *Dred Scott v. Sandford* decision was announced on March 6, 1857, just two days after the presidential inauguration of Democrat and southern sympathizer James Buchanan. The Supreme Court's 7 to 2 majority made several important findings, each to Scott's detriment and to that of all Black Americans. Chief Justice Taney and the Court's majority ruled that Scott was not a citizen and, therefore, did not have standing to be in a federal court at all. That should have been the end of it; you have no right to appear in this court – be gone. But the Court, convinced that the place of slavery and Black people, especially free Black people, had been unresolved before the country for too long, had more to say. Taney declared for the Court that the social and political position of Black people had been worse during the Founding period than it was in 1857; that the descendants of Africans brought to the country as slaves, even if free in 1857, had never been and could never be citizens with the right to sue in federal courts. Finally, Taney declared that Black people "had for more than a century been regarded as beings of an inferior order . . . so far inferior that they had no rights which the White man was bound to respect."[20] The country was listening and some did not like what they heard.

Abraham Lincoln, still smarting from a narrow loss to Democrat Lyman Trumbull in an 1855 Illinois Senate race and organizing for another Senate run in 1858 against Democrat incumbent Stephen A. Douglas, saw the *Dred Scott v. Sandford* decision as a political opportunity, though one that had to be played carefully. Judge Douglas, as Lincoln usually called the senator, had already spoken in support of Chief Justice Taney's majority opinion declaring that Scott was not and could not be a U.S. citizen.[21] Lincoln challenged Taney and Douglas by favorably citing key points from Associate Justice Benjamin Curtis' dissenting opinion in *Dred Scott*.[22] First, Lincoln joined Curtis in arguing that Taney and the majority had simply been wrong on critical historical facts underpinning their conclusions.

Chief Justice Taney argued that Black residents, slave and free, had been no part of "the people," by and for whom the Declaration of Independence and the Constitution were written. Lincoln drew on Justice Curtis to demonstrate that "in five of the thirteen states, to wit, New Hampshire, Massachusetts, New York, New Jersey, and North Carolina, free negroes were voters, and, in proportion to their numbers, had the same part in making the Constitution that white people had."

Second, Lincoln challenged Taney's argument that Black Americans were even more thoroughly discounted as people and as potential citizens during the Founding period than in the enlightened 1850s. He pointed out that some rights Black people had earlier enjoyed had been repealed, including that two of the five states that once allowed free Black men to vote had since rescinded that right, New Jersey and North Carolina, and that in New York it had been "greatly abridged; while it has not been extended, so far as I know, to a single additional State." And third, Lincoln closed by trying to disarm Judge Douglas of his principal political cudgel – miscegenation and interracial marriage. With a political race looming and anti-Black sentiment widespread in Illinois and across the Midwest, Lincoln rejected "mixing blood by the white and black races: agreed for once – a thousand times agreed. There are white men enough to marry all the white women, and black men enough to marry all the black women; and so let them be married." And then Lincoln deftly turned the charge, not of desiring interracial marriage, but interracial sex and the attendant births, against his opponents in the South's and in Senator Douglas' Democratic Party. Pointing to the 1850 census, Lincoln noted the presence of 405,751 mulattos in the nation, almost all in the slave states, or escapees from them, and "nearly all have sprung from black slaves and white masters."[23] Lincoln knew that in a fight, especially a political fight, it can be just as important to parry a blow as to land one – it's not me and my people that you need to be worried about here, it's you and your people. Despite Lincoln's protests, the *Dred Scott* decision was, for a time, the law of the land. Though we and history may judge that Lincoln won the debate, Douglas won the election and his views held the field as these sectional tensions broke the Union.

Black Citizenship and Suffrage in the Civil War and Reconstruction

The Civil War and Reconstruction have often been called the Second American Revolution or the Second Reconstruction. Like the first, it expanded liberty and civil rights through constitutional and legal reforms that this time ended slavery, made Black residents birthright citizens, awarded suffrage to Black men, pledged protection to Black persons and property, and promised equal access to public places, services, and opportunities. The Founders' Constitution, with its regional compromises in favor of states' rights and slavery, did not survive the war. Lincoln and his Republican Party implanted national commitments to liberty, equality, and due process of law in the Constitution, but, as with the first revolution, reverence for existing institutions precluded a root and branch approach to reform.[24] And again the social and political forces opposed to racial equality proved determined and powerful.

As the Civil War turned in the Union's favor and Black soldiers were allowed to join the ranks, hopes were high. On April 6, 1863, Frederick Douglass exulted that, "Once the black man get upon his person the brass letters U.S., let him get an eagle on his button, and a musket on his shoulder, and bullets in his pocket, and there is no power on the earth that can deny that he has earned the right to citizenship."[25]

In early October 1864, with the Emancipation Proclamation in place, Sherman having taken Atlanta, and Lincoln's reelection assured, Douglass and a national convention of anti-slavery activists gathered in Syracuse to survey the road ahead. In Douglass' speech, entitled "The Cause of the Negro People" and the convention's "Address to the American People," suffrage was described as "the keystone to the arch of human liberty."[26] Yet few Black voters, including Black soldiers, were allowed to cast their ballots for Lincoln or anyone else. Nineteen states allowed soldiers to vote at the front, but few Black soldiers qualified to do so in their states.[27] Only New England – Maine, Vermont, New Hampshire, Massachusetts, and Rhode Island – permitted Black suffrage; the other thirty-one states did not. The right to vote, how open or how limited it should be, has always been a contested question in American politics.[28]

War's end brought a decade-long rush to constitutionally and legally establish Black citizenship and suffrage before the moment so long fought for passed. Between 1865 and 1875 Congress adopted and the states ratified the Thirteenth, Fourteenth, and Fifteenth Amendments, and Congress passed three enforcement acts and the Civil Rights Acts of 1866 and 1875.[29] These constitutional and legal protections for Black rights were both fundamental and fragile. As the historian John Haller has written, "A political and military solution, implemented by the Thirteenth, Fourteenth, and Fifteenth Amendments, a civil rights act, and several force bills, had answered the Negro question and had established through law his position in the order of American society."[30] And so it seemed so long as Northern troops stood guard on Southern ground.

The Thirteenth Amendment (1865) superseded the Emancipation Proclamation to end slavery throughout the nation. The Fourteenth Amendment (1868) declared, contrary to the *Dred Scott* decision, that Black people were birthright citizens of the United States deserving the same equal protection and due process rights as White citizens. The Fifteenth Amendment (1870) appeared firmly to set "the keystone to the arch of human liberty" by promising Black men the right to vote. The Force Acts put the Union army behind Congress' determination that the South be reconstructed to make social, political, and economic space for the new Black citizens. And finally, the expansive Civil Rights Act of 1875 declared full social equality, guaranteeing that: "All persons within the jurisdiction of the United States shall be entitled to the full and equal enjoyment of the accommodations, advantages, facilities, and privileges of inns, public conveyances . . ., theaters, and other places of public amusements; . . . applicable alike to citizens of every race and color; regardless of any previous condition of servitude."

The post-Civil War Reconstruction Era (1865 to 1877) allowed a brief flowering of Black political participation and appointment and election to political office at the local, state, and national levels. This flowering wilted quickly and was memory by the end of the nineteenth century. The historian Darlene Clark Hine has calculated that about 700,000 Black Americans qualified as voters at some point between 1865 and 1900, though their numbers fell over time.[31] Over that same period, Henry Louis Gates, Jr., Robert Putnam, and others have concluded that 2,000 Black citizens held political office in the South from local sheriff, to state legislators and governors, to members of both houses of Congress.[32] David Woodard found that 260 Black Americans served in Southern state legislatures in 1868, 325 in 1872, before their numbers plummeted to 150 as Reconstruction began coming to an end in 1876 and continued down from there.[33]

Pinckney Pinchback of Louisiana, the first Black man to serve as a state governor during Reconstruction, served for a total of thirty-five days. Two Black men served in the United States Senate and twenty served in the U.S. House in the post-Civil War era. The Mississippi legislature sent Hiram Revels to the U.S. Senate for one year, 1870–1871, while Blanche K. Bruce, also of Mississippi, served a full six-year term from 1875 to 1881. Eight southern states, Virginia, North Carolina, South Carolina, Florida, Georgia, Alabama, Louisiana, and Mississippi, sent Black members to the U.S. House. Pinchback and Bruce were of mixed race, White fathers, Black mothers, while Revels, whose mother was of Scots ancestry, was born into a Black family whose ancestors had been free since before the Revolution. Hispanic members also served in Congress during the nineteenth and early twentieth centuries. Joseph Hernandez served one term from Florida in the U.S. House, 1822–1823, but it was the Mexican-American War (1846–1848), in which the U.S. took the northern half of Mexico and 117,000 Hispanics, that ushered Hispanics into American politics. Yet, for many decades Americans would continue to see their politics in Black and White.

The prospect of Black voting troubled many White Americans and not just those in the South. On the day that ratification of the Fifteenth Amendment was announced in the U.S. House of Representatives, James A. Garfield, House Speaker and future president, declared: "The Fifteenth Amendment confers upon the African race the care of its own destiny. It places their fortunes in their own hands." Making the same point even more sharply, an Illinois newspaper observed that: "The negro is now a voter and a citizen. Let him hereafter take his chances in the battle of life."[34] Many Southern members, only recently restored to their House seats, must have exchanged knowing glances and wry smiles.[35]

The poet Walt Whitman, an admirer of Abraham Lincoln, whom he memorialized after his assassination in "O Captain, My Captain," was worried in 1874 about immigrant voters and, far more so, about Black voters. Whitman, known, ironically enough, as the "Bard of Democracy," complained: "As if we had not strained the voting and digestive calibre of American Democracy to the utmost for the last fifty years with the millions of ignorant foreigners, we have now infused a powerful percentage of blacks, with about as much intellect and calibre (in the mass) as so many baboons."[36] To be fair, much that Whitman wrote about American democracy in post-Civil War America was celebratory, but not all and his dismissal of Black voters as "so many baboons" suggested the receptivity of the popular culture to such disparagement of the freedmen.

Soon, the nation's highest authorities joined in stripping away the assurances of equal treatment and due process given to former slaves and free Black people after the war. In 1876, the Supreme Court, in *United States v. Reece*, struck down key provisions of the Enforcement Act of 1870 designed to protect the voting rights of citizens. Chief Justice Morrison Waite, writing for an 8-to-1 majority, declared that the language of the Enforcement Act prohibiting interference with a citizen's attempt to vote was too broad to qualify as congressional implementation of the Fifteenth Amendment. More consequentially, Waite declared that the Fifteenth Amendment, "does not confer the right to suffrage upon anyone," but simply "prevents the states, or the United States, . . . from giving preference . . . to one citizen of the United States over another on account of race, color, or previous condition of servitude."[37] *Reece* held that states were entitled to establish and enforce voter registration and election rules so long as those rules did not starkly discriminate on the basis of race, color, or previous condition of servitude. Again, wry smiles and winks.

Although President Garfield did not live to see it – he was shot just four months into office and died in September 1881 – the Supreme Court adopted his dismissive attitude toward protection of Black rights and liberties. In 1883, the Supreme Court combined five cases, which are commonly referred to as the *Civil Rights Cases of 1883*, challenging the social and economic equality guaranteed in the Civil Rights Act of 1875. Briefly, that act promised all citizens equal access to all that society had to offer, including transportation, hotels, restaurants, and amusements. Justice Joseph P. Bradley, writing for a Court again divided 8 to 1, declared that the Thirteenth and Fourteenth Amendments outlawed racially discriminatory state action but did not allow Congress to reach racially discriminatory action by individuals – like hotel and restaurant owners. Justice John Marshall Harlan in lonely dissent argued that the Thirteenth Amendment not only provided for an end to slavery but authorized Congress to legislate against the "badges and incidents" of "slavery and servitude" – like being barred from restaurants and hotels.[38] Bradley would have none of it, instead he lectured hard-pressed Black citizens, writing: "When a man has emerged from slavery, and by the aid of beneficent legislation has shaken off the inseparable concomitants of that state, there must be some stage in the progress of his elevation when he takes the rank of a mere citizen, and ceases to be the special favorite of the laws, and when his rights as a citizen or a man, are to be protected in the ordinary modes by which other men's rights are protected."[39] For Garfield, for Justice Bradley, and for so many Northern White citizens, what Black people deserved was an end to slavery and they had that, asking for more seemed pleading for special favors.

Southern White people waited confidently for Northern attention to fade and for determination to protect the freedmen in their new liberties, not very strong to begin with, to waver. Many White Southerners did not wait at all; a campaign of physical, social, and economic violence through the closing decades of the century met Black freedom, determined to roll it back. As national authorities returned control of the Southern states to their traditional elites after 1876, those elites began a systematic campaign to move Black and many poor White Americans to the fringes of social, political, and economic life. The campaign was largely successful by century's end and would remain in place for decades. The best known aspects of this campaign, most intense in the South but present throughout the country, were a new set of "restrictive Black Codes, and the disenfranchisement of African Americans through poll taxes, literacy tests, and election fraud."[40]

White attitudes were based on a thickening layer of natural and social scientific thinking that supplemented Charles Darwin's theory of evolution. In 1863, the prominent Harvard geologist and zoologist, Louis Agassiz, declared that while slavery was wrong and Black people deserved freedom, they were "incapable of living on a footing of social equality with the Whites . . . without becoming an element of social disorder."[41] Most White people, even many who thought themselves sympathetic to the former slaves, would have nodded along when Dr. J.F. (John Fulenwider)

Miller wrote scornfully of the freedmen's readiness for suffrage; "A native of Africa and a savage a few generations ago, then a slave for several generations afterwards; this is the man and the race upon whom the high responsibilities of freedom were thrust. . . . Without education of self or ancestry and without preparation of any sort, the new negro was invested with the highest functions of citizenship."[42] Only a few White Americans thought Dr. Miller's judgment too harsh.

Southern states initially sought to reassert White supremacy with the blunt tools of intimidation and violence.[43] As the Pulitzer Prize-winning journalist Douglas Blackmon explained in *Slavery by Another Name*, Southern legislatures rewrote criminal laws to create more violations, many petty, some invented, to jail freedmen and then lease them to private owners of plantations, mines, mills, and timber camps.[44] Other old tools, like residency requirements and poll taxes, were repurposed and some new ones, like grandfather clauses and White primaries, were developed to disenfranchise Black and, as something of a bonus, poor White voters.[45] Mississippi led the way. In 1890, the Mississippi legislature revised the state constitution, in large part to reconstitute the state's electorate around White traditionalists. The "Mississippi Plan" involved early and complicated registration requirements, a two-dollar poll tax, a literacy requirement, a grandfather clause, criminal disenfranchisement, and a requirement that only registered voters could serve on juries. Over the next two decades, every Southern state, as well as many border states and others, picked from this new and expanded smorgasbord of disenfranchisement options to limit, shape, control, and ultimately bleach, their electorates.[46] Black and as many as a quarter of Southern White citizens disappeared from the voter rolls – suffrage, "the keystone to the arch of human liberty," had been removed and the whole edifice of Black hope for freedom and equality crumbled and lay in ruins for half a century.[47] Darlene Clark Hine explained the motivation behind disenfranchisement as a firm determination to nip Black aspiration in the bud: "Just as slave masters had viewed the existence of a class of free blacks as a threat to the preservation and justification of slavery, so the proponents of disenfranchisement found the existence of a few blacks who qualified to vote in general elections, despite virtually insurmountable obstacles, to threaten the concept of white supremacy."[48] It could not be suffered and so would not be allowed.

The Fight to Register and to Vote

The long-running fight to overcome the social, economic, and political elements of Jim Crow segregation went on for decades. Black leaders, often associated with the still fledgling National Association for the Advancement of Colored People (NAACP), prepared for a new battle in an old war. Their goal was to restore suffrage for Black Americans and to build a broader structure of rights and opportunities on that foundation. Moorfield Storey, a White Boston lawyer, former President of the American Bar Association and first President of the NAACP, said of Black suffrage in 1920: "In the long run only voters have rights in this country. The politicians . . . have no thought to spare for any class that has no vote." William H. Hastie, two or three generations younger than Storey and a fledgling NAACP lawyer in the 1920s, became the nation's first Black federal judge and later was NAACP co-counsel with Thurgood Marshall on the critical voting rights case, *Smith v. Allwright* (1944). Hastie seconded Storey in a 1973 interview looking back to his early days in the NAACP, saying: "We all felt then that the things we were doing in education or housing or residential segregation and so on, would not amount to much unless the blacks in the South were effectively franchised . . ."[49]

Over the first four decades of the twentieth century, the Texas legislature, like most other Southern legislatures, mandated and then session by session refined and tightened a Whites-only party primary election system. The White primary initially was a county option, but some counties, like San Antonio's Bexar (pronounced *bear*) County, continued to allow Black citizens to vote in primaries and in some non-partisan city elections. The 1923 Texas legislature finally lost its collective patience and dropped all pretense, mandating that "in no event shall a negro be eligible to participate in a Democratic Party primary election held in the State of Texas" – what Fifteenth Amendment! Lawrence A. Nixon, a physician, pharmacy owner, and a founding member of the El Paso NAACP, challenged the new law by, poll tax receipt in hand, presenting himself to vote in the 1924 Democratic primary. The election judge, C.C. Herndon, a friendly acquaintance of Dr. Nixon's, politely refused him a ballot and Nixon sued. *Nixon v. Herndon* eventually wended its way to the Supreme Court where Justice Oliver Wendell Holmes, writing for a unanimous Court, found for Nixon and the NAACP. Holmes made the obvious point that the 1923 law prohibiting Black voting in the Democratic primary was "state action" in violation of Nixon's and other Black peoples Fourteenth Amendment guarantee of equal protection of the laws.[50]

The Texas legislature, full of shrewd legal minds, decided to strike all the laws dealing with primary elections and ultimately to leave primary election design and administration to the political parties – private entities, not state agencies or actors. In *Grovey v. Townsend* (1935), Justice Owen Roberts, writing for a unanimous Court, allowed this subterfuge to stand, arguing that the Texas Democratic Party was a private organization, not a state agency, and hence not subject to the Fourteenth and Fifteenth

Amendments. The national NAACP and its Texas branch waited for just the right case, and for fortunate changes in the membership of the Court, to again challenge restrictions on Black suffrage. They found both in a case that came to be known as *Smith v. Allwright*.

Dr. Lonnie Smith was a Houston dentist and NAACP activist who tried to vote in the 1940 Democratic primary. Election Judge S.E. Allwright denied him a ballot and Smith, with the assistance of the national NAACP and its co-counsels, Thurgood Marshall and William Hastie, sued. By early 1944 the issue of Black suffrage was again before the U.S. Supreme Court. Smith and his lawyers had lost in the lower courts, where the judges were following what they took to be the relevant precedents, but prevailed in the High Court. Writing for an 8-to-1 Court (Justice Owen Roberts, the author of *Grovey v. Townsend* dissenting), Justice Stanley F. Reed declared that Texas had violated Black voters' Fourteenth and Fifteenth Amendment rights. The majority said: "We think that this statutory system for the selection of party nominees for inclusion on the general election ballot makes the party which is required to follow the legislative directives an agency of the state."[51] Not all at once, but over the next few decades, the keystone to the arch of human liberty was gingerly slipped back into place.

With *Smith v. Allwright*, Black voters, particularly in the South, were again to be allowed to cast the ballots that had been promised them in the Fifteenth Amendment, briefly allowed in the late nineteenth century, and then denied for decades. More than half of eligible Black voters had cast ballots in 1880 but just 2 percent did in 1912.[52] In *Stony the Road*, the African-American Studies scholar Henry Louis Gates, Jr. pointed out that by the early twentieth century "Louisiana had fewer than 6,000 registered black voters, down from a high of 130,000, and Alabama had 3,000, down from 181,000. These figures were typical of other states in the former Confederacy."[53]

Northern Black voters, their numbers relatively small before the Great Migration, and the few mostly urban Black voters in the South clung to the Republican Party. The Republicans had been the party of the Union and Black emancipation, so Frederick Douglass defined partisan choice for Blacks as simple: "The Republican party is the ship, all else is the sea."[54] As late as Franklin D. Roosevelt's first election as president in 1932, Black voters stood firmly Republican, but a seismic shift was soon underway. Though their participation in them was only limited, Black citizens did benefit from various New Deal programs. They also noted Roosevelt's inclusion of Black officials at the sub-cabinet level throughout the administration and many were thrilled by Eleanor Roosevelt's endorsement of anti-lynching legislation in 1934. When Roosevelt died in 1945 Black citizens mourned and braced themselves; like Lincoln, FDR had been an ambivalent champion, but he had been a champion. Harry S. Truman, initially little known to most Black people, soon proved to be bolder than FDR on race. In 1947, Truman became the first president to address a meeting of the NAACP. Truman declared: "We can no longer afford the luxury of a leisurely attack upon prejudice and discrimination. . . . we cannot, any longer, await the growth of a will to act in the slowest State or the most backward community. Our National Government must show the way."[55]

Restoring Black rights to register and vote was not a decision, it was a process. Modern voter rolls, such as we would think of them today, barely existed in the nineteenth century. Tax rolls and the sheriff's nod of recognition sufficed for much of the century. Over the first several decades of the twentieth century, voter registration in the states became more uniform and regularized and so we have some data beginning in the 1920s, good data from the 1940s, and excellent data from the 1960s. These voter registration data come in two flavors; one is the proportion of the voting-age population (VAP), those over eighteen, who are registered to vote, and the other is the proportion of the U.S. citizen population (CP) over eighteen that is registered to vote. VAP is easier to calculate through the census and its annual updates; all you need to know is how many persons in the country are over eighteen and how many of those are registered to vote. The citizen population over eighteen is somewhat harder to calculate, because there are legal resident aliens in the country and illegal aliens; neither group entitled to vote. Here we use VAP, both because the data go back further and because it better reflects the limited but growing impact that Hispanics and Asians have on our elections.

Between 1920 and 1940, the vast majority of Black citizens still lived in the South and only 3 percent of them were registered to vote. Few gains were made until the Supreme Court struck down the White primary in *Smith v. Allwright* (1944) and then even greater gains were made when LBJ and the Democratic Congress passed the Voting Rights Act of 1965. From 3 percent in 1940, Black voter registration in the South jumped to 12 percent in 1947, 25 percent in 1956, and 29 percent in 1960.[56] A million new Black voters joined the rolls in the immediate wake of the Voting Rights Act of 1965 and by the end of the 1960s two-thirds of Black Americans were registered to vote.[57] Remarkably, once the momentum of LBJ's Great Society was spent and the conservative backlash of the Nixon administration began, Black voter registration stalled. From 66.2 percent in 1968, Black voter registration only twice broke higher, 66.3 in 1984 and 68.5 in Obama's reelection, before settling at 64.7 in 2020, slightly lower than it had been half a century earlier.[58]

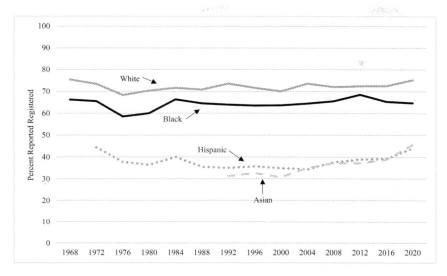

FIGURE 3.1 Percent Reported Registered in Presidential Elections by Race and Ethnicity, 1968–2020

Source: U.S. Census Bureau, Current Population Survey, "Reported Voting and Registration, by Race, Hispanic Origin, Sex, and Age," Tables 2.1, 2.3, 2.4, 2.5, 2.6, November 1964–2020.

Several key points in Figure 3.1 deserve to be highlighted. The percentage of White and Black citizens registered to vote has been steady for decades at 70 to 75 percent of White citizens and at 60 to 66 percent for Black citizens, except for Obama's 2012 reelection when Black registration rose to 68.5. Black voter registration has trailed White registration by 5 to 10 points since 1968. Hispanic voter registration was 44.4 percent in 1972, the first time it was measured, and 44.1 percent in 2020; over the intervening half century it ranged between 35 and 40 percent of the Hispanic population over age eighteen. Asian voter registration, recorded for the first time in 1992 climbed unevenly from the low 30s into the high 30s by 2016 to an all-time high of 45.7 percent in 2020. Both Hispanic and Asian voter registration numbers are expected to continue rising, probably slowly, as non-citizens become citizens, members of these young populations reach eighteen, and as experience and acculturation make people more familiar and comfortable.[59] One can hardly miss the glacial stability, the complete lack of improvement, in voter registration levels over the past half century. To say that voter registration has not been a priority would be something of an understatement.

Voter Turnout by Race

Figure 3.2 traces voter turnout in presidential elections by race and ethnicity since 1964. First, the trajectories of the White, Black, and Hispanic turnout numbers are very similar; high in 1964 for White and Black voters and for Hispanics in 1972, dropping about 10 points by 1996 and 2000, and then rising back to 1964 levels by 2020. The Asian trajectory, which does not start until 1992, shows a slow upward trend until it jumped in 2020. But overall, Figure 3.2 shows no improvement in voter turnout. Second, over the entire period of nearly six decades, White turnout has exceeded Black turnout by an average of nearly 10 points, 64.5 to 55.1, while Hispanics and Asians have turned out at 31.3 and 31.0 percent respectively, less than half of White turnout.[60] And third, since the Hispanic and Asian populations are the nation's fastest growing, while the Black population is slow growing and the White population is flat, a continuing decline in White voter dominance and a reciprocal rise in minority voter influence seems likely.

Next, in Figure 3.3, we show how the voter turnout numbers translate into votes cast in presidential elections by race and ethnicity and here we find a great source of White anxiety. In 1948, the U.S. was still effectively

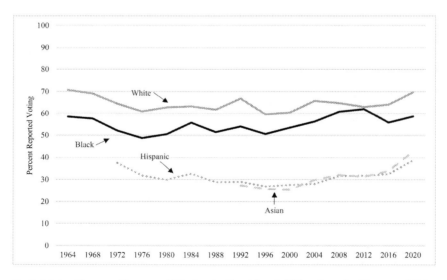

FIGURE 3.2 Percent Reported Voting in Presidential Elections by Race and Ethnicity, 1964–2020

Source: U.S. Census Bureau, Current Population Survey, "Reported Voting and Registration, by Race, Hispanic Origin, Sex, and Age," Tables 2.1, 2.3, 2.4, 2.5, 2.6, November 1964–2020.

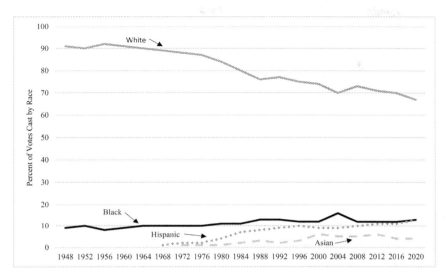

FIGURE 3.3 Percent of Votes Cast in Presidential Elections by Race and Ethnicity, 1948–2020

Sources: 1948–2012: American National Election Study (ANES), Social Characteristics, Table 1A.3, "Race," https://www.electionstudies.org/resources/anes-guide/; 2016–2020: Roper Center.

a biracial society. Hispanic and Asian numbers were small, and Black people, post-*Smith v. Allwright*, were only beginning to return to the electorate in large numbers. In 1948, White voters cast 91 percent of all votes cast for president and Black voters cast the other 9 percent. Those proportions held through 1964, at 90 and 10 percent, but then, by steady increments, Hispanics and Asians began to cast more ballots. The White share of votes cast in presidential elections fell to 80 percent in 1984 and 70 percent by 2004. The Black share of the vote held at 10 or 11 percent into the 1980s before ticking up to 12 or 13 percent in more recent elections. The Hispanic share, 1 percent in 1968, hit 7 percent in 1984, and 13 percent in 2020. Asian numbers have risen from 1 percent in 1972 to 4 percent in 2016 and 2020. Given the ongoing demographic changes projected by the census, these numbers, from the White perspective, will continue to deteriorate.

Finally, to close our discussion of voter registration and turnout we look at the partisan choices that voters have made since 1948. Figure 3.4 tracks the percent of voters by race and ethnicity that have gone to the Democrats in each election cycle; the remainder in each case is the percent that voted Republican. From 1870 well into the 1930s most Black voters opted for the Republicans – the party of Lincoln. Some Black voters chose FDR and

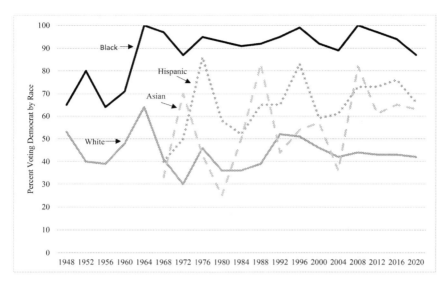

FIGURE 3.4 Percent Voting Democrat in Presidential Elections by Race and Ethnicity, 1948–2020

Sources: 1948–2016: American National Election Study (ANES), Presidential Vote Choice, Table 9A.1, "Presidential Vote 2 Major Parties;" 2020: Edison Research, Exit Polls.

the Democrats during the Great Depression, but everyone knew that the Democrats' Southern wing was deeply racist. Democrat leaders were aware that they had a delicate political situation on their hands; so they moved cautiously, but they did move. In October 1947, President Truman's Committee on Civil Rights delivered a report entitled "To Secure These Rights." The report called for better protection of voting rights, an anti-lynching bill, and equal implementation of the Bill of Rights. The report met stern opposition in Congress, forcing Truman to desegregate the armed forces by executive order, and splintering the Democratic Party before the 1948 presidential election.

White voters, and especially Southern White voters, began moving away from the Democratic Party, a process that would continue for decades. Truman held a slight majority of the White vote in 1948 and LBJ enjoyed a blow-out win in 1964, but otherwise Republicans have carried the White vote. The explanation for this dramatic partisan redistribution, while not hard to find is hard to look at. In response to *Brown v. Board of Education* (1954) and a weak Civil Rights Act (1957), William F. Buckley, a young conservative leader and founder of *National Review*, wrote a remarkable editorial entitled "Why the South Must Prevail." Speaking for much of the conservative opinion of the day, Buckley wrote that: "The central question that emerges ... is whether the White community in the South is entitled to take such measures as are necessary to prevail, politically and culturally, in areas in which it does not prevail numerically? The sobering answer," Buckley declared, "is Yes – the White community is so entitled because, for the time being, it is the advanced race."[61] Still, Black voters moved toward the Democratic party, long the party of the White South, with trepidation. After John and Robert Kennedy somewhat belatedly befriended Martin Luther King in the run-up to the 1960 election, Black voters developed an overwhelming commitment to the Democratic Party.[62] Hispanic and Asian voters have been more volatile but have increasingly chosen the Democrats in presidential elections by about two-to-one.[63] A White electorate, slowly shrinking, leaning toward the Republican Party, and minority electorates, holding their own or growing, leaning toward the Democratic Party, explain much of the tension in modern American politics.

The Civil Rights Era Gains and White Reaction

The Roosevelt/Truman Democratic coalition of the 1930s through the 1950s was made up of conservative White Southerners, liberal White Northerners, and Black voters increasingly attracted by the modest benefits allowed to them by New Deal policies. As Black voters moved steadily from the Republican to the Democratic party, White Southerners in particular saw a challenge to Southern racial mores. Nonetheless, through the 1950s and into the early 1960s, almost 50 percent of White Americans identified with the Democratic party compared to less than a third that identified with the Republicans.

But Lyndon B. Johnson was the last Democratic presidential candidate to win a majority of the White vote. Johnson's Great Society program, often called the third Civil Rights Revolution, headlined by the Civil Rights Acts of 1964 and 1965, the Voting Rights Act of 1965, and the Fair Housing Act of 1968, made the Democratic party the party of Black America. As Southern Blacks joined the electorate in growing numbers, White Southerners pulled back, first voting Republican for president, then for U.S. senators and suburban House members, while sticking with Democrats for state and local offices. Before the 1960s were over, Black voter registration in Mississippi had risen from 7 percent to 67 percent, in Alabama from 19 percent to 61 percent, in Georgia from 27 percent to 60 percent, and in Louisiana from 32 percent to 61 percent.[64]

As during the early national period and the post-Reconstruction era, Black gains in the mid-twentieth century sparked White resistance. In fact, the backlash to Black political and social gains developed early, and has built in waves over the past half century and more. On January 14,

1963, George Corley Wallace was sworn in as governor of Alabama; in his inaugural address he famously called for "segregation now, segregation tomorrow, segregation forever." Many Americans saw Wallace as an embarrassing throwback, especially with the urbane John F. Kennedy in the White House, but many others saw Kennedy as a threat and Wallace as a bold defender of traditional values, of which White supremacy was the sometimes spoken, often unspoken, linchpin. In November 1963, just days before Kennedy was assassinated, Wallace declared his intention to oppose him for the Democratic presidential nomination in 1964. Lyndon B. Johnson succeeded to the presidency upon Kennedy's death and won the 1964 Democratic nomination, but Wallace galvanized millions, winning 30 percent of the Democratic primary vote in Indiana, 42 percent in Maryland, and 34 percent in Wisconsin. Arizona Senator Barry Goldwater, the Republican nominee in 1964, studied Wallace's impact on conservative White voters and hoped to split the Democratic vote by drawing White Southerners to the Republican party. Goldwater lost decisively, carrying only six states, his native Arizona and five states in the deep South – South Carolina, Georgia, Wallace's Alabama, Mississippi, and Louisiana. Nonetheless, the Southern strategy was born.[65]

Richard Nixon successfully rode the Southern strategy into the White House in 1968. Nixon's chief political strategist in the 1968 campaign was Kevin Phillips. Phillips' 1969 book *The Emerging Republican Majority* explained the opportunity Republicans saw to reorganize the electorate to their long-term benefit. Phillips argued that White Southerners could be separated from their historic Democratic Party commitments by highlighting the growing presence of Black people in their party. In a February 1970 speech at Yale University, Phillips explained that a new Republican majority coalition was possible: "the nature of the majority – or potential majority – seems clear. It is largely white and middle class. It is concentrated in the South, the West, and suburbia."[66] But the prospect of the new Republican majority was seriously clouded by a states' rights Democrat.

George Wallace has largely faded from the American popular imagination, but his insight into the prejudices and fears of the White working class has not. In fact, despite an assassination attempt that left him paralyzed and wheelchair bound, Wallace sought the Democratic nomination again in 1972, winning Tennessee (68 percent), Michigan (51 percent), North Carolina (50 percent), running first in every county in Florida and carrying 42 percent of the statewide vote. South Dakota Senator George McGovern defeated Wallace elsewhere to win the nomination before suffering an historic loss to President Nixon in the general election. Nixon easily carried the South in the general election. Ronald Reagan also adopted the Southern strategy in 1980 and 1984. Even more starkly, Connecticut-born

Texan George H.W. Bush won the presidency in 1988 behind a race-baiting strategy developed by South Carolinian Lee Atwater and featuring the famously noxious "Willie Horton" ad.[67] As political scientists Desmond King and Rogers Smith have noted, "since the 1970s, today's racial policy alliances have become more and more fully identified with the two major parties. . . . this overlay of opposing parties, opposing economic ideologies, and opposing racial alliances has contributed to the heightened polarization that wrenches apart modern American politics."[68]

Moreover, as in all conflicts, new tactics and weapons can be decisive. The weapons deployed for White racial advantage in the 1970s, racial gerrymandering, multimember election districts, at-large elections, and primary election runoffs, are still commonly used to secure White majorities. More recently, voter roll purges, limits on early voting, voting by mail, voting hours, and drop boxes have constrained many voters of color.[69] And again, when the social and political tide turned against Black equality and empowerment, the high court affixed its imprimatur. Justice Lewis Powell, writing for the majority in the first major reverse discrimination case, *Bakke* in 1973, echoed Justice Bradley from a century earlier in the *Civil Rights Cases of 1883*, intoning: "It is far too late to argue that the guarantee of equal protection to all persons permits the recognition of special wards entitled to a degree of protection greater than that accorded others."[70]

Of course, the opposing policy coalitions that King and Smith describe do not operate just, or even mainly, at the national level, they divide the states into red and blue. Red states seek to limit and channel voting while blue states seek to facilitate it. By 2023, thirty-six states, mostly but not exclusively red, had enacted some form of voter ID. Forty-six states, mostly but not exclusively blue, allow no excuse early voting in some form, twenty-two states allow voter registration on election day, forty states allow online voter registration, and five states conduct all-mail voting.[71] Of course, both red and blue states adopt the voting rules that they believe will benefit them. Yet, it still makes a difference whether you think your benefit lies in limiting or promoting voter registration and turnout.

The Ongoing Partisan and Racial Polarization of American Politics

Experts think of polarization, in this case partisan polarization, as the deep psychological and behavioral division between Democrats and Republicans. Partisan polarization has risen and fallen over the course of American history. We assume, for example, though we do not have good measures (other than deaths on the battlefield) that polarization reached all-time highs in the era of the Civil War and Reconstruction. However, we do have an intriguing measure of partisan conflict or polarization between 1891 and last month. The Federal Reserve Bank of Philadelphia and Professor Marina Azzimonti of Stony Brook University maintain a partisan conflict index constructed from newspaper databases. The index shows high partisan conflicts in the 1890s and 1900s, moderating from World War I (1914–1918) through the mid-1960s, before beginning a steady climb. Early twentieth-century conflict peaks were matched in the 1970s and 1980s, with new all-time highs reached during the Obama years, before spiking again, to even newer all-time highs early in Donald Trump's term.[72] The index has been notably more subdued during the Biden years.

Scholars have sought to determine whether partisan polarization is driven by the influence of grassroots opinion on party elites or by signaling from partisan elites to the grassroots and which party, if either, has moved furthest toward its fringe. There is a consensus, not perfect of course, but substantial, that polarization is driven by elite signaling rather than by elites responding to an energized and demanding base and that the Republican party has moved much further to the right than the Democrats have moved to the left. Thinking just for a moment about the 2020 presidential candidates, Trump and Biden, should provide evidence for both points for all but the most closed-minded partisans. Trump changed more long-held Republican party positions than Biden did Democrat positions, and Republican support for the "big lie" and unwillingness to look closely at the January 6, 2021, Capitol insurrection provide further evidence.[73]

Critically, scholars have shown that the speed and degree of polarization in U.S. politics over the last four decades is greater than polarization in other wealthy democracies, some of which, Australia, Norway, Sweden, Germany, the U.K., have experienced declines in polarization, and that race and ethnicity have become more central to partisan divisions in the U.S.[74] Of course a close look at the Obama elections of 2008 and 2012 will highlight the continuing and even enhanced role of race in American electoral politics, but we will review those elections a little later in this chapter, so here we look at our most recent national elections, 2016 and 2020: Trump's election and, for a time at least, defeat.

Not surprisingly, Isabel Wilkerson watched the 2016 election with a weather eye out for race, caste, and hierarchy – and she saw them clearly. Wilkerson wrote: "The 2016 election became a remarkable blueprint of caste hierarchy in America, from highest to lowest status, in a given group's support of the Republican: White men voted for Trump at 62 percent. White women at 53 percent. Latino men at 32 percent, Latina women at 25 percent. African-American men at 13 percent, and black women at 4 percent."[75] The 2020 election showed very similar patterns in voting by race and ethnicity. The Pew Research Center reported that White men voted for Trump at 57 percent; White women at 53 percent; Hispanic men voted Republican at 40 percent; Hispanic women at 37 percent. Black men voted for Trump at 12 percent and Black women at 5 percent. Because Trump did less well with White voters and just a bit better with minorities, the close races in Wisconsin, Pennsylvania, Arizona, and Georgia, and with them the presidency, fell to Biden in 2020.

Minority Elected Officials

In the last third of the nineteenth century, up to 700,000 Black voters cast ballots in local, state, and national elections, thousands of Black officeholders served at all levels of government, including nearly two dozen Black members of the United States Congress. But before the door could be secured fully open, it began to swing closed. Once George Henry White of North Carolina left the House in 1901, only one congressional district, Illinois' first, representing the southside of Chicago, sent Black members to Congress; three in a row, Oscar DePriest (1929–1935), Arthur Mitchell (1935–1943), and William Dawson (1943–1970). The Hispanic presence in the House was restored by New Mexico's Dennis Chávez. Chávez served two terms in the U.S. House (1933–1937) before being elected to the U.S. Senate in 1936 where he served until 1970. In 1961, San Antonio sent Henry B. González to the U.S. House and in 1963 Los Angeles sent Edward R. Roybal. González served thirty-seven years and Roybal thirty years in distinguished careers.

In the modern era, the number of Black and Hispanic elected officials in the U.S. has risen substantially. In 1970 there were 1,469 Black officials in the U.S., by 1990 there were 7,335, and by 2010 there were over 10,000.[76] The number of Hispanic elected officials has also grown, but even today, when Hispanic population numbers exceed Black population numbers, the number of Hispanic officials continue to lag Black numbers. In 1974, there were 1,539 Hispanic elected officials in the U.S.[77] By 1985 the number had nearly doubled, to 3,147, by 2000 to 5,019, and by 2019 to 6,832. In 2021, Texas claimed 2,808 (40 percent), California claimed 1,833 (26 percent), and New Mexico 649 (9 percent), for 75 percent of all Hispanic elected officials in the U.S.[78]

Black, Hispanic, and Asian numbers in Congress have also increased. Figure 3.5 presents the increases since 1953. Black numbers took two jumps, one during the Civil Rights Revolution of the 1960s and another in the Clinton years of the 1990s, but have been largely flat since. Hispanic membership in Congress has grown more rapidly since the early 1990s and Asian numbers have grown slowly but steadily.

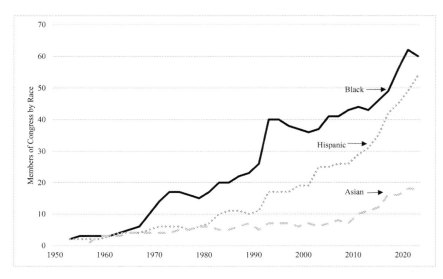

FIGURE 3.5 Number of Black, Hispanic, and Asian Members of Congress, 1953–2023

Sources: 1953–2022: Brookings Institution, *Vital Statistics on Congress*, updated November 21, 2022, https://www.brookings.edu/multi-chapter-report/vital-statistics-on-congress; 2023: Katherine Schaeffer, "Changing Face of Congress in 8 Charts," Pew Research Center, February 7, 2023.

While a steadily increasing number of minority politicians served in national office, often from minority-heavy districts in Chicago, Miami, or San Antonio, few Americans, especially White Americans, even allowed themselves to consider the possibility of a Black, Hispanic, or Asian president. But change was afoot. One stream of data that slowly turned hopeful comes from the Gallup organization, which asked in 1958 and then regularly thereafter: "if your party nominated a generally well-qualified man for president and he happened to be a negro, would you vote for him?" In 1958, a majority (53 percent) said no, while 37 percent said yes, and 10 percent were stunned into silence by the question. But the numbers began, haltingly at first, to climb. By 1967, 53 percent of respondents said yes, 41 percent said no; by 1999, 95 percent said yes.

Just a few key points: in 1958, almost two-thirds of Americans and more White citizens, still seething over *Brown v. Board*, answered no or declined to answer. But the 1960s brought change; by 1969 two-thirds of respondents answered yes and a third answered no or no opinion. The Clinton years brought even bigger change. Often called America's first Black president because of his evident comfort among and familiarity with Blacks, Clinton brought more Blacks into government at higher levels than

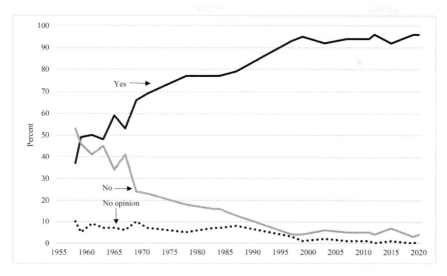

FIGURE 3.6 Would You Vote for a Black Man for President, 1958–2020

Source: https://www.news.gallup.com/poll/4729/presidency.aspx. See also Tom W. Smith, "Trends in Willingness to Vote for a Black and a Woman for President, 1972–2008," GSS Social Change Report, no. 55, August 2009.

any previous president. By the time Clinton left office in 2000, 95 percent of Americans said they could vote for a Black president. Clinton deserves a lot of credit for normalizing the Black presence in high office and society more generally – remember the sax and shades on *Arsenio Hall*. But Clinton, like Lincoln, FDR, and so many before felt the electoral need to separate from Black Americans – the "Sister Souljah moment" – in order not to alienate too many White Americans.

And, of course, at the very top of the heap of Black elected officials are President Barack Obama (2009–2017) and Vice President Kamala Harris (2021–2025). Both Obama and Harris were biracial. Obama had a Black father and White mother, and Harris had a Black father and South Asian mother. Both chose to identify as Black. But it is instructive to pause for a moment and ask whether either had the choice of seeing themselves (and being seen as) White, Asian, or Black, or was Black the only choice allowed them – one drop?

Barack Obama, a former Illinois state senator and one term U.S. senator, won the Democratic Party nomination and the presidency in 2008. Black Americans turned out at the polls in unprecedented numbers, the first time in American history that they had a chance to vote for one of their own for president in a general election. Obama won comfortably over Arizona Senator John McCain as the national economy went into a deep economic decline now commonly referred to as the "Great Recession." Ominously, though, Obama won only 43 percent of the White vote in 2008 while running up huge margins among Black (95 percent), Hispanic (73), and Asian (82) voters. In 2012, Obama won reelection, though a bit more narrowly, securing just 39 percent of the White vote, while carrying 93 percent of the Black vote, 73 percent of the Asian vote, and 71 percent of the Hispanic vote.[79] Kamala Harris, a former attorney general of California and one term U.S. senator, was selected by Democratic presidential candidate Joe Biden in 2020 as his vice presidential running mate. She was widely seen as capable, inexperienced, and as a possible Democratic presidential nominee after Biden.[80]

As we shall see in more detail in the next chapter, entitled "Race, Ethnicity, and the American Mind," Black candidates for high office must squeeze through a narrow door in regard to their depiction of American history and culture. Black candidates running in majority Black cities or congressional districts can challenge racial discrimination unequivocally, while Black candidates running in majority White districts, for a governorship, or for the presidency must tell a more reassuring and even congratulatory story of racial progress. In 2008, Barack Obama was the first Black candidate ever to win the nomination of his party for president. Obama's race, always a presence in the campaign, became the dominant issue when tapes surfaced of his longtime pastor, the Rev. Jeremiah Wright, damning America for its treatment of Black Americans and of people of color around the world. Crisis engulfed the Obama campaign for a full two weeks – did he know, did he agree, did he too damn America for slavery, Jim Crow, and discrimination? – before the candidate spoke in a high-stakes, primetime, national address. The address was brilliant; it saved the campaign by expressing an American story focused on early wrongs, historic progress, and future unity.

Obama began by trying to contextualize the nation's racial history; saying, "We do not need to recite here the history of racial injustice in this country. But we do need to remind ourselves that so many of the disparities that exist between the African-American community and the larger American community today can be traced directly to inequalities passed on from an earlier generation that suffered under the brutal legacy of slavery and Jim Crow." Where Rev. Wright went wrong, Obama argued, was that he "sees white racism as endemic, and . . . elevates what is wrong with America above all that we know is right with America."

What had been wrong with America, slavery and Jim Crow, had been overcome, and what was right with America was the willingness to change, to continue the fight for progress. Obama argued that,

> The profound mistake of Reverend Wright's sermons is not that he spoke about racism in our society. It's that he spoke as if our society was static;

as if no progress had been made; as if this country – a country that has made it possible for one of his own members to run for the highest office in the land . . . – is still irrevocably bound to a tragic past. But what . . . we have already achieved gives us hope . . . for what we can and must achieve tomorrow.

Finally, Obama reassured his listeners that the path of future progress would not be trodden just by African-Americans but by all Americans. For African-Americans the path forward meant "continuing to insist on a full measure of justice in every aspect of American life. But is also means binding our particular grievances – for better health care and better schools and better jobs – to the larger aspirations of all Americans. . . . And it means taking full responsibility for our own lives." While it may seem heartless to describe the modern deficiencies in Black income, education, health care, and housing that flow from slavery, Jim Crow, and past discrimination as Black Americans' "particular grievances," doing so was an important element of resolving White doubts. So was his reassurance that despite wanting to see more racial progress, he loved America today; in the most famous line of his speech Obama intoned, "I will never forget that in no other country on earth is my story even possible."[81]

Few other Black candidates for high office have had the opportunity to address a statewide, let alone a national, audience on race in American history; when they do address the topic they tend to trace Obama's footsteps, though with variations between Democrats and Republicans. Wes Moore, a Black Democrat, was elected Governor of Maryland in November 2022. As the first Black governor in the state's history and just the third nationally since Reconstruction, Moore was afforded the star treatment in *Time* magazine. When asked about the nation's fraught history on race, Moore said,

> I can tell you countless instances of this country's history of brutality, . . . But if I do that without also talking about the other elements of its history, that's a selective memory that I think is dangerous. Because . . . I can literally be the grandson of a man that the Ku Klux Klan ran out, and . . . be a person who's about to become the first Black governor in the history of the state. Both of these things are true. And we can't look at one without understanding the other.[82]

True enough; it was true when Obama made a similar point and it is true for Moore as well. But it is also true that one side of that balance marks the brutalization of a people while the other represents the rise of a person.

Perhaps even a bit more difficult is the political task of a Black Republican running for high office before a majority White electorate. South Carolina Republican Senator Tim Scott, speaking before a largely White Charleston County GOP meeting, declared that, "If you want to understand America . . .; you need to understand and appreciate the devastation brought upon African Americans. But if you stop at our original sin, you have not started the story of America, because the story of America is not defined by our original sin. The story of America is defined by our redemption."[83] Note that though "our original sin" is mentioned, the "story of America" is said to begin after that sin has been redeemed. The claim that American history began after the end of slavery is puzzling, though perhaps somehow comforting to a Charleston, South Carolina, audience; but perhaps even more puzzling is that our "redemption," unmerited as evangelicals might say, is in hand.[84]

The end of slavery took a Civil War to secure and the struggle for Black suffrage had to be won and lost several times, especially in the South, before it was secured more fully in the *Smith v. Allwright* case and in the Voting Rights Act of 1965. These struggles were so hard and lasted so long because White America rejected Black equality and opportunity well into the twentieth century. Somewhere in there redemption must have been won because in the middle decades of the century Americans began to tell pollsters they could vote for a Black president, and more minorities began being elected and appointed to high office. Had something changed? If so, what and by how much? In Chapter 4 we explore U.S. public opinion on a broad range of topics to see when and to what extent racial attitudes have moderated. We show that they have, to some extent, though racial tensions still exist and, in some ways, have hardened.

Notes

1 Yascha Mounk, *The Great Experiment: Why Diverse Democracies Fall Apart and How They Can Endure* (New York: Penguin Press, 2022), 8–10.
2 John Lewis, "Opinion: Together, You Can Redeem the Soul of Our Nation," *New York Times*, July 30, 2020, A23.
3 Wang Xi, "Citizenship and Nation-Building in American History and Beyond," *Social and Behavioral Sciences* 2 (2010): 7019. See also Wang Xi, *The Trial of Democracy: Black Suffrage and Northern Republicans* (Athens: University of Georgia Press, 1997); Thomas Piketty, *A Brief History of Equality* (Cambridge, MA: Harvard University Press, 2022), 226–227.
4 Gordon S. Wood, *Empire of Liberty: A History of the Early Republic* (New York: Oxford University Press, 2009), 155.
5 Richard F. Bensel, *Yankee Leviathan: The Origins of Central State Authority in America, 1859–1877* (New York: Cambridge University Press, 1990), 63.
6 Kermit Roosevelt III, *The Nation That Never Was: Reconstructing America's Story* (Chicago, IL: University of Chicago Press, 2022), 171. See also Edward J.

Larson, *American Inheritance: Liberty and Slavery in the Birth of a Nation, 1765–1795* (New York: Norton, 2023), 87, 96–97.
7 Calvin Jillson, "Constitution-Making: Alignment and Realignment in the Federal Convention of 1787," *American Political Science Review* 75, no. 3 (1981): 598–612. See also Rogan Kersh, *Dreams of a More Perfect Union* (Ithaca, NY: Cornell University Press, 2001), 102–103; David Hackett Fischer, *African Founders: How Enslaved People Expanded American Ideals* (New York: Simon & Schuster, 2022), 179.
8 Calvin Jillson, *Constitution-Making: Conflict and Consensus in the Federal Convention of 1787* (New York: Agathon Press, 1988).
9 Noah Feldman, *The Broken Constitution: Lincoln, Slavery, and the Refounding of America* (New York: Farrar, Straus, and Giroux, 2021), 8–9. See also Harry V. Jaffa, *A New Birth of Freedom: Abraham Lincoln and the Coming of the Civil War* (New York: Rowman and Littlefield, 2000), xi.
10 Matthew Desmond, "Capitalism," in *The 1619 Project*, ed. Nikole Hannah-Jones, Caitlin Roper, Ilena Silverman, and Jake Silverstein (New York: The New York Times Co., 2021), 169. See also Jill Lepore, *This America: The Case for the Nation* (New York: Liveright, 2019), 31; Richard F. Bensel, *Sectionalism and American Political Development, 1880–1980* (Madison: The University of Wisconsin Press, 1984), xviii–xix, 6, 22–24.
11 Kate Masur, *Until Justice Be Done: America's First Civil Rights Movement, from the Revolution to Reconstruction* (New York: W.W. Norton, 2021), 8–9.
12 Tyler Stovall, *White Freedom: The Racial History of an Idea* (Princeton, NJ: Princeton University Press, 2021), 121, see also 158–159.
13 Marc W. Kruman, *Between Authority and Liberty: State Constitution Making in Revolutionary America* (Chapel Hill: University of North Carolina Press, 1997), 7, 106–107.
14 Masur, *Until Justice Be Done*, 209, 211–212. See also Fischer, *African Founders*, 95–96; Van Gosse, *The First Reconstruction: Black Politics in America from the Revolution to the Civil War* (Chapel Hill, NC: University of North Carolina Press, 2021), 6–7.
15 Michael C. Dawson, *Behind the Mule: Race and Class in African-American Politics* (Princeton, NJ: Princeton University Press, 1994), 54, 101.
16 Masur, *Until Justice Be Done*, 58; Gosse, *The First Reconstruction*, 106, 150, 154, 173.
17 David W. Blight, *Frederick Douglass: Prophet of Freedom* (New York: Simon & Schuster, 2018), 94.
18 John M. Blassingame, ed., *The Frederick Douglass Papers*, 4 vol. (New Haven, CT: Yale University Press, 1982), 2:60.
19 David Herbert Donald, *Lincoln* (New York: Simon & Schuster, 1995), 199–202.
20 U.S. Supreme Court, *Scott v. Sandford*, 60 U.S. 19 How. 393, 1856. See also Jared A. Goldstein, *Real Americans: National Identity, Violence, and the Constitution* (Lawrence, KS: University Press of Kansas, 2022), 31, 39; Harry V. Jaffa, *Crisis of the House Divided: An Interpretation of the Issues in the Lincoln-Douglas Debates* (Chicago, IL: University of Chicago Press, 1959, 1982), 32, 60.
21 Donald Yacovone, *Teaching White Supremacy: America's Democratic Ordeal and the Forging of Our National Identity* (New York: Pantheon Books, 2022), 52.
22 Feldman, *The Broken Constitution*, 284.
23 Roy P. Basler, ed., *The Collected Works of Abraham Lincoln*, 9 vol. (New Brunswick, NJ: Rutgers University Press, 1953), 2:403–404, 407–408.

24 Feldman, *The Broken Constitution*.
25 "Speech of Frederick Douglass," *Liberator* (1863–1865) 33, no 30 (July 24, 1863): American Periodicals, 118. See also Theodore R. Johnson, *When the Stars Begin to Fall: Overcoming Racism and Renewing the Promise of America* (New York: Grove Press, 2021), 79.
26 Philip S. Foner, ed., *The Life and Writings of Frederick Douglass*, 4 vol. (New York: International Publishers, 1952), 3:420.
27 Blight, *Frederick Douglass*, 444.
28 George Packer, *Last Best Hope: America in Crisis and Renewal* (New York: Farrar, Straus, and Giroux, 2021), 159. See also Yacovone, *Teaching White Supremacy*, 67.
29 Darlene Clark Hine, *Black Victory: The Rise and Fall of the White Primary in Texas* (Columbia, MO: University of Missouri Press, 2003), 53–55. See also Michelle Alexander, *The New Jim Crow: Mass Incarceration in the Age of Colorblindness* (New York: The New Press, 2010; 10th anniversary ed., 2020), 36.
30 John S. Haller, Jr., *Outcasts from Evolution: Scientific Attitudes of Racial Inferiority* (Carbondale, IL: Southern Illinois University Press, 1971, 1995), 79. See also Xi, "Citizenship and Nation-Building," 7022.
31 Hine, *Black Victory*, 52.
32 Henry Louis Gates, Jr., *Stony the Road: Reconstruction, White Supremacy, and the Rise of Jim Crow* (New York: Penguin Books, 2020), 8. See also Robert D. Putnam, *The Upswing: How America Came Together a Century Ago and How We Can Do It Again*, with Shaylyn Romney Garrett (New York: Simon & Schuster, 2020), 201; Peniel E. Joseph, *The Third Reconstruction: America's Struggle for Justice in the Twenty-First Century* (New York: Basic Books, 2022), 17; Olivia B. Waxman, "Reconstruction's Black Politicians," *The Economist*, February 28–March 7, 2022, 26.
33 J. David Woodard, *The New Southern Politics* (Boulder, CO: Lynne Reinner, 2006), 132.
34 Ibram X. Kendi, *Stamped from the Beginning: The Definitive History of Racist Ideas in America* (New York: Bold Type Books, 2017), 248.
35 Leon F. Litwack, *Trouble in Mind: Black Southerners in the Age of Jim Crow* (New York: Vintage Books, 1998), xiii.
36 Floyd Stovall, ed., *The Collected Writings of Walt Whitman*, vol. 2 (New York: New York University Press, 1964), 762. See also Eddie S. Glaude, Jr., *Begin Again: James Baldwin's America and Its Urgent Lessons for Our Own* (New York: Crown Books, 2020), 73; Yacovone, *Teaching White Supremacy*, 47.
37 *United States v. Reece*, 92 U.S. 214 (1876), see https://www.oyez.org/cases/1850-1900/92US214. See also Kersh, *Dreams of a More Perfect Union*, 232–235.
38 Paul M. Rego, *Lyman Trumbull and the Second Founding of the United States* (Lawrence, KS: University Press of Kansas, 2022), 196.
39 *The Civil Rights Cases*, 109 U.S. 3 (1883), see https://www.oyez.org/cases/1850-1900/109US3.
40 Putnam, *The Upswing*, 201; Chandler Davidson, *Race and Class in Texas Politics* (Princeton, NJ: Princeton University Press, 1992), 5–8.
41 Elizabeth Cory Agassiz, ed., *Louis Agassiz: His Life and Correspondence*, vol. 2 (Boston: Houghton Mifflin and Company, 1886), 607; see also Haller, *Outcasts from Evolution*, 85; Yacovone, *Teaching White Supremacy*, xix–xx, 37–39, 326.

42 J.F. (John Fulenwider) Miller, "The Effects of Emancipation Upon the Mental and Physical Qualifications of the Negro in the South," *North Carolina Medical Journal* (November 1896): 292.
43 Earl Black and Merle Black, *The Rise of Southern Republicans* (Cambridge, MA: Harvard University Press, 2002), 11, 41–44.
44 Douglas A. Blackmon, *Slavery by Another Name: The Re-Enslavement of Black Americans from the Civil War to World War II* (New York: Anchor Books, 2009).
45 Allan J. Lichtman, *The Embattled Vote in America: From the Founding to the Present* (Cambridge, MA: Harvard University Press, 2020), 94, 137.
46 Gillian Brockell, "Some Call Voting Restrictions Upheld by Supreme Court Jim Crow 2.0," *Washington Post*, July 2, 2021. See also Litwack, *Trouble in Mind*, 224–225.
47 David Levering Lewis, *W.E.B. Du Bois: A Biography, 1868–1963* (New York: Henry Holt and Company, 2009), 79–91, 181.
48 Hine, *Black Victory*, 140. See also Charles M. Blow, "Welcome to Jim Crow 2.0," *New York Times*, July 15, 2021, A21; Litwack, *Trouble in Mind*, 220; Dawson, *Behind the Mule*, 52, 55.
49 Hine, *Black Victory*, 108, see also 164.
50 Alexander Keyssar, *The Right to Vote: The Contested History of Democracy in America* (New York: Basic Books, 2000), 247–249.
51 *Smith v. Allwright*, 321 U.S. 649.
52 Desmond King, et al., eds., *Democratization in America: A Comparative-Historical Analysis* (Baltimore, MD: Johns Hopkins University Press, 2009), 139.
53 Gates, *Stony the Road*, 186–187. See also Litwack, *Trouble in Mind*, 225.
54 Lerone Bennett, Jr., *Before the Mayflower: A History of the Negro in America, 1619–1962* (Chicago, IL: Johnson Publishing Company, 1962; Eastford, CT: Martino Fine Books, 2016), 302.
55 *Public Papers of the Presidents of the United States, Harry S. Truman*, vol. 4 (Washington, D.C.: U.S. Government Printing Office, 1964), 311–313.
56 Stephen B. Oates, *Let the Trumpets Sound: A Life of Martin Luther King, Jr.* (New York: HarperCollins, 1982), 325.
57 John Lewis and Archie E. Allen, "Black Voter Registration Efforts in the South," *Notre Dame Law Review* 48, no. 1 (1972): 105–132.
58 Hine, *Black Victory*, 18–19, 253–254. See also Heather McGhee, *The Sum of Us: What Racism Costs Everyone and How We Can Prosper Together* (New York: OneWorld, 2021), 158.
59 Lisa Garcia Bedolla, *Latino Politics*, 2nd ed. (New York: Polity, 2014), 19–22. See also Neil Foley, *Mexicans in the Making of America* (Cambridge, MA: Harvard University Press, 2014), 224.
60 Theodore J. Davis, Jr., *Black Politics Today* (New York: Routledge, 2011), 104.
61 William F. Buckley, "Why the South Must Prevail," *National Review*, August 25, 1957.
62 Johnson, *When the Stars Begin to Fall*, 124. See also Ismail K. White and Chryl N. Laird, *Steadfast Democrats: How Social Forces Shape Black Political Behavior* (Princeton, NJ: Princeton University Press, 2020), 197; Tasha Philpot, *Conservative but Not Republican: The Paradox of Party Identification and Ideology Among African Americans* (New York: Cambridge University Press, 2017), 129–131.
63 F. Chris Garcia and Gabriel Sanchez, *Hispanics and the U.S. Political System: Moving into the Mainstream* (New York: Routledge, 2007), 129–130.

64 Alexander, *The New Jim Crow*, 47.
65 Black and Black, *The Rise of Southern Republicans*, 139, 210–211.
66 Joseph E. Lowndes, *From the New Deal to the New Right: Race and the Southern Origins of Modern Conservatism* (New Haven, CT: Yale University Press, 2008), 133. See also Thomas Byrne Edsall, *The Point of No Return: American Democracy at the Crossroads* (Princeton, NJ: Princeton University Press, 2023), 201–202; Kevin P. Phillips, *The Emerging Republican Majority* (Arlington, VA: Arlington House, 1969), 3.
67 Nancy DiTomaso, *The American Non-Dilemma: Racial Inequality Without Racism* (New York: Russell Sage Foundation, 2013), 145–148. See also Ashley Jardina, *White Identity Politics* (New York: Cambridge University Press, 2019), 248.
68 Desmond S. King and Rogers M. Smith, *Still a House Divided: Race and Politics in Obama's America* (Princeton, NJ: Princeton University Press, 2011), 10–11.
69 Eduardo Bonilla-Silva, *Racism Without Racists: Color-Blind Racism and the Persistence of Racial Inequality in America*, 5th ed. (Lanham, MD: Rowman and Littlefield, 2018), 3, 30. See also Michael Omi and Howard Winant, *Racial Formation in the United States*, 3rd ed. (New York: Routledge, 2015), 234.
70 *Regents of the University of California v. Bakke*, 438 U.S. 265 (1978), 295. See also Adam Harris, *The State Must Provide: Why America's Colleges Have Always Been Unequal—and How to Set Them Right* (New York: Ecco/HarperCollins, 2022), 210–211.
71 Lichtman, *Embattled Vote*, 186–187. See also Ian Haney López, *Dog Whistle Politics: How Coded Racial Appeals Have Reinvented Racism and Wrecked the Middle Class* (New York: Oxford University Press, 2015), 160.
72 "Partisan Conflict Index," https://www.philadelphiafed.org/surveys-and-data/real-time-data-research/partisan-conflict-index. See also Jeff Sommer, "Political Strife is High, but the Market Doesn't Care," *New York Times*, July 23, 2017, Bu3.
73 Putnam, *The Upswing*, 86, 92, 99.
74 Levi Boxell, Matthew Gertzkow, and Jesse M. Shapiro, "Cross-Country Trends in Affective Polarization," National Bureau of Economic Research, Working Paper 26669, revised June 2020, https://www.nber.org/papers/w26669. See also Alan I. Abramowitz, *The Great Alignment: Race, Party Transformation, and the Rise of Donald Trump* (New Haven, CT: Yale University Press, 2018).
75 Isabel Wilkerson, *Caste: The Origins of Our Discontents* (New York: Random House, 2020), 330. See also Michael J. Sandel, *The Tyranny of Merit: What's Become of the Common Good?* (New York: Farrar, Straus, and Giroux, 2020), 101–102.
76 Bonilla-Silva, *Racism Without Racists*, 29.
77 Foley, *Mexicans in the Making of America*, 189.
78 Census Bureau, *Statistical Abstract of the United States*, 2023 online edition, Elections, Table 475.
79 Jardina, *White Identity Politics*, 218; see also "Special Report: Race in America," *The Economist*, May 22, 2021, 7.
80 Christina Greer, "Dear Kamala Harris: It's a Trap," *New York Times*, June 30, 2021, A22.
81 NPR, "Barack Obama's Speech on Race," March 18, 2008, www.npr.org/templates/story/story.php?storyId=88478467.
82 Molly Ball, "Politics: Where Wes Moore Comes From," *Time*, February 27–March 6, 2023, 42–49.

83 Jonathan Weisman, "Senator Brings Message of Unity Within a G.O.P. That Is Spoiling for a Fight," *New York Times*, February 18, 2023, A10.
84 Jonathan Weisman and Trip Gabriel, "Racism as Narrative, Not an Issue, for G.O.P. Candidates of Color," *New York Times*, June 2, 2023, A1, A15. See also Jonathan Weisman, "Scott Defends Racial Views in Interview of 'The View,'" *New York Times*, June 6, 2023, A14.

4
RACE, ETHNICITY, AND THE AMERICAN MIND

> "We who are dark can see America in a way that white Americans can not."
>
> W.E.B. Du Bois, 1926 NAACP annual meeting, Chicago

One of the most evocative ideas of the last several decades is Benedict Anderson's "imagined communities." *Imagined Communities* was the title of Anderson's 1983 book on the rise of national communities, which he described as a particular kind of cultural artifact; the joint creation of those considered to be a people. This idea of an imagined community is just what Thomas Jefferson had in mind when he described the luminous claims of the Declaration of Independence – "that all men are created equal, that they are endowed by their Creator with certain unalienable Rights, that among these are Life, Liberty, and the pursuit of Happiness" – as "an expression of the American mind," resting "on the harmonizing sentiments of the day."[1] These were, of course, the harmonizing sentiments of the White American mind, but were they more than that? In fact, imagined communities have been variously described – sometimes as open, sometimes as closed.

Anderson's imagined community connects easily in our minds with the concept, popularized by Martin Luther King, Jr., "the beloved community." King, the most significant civil rights leader of the mid-twentieth century, envisioned defeating racism, sexism, and exclusion through an ever-expanding community of love, care, and inclusion. But a careful reading will show that Anderson was much more doubtful, even

DOI: 10.4324/9781003449188-4

skeptical, about the range and breadth of community; in fact, Anderson and King were talking about quite different social processes. For King, the beloved community was at least potentially general, universal, inclusive; for Anderson, the imagined community was decidedly bounded, particular, exclusive. Race, like nationalism, was for Anderson a cultural artifact "both limited and sovereign," bounded and internally cohesive. Anderson ominously concluded that "racism dreams of eternal contaminations," eternal exclusions for cause and with prejudice.[2] Sadly, Anderson's bounded and exclusive "imagined community," with its "eternal contaminations," describes the divided American mind on race much better than does Martin Luther King's expanding and inclusive "beloved community."

What makes community and race such a volatile mix, especially in America but not just in America, is that: "Communities . . . have a history – in an important sense they are constituted by their past – . . . And if the community is completely honest, it will remember stories not only of suffering received but of suffering inflicted – dangerous memories, for they call the community to alter ancient evils."[3] As we shall see throughout this chapter, one of America's singular failures as a national community has been and remains its unwillingness to admit and address in our national story the "ancient evils" of "suffering inflicted." Just a moment's pause will allow us to remember that both Jefferson and Lincoln, with many more in their respective generations and after, thought that the "ancient evils" of slavery and the scars still remaining from them would always divide Black and White Americans.[4]

Anderson's insights will help clarify the origins of some patterns we have already seen. In earlier chapters we saw that racial hierarchy and the tensions and hatreds that flow from them have characterized American history from its earliest days. We also saw a pattern of advance and retreat in racial policy and practice, identified as extended periods of a couple of decades of racial progress around peaks, including the American Revolution, the Civil War and Reconstruction, and the Civil Rights Revolution of the mid-twentieth century. But advances were never unopposed. After each advance, the old racial order reasserted itself, working to slow and even reverse recent changes, taking back some though not all gains, and leaving the old hierarchy of races still in place.

Here, we ask where the American mind has rested in recent decades and even today on matters of race in public opinion and in public policy. Fortunately, public opinion polling, with its roots in the 1920s and 1930s, has been ubiquitous since the 1950s. While frequently frustrating and opaque, the best public opinion polls provide us with fascinating information on what Americans think about race and, occasionally, even why they think it. As we will see, opinions within the broad American public on race have not so much changed as evolved, leaving the architecture of the old order still visible in hierarchy, animus, suspicion, and denial. Before we look at public opinion data, we listen to Frederick Douglass, W.E.B. Du Bois, James Baldwin, and others on the historical American mind and how it has been divided by and about race.

The Historical American Mind

It is quite likely that no American has understood better than Frederick Douglass the deep divisions and violent conflicts within the nation's psyche regarding race. Douglass closely watched White America's grudging reaction to Black Americans as they moved from slavery to a cramped and narrow freedom. Before the Civil War, in an 1854 commencement address at Western Reserve College, Frederick Douglass declared that, "when men oppress their fellow-men, the oppressor ever finds, in the character of the oppressed, a full justification for his oppression."[5] Douglass knew that if White Americans did not respect Black Americans, they could not sympathize with them, come to know them; they could not form a community with them either in imagination or in history. During the war, Douglass observed that: "The public mind is widely and deeply agitated; and bubbling up from its perturbed waters, are . . . poisonous miasma demand[ing] a constant antidote."[6] The poisonous miasma that the war brought bubbling up from the White mind was uncertainty, fear, even disgust at the prospect of Black freedom and equality. Hence, Douglass worried that whether the war brought victory or defeat to the Union, it would bring suffering to Black Americans, especially the former slaves. When the South was defeated, Douglass cautioned his listeners, saying: "Think you, that because they are for a moment in the talons and the beak of our glorious eagle . . . that they are converted? . . . better wait and see what new form this old monster will assume."[7] Slavery was dying, if not gone, but Douglass knew that racial oppression, that "old monster," might take a "new form," particularly if the "glorious eagle" of national power turned its gaze elsewhere. Depending on White Americans to support Black freedom was a fool's bet; so Black leaders remained alert to betrayal. As Reconstruction waned, the Reverend Samuel T. Spear warned in the New York *Independent* that, "Negrophobia . . . is a prevalent characteristic of the white American mind."[8] Soon that White American mind would turn its thoughts to reconciliation.

Four decades after Douglass warned of White supremacy's tenacity and resilience, W.E.B. Du Bois delivered a speech modestly entitled, "The Address to the Country" at the Niagara Movement's 1906 national meeting.

Du Bois warned that White people could not enjoy the full benefit of the nation's founding values and civil protections if they continued to deny them to their Black fellow citizens. Du Bois declared: "The battle we wage is not for ourselves alone but for all true Americans. It is a fight for ideals, lest this, our common fatherland, false to its founding, become . . . a byword . . . among the nations for its sounding pretensions and pitiful accomplishments."[9] Another two decades on, with the battle to realize American ideals for the nation's Black citizens still not won, Du Bois observed ruefully that, "We who are dark can see America in a way that white Americans can not."[10] Douglass had said our White fellow-citizens do not know us; here Du Bois added but we know them.

Black leaders and intellectuals have long understood the two-sided, even double-edged, promise that the American political culture, the White American sense of society and self, held for Black Americans. Even though America might denigrate and deny Black people, Black people could not denigrate and deny America – call her promises of openness and opportunity a lie – or she would turn away. The American story and its promise had to be praised, accepted as real, if there were to be any chance that she would listen. Because, as the historian Michael Kazin observed, "It is difficult to think of any [American] . . . reformer who repudiated the national belief system and still had a major impact on U.S. politics and policy." As Benjamin Banneker, Frederick Douglass, Martin Luther King, Jr., and many others have known, "Americans who want to transform the world have to learn how to persuade the nation."[11] They have also known that no matter how soothingly the Black community might speak, the nation and its White majority might not deign to listen.

The dominant culture's focus on individualism held that "success came ultimately to the hardworking, the sober, the honest, and the educated – to those who adopted a work ethic of diligence, perseverance, . . . thrift, cleanliness, and temperance; and led moral, virtuous, Christian lives."[12] America promised success and security, maybe not immediately, but ultimately to all willing to prepare well, work hard, and play by the rules. Booker T. Washington argued that the promise was real, but Douglass and many others knew better. Most Black citizens understood that try as they might, success was denied them. Egalitarianism and communalism softened individualism for Black Americans who well knew that their comfort and security was in their own community – individualism meant exposure and vulnerability.[13] White people denied Black people all opportunity and then pointed to Black poverty and said, "I told you so." Like a funhouse mirror, the nation's culture inflated Whites and deflated Blacks.

The longer White and Black Americans looked into the mirror and saw themselves inflated and diminished, the harder it was for either to recall that the images were not real. The Black historian Carter G. Woodson, the second Black person to receive a Ph.D. from Harvard, after Du Bois, wrote in his 1933 book, *The Mis-Education of the Negro*, that: "It is well understood that . . . by the teaching of history the white man could be further assured of his superiority, . . . If you can control a man's thinking you do not have to worry about his action."[14] The brilliant James Baldwin, poet, novelist, and essayist, always insightful if not always consistent, agreed with Woodson that White control of the narrative – the history – of American life imprisoned Black people. Baldwin wrote in his most famous essay, "Everybody's Protest Novel" (1949), that a racially fraught national mythology located and constrained Black people, saying, "It is the peculiar triumph of society – and its loss – that it is able to convince those people to whom it has given inferior status of the reality of this decree so that the allegedly inferior are actually made so, insofar as societal realities are concerned."[15] Du Bois, Woodson, and Baldwin knew and warned that Black people were raised in a White dominated society and so drew many of their referents and presumptions, even when negative and prejudiced in regard to themselves, from that society.

The American culture held out to Black citizens a vision of success that most could not achieve and then bid them own their failure.[16] But James Baldwin and Martin Luther King both argued that the dominant culture was harmful, perhaps just as harmful, to White people as to Black people. If society's dominant narrative is distorted and incomplete, even a lie, though flattering to some and unflattering to others, it is still a lie that distorts reality for everyone. King described the frustration he felt in dealing with the White leaders of Montgomery, Alabama, during the city bus boycott of 1956. They were impervious to calls for justice because it had been: "instilled in them that the Negro is inferior. Their parents probably taught them that; the schools they attended taught them that; the books they read, even their churches and ministers often taught them that. The whole cultural tradition under which they have grown – a tradition blighted with more than 250 years of slavery and more than 90 years of segregation – teaches them that. . . . So these men are merely the children of their culture."[17] Others made a similar point less generously. A Black teacher in Louisiana said to Robert Penn Warren, the great novelist and author of *All the King's Men*: "You hear some white men say they know Negroes. Understand Negroes. But it's not true. No white man ever born ever understood what a Negro is thinking. What he's feeling."[18] Just over a century earlier, Frederick Douglass had said something very similar. Both knew that no understanding meant no community, no common purpose.

In the end, we do not need to agree with Du Bois, Baldwin, and King that because Black people stand somewhat apart from the dominant culture they have a deeper understanding of it than White people to assume that those systematically disadvantaged by a culture will spend more time delving into its weaknesses and inconsistencies than those systematically advantaged by it. As Baldwin wrote, "No curtain under heaven is heavier than the curtain of guilt . . . behind which white Americans hide. . . . The American curtain is color. Color." White Americans, he contended, are "aware that the history they have fed themselves is mainly a lie, but they do not know how to release themselves from it, . . ."[19] Nor, actually, do most White Americans want to be released from this carefully crafted history as it has, and continues, to serve them well. Tragically, White denial of the nation's racial history is the great hurdle that public opinion and public policy ultimately must clear before social justice can be won.[20]

Race in the Deep American Mind

Despite the long-term presence of racial hierarchy in the American mind, we know that that mind has changed over the long course of history. Here we ask how much it has changed and across how broad a front. As we saw in Chapters 1 and 2, perhaps the greatest violation of racial hierarchy, one that could easily be seen but never spoken, was interracial sex, childbearing, and marriage. The first Black people arrived in Virginia in 1619 and social and legal sanctions against interracial intimacy, especially marriage, quickly followed. Social opprobrium, physical punishments for White people as well as Black people, and legal sanctions discouraged but did not stop interracial sex, some voluntary, much not, or the mixed-race births that resulted. Law in the Southern colonies and beyond insured that children's status followed the mother's, and inheritance laws, whoever the father, directed benefits away from the enslaved. Even after the end of slavery, interracial sex and marriage remained socially sanctioned and illegal throughout most of the United States, especially the South and Southwest.

Once modern polling arrived on the scene, few questions were asked earlier or more regularly than Gallup's simple query: "Do you approve or disapprove of marriage between Black people and White people?" As late as 1958, only 4 percent of White adults told the Gallup pollsters that they approved interracial marriage, 94 percent declared that they did not. Nonetheless, also in 1958, high school sweethearts Mildred Jeter, Black and perhaps Native American, and Richard Loving, White, of Caroline County, Virginia, were married in Washington, D.C. Virginia's Racial Integrity Act of 1924 precluded their marriage in Virginia and they were arrested soon after they returned home. The Lovings pled guilty to illegally living as man and wife in Virginia, received a one-year prison sentence, and then the sentence was suspended when they agreed to move to D.C. In 1964, frustrated by their inability to visit family in Virginia and the requirement to live outside the state, the Lovings filed a motion in Caroline County to have the original conviction vacated as a violation of the Fourteenth Amendment equal protection of the laws clause. They also filed suit in the Federal District Court for the Eastern District of Virginia. Caroline County Court Judge Leon M. Bazile found against the Lovings declaring that, "Almighty God created the races white, black, yellow, malay and red, and he placed them on separate continents. . . . The fact that he separated the races shows that he did not intend for the races to mix." The Virginia Supreme Court squirmed, struck down the original sentence and ordered the Lovings to be resentenced by the Caroline County Court. Meanwhile, the Lovings had appealed to the United States Supreme Court, which, on June 12, 1967, overturned their conviction and struck down the Virginia statute prohibiting interracial marriage – 1967! The High Court cited the Fourteenth Amendment equal protection clause.

So what effect did the Supreme Court's finding in *Loving v. Virginia* have on public opinion on interracial marriage? Or perhaps prior movement in public opinion opened the door for the Court. Figure 4.1 charts what is often presented triumphally as public acceptance of racial equality

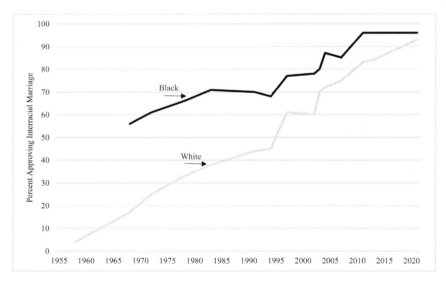

FIGURE 4.1 American Opinion on Interracial Marriage (Approve), 1958–2021

Source: Gallup, https://news.gallup.com/poll/1687/RaceRelations.aspx. See also Justin McCarthy, "U.S. Approval of Interracial Marriage at New High of 94%," Gallup, September 10, 2021.

even in the intimacy of sex and marriage. To some degree it was, but a close look presents a more mixed picture of reluctance and perhaps even ongoing rejection of interracial marriage.

As mentioned above, in 1958 only 4 percent of White Americans approved of interracial marriage; by 1968 White approval was 17 percent and Black approval was 56 percent.[21] That nearly 40-point gap did not close to 30 points until 1991, to 20 points until 1997, and 10 points until 2003. Still, it was 15 points in 2004, 72 percent for White respondents and 87 percent for Black respondents, 12 points in 2013, though it had closed to just 3 points in 2021. Nonetheless, some critics are not buying the change in White opinion as a true change of heart. Sociologist Joe Feagin declared that, "such opinion surveys are seriously limited by the fact that many whites give the pollster *socially desirable* answers that . . . disguise their actual racial framing of society."[22] Moreover, probing the White numbers exposed doubts. Feagin reported follow-up interviews with a group of White respondents showing 80 percent approval, but upon probing only 30 percent were consistently comfortable with interracial marriage.[23]

Finally, the Pew Research Center conducted a poll recognizing the fiftieth anniversary of *Loving v. Virginia*. The survey asked respondents whether they thought interracial marriage was a good thing, bad thing, or did not make much difference for society. The survey reported historical data showing that, "As recently as 1990, roughly six-in-ten nonblack Americans (63 percent) said they would be opposed to a close relative marrying a black person. This share had been cut about in half by 2000 (to 30 percent), and halved again since then to stand at 14 percent today."[24] Yet, opposition remained, among men more than women (13 percent vs. 8), older people (21 percent for over 65 vs. 5 for 18 to 29), the less educated (14 for high school vs. 8 for higher), and party (16 for Republicans vs. 7 for Democrats). Readers will also recall from Chapter 2 that while intermarriage rates are increasing, the least common pairing is Black and White.

A moment's thought will also remind us that while issues of race and justice are always within the American mind, they are not always or even often top of mind.[25] Data from Gallup, not shown here, on the percent of Americans that rated issues of race relations, racial justice, and racism as the number one issue facing the country in each year between 1949 and 2021 – more than seventy years – shows quite clearly that attention to race is periodic rather than continuous. Race does become front of mind as social tensions rise. For example, the period from *Brown v. Board* (1954) through the Civil Rights Acts of 1964 and 1965, the *Loving v. Virginia* decision in 1967, and the Fair Housing Act of 1968 was one period of sustained attention, as has been the period from 2014, when Michael Brown was shot in Ferguson, through the aftermath of George Floyd's killing in Minneapolis in 2020 – between these eruptions is quiescence if not calm. On the other hand, we should not be surprised to find that some people, say Black and Hispanic people, think about race more than others, say White people.

Since 1952, the authoritative American National Election Studies, originally conducted by the University of Michigan, now in a collaborative of Michigan and Stanford, funded by the National Science Foundation (NSF), has asked a national sample to agree or disagree with the following prompt: "Public officials don't care what people think." The question was asked twenty-six times between 1952 and 2020. Every time the question was asked, a greater share of Black than White participants, often by 20 points or more, "agreed" that public officials don't care what people think – until Obama. Remarkably, during the years that Obama spent in the White House, more White than Black participants agreed that public officials don't care. Hispanic opinion has been more volatile, sometimes more despondent even than Black opinion, as in the late 1960s and the Reagan years, but sometimes mirroring White sanguinity rather than Black despair.

Figure 4.2 shows that Black Americans believe, even during periods of racial turmoil like school desegregation in the 1950s, the civil rights demonstrations of the 1960s, and the fairly mild affirmative action fights of the 1970s and beyond, that public officials, presidents, congressmen, governors, all of them, are managing White reaction rather than battling for Black equality. Nonetheless, Black despair of political support is both understandable and still quite remarkable. Most major legal advances for Black people – the end of slavery, desegregation, voting rights, and others – have come from the federal government. This is not to say that Black Americans have not fought and died to push these goals forward, but it is to say that at some point government has had to validate those demands, write them into the constitution and laws, and work to institutionalize those gains. But Figure 4.2 suggests that Black attitudes toward public officials and government reflect the long periods of social stasis that preceded and the backsliding that followed rather than the critical bursts of activism and supportive government action that marked occasional progress.

As we shall see regularly, Black assessments of the responsiveness, really non-responsiveness, of public officials has been more stable than those of White or Hispanic people. Black people have almost always been skeptical of public officials and when hope has been allowed to bloom, usually briefly, it has soon faded. White Americans have become more

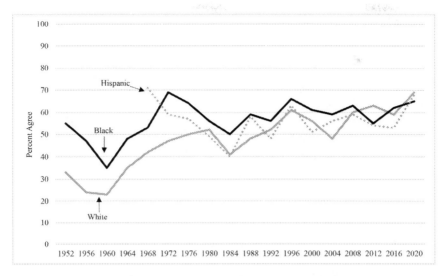

FIGURE 4.2 Public Officials Don't Care What People Think (Percent Responding Agree), 1952–2020

Source: American National Election Studies, 1952–2020, "Public Officials Don't Care What People Think," 5B.3, ANES Guide to Public Opinion and Electoral Behavior.

consistently skeptical of public officials over the last seven decades, especially the last three or four decades, until they actually became more skeptical than Black people as they stared into their television screens to see the nation's first Black president. Hispanic opinion has been volatile throughout with immigration policy, and the political climate surrounding it, apparently the driver. Another reading of Figure 4.2 would be that during the 1960s and 1970s, the height of the modern Civil Rights Revolution, both Black and White people became increasingly convinced that public officials were not listening to them. Likely though Black people wanted the Civil Rights Revolution to press forward, White people wanted it to slow down, and neither thought they were getting what they wanted.

Politicians don't care and race issues are rarely top of the American mind, so how many Black Americans today share the pessimism of Jefferson and Lincoln, and of Douglass and Du Bois? Fortunately, if soberingly, several prominent polling organizations have posed variants of this question to panels of respondents over decades. Gallup has asked: "Do you think relations between Blacks and Whites will always be a problem for the United States, or that a solution will eventually be worked out?" Figure 4.3 presents the share of respondents choosing "Always a problem."

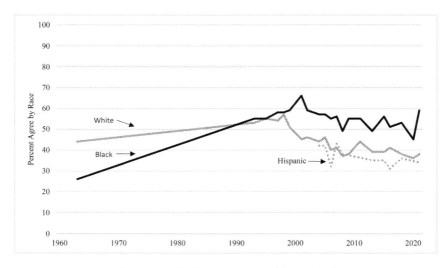

FIGURE 4.3 Race Relations Will Always Be a Problem, 1963–2021
Source: Gallup Historical Trends, https://news.gallup.com/poll/1687/RaceRelations.aspx.

Gallup first asked this question in 1963 and only 26 percent of Black respondents, but 44 percent of White respondents, answered that race would "always be a problem." The question was not asked again until 1993. Over these three decades, which spanned most of the modern civil rights era and the backlash to it, White respondents became slightly more convinced that race would always be a problem and Black respondents became considerably more convinced of that likelihood. The civil rights movement did not make Black respondents more hopeful for the future, it made them less so. In the twenty times Gallup asked this question between 1993 and 2021, an average of 55 percent of Black respondents declared that race relations would "always be a problem" in the U.S. On only three occasions did less than a majority of Black respondents, and never fewer than 45 percent, choose "always be a problem." Over that same period of nearly three decades, an average of 44 percent of White respondents also chose "always be a problem." After 2000 the average dropped to 41 percent, and after 2006 to 39 percent. Still more sanguine were Hispanics. Since they were first polled on this question in 2004, Hispanics declared themselves hopeful that tensions between Black and White Americans would eventually resolve. Between 2004 and 2020, 37 percent of Hispanics chose always a problem. While White and Hispanic respondents saw better days ahead on race relations, fully 59 percent of Black respondents declared that race relations would always be a problem.

Gallup has polled regularly since 2001 on how satisfied respondents were with how Black people in society were treated: very satisfied, somewhat satisfied, somewhat dissatisfied, very dissatisfied, and no opinion. We combine the very and somewhat satisfied responses in Figure 4.4. Clearly, White people have always been more satisfied with how Black people are treated in society than Black people themselves, but after about 2013 the slope of both lines is down, indicating declining satisfaction with how Black people are treated, especially among – shock – Black people. The consistent gap of 20 to 30 points, even 41 points in 2007, is remarkable but not surprising.

Many Black Americans have looked at the nation's history and concluded that change, even a slow crawl toward equality, is impossible. In Chapter 1, we quoted Jefferson's fear of race war, Pennsylvania Rep. Thaddeus Stevens' despair that the nation ever would permit Black equality, and Frederick Douglass's famous query to his Fourth of July audience in 1852, "What, to the American slave, is your fourth of July?" Sadly, the activist and former NFL quarterback Colin Kaepernick, felt compelled to respond to the Fourth of July in 2020 by declaring: "We reject your celebration of white supremacy."[26]

Kaepernick's conflation of that most American of holidays, the Fourth of July, with white supremacy might puzzle momentarily, but just

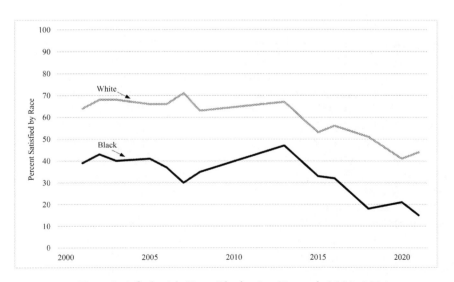

FIGURE 4.4 How Satisfied with How Blacks Are Treated, 2001–2021

Source: Gallup, https://news.gallup.com/poll/1687/RaceRelations.aspx. Those responding very satisfied and somewhat satisfied.

momentarily. Political scientist Ashley Jardina, author of *White Identity Politics*, reminded us that for all of American history: "national identity was explicitly tied to race in order to help create and maintain a certain racial order – an order from which white Americans today implicitly and explicitly benefit. The nation's increasing diversity challenges this definition of America and threatens the mythology and character of the nation that helps maintain whites' power and privilege."[27] Moreover, there is solid empirical evidence that White supremacist activity has been on the rise in America. We easily recall the tiki torch parade in Charlottesville, Virginia, in 2017 and the parading of the Confederate battle flag through the U.S. Capitol during the January 6, 2021 rebellion. In early 2021, the Anti-Defamation League's Center on Extremism released a report that found a twelve-fold rise in White supremacist propaganda – physical fliers, stickers, banners, and posters – since 2017. So there is plenty of room for Black skepticism as to their future role in the American society. The Princeton professor Eddie S. Glaude, Jr., channeling James Baldwin, wrote (note the past tense): "I hoped that one day white people here would finally leave behind the belief that they mattered more. But what do you do when this glimmer of hope fades, and you are left with the belief that white people will never change – that the country, no matter what we do, will remain basically the same?"[28]

Race and Public Policy Preferences

Declining satisfaction among both Black and White Americans, but especially among Black Americans, with how Black people are treated in society raises the question of what might be done. Gallup has polled by race on two questions, one since the early 1990s and the other since the early 2000s, that will provide insight. First, since 1993 Gallup has asked, "Do you think new civil rights laws are needed to reduce discrimination against Blacks, or not?" Black respondents do, White respondents don't. In 1993, White respondents were less than half as likely as Black respondents (33 percent to 70 percent) to believe new civil rights laws were needed to protect equal rights for Black people. Over the next three decades, White support actually dropped, reaching as low as 15 percent in 2011, before rising back into the low 30s by 2015, and then to an unprecedented 53 percent in 2020. Over that same time period, Black support declined into the low 50s before jumping to 69 percent in 2015 and 82 percent in 2020. The killings of young Black men, beginning with Trayvon Martin in 2012 and running through George Floyd in 2020, at least for a time, moved many Americans. Still, much of the increased support for new civil rights laws

Race, Ethnicity, and the American Mind   **113**

came from White Democrats and the well-educated.[29] White Republicans and the less well-educated remained resistant.

The second question, not shown here graphically, was: "Do you generally favor or oppose affirmative action programs for racial minorities?" Though not quite as visceral as the issue of interracial marriage, once civil rights were generally affirmed in the mid-1960s, affirmative action, or whether to provide Black people with contemporary advantages in higher education admissions and job searches, was perhaps the most contested civil rights issue of the late twentieth and early twenty-first centuries. Support for affirmative action, fairly robust for Black and Hispanic Americans and lukewarm for White Americans, has been remarkably stable. For White respondents, support remained in the mid- to high 40s before jumping to 57 percent in 2018 and 2021. For Black respondents, support was much higher but also stable, in a narrow range between 69 and 76 percent the entire time. Hispanics were even more stable, between 62 and 66 percent before jumping to an unprecedented 79 percent in 2021. Prior to ticking up in the last few years, support for affirmative action, even conceptually, was limited among White Americans and even 20 percent to 30 percent of Black and Hispanic Americans had reservations. Despite the increased support of recent years, the Supreme Court struck down affirmative action in college admissions in 2023.

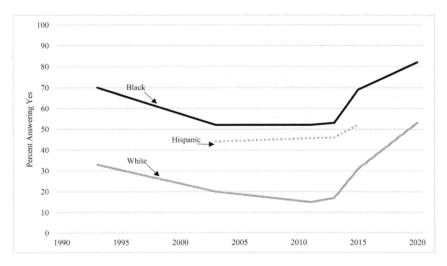

FIGURE 4.5   Are New Civil Rights Laws Needed?, 1993–2020

Source: Gallup, https://news.gallup.com/poll/1687/RaceRelations.aspx.

Before moving more deeply into what polling can show us about different perspectives on fairness, opportunity, and justice by race, we need to spend a moment on an important literature exploring the attitudes that underlie and motivate those views, especially among White people. For more than half a century, scholars have used a number of terms and concepts to describe what University of California, San Diego, sociologist Joseph Gusfield called "status politics." Gusfield, Daniel Bell, Seymour Martin Lipset, and many others since the mid-twentieth century argued that while politics has often been a struggle over material resources, like income, wealth, and property, it has just as often and just as importantly been a struggle over "status," over prestige, and over the prospects of rising or falling in society, the economy, and politics.

More recently, an important article by political scientists Justin Gest, Tyler Reny, and Jeremy Mayer highlighted the idea, especially among White Americans, of "nostalgic deprivation – the discrepancy between individuals' understandings of their current status and their perceptions about their past. This deprivation may be understood in economic terms (inequality), political terms (disempowerment), or social terms – a perceived shift to the periphery of society."[30] Underlying "status politics" or "nostalgic deprivation" is the "feeling that the country and political system is being taken over by out-groups at the expense of the in-group."[31]

Another important stream of scholarship has made the case that while in-group favoritism – historically, of course, this has meant favoritism among White people – has been real, it has not necessarily or even primarily been motivated by racial discrimination. The psychologists Anthony Greenwald and Thomas Pettigrew contend that: "discrimination does not require hostility. Unequal treatment can be produced as readily . . . by helping members of an advantaged group as by harming members of a disadvantaged group."[32] No doubt White parents, with more assets than minority parents, helping their children, or giving their nephew or a member of their church or a neighbor, an advantage in hiring is a form of in-group favoritism and not obviously driven by malice toward out-groups.

Ashley Jardina wrote that, "Much of the work on racial conflict in the United States has focused on white *out-group* attitudes in the form of racial prejudice and racial resentment. . . . My claim is that white racial solidarity is far more consequential for policies that benefit whites, and considerably less associated with policies that benefit or harm racial and ethnic minorities."[33] The sociologist Nancy DiTomaso has also argued that, "one of the most important privileges of being white in the United States is not having to be racist in order to enjoy racial advantage, . . . it is the acts of favoritism that whites show each other . . . that contribute most to continued racial inequality."[34]

Critically though, the fact that strong social networks, access to good jobs, comfortable incomes, and, often, intergenerational wealth help to buttress white privilege and make overt prejudice and discrimination unnecessary to prosperity, "does not mean that the consequences of white identity are innocuous when it comes to racial inequality in the United States. By promoting policies that protect their group, whites are of course seeking to maintain the power and privilege of their group, ultimately preserving a system of inequality."[35] Jardina also noted that about 30 percent of White Americans exhibit a conscious racial identification as White and most of them "embrace their privileged status. . . . they are happy to have such advantages, and they have no desire to relinquish them."[36]

So, White people are sitting atop the nation's racial hierarchy, unwilling to see their status deteriorate. As a result, racial justice advocates have to thread the needle in appealing to them. The Berkeley School of Law professor, Ian Haney López, has noted that most White people are "uninterested in talking about past injustices" or in focusing on "white-against-nonwhite discrimination." Therefore, López advised in favor of class-based, rather than race-based, appeals because surveys showed that "Mentioning that all racial groups would benefit drove up support for investing in education, creating better jobs, and making health care more affordable."[37] Perhaps, but it must be said that White unwillingness to acknowledge and address historical and contemporary consequences of racial discrimination has long been of enormous and negative consequence.[38] Trying to solve deep social problems without speaking their names above a whisper seems an unlikely strategy, but perhaps the only strategy remaining since the Supreme Court assault on affirmative action in college and university admissions.

Race and Public Policy: Jobs, Education, Policing, and Reparations

Now we turn to look at public opinion by race on a number of substantive policy issues. As we do, we should keep in mind an observation by the great early twentieth century social scientist, Max Weber, about the powerful motivation of the privileged to see their privileges as earned, deserved, legitimate. Weber wrote that, "The fortunate man is seldom satisfied with the fact of being fortunate. Beyond this, he needs to know that he has a right to his good fortune. He wants to be convinced that he 'deserves' it, and above all, that he deserves it in comparison with others ... Good fortune thus wants to be legitimate fortune."[39]

Historically, White Americans, and later Hispanics, have been much more convinced than Black Americans themselves that Black people have equal access to jobs in their communities. Although Gallup and others, including the Pew Research Center and CBS News, have asked about fairness for Black people in job opportunities for decades, the pattern of responses has remained quite stable – White and Hispanic respondents see reasonably equal access for Black people while Black respondents do not.

Several points strike the eye in Figure 4.6. First, in 1963, few Americans, well less than half of White respondents (41 percent) and less than a quarter of Black respondents (23 percent) believed that Black people had equal job opportunities with White people. But after the victories of the civil rights movement in the 1960s and 1970s, White respondents became convinced that equal job opportunities were present for Black people in their communities. From 1978 through 2021, three-quarters of White respondents (74 percent) replied that Black people had just as good a chance at jobs in their communities as White people. Nonetheless, White confidence that equality of job opportunities had been achieved has declined in recent years. From a high point of 82 percent, in 1998 and 2009, each of

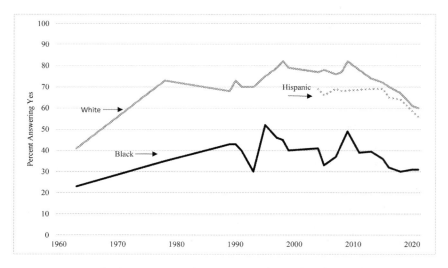

FIGURE 4.6 Do Blacks Have Equal Access to Jobs with Whites?, 1963–2021

Source: Question: "In general, do you think that Blacks have as good a chance as Whites in your community to get any kind of job for which they are qualified, or don't you think they have as a good a chance?" https://news.gallup.com/poll/1687/RaceRelations.aspx.

the last seven measurements of White opinion has slipped, all the way to 60 percent in 2021. The last decade has been especially hard on White denial. Second, Black opinion on equality of job opportunities has tracked an average of nearly 30 points below White opinion. On only one occasion, 1995, did Gallup report that more than half of Black respondents (52 percent) replied that job opportunities were equal. Like White opinion, Black opinion has dipped over the last decade, but from a lower point: from 49 percent in 2009, Black opinion slipped to 31 percent in 2020 and 2021. Finally, since Hispanics were first queried on this issue in 2004, Hispanic opinion on whether Black people have job opportunity equal to White people has tracked about 5 to 10 points below White opinion and 25 to 30 points or more above Black opinion.

Many other polls over the decades have shown similar patterns; White people much more sanguine about Black prospects than are Black people themselves. One fairly entertaining report came from CBS News in June 2014. When a national sample of adults were asked who has a better chance of getting ahead in America, Black or White people, or is it about the same, only 28 percent of White respondents, but 46 percent of Black respondents, reported thinking White people had a better chance. But tellingly, only 5 percent of White respondents and 4 percent of Black respondents reported thinking Black people had a better chance of getting ahead. The rest said about equal. A second question on the same CBS News survey asked how much discrimination against African-Americans respondents thought there was: a lot, some, only a little, or none at all? Again, tellingly, only 5 percent of White respondents and 1 percent of Black respondents replied "none at all."[40] Finally, a Pew Research Center poll from 2013 asked whether respondents believed that Black people were treated less fairly than White people on the job. Only one-sixth of White respondents (16 percent), but more than half of Black respondents (54 percent) responded that Black people were treated less fairly at work.

A similar set of Gallup polls, with one survey in 1962 and then steady administration since 1989, asked respondents whether Black children in their communities had as good a chance as White children at getting a good education. The pattern of responses by race is very similar to that shown in Figure 4.6. White respondents replied almost uniformly yes, of course, while Black respondents replied no! Again, Hispanics track closer to White respondents than to Black respondents. White opinion on Black children's access to a good education was remarkably stable into the twenty-first century, when it began to erode, while Black opinion tracked about 30 points lower throughout. Hispanic opinion on this issue was elicited only between 2004 and 2016 but was as high, sometimes higher, than White opinion.

Several points need to be emphasized. First, over the entire period, 1962 to 2020, 81.3 percent of White respondents affirmed that equal educational opportunity existed for Black children in their communities, while only 53.9 percent of Black respondents, but 75.9 percent of Hispanic respondents agreed. In only one year between 1962 and 2015 did White commitment to the conviction that Black children had educational opportunity equal to White children fall below 80 percent (it was 79 percent in 1979). However, in 2016 it dipped to 75 percent and in 2020 to 64 percent. As with the issue of equal job opportunity, White confidence that equality reigns in America has eroded in recent years. Second, Black support for the proposition that equal educational opportunity reigned in America was more muted throughout and also fell after 2013. Third, Hispanic support for the idea that Black children enjoyed educational equality tracked seven to ten points below White opinion from 2004 through 2008 but above White support after 2013.

Remarkably similar survey data on whether Black people have as good a chance to buy any housing they can afford is available from Gallup from 1989 through 2020. Again, as with jobs and education, White respondents were firmly convinced, at margins of 82 to 86 percent between 1997 and 2015, that Black people had equal access to available housing. But again, after 2015, that conviction among White respondents began to erode, slipping to 66 percent by 2020. Black response tracked 30 points lower throughout the period; 80 percent of White respondents, but just 50 percent of Black respondents, and 71.5 percent of Hispanic respondents thought Black people had equal access with White people to any housing they could afford.[41]

Police, the courts, and prisons are often referred to as social control mechanisms, meaning that they are the institutional tools that leaders have to enforce society's preferences and to punish non-compliance. How society's social control mechanisms interact with Black people as opposed to White people has always been a topic of great concern. Overseers and slave catchers controlled Black people before the Civil War, though, as economic assets, plantation justice served in place of formal punishment by the state. After the Civil War, jails and prisons filled with Black freedmen who had violated White social norms and laws.[42] Douglas Blackmon's prize-winning book, *Slavery by Another Name*, explained how sheriffs, jails, and courts, mostly but not exclusively in the South, directed Black men back into enforced labor, slavery, well into the twentieth century. More recently, references to mass incarceration and even the "carceral state" highlight disproportionate use of imprisonment, particularly of Black and other young minority men, in the U.S. Not surprisingly, Black Americans have always been skeptical of the criminal justice system, rejecting even the term, while most White Americans have accepted its legitimacy and even seen the "thin blue line" as the bulwark of their defense – until quite recently.

Stable patterns of White support for and Black skepticism of police began to change during Barack Obama's presidency. Donald Trump and his "birther" challenge to Obama's legitimacy as a citizen, and, hence, as president, triggered Black alarm. Even more directly, the shooting and death of Michael Brown in Ferguson, Missouri in 2014, and the killing of George Floyd in Minneapolis in 2020, along with many others, prompted an unprecedented movement in opinion on race and policing. The *New York Times* "Poll Watch" has written that "Never in the history of modern polling have Americans expressed such widespread agreement that racial discrimination plays a role in policing – and in society at large."[43]

Five polls were conducted between 1993 and 2016 by the Gallup organization asking: "Do you think the American justice system is biased against black people?" Among White respondents, yes responses actually fell from 33 percent in 1993 to 25 percent in 2013, before jumping to 42 percent in 2015 and 45 percent in 2016. Among Black respondents, yes responses remained stable at 67 and 68 percent between 1993 and 2013 and then moved up to 74 percent in 2015 and 76 percent in 2016. Hispanic numbers remained stable in the low to mid-40s between 2008 and 2016.

While public opinion on racism in policing had been changing for some years, there is no question that the murder of George Floyd on May 25, 2020, set off a firestorm of protest and then of social introspection. As *The Economist* noted: "Mr. Floyd's death, which was filmed by a bystander," actually several bystanders, "sparked the biggest civil rights protests in America's history. Some 20 million Americans took part, flouting COVID-19 restrictions. There were 7,750 protests in over 2,440 places, in every state."[44] A year after Floyd's death and the ensuing protests and demonstrations, an AP/NORC poll showed that the early opinion changes had largely held. "In 2019, just 36 percent of Americans called police violence an extremely or very serious problem. After Floyd was killed, that number increased to 48 percent, and 45 percent" still said so in May 2021. The same poll found that, "Beyond policing, about 8 in 10 Black Americans and about two-thirds of Hispanic and Asian Americans say racism in the U.S. is a very or extremely serious problem. Among white Americans, about half call it that serious."[45]

Highlighting the intense focus on racial justice issues in the wake of George Floyd's killing and Officer Derek Chauvin's conviction for murder, a majority of Americans agree that racism is a serious problem in the U.S. but disagree as to whether enough has been done to combat it. One prominent poll, from the *Wall Street Journal*/NBC News in 2020, found that 56 percent of registered voters agreed that "American society is racist," including 66 percent of women, 65 percent of young people between 18 and 34, and 78 percent of Black people. Moreover, 63 percent of American adults, including 58 percent of White people and 84 percent of Black people believe that "slavery affects the position of black people in society today."[46] Nonetheless, a majority of American adults (54 percent) believe the nation has gotten it "about right" or "gone too far" in giving Black people equal rights. Sixty-two percent of White people, but only 20 percent of Black people reported believing that the U.S. had gotten it about right or gone too far.[47] Recall the earlier discussion of status politics or nostalgic deprivation – I want you to be equal but don't want to give up anything to make you so.[48]

No group affected the changing view of police violence against Black people as much as Black Lives Matter (BLM). BLM is not so much an organization – there are many related organizations – as a broad movement of people and groups advocating against police violence and for Black liberation, equality, and security. The movement began as a social media hashtag, #BlackLivesMatter, following the killing of Trayvon Martin in early 2012 and the acquittal of George Zimmerman in a trial for that crime in 2013. BLM's presence and visibility increased greatly around demonstrations following the killings of Michael Brown and Eric Garner at the hands of the police in 2014, in Ferguson and New York respectively, and in the wake of George Floyd's killing in 2020.

Both long-term observers of U.S. social movements and newer participants in those movements were surprised by the multiracial makeup of the demonstrations. Some White supporters marched with Martin Luther King, Jr. in the 1950s and 1960s, but White people were often a majority of the demonstrators after Floyd's death. One fairly modest study, conducted by a University of Maryland sociologist, Dana R. Fisher, and a University of Michigan political scientist, Michael T. Heaney, interviewed 195 people at demonstrations in three major cities; demonstrators in Washington, D.C. were 65 percent White, 61 percent were White in New York, and 53 percent in Los Angeles. Doug McAdam, author of a classic book on social movements, entitled, *Political Process and the Development of Black Insurgency, 1930–1970*, initially published in 1982, said, "This is utterly different from anything we've seen."[49]

Even more importantly, polls by the Pew Research Center and CNN showed support for BLM holding up, though with some slippage among conservative White people, several months after Floyd's killing and the demonstrations that followed. Pew found overall support for BLM slipping from 67 percent in June to 55 percent in September, though again most of that was among Whites and mostly among conservative Whites. Black support rose one point over that period, from 86 to 87 percent. Support among Hispanics dropped from 77 to 66 percent, among Asians from 75 to 69 percent, and among White people from 60 to 45 percent. Fascinatingly, though perhaps not surprisingly, support for BLM among White adults identifying as Democrats or leaning toward Democrat, support dropped from 92 to 88 percent. Among White people identifying as Republican or leaning Republican, support dropped from 37 to 16 percent.[50] By December 2021, Civiqs' daily tracking poll showed that 85 percent of Democrats supported BLM and 86 percent of Republicans opposed them.[51] Increasing visibility for Black people and Black issues has long unnerved many White Americans.

Finally, reparations, usually understood as cash payments to Black people as at least partial compensation for the losses endured during slavery, Jim Crow, and for more recent discrimination, has always been a distinctively divisive issue. Historically, the evanescent promise of "forty acres and a mule," meaning land and the means to work it, in the immediate wake of the Civil War was an acknowledgement that reparations were due and simply turning former slaves loose without the means to survive, let alone prosper, was unjust and cruel. Yet, White decisionmakers in Washington could not overcome the concern that White property rights, even of former rebels, would have to be sacrificed to do justice to the former slaves. That too would be unjust they held, and so backed slowly, quickly actually, away from reparations. While the idea that justice had been left undone and that reparations were one obvious path to justice never left Black minds, White leaders and citizens remained sullenly resistant.

Nevertheless, as we will see in more detail in Chapter 10, Congressman John Conyers (D-Mich.) introduced HR 40, a bill to establish a Commission to Study and Develop Reparation Proposals for African-Americans in 1989 and reintroduced it in every subsequent Congress until he retired in 2017. Conyers died in 2019, but others, including Sheila Jackson Lee (D-TX), continued the effort. Though committee hearings were held on the bill in 2007 and in 2019, the bill was not successfully passed out of the Judiciary Committee of the U.S. House until April 2021. It has not received a floor vote to date.

Opinion on reparations remains divided and especially negative among White Americans. A Fox News/Opinion Dynamics poll from March 2001 asked: "Do you think the government should or should not make cash payments to black Americans who are descendants of slaves?" Six percent of White respondents answered yes while 55 percent of Black respondents answered in the affirmative.[52] Gallup did two polls, one in

2002, the other in 2019, on the same question and there was some movement. In 2002, Gallup reported numbers identical to Fox – 6 percent of White respondents and 55 percent of Black respondents approved cash payments to descendants of slaves. By 2019, White approval had risen to 16 percent and Black approval had risen to 73 percent. And an AP/NORC Center for Public Affairs research poll in fall 2019 found 15 percent of White respondents and 74 percent of Black respondents favoring reparations.[53]

While public opinion on reparations has not moved much, thinking among Democrat elected leaders, activists, and progressive academics has changed. An initiating spark was Ta-Nehisi Coates' 2014 article in *The Atlantic* entitled "The Case for Reparations." Another was the book, *From Here to Equality: Reparations for Black Americans in the Twenty-First Century*, by William A. Darity and A. Kirsten Mullen. Both take reparations more seriously than previous cursory treatments and ask not just whether it should be done, but how, and at what cost. Some advocates contend for a mix of cash payments and programs intended to improve Black neighborhoods and lives, like targeted job training, educational assistance, and access to home loans. Others call for states and communities to play a role in reparations. California passed a bill in 2020 to study and develop proposals for addressing slavery reparations. In 2023 the study commission produced a 1,100 page report with myriad recommendations, but it was the projected cost of $500 billion that received most of the attention. Republicans dismissed the idea of reparations, while elected Democrats danced. Governor Gavin Newsom (D-CA) noted that reparations were about more than money.[54] Some communities, most notably Evanston, Illinois, have stepped up with programs. Evanston, a relatively affluent city of 75,000, 16 percent Black, began paying out an initial traunch of $400,000 in 2021.[55]

Finally, between 2004 and 2016, Gallup conducted five polls asking a somewhat broader question: "How much of a role, if any, do you think government should have in trying to improve the social and economic position of Blacks and other minority groups in this country?" The national numbers were remarkably stable, though drifting down marginally. In 2004, 40 percent of U.S. adults said government should have a major role, and in 2016 that number was 38 percent. In 2004, 45 percent said a minor role, and in 2016 that number was 40 percent. Respondents who said government should have no role increased from 14 percent in 2004 to 22 percent in 2016. Over the period 2004 to 2016, White respondents moved away from government involvement until in 2016 just one-quarter said major role, half said minor role, and one-quarter said no role. Among Black and Hispanic respondents, a little less than two-thirds said major role, a little less than a third said minor role, and only about one-in-ten said no role.[56] We will explore the economics of the reparations issue more fully in Chapter 10, but for now we might simply observe that a national reparations program remains unlikely.

Race and Persons: Obama, Gates, and Trump

No one will be shocked to hear that people respond differently to public figures depending upon their own and the public figure's race. Not surprisingly, Black hopes were high as Barack Obama secured the Democratic nomination for president in 2008 and prepared for the general election campaign.[57] ABC News and the *Washington Post* asked respondents in June 2008, prior to the general election, and again in January 2010, one year into the new Obama administration, whether his candidacy and then presidency would help or hurt race relations in the country. Prior to the election, 60 percent of Black Americans and 38 percent of White Americans thought Obama would help race relations, but a few, 8 percent of Blacks and 17 percent of Whites, thought he would hurt them, and the rest thought he would not make much difference. By early 2010, Black confidence that Obama would help race relations had waned a bit, falling from 60 to 51, but White confidence, modest to begin with, edged up from 38 to 40 percent. Still, even fewer, 4 percent of Black respondents and 12 percent of White respondents, thought he would hurt race relations.[58]

On November 5, 2008, the day after election day, Gallup asked respondents nationwide whether they thought Obama's election would make race relations a lot better, a little better, no change, a little worse, or a lot worse. Though responses were not broken out by race, 70 percent of Americans chose a little or a lot better, while only 10 percent chose a little or a lot worse, with just 3 percent choosing a lot worse. Between mid-November 2008 and mid-January 2009, CNN and the Opinion Research Corporation collaborated on two polls that produced similarly hopeful results, though there were worrisome differences by race. Just days after the election, 80 percent of African-Americans described Obama's election as "a dream come true" while only 28 percent of White Americans thought so. On the other hand, by mid-January 69 percent of White people and 80 percent of Black people proclaimed that Obama's election opened "a new era" or at least offered hope for "some improvement" in American politics and life. Only 6 percent of White respondents and 5 percent of Black respondents chose worse.[59]

The same Gallup question referred to just above, with race now broken out, was asked three more times, later in 2009, in 2011, and in 2016.

Hope faded, though faster among Whites than Blacks. In October 2009, 39 percent of White respondents chose a little or a lot better, but 23 percent chose a little or a lot worse. Among Black respondents in late 2009, 53 percent chose a little or a lot better while 20 percent chose a little or a lot worse. By the end of Obama's presidency in 2016, just 23 percent of White respondents chose a little or a lot better while 51 percent chose a little or a lot worse. Among Black respondents by 2016, 37 percent chose better and 39 percent chose worse.[60]

One of the purer Rorschach tests on race in America during the Obama years came in July 2009 when Henry Louis Gates, Jr., professor of African American Studies at Harvard, got locked out of his very nice Cambridge, Massachusetts home. While Gates, fifty-eight years old at the time, jiggled door knobs and pried on windows, trying to get into his house, someone reported suspicious activity to the local police – and then it got interesting – and then it blew up. Cambridge police Sgt. James Crowley, White, responded to the scene; though accounts differ, words were exchanged and Gates was arrested for "disorderly conduct." President Obama entered the fray, admitting that he did not know all the facts, but opining that "the Cambridge police acted stupidly." Emotions flared, Obama invited Gates and Crowley to the White House for a July 30 "beer summit," in which then Vice President Biden joined, presumably to balance the racial sides around the picnic table, and ruffled feathers were smoothed.

CNN put a poll in the field the next day, July 31, and in a battery of questions showed that while the principals might have shaken hands and made up, the public was still deeply and predictably divided. When asked whether they thought Officer Crowley had acted stupidly in the incident, 59 percent of Black respondents answered yes, while only 29 percent of White respondents agreed. When asked who they sympathized with more, Professor Gates or Officer Crowley, 61 percent of Black respondents chose Gates while only 29 percent of White respondents did; 45 percent of White respondents chose Crowley while only 19 percent of Black respondents chose the officer. When asked whether a White homeowner would have been arrested under similar circumstances, 66 percent of White respondents said they would while 64 percent of Black respondents said they would not. Asked whether Obama had acted stupidly in commenting on the incident, 63 percent of White respondents said yes and 59 percent of Black respondents said no.[61] Obama later wrote in his memoir, *A Promised Land*, that this event dropped his poll numbers further than any other single event of his presidency.[62]

As Obama neared completion of his second term as president, a Bloomberg Politics Poll and a CNN/ORC Poll asked similar questions,

"Do you think race relations have gotten better, gotten worse, or stayed about the same under the first black president?" CNN/ORC concluded their question a little differently, mentioning Obama by name, as in "since Barack Obama became president?" In these two polls, just 7 to 11 percent of White respondents thought race relations had gotten better, while 15 to 25 percent of Black respondents thought so. Soberingly, 45 to 56 percent of White respondents and 26 to 45 percent of Black respondents declared that race relations had gotten worse.[63]

Two Gallup questions, each asked several times between 2008 and 2016, show hope transforming into disappointment over Obama's caution. As the nation's first Black president, Obama struggled throughout his presidency to be accepted as president of all Americans rather than just as president of Black America. Gallup asked respondents three times, in late 2009, and in the summers of 2011 and 2016, whether Obama administration policies had gone too far, about right, or not far enough to aid the Black community. Opinion among both Black and White respondents changed in fascinating ways. Not too surprisingly, only 5 or 6 percent of Black respondents ever thought Obama policies had gone too far in aiding Black people, but those answering "about right" fell from 55 percent in 2009 to 39 percent in 2016, while Black respondents replying "not far enough" rose from 32 percent to 52 percent. More White respondents always thought that Obama administration policies had gone too far, but the numbers settled from 28 percent in 2009 to 25 percent in 2016. White responses saying "about right" also settled a bit, from 45 percent in 2009 to 39 percent in 2016. And remarkably, the percentage of White people responding that Obama administration policies had not gone far enough in aiding the Black community rose from 16 percent in 2009 to 30 percent in 2016.[64]

Another Gallup survey, again conducted three times, late 2009, and the summers of 2011 and 2016, asked whether the Obama presidency was the most important advance for Black people in the past 100 years, one of the most important, important, or not that important. Among Black respondents, those answering most important declined from 44 percent in 2009 to 21 percent in 2016, while Black people responding "not that important" rose from 6 to 18 percent. Nonetheless, even in 2016, almost 60 percent of Black respondents still saw the Obama presidency as one of the most important developments of the past century or as important. White responses showed a growing sense that the storm had been weathered. White Americans responding "most important" declined from 16 percent in 2009 to 6 percent in 2016, those responding one of the most important dropped from 40 to 21 percent, important rose from

25 to 33 percent, while those responding not that important rose from 17 percent in 2009 to 38 percent in 2016. As the Obama presidency wound down, Black people were disappointed that more had not been done while White people generally were relieved.

It is hard to imagine a political figure more different from Barack Obama than Donald J. Trump. Trump was a divisive public figure long before he was a political figure. He had teased running for office many times over the course of his adult life, but had never followed through. Few thought that he would in 2015, even as he rode down the Trump Tower escalator to declare his candidacy for the Republican presidential nomination. And there was no reason people should have taken him seriously. The first time Trump's name was polled by Hart Research Associates was July 1990; 3 percent of respondents viewed him very positively, another 11 percent somewhat positively, with the remainder neutral or negative. By October 1999, his positives had not budged, still at 3 and 11, while his very negative numbers had risen from 24 to 32 percent. With nowhere to go but up, his numbers did that slowly. Trump broke 10 percent very positive in July 2015, the month after he declared his candidacy, broke 20 percent after his election, and broke 30 only twice before his defeat for reelection in 2020. His negatives always outstripped his positives.[65]

Nor was the public hopeful about Trump's impact on race relations in the U.S. Shortly before Trump's inauguration, Quinnipiac asked respondents whether, "Now that Donald Trump has been elected president, are you more concerned about discrimination and violence against minorities, less concerned, or concerned about the same?" Only half of Republicans (52 percent) were less concerned, while 83 percent of Democrats and half of Independents were more concerned.

Moreover, when NBC News and the *Wall Street Journal*, nearly three years into Trump's presidency, asked whether race relations had gotten better, worse, or stayed the same, only 11 percent of White respondents said better, while 47 said they'd gotten worse, and 41 said they'd stayed the same. Only 5 percent of Black respondents chose gotten better, 86 percent chose gotten worse, and just 9 percent said stayed the same. Hispanics were only a little less negative than Blacks.[66] The explanation is not hard to find; *New York Times* reporters wrote that Trump "regularly uses harsh and violent language that no other American leader employs, vocally supporting the views of white nationalists and even defenders of white supremacy rather than the views expressed by majorities of Americans in polls."[67] Most famously, as the demonstrations, most peaceful, some violent, erupted in the wake of George Floyd's murder, President

Trump tweeted on the evening of May 28, 2020, that "THUGS" were dishonoring Floyd's name. Trump vowed to restore order, ending ominously with "When the looting starts, the shooting starts." Close observers immediately recognized this phrase from the 1960s' civil rights clashes and from George Wallace's 1968 presidential campaign.[68] Trump claimed not to have been aware of that history.

Race has been a structural constant in American politics, but concern with race ebbs, rises, crests, and then ebbs again. When Americans do think about race, they see different realities. White Americans generally see great progress; slavery is long over, segregation a fading memory, the legislation and court decisions of the mid-twentieth century and beyond promised and largely delivered equal opportunity and treatment – little more needs to be done. Black Americans generally agree that if one looks back to the 1860s, the early 1900s, or even the 1950s and early '60s, great improvements have been made. But over the last half century progress has ground to a halt and significant backsliding has occurred in the fundamentals and basics of Black life. Since 1970, Black educational attainment, income and wealth, health and longevity, quality of neighborhoods and housing, and interactions with the criminal justice system have stagnated or deteriorated, compared to the same areas for White Americans. It is to these critical public policy issues we now turn, beginning with education.

Notes

1 Thomas Jefferson, *The Writings of Thomas Jefferson*, Monticello Edition (Washington, D.C.: The Thomas Jefferson Memorial Association, 1904), xvi:118. See also Carl L. Becker, *The Declaration of Independence* (New York: Knopf, 1942), 25.
2 Benedict Anderson, *Imagined Communities: Reflections on the Origins and Spread of Nationalism* (London: Verso, 1983, 2016), 6, 149. See also Gary Gerstle, *American Crucible: Race and Nation in the Twentieth Century* (Princeton, NJ: Princeton University Press, 2001, rev. ed. 2017), 11; Robert Wuthnow, *The Left Behind: Decline and Rage in Small-Town America* (Princeton, NJ: Princeton University Press, 2018), 32; Martin Wolf, *The Crisis of Democratic Capitalism* (New York: Penguin Press, 2023), 17, 38, 326–328.
3 Robert H. Bellah, Richard Madsen, William M. Sullivan, Ann Swindler, and Steven M. Tipton, *Habits of the Heart: Individualism and Commitment in American Life* (Berkeley, CA: University of California Press, 1985), 153. See also Yascha Mounk, *The Great Experiment: Why Diverse Democracies Fall Apart and How They Can Endure* (New York: Penguin Press, 2022), 177.
4 Noah Feldman, *The Broken Constitution: Lincoln, Slavery, and the Refounding of America* (New York: Farrar, Straus, and Giroux, 2021), 25, 271, 323.

See also Michael Wayne Santos, *Rediscovering a Nation: Will the Real America Please Stand Up* (Lanham, MD: Rowman and Littlefield, 2022), 76.
5 Frederick Douglass, "The Claims of the Negro, Ethnographically Considered," Commencement Address, Western Reserve College, July 12, 1854, 15, https://www.loc.gov/resource/rbaapc.07900.
6 John W. Blassingame, ed., *The Frederick Douglass Papers*, series 1, vol. 2 (New Haven, CT: Yale University Press, 1982), 250.
7 Blassingame, *The Frederick Douglass Papers*, series 1, vol. 4, 84–85.
8 William Gillett, *Retreat from Reconstruction, 1869–1879* (Baton Rouge, LA: Louisiana State University Press, 1979), 191.
9 Herbert Aptheker, ed., *Pamphlets and Leaflets by W.E.B. Du Bois* (White Plains, NY: Kraus-Thomson Organization Limited, 1986), 63.
10 Herbert Aptheker, ed., *Selections from the Crisis*, 2 vol. (Millwood, NY: Kraus-Thomson Organization Limited, 1983), 2:444.
11 Michael Kazin, "A Patriotic Left," *Dissent*, October 1, 2002, 42.
12 Leon F. Litwack, *Trouble in Mind: Black Southerners in the Age of Jim Crow* (New York: Vintage Books, 1998), 69–70, 90. See also Joe R. Feagin, *The White Racial Frame: Centuries of Racial Framing and Counter-Framing*, 3rd ed. (New York: Routledge, 2020), 5, see also 104–105.
13 Michael C. Dawson, *Behind the Mule: Race and Class in African-American Politics* (Princeton, NJ: Princeton University Press, 1994), 58, 60, 99–100. See also Theodore R. Johnson, *When the Stars Begin to Fall: Overcoming Racism and Renewing the Promise of America* (New York: Grove Press, 2021), 114; Gerstle, *American Crucible*, xv.
14 Carter G. Woodson, *The Mis-Education of the Negro* (Mineola, NY: Dover, 2005), 551. See also Molly Ball, "A Charter School's Racial Controversy Illustrates the Real Battle for America's Classrooms," *Time*, December 13, 2021, 46–52.
15 James Baldwin, "Everybody's Protest Novel," in *Notes of a Native Son* (New York: The Dial Press, 1963), 19–20. See also Donald Yacovone, *Teaching White Supremacy: America's Democratic Ordeal and the Forging of Our National Identity* (New York: Pantheon Books, 2022), 287–288.
16 Gary Gerstle, *The Rise and Fall of the Neoliberal Order: America and the World in the Free Market Era* (New York: Oxford University Press, 2022), 63.
17 Martin Luther King, *Stride Toward Freedom: The Montgomery Story* (New York: Harper & Row, 1958), 138–139. See also Mounk, *The Great Experiment*, 184.
18 Robert Penn Warren, "Segregation: The Inner Conflict in the South" (1956) in Jon Meacham, ed., *Voices in Our Blood: America's Best on the Civil Rights Movement* (New York: Random House, 2001), 174–175.
19 James Baldwin, "White Man's Guilt," in David R. Roediger, ed., *Black on White: Black Writers on What It Means to be White* (New York: Schocken Books, 1998), 320–323.
20 Wuthnow, *The Left Behind*, 153.
21 Similar poll results were reported by Gertrude J. Selznick and Stephen Steinberg, *The Tenacity of Prejudice* (New York: Harper & Row Publishers, 1969), 171. See also Robert Wuthnow, *Rough Country: How Texas Became America's Most Powerful Bible-Belt State* (Princeton, NJ: Princeton University Press, 2014), 209.
22 Feagin, *The White Racial Frame*, 102.
23 Ibid., 103. See also Gerstle, *American Crucible*, 309.

24 Gretchen Livingston and Anna Brown, "Intermarriage in the U.S. 50 Years After *Loving v. Virginia*," Pew Research Center, May 2017.
25 Johnson, *When the Stars Begin to Fall*, 101.
26 Michael Powell, "Supremacy? Divide Grows Over a Phrase," *New York Times*, October 18, 2020, A1, A22–A23.
27 Ashley Jardina, *White Identity Politics* (New York: Cambridge University Press, 2019), 126.
28 Eddie S. Glaude, Jr., *Begin Again: James Baldwin's America and Its Urgent Lessons for Our Own* (New York: Crown Books, 2020), xvii. See also "Special Report: Race in America," *The Economist*, May 22, 2021, 3.
29 George Packer, *Last Best Hope: America in Crisis and Renewal* (New York: Farrar, Straus, and Giroux, 2021), 125.
30 Justin Gest, Tyler Reny, and Jeremy Mayer, "Roots of the Radical Right: Nostalgic Deprivation in the United States and Britain," *Comparative Political Studies* 51, no. 13 (2018): 1694–1719. See also Rogers M. Smith and Desmond S. King, "White Protectionism in America," *Perspectives on Politics* 19, no. 2 (May 13, 2020): 3.
31 Gest, Reny, and Mayer, "Roots of the Radical Right," 1710. See also Jared A. Goldstein, *Real Americans: National Identity, Violence, and the Constitution* (Lawrence, KS: University Press of Kansas, 2022), 28, 82, 168–170, 178–179; Wolf, *The Crisis of Democratic Capitalism*, 84–87, 106.
32 Anthony G. Greenwald and Thomas F. Pettigrew, "With Malice Toward None and Charity for Some," *American Psychologist* 69, no. 7 (2014): 670.
33 Jardina, *White Identity Politics*, 5, 43.
34 Nancy DiTomaso, *The American Non-Dilemma: Racial Inequality Without Racism* (New York: Russell Sage Foundation, 2013), 6. See also Michael C. Dawson and Megan Ming Francis, "Black Politics and the Neoliberal Racial Order," *Public Culture* 28, no. 1 (2016): 23–62, especially 30.
35 Jardina, *White Identity Politics*, 215.
36 Jardina, *White Identity Politics*, 134, 136, see also 153. See also Robert P. Jones, *White Too Long: The Legacy of White Supremacy in American Christianity* (New York: Simon & Schuster, 2020), 158–163.
37 Ian Haney López, *Merge Left: Fusing Race and Class, Winning Elections, and Saving America* (New York: The New Press, 2019), 103–104, 186. See also Kermit Roosevelt III, *The Nation That Never Was: Reconstructing America's Story* (Chicago, IL: University of Chicago Press, 2022), 206, 223.
38 Timothy Shenk, "The Fiery Brilliance of Obama's Lost Book Manuscript," *New York Times*, October 9, 2022, SR4–5.
39 H.H. Gerth and C. Wright Mills, eds., "The Social Psychology of World Religions," in *From Max Weber: Essays in Sociology* (New York: Oxford University Press, 1958), part III, chap. II, 271.
40 CBS News Poll, June 18–22, 2014, https://www.pollingreport.com/race.htm.
41 See https://news.gallup.com/polls/1687/Race-Relations.aspx.
42 Litwack, *Trouble in Mind*, 11.
43 Giovanni Russonello, "Poll Watch: A 'Seismic Shift' in the Views on Racism in America," *New York Times*, June 6, 2020, A19. See also Nate Cohn and Kevin Quigley, "How Public Opinion Has Moved on Black Lives Matter," *New York Times* interactive, June 10, 2020.
44 "Special Report: Race in America," 1–12.
45 Kat Stafford and Hannah Fingerhut, AP, "Police Violence Still a High Concern," *Dallas Morning News*, May 22, 2021, A2. See also AP/NORC poll of 1,842 adults conducted April 29–May 3, 2021.

46 Sabrina Siddiqui, "Majority of Voters Say U.S. Society is Racist as Support Grows for Black Lives Matter," *Wall Street Journal*, July 21, 2020. See also Packer, *Last Best Hope*, 120.
47 Juliana Menasce Horowitz, "Most Americans Say the Legacy of Slavery Still Affects Black People in the U.S. Today," Fact Tank, Pew Research Center, June 17, 2019.
48 Lawrence D. Bobo and Camille Z. Charles, "Race in the American Mind: From the Moynihan Report to the Obama Candidacy," *The ANNALS, AAPSS* 621 (January 2009): 247–248.
49 Ann Harman and Sabrina Tavernise, "'Utterly Different Scene' at Protests as White Faces Turn Out in Droves," *New York Times*, June 13, 2020, A19. See also Christopher Sebastian Parker, "An American Paradox: Progress or Regress? BLM, Race, and Black Politics," *Perspectives on Politics* 20, no. 4 (December 2022): 1167.
50 Deja Thomas and Juliana Menasce Horowitz, "Support for Black Lives Matter Has Decreased Since June But Remains Strong Among Black Americans," Fact Tank, Pew Research Center, September 16, 2020.
51 https://civiqs.com/results/black_lives_matter?. See also Michael Tesler, "Why Republican Support for Peaceful Racial Justice Protests Was Short-Lived," *FiveThirtyEight.com*, December 7, 2021.
52 Fox News/Opinion Dynamics, March 28–29, 2001, N=905 registered voters nationwide.
53 Kevin Freking, AP, "Slavery Reparations Bill Poised to Advance," *Dallas Morning News*, April 5, 2021, A4.
54 Kurtis Lee, "California Contemplates Billions in Reparations," *New York Times*, December 2, 2022, A1, A17. See also Trip Gabriel, Maya King, Kurtis Lee, and Shawn Hubler, "Democrats Are in a Bind Over Reparation Calls," *New York Times*, May 28, 2023, A1, A14.
55 Susan Berfield and Jordyn Holman, "The Evanston Reparations Experiment," *BusinessWeek*, May 31, 2021.
56 Gallup, "Race Relations," https://news.gallup.com/poll/1687/Race-Relations.aspx.
57 Claude A. Clegg III, *The Black President: Hope and Fury in the Age of Obama* (Baltimore, MD: Johns Hopkins University Press, 2021).
58 ABC News/*Washington Post* Poll, June 12–15, 2008, N=1,125 adults nationwide; and January 12–15, 2010, N=1,083 adults nationwide. See https://pollingreport.com/race.htm.
59 Paul Steinhauser, "In Poll, African-Americans Say Election a 'Dream Come True,'" November 11, 2008, https://cnn.com/2008/POLITICS/11/11/obama.poll; CNN/Opinion Research Corporation Poll, January 12–15, 2009, N=1,245 adults nationwide. See https://www.pollingreport.com/race2.htm. See also Peniel E. Joseph, *The Third Reconstruction: America's Struggle for Racial Justice in the Twenty-First Century* (New York: Basic Books, 2022), 46.
60 Gallup Historical Trends, https://news.gallup.com/poll/1687/Race-Relations.aspx.
61 CNN/Opinion Research Corporation Poll, July 31–August 3, 2009, N=1,136 adults nationwide.
62 Barack Obama, *A Promised Land* (New York: Crown Books, 2020), 397.
63 Bloomberg Politics Poll, December 3–5, 2014, N=1,001, and CNN/ORC Poll, February 12–15, 2015, N=1,027. See https://www.pollingreport.com/race.htm. See also Gerstle, *American Crucible*, xiv.

64 Gallup, "Race Relations," https://news.gallup.com/poll/1687/Race-Relations.aspx.
65 Hart Research Associates/Public Opinion Strategies/Vision Strategy & Insights, Study #200356, NBC News/*Wall Street Journal* Survey, July 2020.
66 NBC News/*Wall Street Journal* Poll, August 10–14, 2019, N=1,000 adults nationwide.
67 Jonathan Martin, Maggie Haberman, and Katie Rogers, "Political Memo: As Americans Shift on Racism, President Digs In," *New York Times*, June 10, 2020, A1, A18. See also Glaude, *Begin Again*, 21.
68 Johnson, "Snide and Prejudice," *The Economist*, June 13, 2020, 68.

5
RACE, EDUCATION, AND SOCIAL COMPETITION

> "Those were wonderful days, directly after the war! Suddenly, as if at the sound of a trumpet, a whole race that had been slumbering for centuries in barbarism awoke and started off one morning for school."
> Booker T. Washington, 1910, "A University Education for Negroes"

Public education in America was a decidedly regional commitment, made by New England from the 1630s and the Old Northwest and Midwest after the Revolution, but abjured in the South until the 1870s and beyond. Over the course of the nation's history, public education experienced three major waves of expansion and innovation after independence. The first major wave, the common school or public grade school movement, spanned the late eighteenth century and most of the nineteenth century but did not reach much of the South, especially the rural South, until decades after the Civil War. The second wave, building slowly throughout the nineteenth century but only gaining momentum late in the century, was the public high school movement. The high school movement was not fully consolidated until the 1930s when the depression killed jobs and made staying in school the best option for many. The third major wave of educational expansion, the college movement, began early but built slowly. The Land Grant College Act, initiated by the Lincoln administration, spurred expansion but the real surge came with the post-World War II generation of G.I. college-goers and continued to build through the 1970s before slowing thereafter. [1]

At every stage of American history, the acknowledged importance of education for some, even if not initially for all, has been undercut and

DOI: 10.4324/9781003449188-5

disrupted by the cultural presumptions and practical politics of race. Over most of that history, race and region overlapped as nine in ten Black people lived in the South, and the South stood adamantly against public schools, especially for Blacks, slave or free. After the Civil War and Reconstruction, public schools did come to the South, on a segregated basis, but Black schools were funded at about half the level of White schools. The Civil Rights Revolution of the mid-twentieth century, including the monumental school desegregation case *Brown v. Board of Education* (1954), the Civil Rights Acts of 1964 and 1965, and the Elementary and Secondary Education Act of 1965, produced real progress. Segregation declined and school funding became more equal. However, since the 1980s, progress has stalled, segregation has steadily reasserted itself, and educational attainment by race, especially now at the college level, has stagnated.

Education in Early America

The movement for free public schools began in colonial New England, was then carried by settlers into the Old Northwest and then the Midwest, and then diffused slowly and unevenly through the South and West after the Civil War. There were always private tuition-driven schools for those who could afford more than the public schools offered or where no public schools yet existed. In the South, private schools were almost the only option until after the Civil War and even then, due to poverty and race, public schools arrived late and were accepted only with suspicion.[2]

The high school movement became the focus of educational reform in the late nineteenth and early twentieth centuries. The first public high schools in what would become the U.S. were the Boston Latin School (1635), the Hartford Public High School (1638), and the Cambridge Latin School (1648). Only twenty of the first hundred public high schools – the hundredth was not established until 1868 – were in the South and most of those were in the peripheral South. Fully twenty-five of the first hundred public high schools were located in Massachusetts. From the founding of the Boston Latin School through most of the nineteenth century, high schools, which usually started after what we would now think of as sixth grade, were designed for students intending to go directly to college, so their curricula focused on Greek, Latin, the classics, and the sciences broadly understood. Higher education also began in New England, with the founding of Harvard (1636), Yale (1701), and Princeton (1746). William and Mary (1693) stood virtually alone in the South until the founding of the University of Georgia (1785), the University of North Carolina (1789), and Jefferson's beloved University of Virginia (1819).

The North's commitment to public education was evident in the Northwest Ordinance of 1787. Written in the Confederation Congress as the Federal Convention of 1787 struggled through a hot Philadelphia summer to produce a new Constitution, the Northwest Ordinance laid out the political and social structure of the territory north of the Ohio River. Each town was to have a central square with a church on one end and a school on the other. Explaining and extolling the priority given to church and school in the territory, the Northwest Ordinance declared: "Religion, morality, and knowledge being necessary to good government and the happiness of mankind, schools and the means of education shall forever be encouraged." Just a few decades later Alexis de Tocqueville made a slightly different but closely related point, saying, "Town meetings are to liberty what primary schools are to science; they bring it within the people's reach, they teach men how to use and how to enjoy it."[3]

The South took a different, more elitist, view of education, reserving it mostly for those who could afford it. Wealthy plantation owners hired tutors for their children, perhaps the children of the White overseer, sometimes joining with neighboring plantations to share the cost, but in the largely rural and agricultural region, free public schools, even for White children, were uncommon. Moreover, at least seven states, Alabama, Georgia, both Carolinas, Louisiana, Missouri, and Virginia, made it illegal to educate slaves.[4]

By the mid-nineteenth century, even before the grade school boom, the U.S. had higher literacy rates and more children in school than any other nation in the world, but there were stark differences by region and by race. In 1857, North Carolina's Hinton Rowan Helper wrote a book entitled *The Impending Crisis of the South*, in which he highlighted the North's greater commitment to public education, noting that in Massachusetts, for instance, there were 1,462 public libraries; in Virginia, just 54. In Michigan, 417; in North Carolina, 38. Pennsylvania had 9,061 public schools; Mississippi, 782.[5] And no one will be surprised to hear that while Northern White citizens enjoyed more education and higher literacy rates than Southern White citizens, it was Black people, and especially enslaved Black people that suffered near complete denial of educational opportunity. The historians Roger Ransom and Richard Sutch reported that, "Probably no more than 2 to 5 percent of adolescent and adult slaves could read and write on the eve of the Civil War, and those were largely self-educated. In 1870, after emancipation, less than 10 percent of blacks over the age of twenty could read and write in the Five Cotton States. By contrast, over 80 percent of adult whites in those states were literate."[6]

Finally, it is critical to remember that while schools are important, so are what they teach and what they leave out. Even after the South began to provide public education in the closing decades of the nineteenth century, those schools taught the nobility of the Lost Cause and the destructive folly of Black citizenship and political participation.[7] Moreover, they did so in segregated schools in which funding levels and teacher pay in the Black schools were half what they were in the White schools, and hand-me-down textbooks, when they were available at all, taught lessons flattering to the White majority. As the author William Humphrey wrote in *No Resting Place* (1989): "History is heavily edited for schoolchildren and, for most of us, commencement puts an end to study. This way we go through life with notions of our past which, for depth, complexity, subtlety of shading, rank with comic books."[8] Here we try to provide a little more of that shading.

Schooling After Emancipation

Anticipation of better days was rampant among Black citizens after the Civil War, but defeated White southerners were sullen and angry. Thomas Woodrow Wilson (1856–1924), the nation's twenty-eighth president, was born in the South, raised mostly in Georgia during the Civil War and Reconstruction, before earning a B.A. from Princeton and a Ph.D. in history and political science from Johns Hopkins in 1886. He taught briefly at Bryn Mawr College and Wesleyan University before joining the Princeton faculty in 1890. He wrote regularly in scholarly journals, elite opinion magazines, and he published a number of widely read books. In 1902, Wilson was appointed President of Princeton, in 1910 he was elected governor of New Jersey, and in 1912 he defeated the incumbent president William Howard Taft and the former president Theodore Roosevelt to become President of the United States from 1913 to 1921. Wilson was one of the nation's intellectual leaders years before he went actively into politics.

So, the nation's White intellectual elite read closely when Wilson wrote a long article entitled, "The Reconstruction of the Southern States," in the January 1901 issue of *Atlantic Monthly*. Wilson spoke for most White citizens, North as well as South, when he endorsed the White South's rejection of Reconstruction and denigrated the Black South's hopes for freedom and equality. Critically, Wilson described the freedmen as "unpracticed in liberty, unschooled in self-control; . . . excited by a freedom they did not understand, exalted by false hopes; . . . sick of work, covetous of pleasure, – a host of dusky children untimely put out of school."[9] Wilson's White readers would have nodded along throughout. But his Black readers would have been saddened by most of it, until outraged by the final phrase, "a host of dusky children untimely put out of school," knowing that he meant not children but adults untimely put out of the school of slavery before

136 Race, Education, and Social Competition

their education in civilization was complete. In Wilson's mind, perhaps in the White American mind, the slaves had been freed too soon.

As a result, freedom brought euphoria and dread to Black Americans, especially in the South. The dread far outlasted the euphoria. As we noted in the headnote to this chapter, Black educator Booker T. Washington, founder and longtime President of the Tuskegee Institute, described the heady, euphoric postwar days; declaring: "Those were wonderful days, directly after the war! Suddenly, as if at the sound of a trumpet, a whole race that had been slumbering for centuries in barbarism awoke and started off one morning for school."[10] The dread arose both from an awareness that schools had to be built and teachers educated or found before they could begin their work and because White Southerners continued to oppose Black education both in principle and for what they took to be good practical reasons.

Table 5.1 displays the rise in enrollment, beginning just after the Civil War, first in elementary schools, then in high schools or secondary schools, and then in colleges and universities. Elementary school enrollments grew

TABLE 5.1 Enrollment in Elementary, Secondary, and Post-Secondary Schools, 1869–2023 (in thousands)

Year	Elementary K–8	Secondary 9–12	Post-Secondary	Total
1869	6,792	80	52	6,924
1879	9,757	110	116	9,983
1889	14,036	298	157	14,491
1899	16,225	630	238	17,093
1909	18,340	1,032	355	19,727
1919	20,864	2,414	598	23,876
1929	23,589	4,740	1,101	29,430
1939	20,985	7,059	1,494	29,538
1949	22,095	6,397	2,659	31,151
1959	31,551	9,306	3,640	44,497
1969	36,713	14,337	8,005	59,055
1985	31,229	13,750	12,247	57,226
1990	34,388	12,477	13,819	60,684
2000	38,592	14,781	15,312	68,685
2010	38,709	15,979	21,019	75,707
2020	38,551	16,818	18,992	74,361
2023	38,301	17,116	19,851	75,268

Source: National Center for Education Statistics, *Digest of Education Statistics*, Table 105.30, "Enrollment in Elementary, Secondary, and Postsecondary Institutions, . . . Selected Years, 1869–70 through 2030."

rapidly, more than doubling between 1869 and 1889, as a greater share of youngsters went to school. High schools were relatively few until the 1890s but enrollment exploded thereafter, growing eleven-fold between 1899 and 1939, while colleges and universities saw their most explosive growth in the 1960s and 1970s. Enrollment growth at all levels has slowed markedly since 2000.

When the guns fell silent and emancipation became the law, more than 95 percent of Black people were illiterate. Seventy-five percent remained illiterate at the end of the century, mainly because White Southerners wanted it that way. Henry Louis Gates, Jr. memorably quoted one Southern planter, who claimed to be quoting a "little colored girl," as observing that, "'You can't get clean corners and algebra into the same nigger.' . . . The world demands *clean corners*; it is not so particular about *algebra*."[11] More critical even than clean corners was a dependable supply of compliant field labor and "Illiteracy . . . helped to trap the black farmer in southern agriculture."[12] An academic justification and gloss was put on these attitudes and convictions by the British polymath Herbert Spencer and his North American social Darwinist allies, led by Yale's William Graham Sumner. Spencer was the dominant social scientist of the mid-nineteenth century, publishing *Principles of Psychology* in 1855 and following that many other books with his massive *Principles of Sociology* in 1873. Spencer reported approvingly that one of the reasons offered in the U.S. for not educating Black children along with White children was that they steadily fell behind, "their intellects being apparently incapable of being cultured beyond a particular point."[13] White Southerners were untroubled by Spencer's conclusions as Black training, if not education, could and always had encompassed just two economic roles: domestic service, those clean corners, and fieldwork. Only a few Black people worked as teachers, doctors, tradesmen, or skilled craftsmen, always serving the Black community.

After the war, a few schools were set up by Black freedmen and before long Northern missionaries and teachers began to arrive. The U.S. government's Freedmen's Bureau established more than a thousand primary schools and several colleges, including Atlanta University, Fisk University, and Howard University, between 1865 and its dismantlement in 1872.[14] By the end of 1865, 90,000 Black students were enrolled in Freedmen's schools and, though funding and attendance began to wane by 1870, the Black quest for education did not abate. Nonetheless, when Reconstruction itself ended in 1877 and Southern White control of state governments was restored across the region, many Black schools were closed and state funding was steadily squeezed for those that remained.

138 Race, Education, and Social Competition

Education of students, then and now, was and is directly impacted by the strengths and deficiencies of the families and communities from which the students come. While enthusiasm for school is important, precursors to effective learning are either present or not when the child first passes through the schoolhouse door. Literate, financially stable parents can help students in myriad ways that illiterate, impoverished parents simply cannot. Moreover, family and community strengths and deficiencies, perhaps especially deficiencies, can constrain outcomes literally for generations especially if the education delivered is itself poor.

The 1870 census was the first in which Black people were recorded as citizens and the details of their lives, including education and literacy levels, were noted along with those of White people. The 1870 census found that 80 percent of Black Americans ten and older nationally, and 84 percent of Southern Black Americans, were illiterate, as were 11.5 percent of White Americans and, again, a higher proportion (15.5 percent) of Southern White Americans. Illiteracy rates for Black Americans ten and over nationally were 70 percent in 1880, while for Southern Black Americans they were 72 percent. By 1900, 45 percent of Black Americans nationally and 51 percent in the South were illiterate.[15]

Illiteracy, especially in the South, fell slowly for several reasons. Mainly it was because illiterate adults usually remained illiterate, rarely

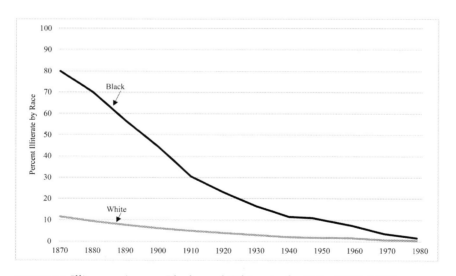

FIGURE 5.1 Illiteracy Among Blacks and Whites in the U.S., 1870–1979

Source: National Center for Education Statistics, *120 Years of American Education: A Statistical Portrait*, January 1993, 21, Table 6, https://nces.ed.gov/pubs93/93442.pdf.

learning to read and write later in life. So only young people remaining in school at least through third grade added much to the literate population, which was a slow year-to-year accretion.[16] In 1900, while 45 percent of Black people reaching ten years old in the South were illiterate, 87 percent of their grandparents who had reached ten in the 1830s remained illiterate.

A second powerful reason for stubbornly high illiteracy rates among the Black population was that White people preferred Black people to remain illiterate. Critically, White Americans were concerned that education would render Black people unfit for local purposes – so they acted to limit their education. As the historian David Levering Lewis explained, "The creed of the 1890s held that it was a dangerous conceit to expose black people" to too much education, "thereby 'spoiling' them for the natural order of southern society in which their place was as . . . industrious farmhands, primary school teachers, and occasional merchants."[17] One Arkansas planter in 1900 explained: "My experience has been that when one of the younger class gets so he can read and write and cipher, he wants to go to town. It is rare to find one who can read and write and cipher in the field at work."[18] Not only did literate Black people leave the fields for town, often they just kept going. White Southerners knew that "migration and education were positively correlated . . . and disproportionate shares of black migrants were literate."[19]

Other Southern leaders had deeper and more visceral concerns. Jefferson's fear of race war was still very much on White southern minds. J. Thomas "Cotton Tom" Heflin, delegate to the Alabama Constitutional Convention of 1901, declared that Black education was foolishly dangerous because "some day the clash will come . . . I do not believe it is incumbent upon us to lift him up and educate him on an equal footing that he may be armed and equipped when the combat comes."[20] Heflin's concerns were not uncommon. His performance in the convention helped him become Alabama Secretary of State in 1903, member of the U.S. House from 1904 to 1920, and U.S. Senator from 1920 to 1931. Heflin was no outlier, he became political royalty in Alabama. His White supremacist views did not detract from his prestige, they were its foundation. Cotton Tom's nephew, Howell T. Heflin, served in the Senate from 1978 to 1996.

Nor could Black Americans look to the federal courts when Southern states denied them equal educational opportunities. The case that eventually reached the U.S. Supreme Court as *Cumming v. Richmond County Board of Education* (1899) from Georgia, Alabama's neighbor to the east, made that clear. In 1890, the high school movement was just getting underway across the nation and still unsettlingly new in the South.

Just 6 percent of young people received a high school diploma in 1890 and only about 0.5 percent of young Black people did. Ware High School in Augusta, Georgia, was the only high school in the state open to Black students. When finances tightened, the Richmond County School Board closed Ware in order to better serve the White students in the district. Just two years after the Supreme Court decided in *Plessy v. Ferguson* (1896) that Louisiana and other states could enforce "separate but equal" train travel so long as both Black and White people had access to the trains, the *Cumming* case arrived at the High Court. John Marshall Harlan, the lone dissenter in the *Plessy* case, which might have given the plaintiffs some hope, wrote for a unanimous Court. With Ware closed, there was no Black high school, so the Court found no violation of the Fourteenth Amendment's equal protection clause – poof! Justice Harlan held that, "the education of people in schools maintained by state taxation is a matter belonging to the respective states." Justice Harlan then mockingly told the plaintiffs that if they had presented evidence that "the board's refusal to maintain . . . [a black high school] was in fact an abuse of its discretion and in hostility to the colored population because of their race, different questions might have arisen in the state court."[21] Apparently, Justice Harlan thought the plaintiffs had neglected to mention that they believed they and their children had been discriminated against in violation of the Fourteenth Amendment because of their race.[22] Such condescension toward Black people by the federal courts has been common throughout American history.

Where schools did stay open, attendance and per capita student funding varied dramatically by race. School attendance improved faster than school funding for obvious reasons: freed Black Americans sought schooling for which White Americans were reluctant to pay. As historians William Collins and Robert Margo observed:

> In 1870, approximately half of white children . . . had attended school during the . . . year but only 9.1 percent of black children had attended school. Regional breakdowns reveal that black and white attendance rates were considerably lower in the South (7.4 percent for blacks, 31 percent for whites) than outside the South (34.4 for blacks, 60.1 percent for whites). . . . The [national attendance] rate for blacks more than doubled between 1870 and 1880, and it doubled again between 1880 and 1910.

Southern attendance rates for Black children increased more than six-fold, from 7 percent in 1870 to 45 percent in 1910, while they doubled for White children, rising from 31 percent to 62 percent.[23]

Black schoolchildren in the South after Reconstruction, and even more so after Black men were forced out of the electorate, suffered from two invidious spending gaps. First, by 1890 schools in the North spent an average of twice as much per pupil as schools in the South. And as David Levering Lewis has noted, "If the North-South gap in educational expenditures was great, a comparable gap grew with each passing year between public money spent for the education of white and black children below the Mason-Dixon line. By 1900, the average was twice as much for white children, and in the following decade the disparity would widen cruelly."[24] Similar gaps existed between salaries paid to White and Black teachers in the nation and its Southern region and they too grew after 1900. Against this determined opposition to Black education, even those few White Americans, such as Jabez Curry of Virginia, who had worked actively on behalf of the cause withdrew from the fight, giving the regional consensus its way.[25]

Education and Race from Jim Crow to *Brown v. Board*

At the dawn of the twentieth century, banks of darkening clouds still hung over the South. Blacks had been squeezed from the electorate and Whites were intently locking down Jim Crow. One-fifth of White Southerners and half of Black Southerners were illiterate, schools were poor throughout the region, and Black schools and teachers received half the funding and pay that White schools and teachers in the region received.[26] Improvements came slowly between 1910 and 1940. Scholars have shown that per-pupil expenditures in Southern schools as a percentage of the U.S. average largely held steady in several states. Alabama spent 33 percent of the national average in 1910 and 37 percent in 1940; Arkansas slipped back from 37 percent to 34 percent; Georgia advanced tentatively from 38 percent to 42 percent; while Mississippi held firm at 31 percent from 1910 to 1940. Other Southern states did better; Florida improved from 51 percent to 71 percent; North Carolina advanced from 28 percent to 49 percent; while others watched and waited.[27] National institutions did little to push the South toward educational equity.

The full social and economic mobilization of World War II finally brought its own insistent demand for change. Mobilization was an all-hands-on-deck call to American young adults, men for the military and more young women than ever before for industry. Strikingly, the National Education Association (NEA) reported that 12 percent of potential military recruits nationally were rejected for illiteracy and that eight states, all in the South – South Carolina, Louisiana, Georgia, Mississippi, Alabama, Arkansas, Virginia, and North Carolina – had their recruits rejected at twice the national rate.[28] The NEA report drew a straight line from low per capita spending to illiteracy and rejection from military service. Similar educational limitations affected those who attempted to join the industrial effort to fight and win the war. Southern state leaders increasingly came to realize that dedication to Jim Crow, with its vast inequalities between urban and rural schools and Black and White schools, had left their region far behind in the educational race for economic competitiveness. What, given the region's commitment to White supremacy and racial segregation, could they do?

Another heavy blow to Southern pride was delivered by President Harry S. Truman's 1947 Commission on Higher Education for American Democracy. Just as millions of G.I.'s, mostly White, were pouring onto college and university campuses barely prepared to receive them, the Truman Commission projected that within little more than a decade half of American youth, including many women, might benefit from college training. The Commission, while not mentioning the South directly, wrote: "If the ladder of educational opportunity rises high at the doors of some youth and scarcely rises at all at the doors of others, while at the same time formal education is made a prerequisite to occupational and social advance, then education may become the means, not of eliminating race and class distinctions, but of deepening and solidifying them."[29] The South realized itself to be at a crucial juncture; it wanted racial segregation but knew increasingly that it needed educational advancement. For another decade and a half, it struggled, unsuccessfully, to have both. The 1950 census found that: "Thirteen states had populations greater than 10 percent black, and all thirteen of those states had racially segregated schools."[30] All were in the greater South. Finally, a study conducted during the early 1950s declared that "Through much of the South, a public-school system hardly existed. The funding disparity between urban and rural schools and between white and black schools created great unevenness."[31]

Black teachers were paid less than White teachers in the late nineteenth century and the gap stayed wide into the 1940s. Historian Robert Margo's benchmark study of teachers' salaries in seven Southern states in 1910 found that Black salaries ranged from 49 percent to 59 percent of White salaries. Margo also found that within states, Black teacher salaries were lower the higher the proportion of the Black population within the school district.[32] Little changed in school funding generally or teacher salaries specifically until World War II; then war mobilization brought rapid change. Margo reported that between 1942 and 1954 Black teachers' salaries jumped from 61 percent to 92 percent of White teachers' salaries, while per pupil expenditures for Black students jumped from 45 percent in 1940 to 78 percent of funding for White students in 1954.[33] After the war, pressure to become more economically competitive continued to force educational

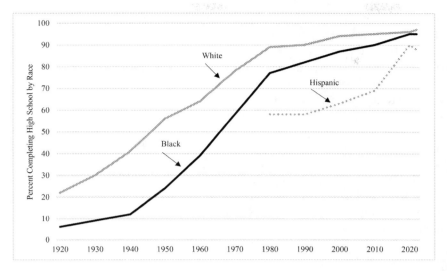

FIGURE 5.2 High School Completion by Age (25–29), Race, and Ethnicity, 1920–2022

Source: *Digest of Education Statistics*, 2022, Table 104.20, "High School Completion – Persons 25–29," https://nces.ed.gov/programs/digest/d22/tables/dt22_104.20.asp.

and other social reforms on the South. The Supreme Court decision in *Brown v. Board*, handed down in May 1954, added to the pressures for change, but resistance remained stout.

Nonetheless, visible progress was made on some fronts, probably most importantly on high school graduation rates. Few Americans went to and graduated from high school before the early twentieth century. Figure 5.2 shows that gaps in high school graduation rates by race and ethnicity narrowed over the course of the twentieth century. In 1920, 22 percent of White people aged 25 to 29 years old had graduated from high school, while just 6 percent of young Black people had graduated. As late as 1950, more than twice as many White people as Black people (56 percent to 24) graduated, but then the gap began to close, though some differences by region and race remained and still remain.[34] By 1980 the gap had shrunk to 12 percent, 8 percent by 1990, 7 percent by 2000, 5 percent by 2010, and just two points in the most recent data. These important gains were not uncontested and the fight continues.

Brown v. Board and the Civil Rights Era

The constitutional doctrine that "separate but equal" public facilities were no violation of the Fourteenth Amendment's "equal protection of the laws" clause, established in *Plessy v. Ferguson* (1896), held into the mid-1930s and then slowly began to crumble. In a series of cases dealing with segregation in higher education, including *In re Gaines* (1938), *McLaurin v. Oklahoma* (1950), and *Sweatt v. Painter* (1950), the Supreme Court held that separate but equal required that states offering graduate programs to White students must also offer them to Black students. Simultaneously, a series of public school cases required that Black and White public schools must increasingly be equal in facilities, funding, curricula, and teacher pay. In the early 1950s, seventeen states, mostly in the broader South and the District of Columbia, mandated separate schools for Black students and White students. Other states fostered racially segregated schools through a variety of devices, including strategically placing schools in the middle of racially discrete neighborhoods, without legally mandating racial segregation.[35]

The landmark public school desegregation case was *Brown v. Board of Education of Topeka, Kansas* (1954). *Brown v. Board* was actually a set of four similar cases raising the fundamental question: can racially separate schools, even when they are truly equal, provide the equal protection of the laws guaranteed to all Americans, including schoolchildren? In the lore that surrounds *Brown v. Board*, great attention has been paid to the fact that the NAACP's lead counsel, Thurgood Marshall, later to be Solicitor General of the United States (1965–1967) and the first Black Justice on the High Court (1967–1991), argued for the plaintiffs. Marshall won twenty-nine of the thirty-two cases he argued before the Supreme Court. Less remarked upon is the fact that the defendants, mostly Southern states, were represented by John W. Davis of West Virginia. Davis, who would be dead within a year, was and long had been one of the nation's leading corporate and constitutional lawyers. Davis had been Solicitor General of the United States (1913–1918) in the Woodrow Wilson administration, Ambassador to the United Kingdom (1918–1921), and the Democratic party nominee for president in 1924. Davis' presidential defeat led him back to the law. Over six decades he argued 140 cases before the Supreme Court, seventy-three as Solicitor General and sixty-seven as a private attorney. Most famously, Davis represented the winning side in *Youngstown Sheet and Tube Co. v. Sawyer* in which the Court ruled against President Truman's wartime seizure of the nation's steel industry. Both Marshall and Davis were formidable advocates.

President Eisenhower, a Republican, had campaigned hard in the South in 1952 and knew he would have to do so again in 1956. Eisenhower worried that his recent appointee and fellow Republican, Chief Justice Earl Warren, a Californian, might not appreciate the social and political implications of the *Brown* case, so at a White House dinner Eisenhower had the states' rights Democrat Davis seated next to Warren. After the dinner, Eisenhower took Warren briefly aside, praised Davis again as he had during the dinner, and observed that White Southerners "are not bad people. All they are concerned about is to see that their sweet little girls are not required to sit in school alongside some big black bucks."[36]

In the face of deeply ambivalent official and public opinion, the Supreme Court unanimously decided that racially separate schools were inherently and unconstitutionally unequal. Chief Justice Warren's opinion, in overturning *Plessy* and a long train of legal precedents that flowed from it, drew on psychological, sociological, and political arguments leading to the conclusion that racially separate schools were damaging to Black children. Warren wrote that: "Segregation of white and colored children in public schools has a detrimental effect upon the colored children." Therefore, Warren concluded, "in the field of public education the doctrine of separate but equal has no place. Separate educational facilities are inherently unequal. . . . The plaintiffs . . . have been deprived of the equal protection of the laws guaranteed by the Fourteenth Amendment." Finally, Warren argued, much as Gunnar Myrdal had in *The American Dilemma* (1944), that White children's commitment to American values was at risk from segregation just as much or more than were those of Black children. Citing contemporary social science, Warren warned that "confusion, conflict, moral cynicism, and disrespect for authority may arise in children as a consequence of being taught the moral, religious and democratic principles of justice and fair play by the same persons and institutions who seem to be acting in a prejudiced and discriminatory manner."[37]

Eisenhower supported the Court's ruling in *Brown v. Board* only very reluctantly and in 1955 the Court decided *Brown II*, the implementation schedule, allowing states and their school districts to proceed "with all deliberate speed." Many in the South and beyond sensed a lack of commitment to school desegregation on the part of federal authorities. Some districts in the Upper South proceeded to desegregate, but the Lower South, the states of the old Confederacy, dug in for what came to be a fifteen-year struggle known in the history books as Massive Resistance. Moreover, a resentful public, North and South, worried about what change might mean for their children and communities. The law professor and historian of education Justin Driver reported that a poll conducted by *Scientific American* in December 1956 asked whether most Black people were being treated fairly in the U.S.; 79 percent of White Southerners and 65 percent of White Northerners responded that Black people were being treated fairly. A Gallup poll in 1959 found a majority responding that states should be able to decide whether their schools were segregated by race or not.[38] When John F. Kennedy succeeded Eisenhower as president, advocates for social change saw a warmer countenance but little real change as Kennedy sensed the same sullen resistance as Eisenhower had.

Following President Kennedy's assassination in Dallas, Texas, in November 1963, Vice President Lyndon B. Johnson assumed the presidency with the mission of energizing and expanding Kennedy's domestic policy programs, especially in the fraught domain of civil and voting rights for the nation's long-suffering minorities. Johnson was an unlikely volunteer for this mission; a rough cut Southern senator from Texas, former Senate majority leader, and initially reluctant vice presidential candidate, he was, on the other hand, a legislative mastermind. Once he had secured his own election as president in 1964, he triggered a legislative avalanche that included the Civil Rights Act of 1965, the Voting Rights Act of 1965, the Elementary and Secondary Education Act (ESEA) of 1965, and much more. Though the title alone might not suggest it, the ESEA was as important for integration and equal school funding as the Voting Rights Act was for minority political participation and officeholding.

The ESEA provided federal education funds to school districts with large numbers of low-income students, many of them in the South, providing that the districts were operating on a non-discriminatory basis. Many were not, of course, so poor Southern school districts faced the excruciating

TABLE 5.2 Percent of Black Elementary and Secondary School Students Going to School with Any White Students in Eleven Southern States, 1954–1973

Year	Percentage	Year	Percentage
1954–55	0.001	1964–65	2.25
1955–56	0.115	1965–66	6.1
1956–57	0.144	1966–67	15.9
1957–58	0.151	1967–68	25.8
1958–59	0.132	1968–69	39.6
1959–60	0.160	1969–70	62.0
1960–61	0.162	1970–71	84.3
1961–62	0.241	1971–72	87.8
1962–63	0.453	1972–73	91.3
1963–64	1.170		

Note: The states are Alabama, Arkansas, Florida, Georgia, Louisiana, Mississippi, North Carolina, South Carolina, Tennessee, Texas, and Virginia. Author estimates for 1969–1970 and 1971–1972 interpolated from surrounding data.

Sources: 1954–1967: Southern Education Reporting Service, "A Statistical Summary, State by State, of Segregation-Desegregation in the Southern and Border Area from 1954 to Present," 2, 40–44; 1968–1973: U.S. Bureau of the Census, *Statistical Abstract of the United States, 1971, 1975,* Table 176, 206.

choice of maintaining segregation and foregoing the federal money – or opening up. Many held out into the early 1970s, all the time watching money flow to other districts, until they grumblingly succumbed.[39] The most striking result of the movement of the Congress and executive branch into the civil rights fight in support of the courts was that the percentage of Black schoolchildren attending school with White children in the South rose from 1.2 percent in 1963 to 91.3 percent in 1972. By 1972, 44 percent of Black students in the South were attending majority White schools. These proportions were the highest in the nation.

Sadly, and not for the first time in our history, judicial backsliding began soon after the floodtide of the Great Society had run its course. In *Milliken v. Bradley* (1974), a Detroit area school busing case, the Supreme Court held that courts could not mandate multi-district, area-wide busing plans to desegregate schools unless those school districts could be shown to have caused the segregation. Busing for desegregation continued in some districts into the 1980s, but the Reagan administration's increasing opposition to busing slowly turned the tide against it. After a series of decisions in the 1990s released school districts from court-ordered desegregation plans, the *coup de grâce* to purposeful school desegregation was administered by Chief Justice John Roberts in the 2007 case *Parents Involved in Community Schools v. Seattle School District #1*. Seattle school administrators used student school assignments to balance campus populations by race. Writing for a narrow 5–4 majority, Roberts found against the school district and its student assignment plan, famously saying that "The way to stop discrimination on the basis of race is to stop discriminating on the basis of race."[40]

Scholars have sought to measure the impact on the racial composition of schools of removing tools designed to promote desegregation. Not surprisingly, studies find a slow resegregation of public schools, especially in the nation's large urban school districts. One major study released by a research collaboration between the University of Southern California and Stanford, reported a "Segregation Index" tracking data from 1991 through 2020. Segregation in large U.S. school districts increased by 35 percent over the three decades after 1991 and seems unlikely to turn around without policies and programs carefully designed to make it do so.[41]

Public authorities, from Congress to local school boards, have largely stood by while public schools resegregated. The legal scholar Sheryll Cashin has reported that, "Public schools are more racially segregated than they have been at any point in the last fifty years. Most Black and Latinx public school students attend majority-minority schools. Nearly 40 percent of Black students attend schools . . . with more than 90 percent students of color."[42] A 2019 Gallup poll asked respondents whether they thought "racial concentration or segregation in U.S. public schools" was a very serious, moderately serious, or not very serious problem. Very or moderately serious were the choices of 57 percent of adults, while not very serious was chosen by 41 percent. But two-thirds of Black and Latino respondents chose very or moderately serious, while only half of White respondents did. Three-quarters of Black and Hispanic respondents said the government should do more, while only 43 percent of White respondents agreed.[43] White Americans are far more likely to decry segregation, or inequality more broadly, than they are to approve specific policies for redressing them.

As always, racial segregation isolates minority students and makes them vulnerable in myriad ways. For example, the 2020–2022 COVID-19 pandemic hit poor and minority students and school districts harder than wealthier students and districts. Researchers at Harvard and Brown analyzed COVID-era school performance and found that "student progress in math decreased by about half in classrooms located in low-income ZIP codes, by a third in . . . middle-income ZIP codes and not at all in high-income ZIP codes. . . . because of disparities in access to computers, home internet connections and direct instruction from teachers."[44] Parents, scholars, and public officials were well aware of the close connections between race, wealth, and education long before COVID exacerbated these problems and made them more starkly visible.

Race and the Rise of Higher Education in the U.S.

Very few Americans of any race went to college during the nineteenth century. The proportion of seventeen-year-olds graduating from high school each year did not break 3 percent until 1890 but two-thirds of those went on to college and they were overwhelmingly White. Colleges were generally fed by the growing number of urban public and private high schools around the country, while the prestigious private colleges and universities in the East were fed by a small number of private boarding schools catering to the WASP elite. Admissions decisions to the elite colleges and universities hinged on the right private school roots, social status, wealth, and the family's history with the institution.

Earlier we noted that the colonists of early New England founded public schools and private schools and colleges soon after stepping off the ships from England. Other colonies in the Middle Atlantic and Upper South follow later. A thin stream of Black college graduates, beginning with Alexander Twilight of Vermont's Middlebury College, totaled about forty by 1865; all from colleges in the North and Midwest. A few Black colleges were established in the North, including Pennsylvania's Lincoln University

(1854) and Ohio's Wilberforce University (1856). Kentucky's Berea College was explicitly established as an interracial college in 1855. Then in the wake of the Civil War, the Freedmen's Bureau helped establish more Black colleges, including Atlanta University (1865), Fisk University (1867), and Howard University (1867). The Lincoln administration's Morrill Land Grant College Act (1862, renewed and expanded in 1890), so critical to the establishment and growth of White colleges and universities, largely ignored Black colleges. And things were even bleaker in regard to Black higher education in the South. W.E.B. Du Bois, the first Black Ph.D. from Harvard in 1895, declared in 1898 that: "There does not exist to-day . . . a single first-class fully equipped institution devoted to the higher education of Negroes; not more than three Negro institutions in the South deserve the name of *college* at all."[45] Only 3 percent of college students were Black as late as 1947 and 85 percent of them attended one of 105 historically Black colleges and universities (HBCUs).[46]

The elitist roots of American higher education eroded slowly over the depression era of the 1930s and then more rapidly after World War II when the G.I. Bill brought millions of veterans to campus, most of them White but many the first in their family to attend college. Grades and test scores, as opposed to family background, did not become critical until mid-century.[47] The three decades between the mid-1940s and the late 1970s saw a remarkable expansion, though not exactly democratization, of American higher education. Institutions expanded while struggling to meet the new demand, admissions requirements were modest, and state governments stepped up with public funding allowing tuition paid by students and families to remain low.

At the national level, Congress passed and presidents signed the G.I. Bill (1944) – officially titled the Servicemen's Readjustment Act – the National Defense Education Act (1958), and the Higher Education Act (1965), including the critical Pell Grant program of college loans to students with financial needs. The broad intent of these programs, as described by President Lyndon B. Johnson at the signing of the Higher Education Act at Southwest Texas State College, his alma mater, was to make a new and explicit promise to the nation's students; Johnson encouraged the nation's parents to "look into the faces of your students and your children and your grandchildren . . . Tell them that a promise has been made to them. Tell them that the leadership of your country believes it is the obligation of your Nation to provide and permit and assist every child born in these borders to receive all the education that he can take." For many White students, much of what the President said rang true; less so for Black and other minority students. They were generally denied access to the G.I. Bill. Having emerged from their still segregated high schools, they were less well prepared, and their families were much less able to help them shoulder the costs.[48] For Black and other minority Americans, the door to college was not exactly open, but it was no longer locked.

The 1940s through the 1970s was an era of unprecedented access to college for young, mostly White, Americans. College was cheap to middle-class students and families and help affording it was increasingly available to those needing it. The economists Claudia Goldin and Lawrence F. Katz wrote that: "College costs relative to family income came down rapidly in the 1940s and 1950s as incomes soared and college tuition rose more slowly. Both tuition and family income increased at about the same rate from the 1950s to 1980. . . . During the great expansion of college-going from the 1950s to the 1970s, tuition at a public university was about 4 percent of the median family income."[49] College costs remained manageable for students and families because state governments stepped up to support public colleges and universities with public funds. The lawyer and progressive advocate Heather McGhee has written that: "In 1976, state governments provided six out of every ten dollars of the cost of students attending public colleges. The remainder translated into modest tuition bills – just $617 at a four-year college in 1976, and a student could receive a federal Pell Grant for as much as $1,400 against that and living expenses."[50] In the mid-1970s, Pell Grants paid almost 80 percent of tuition, fees, and living expenses of the average four-year state college. These investments by national and state governments and by students and their families paid huge dividends, making the U.S.'s educational attainment levels the highest in the world. Political scientist Suzanne Mettler observed that: "In the middle decades of the twentieth century, the United States experienced a meteoric rise in the rate of people earning four-year college degrees, as it soared from 6 percent of twenty-five to twenty-nine-year-olds in 1947 to 22.5 percent in 1977" – quadrupling over just thirty years.[51] Critically though, even during these decades of growth in higher education, Blacks and other minorities started with lower high school graduation rates, limited access to government assistance programs, and family incomes only 50 to 60 percent of White family incomes. And then, as minorities finally began working their way over and around these hurdles, the rules of the game changed to everyone's detriment, especially theirs.

The 1980s brought a reassessment of the scope, role, and responsibilities of government, federal and state, that continued through the first two decades of the twenty-first century. Enrollment stagnated, government support shrank, tuition costs rose faster than inflation or family incomes, student debt became an increasing concern, and the numbers of students earning degrees plateaued and then began a renewed but slower rise. Instead of the 80 percent of tuition, fees, room, and board that Pell Grants covered in 1976, Pell Grants covered just half of the average four-year college bill for tuition, fees, room, and board by 1988 and by 2020 it covered just 29 percent.[52] In 2018, the National Center for Higher Education Management Systems reported that the percent of family income needed to pay for a year at a public four-year institution was 18.2 percent.[53] Meanwhile, state appropriations declined by 14.6 percent, adjusted for inflation, between 2001 and 2020.[54]

A majority of state colleges now rely on tuition for a majority of their funding. Though the percent of twenty-five to twenty-nine year olds earning a B.A. increased from 6 percent in 1940 to 22.5 percent in 1980, 29 percent by 2000, and 39 percent by 2021, the doors were not equally open to everyone. As the philosopher and ethicist Michael Sandel reported, the nation's elite universities went from admitting about 20 percent of applicants in the early 1980s to about 5 percent by 2019.[55] More importantly, even at the public universities that most students attend, more and more of the cost of attendance fell on students and their families. Suzanne Mettler and many others have concluded that, "our system of higher education has gone from facilitating upward mobility to exacerbating social inequality."[56]

Table 5.3 highlights differences in educational attainment, B.A. or higher, by race and ethnicity over the past eight decades. In 1940 and 1950, young White people attained college degrees at more than three times the rate that young Black people did. In the half century beginning in 1960, White people earned college degrees at twice the rate Black people did and

TABLE 5.3 Percent of Persons 25 to 29 with B.A. or Higher by Race and Ethnicity, 1940–2022

Year	Total	White	Black	Hispanic	Asian
1940	5.9	6.4	1.6		
1950	7.7	8.2	2.8		
1960	11.0	11.8	5.4		
1970	16.4	17.3	10.0		
1980	22.5	25.0	11.6	7.7	
1990	23.2	26.4	13.4	8.1	
2000	29.1	34.0	17.8	9.7	
2010	31.7	38.6	19.4	13.5	55.8
2020	39.2	44.6	27.7	24.9	72.0
2022	39.6	45.5	28.3	25.0	71.6

Source: Department of Education, National Center for Education Statistics, *Digest of Education Statistics*, Table 104.20, "Percent of Persons 25 to 29 with Selected Levels of Educational Attainment, by Race/Ethnicity," https://nces.ed.gov/programs/digest/d21/tables/dt21_104.20.asp.

at three times the rate Hispanics did. Asians enter our data in 2010 at rates 50 percent higher than White people. In the most recent data, White people earned degrees at rates 1.6 times and 1.8 times higher than Black people and Hispanics did.

Not surprisingly, as college has gotten more expensive for students and their families, questions have been raised about whether college is "worth it" and what might be done to limit or redirect the cost. Studies have repeatedly found that college is worth it, but that care must be taken with where you go to school, what major you choose, and how much debt you take on. Holders of a B.A. earn about $78,000 annually, those in cities earn $95,000, compared to the average high school grad who earns $45,000. And, as always, incomes vary by race and ethnicity even for those with the same level of education.[57]

Race and Issues in Contemporary American Education

The civil rights battles of the 1950s and 1960s produced a conservative backlash. As a result, American education, both public education and higher education, has languished since the late 1970s. After decades of rapid growth, high school graduation rates in the U.S. dropped from 77 percent in 1970 to as low as 67.5 in 1997, before slowly rising to 87 in 2020. Moreover, the percentage of high school graduates who went on to college the next year also languished. From 52 percent in 1970, to 60 percent in 1990, a high point of 70.1 percent was attained in 2009, before dropping to 62.7 in 2021 due to rising costs and the pandemic. In the cases both of high school graduation rates and college attendance rates, family wealth and income have come to play larger and larger roles.

Because public elementary and secondary schools are financed with a mix of local property taxes, state funds, and about 10 percent federal money, schools in wealthy, usually White, neighborhoods start out way ahead. Wealthy communities tend to draw their school district boundaries strategically to include high property value neighborhoods and exclude poor neighborhoods. State and federal funds often reduce financial disparities between rich and poor neighborhoods and their public schools, but they by no means eliminate them. Stunningly, the journalist George Packer has reported that, "By kindergarten, upper-class children are already a full two years ahead of their lower-class counterparts, and the achievement gap is almost unbridgeable."[58] Unbridgeable because inequalities build from school year to school year. Cashin has disclosed that in 2016, "overwhelmingly white school districts received $23 billion more in state and local funding than majority non-white districts that service about the same number of children."[59] Schools serving wealthy families and neighborhoods experience robust high school graduation and college attendance rates, while those serving poor families and neighborhoods struggle.

Similar dynamics of race and class are evident in higher education. Race and class hierarchies privilege some, almost always Whites and more recently Asian students, and challenge or exclude others, usually Black and Hispanic students.[60] The higher up those hierarchies you look, the Whiter and wealthier they become. Suzanne Mettler has noted that "students from high income backgrounds increasingly attend elite private universities and colleges and the flagship public universities – those with national and international reputations."[61] More than a decade ago, *New York Times* columnist Frank Bruni wrote that "roughly 75 percent of the students at the 200 most highly rated colleges came from families in the top quartile of income. . . . Only 5 percent came from families in the bottom quartile."[62] More recently, Michael Sandel made the same point, writing that: "more than two-thirds of students at Ivy League schools come from the top 20 percent of the income scale; . . . Despite generous financial aid policies, fewer than 4 percent of Ivy League students came from the bottom fifth." Sandel concluded that, "higher education has become a sorting machine that promises mobility on the basis of merit but entrenches privilege."[63] As always, wealth means resiliency and poverty means vulnerability.

During the COVID-19 pandemic, minority students, always living closer to the financial edge, left college or failed to go straight from high school to college in greater number than White students. Total undergraduate enrollment dropped 9.4 percent between spring 2020 and spring 2022. Predictably, enrollment at elite colleges and flagship public universities, with the mostly White and financially privileged student bodies, held up well, enrollment at regional four-year schools and community colleges, where most minority students go, fell furthest. Even more predictably, when new first-time student enrollment began a modest recovery in spring 2022, Black enrollments continued falling.[64]

Not only does college attendance vary by class and race, so do rates of college completion. The six-year graduation rate for students entering college seeking a B.A. in 1996 was 55 percent. Sixty-three percent of the cohort entering college in 2013 had earned a B.A. by 2019. Over this quarter century period, a greater percentage of White than Hispanic and Black students earned their degrees within six years of entry. Of the 1996 cohort, 58 percent of White students, 46 percent of Hispanic students, and 39 percent of Blacks students earned their B.A.s within six years. Of the 2013 cohort, 67 percent of White students, 58 percent of Hispanic students, and 44 percent of Black students earned their degrees by the six-year mark. Just as importantly, students in the 2013 cohort, graduating by 2019, won degrees at much higher rates in the more prestigious colleges and universities. Universities accepting 25 percent or less of their applicants saw 89 percent of their students graduate in six years or less. Schools admitting 50 to 75 percent of applicants graduated almost 65 percent of their admittees, but open enrollment schools, those that admit all applicants, graduated just 29 percent of theirs within six years.[65]

As we have come to expect, there are great differences in median income by both education level and race, showing that more education is valuable economically for all races, but not equally valuable for all races. The U.S. Bureau of Labor Statistics provides excellent data back to 1979. First, in 1980, adults twenty-five and over with a B.A. degree or higher enjoyed wages 41.4 percent higher than those with just a high school degree. This education premium increased steadily for several decades before leveling off. By 1990 the education premium was 65.3 percent; by 2000 it was 76.4 percent; by 2010 it was 82.8 percent; and in 2020 it was 82 percent. Over the course of a working lifetime, the educational earnings premium is huge – so, yes, going to college is worth it, it does pay, and it pays handsomely.[66]

But again, the college earnings premium varies by race.[67] Stunningly, if a young Black person born into the bottom economic quintile manages to earn a four-year college degree, there is still only "a 40 percent chance that she'll make it into one of the top two quintiles" of income earners.[68] And as *Washington Post* journalists Heather Long and Andrew Van Dam have written, "The typical black household headed by someone with an advanced degree has less wealth than a white household with only a high school diploma."[69] Finally, because Black families have less annual income and net worth than White families, Black students, though not Hispanic students, come out of college, degree in hand or not, with more student debt. The authoritative Federal Reserve 2019 Survey of Consumer Finances reported that White students owed $23,000, Black students owed $30,000, and Hispanic students owed $17,600. Moreover, four years after graduation, Black borrowers owed more and White borrowers owed less than their loan balances at graduation.[70]

In 2023, after a half century-long battle, the Supreme Court threw its decisive weight behind the vision of a colorblind society – ready or not. In two landmark cases on the legality of race-based affirmative action in college admissions, involving Harvard and the University of North Carolina, Chapel Hill (UNC), the High Court declared that the equal protection clause of the Fourteenth Amendment required that applicants be treated as individuals, neither advantaged nor disadvantaged as members of a race or ethnicity, in the admissions decision. Though Harvard, UNC, and colleges across the country, especially elite colleges and universities that have the luxury of crafting their incoming classes from deep pools of applicants, scrambled to develop admissions procedures that would produce diverse classes, experts almost universally assumed that minority numbers at elite institutions would fall. Once again, Black and Hispanic students, their families, and their futures were to compete on a field increasingly tilted against them. Many Black students were expected to find their way back to the friendlier confines of the historically Black colleges and universities (HBCUs).

But the financial health of Black higher education is not robust. While a few colleges were established for Black students in the North before the Civil War, most HBCUs were established in the South after the war because White colleges were not open to Black people. The first in the South, by just a matter of months, was Atlanta University, established late in 1865, followed shortly thereafter by Nashville's Fisk University. When W.E.B. Du Bois arrived as a student at Fisk in 1885, he found that "With one admired African-American exception, the faculty of fifteen . . . was white, northern, deeply religious, overwhelmingly Congregationalist, and of impeccable abolitionist credentials."[71] And so it remained with most HBCUs into the twentieth century. While numbers are a bit uncertain, there were about ninety HBCUs in 1900, mostly in the South. There seem to have been 121 HBCUs by the 1930s and 128 in 1970. Then their numbers began to decline. In a prominent 1971 *Yale Law Review* article on the need for affirmative action at majority White institutions, Robert M. O'Neil noted that "as many as 50 of the 128 black institutions. . . . might have to close from lack of funds."[72] By 1991 the number of HBCUs was down to 107 and today it stands at 100. In 2022, Lincoln College, established in Lincoln, Illinois, in 1865, closed its doors for the final time, done in by the pandemic. Nonetheless, HBCUs produce "80 percent of Black judges, 50 percent of Black lawyers and doctors, and 25 percent of Black science, technology, math, and engineering graduates."[73] They do this on a relative shoestring.

In 2021, *BusinessWeek* reported that U.S. college endowments totaled $630 billion, of which $4 billion was held by HBCUs. Harvard alone had an endowment of $42 billion, more than ten times that of the HBCUs, and Yale held $31 billion. Howard University, the HBCU with the largest endowment, held $712 million.[74] While endowments will remain a challenge for many HBCUs, government and philanthropists have stepped forward with some aid. The Biden administration's economic stimulus package contained $5 billion for HBCUs, including $1.6 billion in debt relief. Philanthropists have also discovered HBCUs; MacKenzie Scott (formerly Bezos) gave $500 million to twenty HBCUs and others added $180 million during 2020–2021. Another $124 million was pledged in 2023. While these are big numbers and certainly welcome, many smaller, rural schools will still struggle and more may well go under.[75]

Finally, questions of race and inequality continue to permeate American history and, critically, the teaching of American history in the nation's public schools, colleges, and universities. Most recently, conservatives and liberals have faced off over the role, if any, of critical race theory (CRT) in the nation's public schools and universities. CRT was developed in the 1970s, initially in law schools, as an analytical framework for studying the role of race in American history and the infusion of racial hierarchy into American law, institutions, and culture. Its basic assumption is that racial hierarchies, with their systematic advantages for White people and disadvantages for people of color, infuse American life and that close scrutiny will uncover them so that they can potentially be redressed. Liberals and progressives believe that racism remains a broad problem in America, even if they do not see it as quite so embedded, hidden, and pervasive as CRT would have it. Conservatives believe that society is better served if young people are taught a more optimistic and uplifting view of American history in which freedom and opportunity have been extended over time to all Americans.[76]

Red state governors and legislatures have been active in combatting CRT broadly defined to include multiculturalism, racial sensitivity training, ethnic studies curricula, and much more. In 2021, the Idaho legislature passed a bill forbidding teaching that "individuals, by virtue of sex, race, ethnicity, religion, color, or national origin, are inherently responsible for actions committed in the past by other members of the same sex, race, ethnicity, religion, color, or national origin."[77] Senator Brandon Creighton introduced a bill in the Texas Senate that banned teaching that, "an individual, by virtue of his or her race or sex, is inherently racist, sexist, or oppressive, whether consciously or unconsciously." Clay Robison, spokesman for the Texas State Teachers Association countered that Sen. Creighton's bill and others like it, "try to ignore or downplay the racism, sexism and other injustices in our state's and nation's history, but students must be encouraged to fully explore and understand those injustices if Texas is to provide an equitable future for a rapidly diversifying population."[78] Similar battles are occurring across the country.

The question underlying conservative concern over CRT is whether anyone alive today has any responsibility for what others did decades and centuries ago? More pointedly, do White people today bear any responsibility for slavery, Jim Crow segregation, or plain vanilla racial discrimination and their historic and ongoing consequences or not? CRT and liberalism more generally answer yes – White privilege, with advantages and opportunities carried down through the generations, is real and simply denying it or ignoring it will not address past injustices or heal society. Conservatives contend that any discrimination that occurred in the past was wrong and must not be repeated in new forms like affirmative action or CRT that blame Whites today for things that happened long ago. Should we, especially in our schools and colleges, teach a race-conscious or colorblind view of history and society?

Battles over education, who should have access to it and how it should be paid for, evidently are battles over who will occupy which social and economic roles, high and low, later in life. In slavery White owners assigned Black roles and even after emancipation White people strictly limited education so Black people had no choice but to fill their socially assigned roles in domestic service and fieldwork. During Jim Crow underfunded minority schools produced underskilled graduates who posed little competitive threat to better educated White workers. Today, few question that high quality public schools and colleges are required to prepare the skilled workforce of the future. Now we turn our attention to the financial and economic consequences of the undeniable fact that our educational system prepares some better than others for what the future holds.

Notes

1 Claudia Goldin, "America's Graduation from High School: The Evolution and Spread of Secondary Schooling in the Twentieth Century," *The Journal of Economic History* 58, no. 2 (June 1998): 345–374, see especially 371.
2 Donald Yacovone, *Teaching White Supremacy: America's Democratic Ordeal and the Forging of Our National Identity* (New York: Pantheon Books, 2022), xv, 84.
3 Alexis de Tocqueville, *Democracy in America* (New York: Vintage Books, 1954), 1:63.
4 Adam Harris, *The State Must Provide: Why America's Colleges Have Always Been Unequal – And How to Set Them Right* (New York: HarperCollins, 2021), 3, 35.
5 Hinton Rowan Helper, *The Impending Crisis of the South: How to Meet It* (New York: Burdick Brothers, 1857), 288–289. See also Yacovone, *Teaching White Supremacy*, 101.
6 Roger L. Ransom and Richard Sutch, *One Kind of Freedom: The Economic Consequences of Emancipation*, 2nd ed. (New York: Cambridge University Press, 2001), 15.
7 Leon F. Litwack, *Trouble in Mind: Black Southerners in the Age of Jim Crow* (New York: Vintage Books, 1998), 71, 76.
8 William Humphrey, *No Resting Place* (New York: Delacourt Press, 1989), 3–4.
9 Woodrow Wilson, "The Reconstruction of the Southern States," *Atlantic Monthly*, January 1901, 6.
10 Booker T. Washington, "A University Education for Negroes," *The Independent* 68, no. 3 (March 24, 1910): 613. See also Joe M. Richardson, *A History of Fisk University, 1865–1946* (Tuscaloosa, AL: University of Alabama Press, 1980), 7.

11 Henry Louis Gates, Jr., *Stony the Road: Reconstruction, White Supremacy, and the Rise of Jim Crow* (New York: Penguin Books, 2020), 83, quoting N.S. Shaler, "The Negro Problem," *The Atlantic*, November 1884, https://www.theatlantic.com/magazine/archive/1884/the-negro-problem/531366/.
12 Ransom and Sutch, *One Kind of Freedom*, 31.
13 Herbert Spencer, *The Principles of Psychology*, 2nd ed. (New York: D. Appleton and Company, 1897), 1:368.
14 Harris, *The State Must Provide*, 40, 69, 80.
15 William J. Collins and Robert A. Margo, "Historical Perspectives on Racial Differences in Schooling in the United States," National Bureau of Economic Research, Working Paper 9770, June 2003, 5–6. See also Ransom and Sutch, *One Kind of Freedom*, 27–28; Robert A. Margo, *Race and Schooling in the South, 1880–1950: An Economic History* (Chicago, IL: University of Chicago Press, 1990), 6; Richard F. Bensel, *The Political Economy of American Industrialization, 1877–1900* (New York: Cambridge University Press, 2000), 34–37. 218, 305.
16 Margo, *Race and Schooling*, 9.
17 David Levering Lewis, *W.E.B. Du Bois: A Biography, 1868–1963* (New York: Henry Holt and Company, 2009), 156.
18 Gavin Wright, *Old South, New South: Revolutions in the Southern Economy Since the Civil War* (Baton Rouge, LA: Louisiana State University Press, 1997), 14, 79–80.
19 Trevon D. Logan, "Health, Human Capital, and African American Migration Before 1910," National Bureau of Economic Research, Working Paper 14037, May 2008, 2.
20 Litwack, *Trouble in Mind*, 93.
21 *Cumming v. Richmond County Board of Education*, 175 U.S. 529, 1899, supreme.justia.com/cases/federal/us/175/528/. See also Litwack, *Trouble in Mind*, 58.
22 Justin Driver, *The Schoolhouse Gate: Public Education, the Supreme Court, and the Battle for the American Mind* (New York: Pantheon Books, 2018), 32–34.
23 Collins and Margo, "Historical Perspectives," 10 and Table 4.
24 Lewis, *W.E.B. Du Bois*, 90.
25 Litwack, *Trouble in Mind*, 201.
26 Gene B. Preuss, *To Get a Better School System* (College Station, TX: Texas A&M University Press, 2009), 23. See also Robert D. Putnam, *The Upswing: How America Came Together a Century Ago and How We Can Do It Again*, with Shaylyn Romney Garrett (New York: Simon & Schuster, 2020), 102.
27 Wright, *Old South, New South*, Table 3.10, 80; see also Peter H. Lindert and Jeffrey G. Williamson, *Unequal Gains: American Growth and Inequality since 1700* (Princeton, NJ: Princeton University Press, 2016), 188–189.
28 Preuss, *To Get a Better School System*, 69. See also Gary Gerstle, *American Crucible: Race and Nation in the Twentieth Century* (Princeton, NJ: Princeton University Press, 2001, rev. ed. 2017), 87.
29 U.S. President's Commission on Higher Education, *Higher Education for Democracy* (New York: Harper & Brothers, 1949), 36.
30 Driver, *The Schoolhouse Gate*, 254.
31 Numan V. Bartley, *The New South, 1945–1980: The Story of the South's Modernization* (Baton Rouge, LA: Louisiana State University Press, 1996), 149. See also Calvin B. Hoover and B.U. Ratchford, *Economic Resources and Policies of the South* (New York: Macmillan, 1951), 31; Richard F. Bensel, *Sectionalism*

and American Political Development, 1880–1980 (Madison: The University of Wisconsin Press, 1984), 181, 401.
32 Robert A. Margo, "Teacher Salaries in Black and White: The South in 1910," *Explorations in Economic History* 21 (1984): 309, 324. See also Preuss, *To Get a Better School System*, 49–50.
33 Margo, *Race and Schooling*, 24–25, 56.
34 Goldin, "America's Graduation from High School," 349–352.
35 Richard Rothstein, *The Color of Law: A Forgotten History of How Our Government Segregated America* (New York: Liveright, 2018), 132–134.
36 Bernard Schwartz, *Super Chief: Earl Warren and His Supreme Court: A Judicial Biography* (New York: New York University Press, 1983), 112–113.
37 *Brown v. Board*, 347 U.S. 483 (1954), oyez.org/cases/1940–1955/347us483.
38 Driver, *The Schoolhouse Gate*, 255.
39 Gerald N. Rosenberg, *The Hollow Hope: Can Courts Bring About Social Change?* (Chicago, IL: University of Chicago Press, 1991), 99.
40 *Parents Involved in Community Schools v. Seattle School District #1*, 551 U.S. 701 (2007).
41 "The Segregation Index," https://socialinnovation.usc.edu/segregation.
42 Sheryll Cashin, *White Space, Black Hood: Opportunity Hoarding and Segregation in the Age of Inequality* (Boston, MA: Beacon Press, 2021), 138.
43 Justin McCarthy, "Most Americans Say Segregation in Schools Is a Serious Problem," Gallup, September 17, 2019.
44 Dana Goldstein, "Virus Closures Leave Students Falling Behind," *New York Times*, June 6, 2020, A1, A7.
45 W.E.B. Du Bois, "The Study of the Negro Problems," *Annals of the American Academy of Political and Social Science* 11 (January 1898): 22.
46 Harris, *The State Must Provide*, 113.
47 Michael J. Sandel, *The Tyranny of Merit: What's Become of the Common Good?* (New York: Farrar, Straus and Giroux, 2020), 156, 166.
48 Dorothy A. Brown, *The Whiteness of Wealth: How the Tax System Impoverishes Black Americans—And How We Can Fix It* (New York: Crown Books, 2021), 15.
49 Claudia Goldin and Lawrence F. Katz, *The Race Between Education and Technology* (Cambridge, MA: Harvard University Press, 2010), 278.
50 Heather McGhee, *The Sum of Us: What Racism Costs Everyone and How We Can Prosper Together* (New York: OneWorld, 2021), 41.
51 Suzanne Mettler, *Degrees of Inequality: How the Politics of Higher Education Sabotaged the American Dream* (New York: Basic Books, 2014), 21.
52 Brown, *The Whiteness of Wealth*, 126.
53 See higheredinfo.org/contact.php.
54 State Higher Education Finance 2020, shef.sheeo.org/wp-content/uploads/2021/05/SHEEO_SHEF_FY20_Report.pdf.
55 Sandel, *The Tyranny of Merit*, 61.
56 Mettler, *Degrees of Inequality*, 4, 7–8, 39, 190. See also Nicholas Kristof, "The American Dream Is Leaving America," *New York Times*, October 26, 2014, SR13.
57 Anna Helnoski, "College Remains a Good Bet," *New York Times*, July 18, 2021, 3D.
58 George Packer, *Last Best Hope: America in Crisis and Renewal* (New York: Farrar, Straus, and Giroux, 2021), 89.
59 Cashin, *White Space, Black Hood*, 127.

60 Jennifer Hochschild and Nathan Scovronick, *The American Dream and the Public Schools* (New York: Oxford University Press, 2004), 23. See also Mark Robert Rank, Thomas A. Hirschl, and Kirk A. Foster, *Chasing the American Dream: Understanding What Shapes Our Fortunes* (New York: Oxford University Press, 2014), 107.
61 Mettler, *Degrees of Inequality*, 30.
62 Frank Bruni, "Class, Cost and College," *New York Times*, May 18, 2014, SR3.
63 Sandel, *The Tyranny of Merit*, 10–11, 24, 155.
64 Stephanie Saul, "Enrollment in Colleges Fell in Spring," *New York Times*, May 27, 2022, A16.
65 National Center for Education Statistics, *Digest of Education Statistics*, Table 326.10; see also Brown, *The Whiteness of Wealth*, 97–100.
66 Bureau of Labor Statistics, bls.gov/charts/usual-weekly-earnings/usual-weekly-earnings-over-time-by-education.htm. See also David Leonhart, "Is College Worth It? Clearly, Yes, New Data Says," *New York Times*, May 27, 2014, A3.
67 Michael Omi and Howard Winant, *Racial Formation in the United States*, 3rd ed. (New York: Routledge, 2015), 43. See also Steve Lohr, "Gains by Black Workers Face Limits, Study Says," *New York Times*, September 5, 2023, B5.
68 Paul Tough, "Who Gets to Graduate," *The New York Times Magazine*, May 18, 2014, 54.
69 Heather Long and Andrew Van Dam, "The Black-White Economic Divide Is As Wide As It Was in 1968," *Washington Post*, June 4, 2020.
70 Judith Scott-Clayton and Jing Li, "Black-White Disparity in Student Loan Debt More Than Triples After Graduation," Brookings Institution, October 20, 2016. See also Rodney A. Brooks, *Fixing the Racial Wealth Gap* (Suffolk, VA: August Press, 2021), 86.
71 Lewis, *W.E.B. Du Bois*, 49.
72 Robert M. O'Neil, "Preferential Admissions: Equalizing the Access of Minority Groups to Higher Education," *Yale Law Journal* 80, no. 4 (March 1971): 743.
73 Harris, *The State Must Provide*, 6.
74 "Bridging the Endowment Gap," *BusinessWeek*, May 31, 2021.
75 Stephanie Saul, "Thriving or Not, Black Colleges Seize Moment," *New York Times*, July 19, 2021, A1, A15. See also Melissa Korn, "Historically Black Colleges Get Big Gifts," *Wall Street Journal*, September 14, 2023, A2.
76 Cara Fitzpatrick, *The Death of Public School: How Conservatives Won the War over Education in America* (New York: Basic Books, 2023).
77 Leah Asmelash, "Idaho Moves to Ban Critical Race Theory Instruction in Public Schools, Including Universities," *CNN*, April 28, 2021.
78 Duncan Agnew, "GOP Lawmakers Want to Ban 'Woke Philosophies' Like Critical Race Theory in Texas Schools," *Texas Tribune*, May 5, 2021.

6
INCOME, WEALTH, AND RACE IN AMERICA

"Instead of a horizontal division of classes, there was a vertical fissure, a complete separation of classes by race, cutting square across the economic layers."

W.E.B. Du Bois, 1940, *Dusk of Dawn*

Sometimes progress is so slow and halting as really not to deserve the name. So it has been with the languid and uneven rise of Black income and wealth as a proportion of White income and wealth over the course of American history. Studies have concluded that in slavery Black people received for sustenance less than half to only one-fifth of the value that their labor produced and free Black people during the nineteenth century made about half what White people made. Today, Black Americans make about 60 percent of what White Americans do and have 10 to 15 percent of White wealth. Hispanics do about the same or just a little better. This is what Du Bois was describing in the headnote immediately above; a U.S. labor market fissured along racial lines with the White income and wealth strata elevated well above the Black and Hispanic income and wealth strata. As we shall see, Black people made income and wealth gains relative to White people following the end of slavery, during the 1940s, and during the 1960s and early 1970s. By contrast, during Jim Crow, the 1930s, and since the late 1970s, Black people lost ground against White incomes and wealth. As a result, over the long course of American history, gains in Black incomes and wealth compared to White incomes and

DOI: 10.4324/9781003449188-6

wealth have been modest at best. America has had a two-tier economy, separated by race and ethnicity, since its earliest days.

Race and Wealth Creation in Colonial America

Early settlers into British North America, especially during the late sixteenth and early seventeenth centuries, faced great hardship; the Roanoke Colony was lost without a trace and the colonists at Jamestown and on the Massachusetts Bay suffered greatly. During the middle decades of the seventeenth century, population expanded, local agricultural practices were learned and refined, resupply and trading regimes were established, communities stabilized, and wealth began to grow and accumulate. Once the Upper and Lower South, Maryland to Georgia, had been wrestled from the Native American tribes of the region, the plantation system of slave-produced cash crops spread without resistance. Initially, land was plentiful, cheap, and productive, slave importation was unrestricted, and planter profits, first in tobacco, sugar, and rice, later in cotton, were volatile but often high.

By the late seventeenth century, Britain's North American colonies were, on a per capita basis, as wealthy as England and that wealth was more equally distributed.[1] On the eve of the American Revolution, Britain was the world's richest and most economically dynamic nation, but its wealth was concentrated among its nobility and a narrow urban commercial elite. In North America, at least outside the South, the elite was smaller and wealth was more equally spread among the agricultural many.[2] Among the White colonists, hierarchy certainly existed, between White men and women, between wealthier and poorer White men, and sometimes between White cultural, religious, and language majorities and minorities, but these hierarchies were more permeable and less permanent than the older hierarchies in Europe. Moreover, labor scarcity and free or cheap land created abundant opportunity and an ongoing scramble to make the most of it. The economists Peter Lindert and Jeffrey Williamson have asserted that, "there was no documented place on the planet that had a more egalitarian distribution [of income] in the late eighteenth century."[3]

This happy tale of early adversity and well-earned, hard won prosperity was, of course, clouded by the early presence and growing role of slavery in colonial economic life. Rather than simply an isolated element of Southern life, slavery and the wealth it produced also drove colonial economic development through the Northern service industries of banking, insurance, transportation, and shipping. More than a century ago, Princeton professor and future president, Woodrow Wilson, explained the deep Northern involvement in the transatlantic slave economy, writing: "Out of the cheap molasses of the French islands, . . . [New England] made the rum, with which she bought slaves for Maryland, Virginia, and the Carolinas, and paid her balances to the English merchants."[4] More recently, the sociologist Joe Feagin has made the remarkably broad claim, undercut just a bit by a stray "probably," that Black slave labor provided the foundation of U.S. national wealth creation, declaring that "if there had been no African American enslavement, there probably would not have been the huge North American wealth generation . . . . Enslaved workers cultivating cotton, tobacco, rice, sugar, and other major crops generated huge amounts of economic capital, much of which then circulated throughout European and North American banking and other economic institutions."[5]

As a result, on the eve of the American Revolution, the average White American enjoyed greater prosperity than common people anywhere in the world, but the new society was riven, weakened, made less cohesive and more vulnerable, by racism and human slavery. And then, as has occurred throughout history, war not only brought death and destruction from outside, it brought internal division as well. Some of the most vicious fighting of the American Revolution, as much civil war as fight for independence, occurred in the South with the slaves subject to threats and promises from all sides. The last quarter of the eighteenth century, including not just the disruptions of the revolution (1774–1781), but the tumultuous Confederation period (1781–1789), and the growing pains of the early national period (1789–1800), saw real income drop by about 20 percent, falling behind real income in Britain.[6] Rebuilding growth and prosperity depended upon White supremacy and the enforcement of Black subordination. Near the end of the nineteenth century, W.E.B. Du Bois looked back on this period to note, even somewhat more expansively than Feagin above, that, "Black labor became the foundation stone not only of the Southern social structure, but of Northern manufacturing and commerce, of the English factory system, of European commerce, of buying and selling on a worldwide scale."[7]

The economists William Darity and Kirsten Mullen also have pointed out how thoroughly the colonial and early national economies were integrated with the broader Atlantic trade. They noted that, "Providing provisions . . . for the vast plantations of the U.S. south, the Caribbean, and South America required the efforts of staggering numbers of financiers, merchants, shippers, insurers, real estate brokers, auctioneers, and laborers." The Midwest provided the agricultural products and food; the Northeast provided the commercial support services that allowed the slave economies of the South and beyond to concentrate on high-value cash crops. Hence, Darity and Mullen concluded that, "The slave trade and slavery laid the economic foundation for what is now one of the richest countries in the world."[8] The U.S. economy before the Civil War, and not just the economy of the South, can fairly be characterized as a slave economy. Even after the Erie Canal connected the Midwest through the Great Lakes to New York and the East Coast in 1825, most farm goods raised west of the Appalachians were sold down river to feed slaves on Southern plantations, thus freeing those slaves to grow more profitable cash crops like sugar, rice, and cotton. The high profit margins of the South's large plantations meant that they supplied the liquidity, the finance capital, that drove development of the broader U.S. economy, Du Bois would even say the broader Atlantic economy, during its early industrial phase.

Race, Wealth, and Value in Antebellum America

Slave labor was the foundation of Southern agricultural production. Ninety-four percent of slaves worked in the rural economy, and just 6 percent in urban craft and personal service jobs.[9] In the Northern states, slavery existed through much of the colonial period before being prohibited by state constitutions and laws over the first third of the nineteenth century. Frederick Douglass, an escaped slave and later the most prominent nineteenth-century advocate of Black people in slavery and then in their limited freedom described Black life in the North in terms of what modern social scientists call the "linked-fate" hypothesis. The "linked-fate" idea, developed by Michael Dawson in *Behind the Mule* (1994), highlights the deep sense among Black people that what impacts the community affects its individual members in ways that define, restrict, and limit them.[10] Douglas anticipated Dawson by nearly 150 years, declaring in his 1848 "An Address to the Colored People of the United States," that: "In the Northern states, we are not slaves to individuals, not personal slaves, yet in many respects we are slaves to the community. . . . It is more than a figure of speech to say, that we are as a people chained together."[11] In the South, masters took all the value created by slaves except what was required to keep them alive and working, while in the North, employers paid Black employees half, sometimes a little more, sometimes a little less, of what they paid White employees, "the community" pocketing the difference.

As in the Revolutionary War, in the Civil War, conflict was particularly destructive of Southern wealth. Prior to the Revolutionary War, the South was the rising nation's wealthiest region, but the British Southern campaigns (1778–1781) wrought great damage and reduced average slaveholding and, hence, average wealthholding. In 1774, the South had income per capita of 24 percent above the national average. By 1800, its lead had fallen to 9 percent above the national average, and then to 15 percent below the national average in 1840 and 21.5 percent below in 1850.[12] And then the Civil War, in which the South was devastated demographically, socially, and economically, dropped southern per capita income to half the national average. Most of the financial losses were borne by White people because Black remuneration had always been held to a minimum by White owners in order to buttress their own finances.

While per capita wealth in the South fell below the national average during the first half of the nineteenth century, it also became more uneven. Great wealth and poverty, even among the White population to say nothing of the enslaved Black masses, lived side by side. The 1619 Project's Matthew Desmond wrote that, "By the eve of the Civil War, the Mississippi Valley was home to more millionaires per capita than anywhere else in the United States. . . . In 1860, two in three men with estates valued at $100,000 or more lived in the South, and three-fifths of the country's wealthiest men were enslavers."[13] Yet, per capita income in the South, despite rising cotton process in the 1950s, was 14 percent below the national average in 1860.

All slaves, men, women, children, and the elderly, worked. Young slaves, boys and girls, went to the fields at six or seven, first serving as water carriers and messengers and then shouldering increasingly heavy duties at ten to twelve.[14] Women worked in the fields beside men, sometimes thinking of these men as husbands, and were equally subject to the overseer's orders and discipline. One of the great tragedies of slave life was that parents could not shelter their children and husbands and wives could not protect each other. All were at the orders, and ultimately the disposal, of White masters and overseers. In the North, the oppression was more than stifling but less than total. For example, when still a slave in Baltimore, Frederick Douglass was leased out as a caulker to Price's shipyard where he made $6 to $9 a week, "depositing most of his wages with Hugh Auld every Saturday night." Dock owners pitted White against Black workers to drive down the wages of both and after Douglass' escape to freedom in New England, White caulkers in New Bedford threatened to walk off the job if the Black newcomer was hired.[15]

Free Black people in the North experienced their own grave economic challenges. The historian Van Gosse has described a free Black workforce, about 10 percent of all Black workers, divided between a top fifth engaged in personal services, often for wealthy Whites and other comfortable Blacks, and a bottom 80 percent engaged in poorly paid physical labor. The fortunate few served as barbers and stylists, perfumers, tailors, grocers, butchers, caterers, stewards, and a thin layer of medicos and ministers. A few Black entrepreneurs gained what we would call upper middle-class lifestyles, mixing professionally, though rarely socially, with White clients.

But most free Black people were anything but secure. Gosse explained that, "Because of the abject poverty imposed on most free people of color, their lack of capital and familial resources, and deep social exclusion, all only worsened between 1800 and 1860." Most "surviving . . . in back-alley cellars and shanties in the cities and on the fringe of country life as day laborers and cottagers on stray pieces of land."[16]

An important new study by Ellora Derenoncourt and others has sought to measure the Black/White wealth gap from 1860 through 2020. We will discuss this study more fully below, but for now we will simply note that Derenoncourt and her colleagues found that Black Americans in 1860 held less than two cents in per capita wealth for each dollar, a ratio of 56 to 1, held by White Americans.[17] Eighty-nine percent of Black people were slaves in 1860, of course, so their net worth, by law, was zero. The four-fifths of free Black people living on the economic margins, making half what White people made, also accumulated little wealth. Only the top fifth of free Black workers, about 2 percent of all Black people, lived more comfortably and accumulated some wealth. Nonetheless, per capita net worth of Black Americans in 1860 was less than one-fiftieth of per capita White wealth.

So common, virtually ingrained, was half pay for Blacks that it was continued in military pay during the Civil War. The historian Leon F. Litwack has noted that, "Of the many grievances, the most deeply felt and resented was the inequality of pay – the fact that White privates were paid $13 a month plus a $3.50 clothing allowance, while Blacks received $10 a month, out of which $3.00 might be deducted for clothing." Interestingly, Frederick Douglass, initially a recruiter of Black troops for the Union Army, chided Black people for making too big a deal out of pay differences, saying "Don't you work for less every day than white men get? You know you do," but the differences grated on him too and eventually he ceased recruiting but continued to support the war in other ways.[18]

Racial variation in soldiers' pay was aggravating, but Black and White men knew that far greater sacrifices of blood and treasure were imminent. Increasingly, the idea that justice might demand a blood tribute gained hold. As early as 1844, former president John Quincy Adams, in a speech to Black citizens in Pittsburgh, thundered: "We know the day of your redemption must come. . . . It may come in peace, or it may come in blood; but *whether in peace or in blood,* LET IT COME. . . . Though it cost the blood of MILLIONS OF WHITE MEN, LET IT COME. Let justice be done, though the heavens fall."[19] Adams' sobriquet, "Old Man Eloquent," was well-earned. The abolitionist firebrand John Brown, leader of the failed but galvanizing October 1859 attack on the federal arsenal at Harpers Ferry, drew on the Bible, Numbers 35:33, to declare that: "The land cannot be cleansed of the blood, which is shed therein, but by the blood of him that shed it."[20] Abraham Lincoln sharpened Brown's point in his second inaugural address, saying of the nation's wealth in general and southern White wealth in particular: "if God wills that it [meaning the war] continue until all the wealth piled up by the bond-man's two hundred and fifty years of unrequited toil shall be sunk, . . . so still it must be said, 'The judgments of the Lord, are true and righteous altogether.'"

As Lincoln forecast, the wealth piled up by the slavocracy was sunk, but men differed as to the righteousness of it. Lindert and Williamson recorded that White incomes in the South "fell on average by 30.5 percent. . . . These are huge costs, but they must have fallen mainly on slaveholders and landowners," as poor Whites and slaves had little income to lose. "In prewar 1860, the average per capita incomes in the South were 14 percent below those of the North, while the postwar 1870 gap was 37.8 percent" and falling.[21] White Southerners, irrationally or not, blamed the former slaves for the war and the losses it had brought them. Professors of history and economics Roger Ransom and Richard Sutch contended that, "As a cause of southern poverty, racism may well have been preeminent. . . . [T]he animosity and mutual fear that existed between the races, and in particular the Whites' antagonism toward the Blacks' economic advancement, were at least as powerful as were economic incentives in motivating individual economic behavior."[22] Racism continued to sow division, promote violence, and slow recovery. For decades, White Southerners directed more effort toward reestablishing control over their former bondsmen than they did toward constructing an economy and society in which both races might thrive.

Race, Income, and Wealth During Reconstruction and Jim Crow

Slavery did not end with the Emancipation Proclamation or even with the end of the war; it ended slowly and then only partially. In fact, the grip of slavery seemed to loosen briefly only to tighten again in subsequent decades. Initially, as Union troops appeared and then advanced into the South, slaves rushed toward their lines, but as Union troops moved on, Black people followed or remained behind and were exposed to White wrath. After the war, freedmen and their families sought a new normal, one that looked more like the pre-war White normal. Black citizens sought to withdraw, or at least limit, child and female field work, to allow children some time for school and women some time in the home.[23] White Southerners sought to reestablish control of Black labor and many former slaves had few positive options; "Without land, without tools, without capital or access to credit facilities, the freedmen drifted into a form of peonage: the sharecropping system."[24] It took years of White effort to refasten Black labor to Southern agricultural lands and in the meantime tumult reigned.[25] Over the last third of the nineteenth century a new equilibrium, sullen and grudging on both sides, was reached. Scholars estimate the Black labor output declined by 28 to 37 percent compared to pre-war levels.[26] Black citizens resisted being forced to work and White citizens concluded that Black people would not work without force. Deep poverty and inequality spread throughout the postwar South.

Before the war, half of Southern wealth was held in land and improvements and half in the value of its slave population. Emancipation did not destroy the ability of the now free Black population to labor and create value, but it did transfer ownership and some modest control of Black labor from plantation lords to the individual freedmen themselves. As White Southerners lost their traditional labor force and Black people lost access to land on which to labor, the Southern economy languished for decades; "Per capita output had already fallen sharply with the Civil War, and, . . . the material incomes of blacks had actually increased. Whites had therefore borne the full brunt of that loss."[27] By 1870, falling White wealth, especially in the South, and even very modest accumulation among now free Blacks reduced the wealth gap to 23 to 1. Black people now had four cents for every White dollar in wealth.[28]

White Southerners were, of course, outraged by the results of the war and the deep and dramatic social, political, and economic changes that had already occurred and those they feared would follow. One Florida planter declared, "There is now nothing between me and the nigger but the dollar – the almighty dollar, and I shall make out of him the most I can at the least expense."[29] With the smoke of battle barely cleared, White-dominated Southern state legislatures enacted "Black Codes" that acknowledged Black emancipation, rights to marry, own land, and contract, but also forcefully channeled them back toward agriculture and domestic service, closed off other occupational paths, mandated work under threat of incarceration, and, if incarcerated, threatened public contract labor. Many White Northerners, flush with victory but ready to move on, also enjoined the freedmen to work. The prominent Massachusetts Unionist, Edward Everett Hale, nephew of the Whig and Republican Senator and Secretary of State, Edward Everett, who spoke before Lincoln at the dedication of the Gettysburg National Cemetery in 1863, reminded the freedmen that: "Freedom is not bread and butter, it is not comfort, it is not houses and clothes, it is not a happy life. . . . But freedom is simply the way to get those blessings. It is the right of choice by which the freedman selects one or another course, which he thinks best adapted to secure them."[30]

No one, of course, had to tell the freedmen that they would have to work; work, pitiless, endless work was all they had ever known. One former slave declared: "I know freemen have to work – can't live without work. Dere's great difference between slave and free. When you free you work and de money b'long to yourself."[31] Nonetheless, once the shackles of slavery were removed and the whip, at least for a time, put away, freedmen, and especially their wives and children, did work less – experimenting with no was a new and delicious prospect. White Southerners concluded that Black people were naturally lazy and would not work without compulsion. But hard and insistent reality soon reasserted itself, driving the impoverished freedmen back to the fields.

Emancipation, so full of promise, first and for a long time delivered tragedy to the 90 percent of Black Americans who lived in the South. Happy to be free, yes; but what now? As Ransom and Sutch pointed out, "At the time of his emancipation, the freedman had none of the capital requisites for agriculture. He did not own land, work stock, or farming implements. Set free without human or physical capital, the black nonetheless had one possession. . . . This was his labor."[32] Black leaders like Frederick Douglass, and their White allies like Congressman Thaddeus Stevens, had asked for and been assured of more; the famous "forty acres and a mule," was the promise of land, stock, implements, and seed. But by 1872, when Douglass wrote "Self-Made Man," these helps were no longer in prospect.

Douglass was resigned to the fact that full justice would not be done to Black Americans, especially the freedmen. In words very much like President Lyndon B. Johnson would still need to speak almost a hundred years later, Douglass noted, "It is not fair play to start the negro out in life, from nothing and with nothing, while others start with the advantage of a thousand years behind them." But America was what it was and it would not do more; so Douglass, with worry and doubt in his heart, declared that "the nearest approach to justice for the negro for the past is to do him justice in the present." He asked that America "Throw open to him the doors of the schools, the factories, the workshops, and of all mechanical industries. For his own welfare, give him a chance to do whatever he can do well." And then speaking the American language of social Darwinism and *laissez-faire*, not because it was his preferred language, but because it was the only language he thought White America willing to hear, Douglass said: "allowing only ordinary ability and opportunity, we may explain success mainly by one word and that word is WORK! WORK!! WORK!!! WORK!!!! Not transient and fitful effort, but patient, enduring, honest, unremitting and indefatigable work into which the whole heart is put." To drive home his reassurance to White Americans, he said, "I have been asked, 'How will this theory affect the negro' . . . My general answer is 'Give the negro fair play and let him alone. If he lives, well. If he dies, equally well.'"[33] But as Douglass surely knew and later mourned, America would have none of fair play toward Black people.

Economic historians Robert Fogel and Stanley Engerman, authors of *Time on the Cross*, reported that, "the evidence . . . suggests that the attack on . . . blacks after the Civil War was . . . more cruel than that which preceded it . . . The skill composition of the black labor force deteriorated. . . . The gap between wage payments to blacks and whites in comparable occupations increased steadily from the immediate post-Civil War decades down to the eve of World War II."[34] Nor were the reasons hard to find. Parke Johnston, a former Virginia slave, recalled in 1880 that emancipation "came so sudden on 'em they wasn't prepared for it. . . . turned loose all at once, with nothing in the world, but what they had on their backs, and often little enough of that; men, women, and children . . . walking along the road with nowhere to go."[35] And as the nineteenth century waned, W.E.B. Du Bois made the same point more sharply and more poignantly. In his essay, "The Negro in Business" (1899), Du Bois wrote: "The nation which robbed them of the fruits of their labor for two and a half centuries, finally set them adrift penniless." A decade later, he wrote: "Our people were emancipated in a whirl of passion, and left naked to the mercies of their enraged and impoverished ex-masters."[36]

While Black people in the South groped for a new social, political, and economic dispensation, one that would provide them with real freedom, opportunity, and equality, many White people sought restoration of the old order, just without chattel slavery. Meanwhile, the industrializing North experienced an economic boom that expanded Northern advantages of wealth and income to unprecedented heights. The economist Gavin Wright succinctly described the postwar landscape, saying "as the situation emerged in the 1870s, the South was a low-wage region in a high-wage country."[37] C. Vann Woodward, the leading mid-twentieth century historian of the South, described the misery of the region after the war as "a long and quite un-American experience with poverty. . . . In 1880 the per capita wealth of the South, based on estimated true valuation of property, was $376 as compared with $1,186 per capita in the states outside of the South. In the same year the per capita wealth of the South was 27 percent of that in the Northeastern states."[38] Similarly, economic historians William Collins and Robert Margo reported that: "The southern wage disadvantage moderated to some extent up to 1890, but in the 1890s worsened again, and a substantial wage gap remained in place well into the 20th century."[39]

Without land, tools, capital, and often without income of any kind, the freedmen emerged into a stagnant economy suffering from capital and labor dislocations that would take decades to sort themselves out. The South was poor, White Southerners had lost a great deal and felt themselves aggrieved and impoverished, but Black people were and always remained the poorest Southerners and, hence, the poorest Americans. Still, Black people were not as poor as they and their forebearers had been in slavery. Ransom and Sutch estimated Black income in slavery and freedom, saying "Our calculations suggest that slaves received only 21.7 percent of the output produced on large plantations, . . . Their share of output rose . . . to the approximately 56 percent of output we calculate was received by black sharecroppers and tenant farmers in 1879. . . . As it was, material income increased by nearly 29 percent."[40] Ominously, the Black standard of living in the South again began to deteriorate as Reconstruction ended and Jim Crow segregation took hold. Black people were pushed even further toward the social, political, and economic periphery of Southern

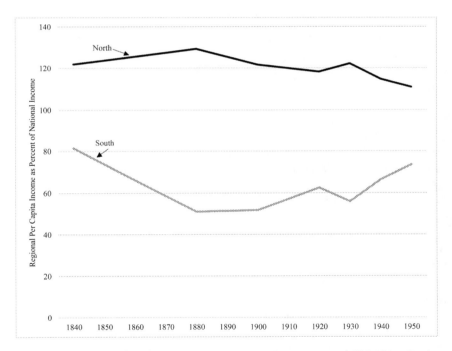

FIGURE 6.1 Regional Per Capita Income as a Percentage of U.S. Per Capita Income, 1840–1950

Source: Richard A. Easterlin, "Interregional Differences in Per Capita Income, Population, and Total Income, 1840–1950," in *Trends in the American Economy in the Nineteenth Century* (NBER and Princeton University Press, 1960), Table D-2, 137. North and South are weighted averages of subregions in Table D-2 with Mountain and Pacific regions excluded.

society – American society – so that by 1890 six out of seven still worked in just two occupational categories: agriculture and domestic service.[41]

The improved economic position of Black people in the South in the wake of the Civil War and Reconstruction and the erosion of those postwar gains during Jim Crow must, of course, be seen within the broader context of an impoverished and still declining region. As the North experienced a postwar boom, the South, focused on its racial tensions, experienced ongoing economic dislocations. Richard Easterlin's calculations of regional per capita income (see Figure 6.1) as a percentage of national per capita income demonstrated the yawning gap between the industrial North and the agricultural South evident before and after the Civil War. The North maintained a huge per capita income advantage from the end of Reconstruction to World War II, after which the gap slowly began to close. As always, Black Southerners were the poorest of the poor.

Race, Income, and Wealth in Early Twentieth Century America

Richard Easterlin's early study (1960) of regional income differences, presented in Figure 6.1, has been foundational to many later studies. His data and analysis have held up quite well, showing a plunge in per capita income in the South prior to and then as a consequence of the Civil War, followed by regional convergence that did not take firm hold until the 1940s. Generations of economists have built on Easterlin's work. In 1979, Charles A. Roberts adjusted Easterlin's income data for regional price differences to see whether the lower cost of living in the South changed the picture at all – it did not; "it was found that no significant differences occurred in either the levels of differences or in the rates of convergence from the original estimates." However, in regard to prices, Roberts noted that, "The convergence of prices is more rapid than the convergence of per capita income."[42] Of course, since the South was the low wage and low price section of the country, trends in which prices rose more rapidly than income was bad for the South and especially for its poorest citizens. In 1999, Kris Mitchener and Ian McLean, extended Easterlin's data through 1980 and added new data concerning labor productivity by state and region. They noted that, "the effects of the Civil War and slavery . . . [on] the southern economy can be seen in estimates of state personal income per capita. . . . of 76 and 72 percent of the national average in 1840 and 1860 respectively . . . but only 51 percent in 1880."[43] They too find that these gaps did not begin to close until well into the twentieth century.

The South in 1900 remained a poor, underdeveloped, mainly agrarian economy. William Collins and Marianne Wanamaker observed that, "At the turn of the twentieth century, real income per worker in the South was less than one-half of that of the rest of the United States."[44] In fact, viewed more broadly, per capita income in the South ranged from less than half the national average to about 55 percent of it between 1870 and 1940. There were brief Southern income gains, for example, when cotton prices rose between 1900 and World War I, but when cotton prices fell after 1920, so did Southern incomes.[45] As late as 1940, seventy-five years after the Civil War ended, the ten poorest states in the nation were all in the South where most Black people still lived.

The South struggled in large part because its White population was more committed to holding the Black population down than to economic growth and prosperity – lest Black people share in it. Only once White hands were pried from Black throats, again by the national government, did Southern economic promise begin to fulfill itself and economic convergence between the regions begin to pick up speed and consistency. Lindert and Williamson have pointed out that, "The first great jump in black relative income came with emancipation and Reconstruction. . . . The second great jump was much later, between 1940 and 1980. . . . Between these two great leaps came the relative stagnation during the long era of Jim Crow . . . . Indeed, the 1870 black-white income ratio was not surpassed until 1950, shortly after World War II."[46]

As the twentieth century opened, 90 percent of Black people still lived in the South, most in the rural South, with the vast majority of employed Black men engaged in agriculture.[47] Black vulnerability was particularly acute in agriculture. The economist Neil Fligstein has noted that, "In 1900, about 60% of white farmers were owners and 40% were tenants, while 80% of black farmers were tenants and only 20% were owners."[48] Between 1900 and 1940, little change took place in Black economic life in the South; "the black-to-white earnings ratio for adult men showed an improvement of just three percentage points, . . . Thus, in 1940, the average annual earnings of black men were about 48 percent of those of white men."[49] Even more remarkably, Collins and Wanamaker reported that "between 1910 and 1930, it appears that blacks' relative gains [those three percentage points mentioned just above] may be accounted for fully by their interregional migration."[50] No hope of gain at home would soon put millions of Black Southerners on the road North.

During the Great Depression of the 1930s, Darlene Clark Hine, African-American historian at Michigan State, explained, "Dire poverty, starvation, homelessness, unemployment, and untold agony were the lot of most black Americans. Already on the bottom step of the economic ladder, they were the first to lose the menial, unskilled, domestic service jobs that whites had allowed blacks to have."[51] Dorothy A. Brown, a legal scholar and federal tax law expert at Emory University, wrote that, "In

1936, more than half of all southern urban black families reported annual incomes of $750 or less, compared with 12 percent of white families."[52] And, of course, urban Black citizens were better off economically than rural Black citizens. Yet, when the Democratic administration of Franklin D. Roosevelt sought to address the distress caused to Americans by the Great Depression, Southern Democrats in the president's own party opposed benefits that might flow to Black Americans. Roosevelt's signature social security program, adopted in 1935, excluded agricultural and domestic service workers, meaning virtually all Black people, especially in the South, due to Southern Democrat resistance in the Congress. When the administration's minimum wage legislation came before Congress in 1937, Texas Democratic congressman Martin Dies warned, "There is a racial question here. . . . And you cannot prescribe the same wage for the black man as for the white man."[53]

By 1938, Roosevelt reluctantly decided to confront the Democratic South, deploying sticks and carrots, to move his domestic program forward. In the 1938 midterm elections, Roosevelt personally campaigned against senior members of his own party responsible for blocking or forcing changes to his policies to suit Southern racial sentiments. To buttress his sticks with carrots, Roosevelt requested in the spring of 1938 that his aides produce a "Report to the President on the Economic Condition of the South." A conference was called in Washington on July 4th to discuss the report. In an opening statement to the conference, Roosevelt declared his "conviction that the South presents right now the nation's No. 1 economic problem." The report itself noted that, "Ever since the War between the States the South has been the poorest section of the Nation. The richest state in the South ranks lower in per capita income than the poorest state outside the region."[54] The South demurred, preferring their traditional social order and poverty to the new egalitarian industrial order and higher incomes that Roosevelt promised.[55] Neither sticks nor carrots worked. Roosevelt failed either to purge his opponents in the 1938 midterms or to convince most Southerners that his big government programs were the path to a better future for the region.[56]

The Great Moderation: Race, Income, and Wealth, World War II to the 1970s

As we have seen and as scholars and journalists now repeat in common refrain, "the deeper explanations" for the income, wealth, and opportunity gaps between Black and White people "lie in the history of slavery, discrimination, and racial segregation."[57] *The Economist* magazine introduced a 2020 story on Black-White economic differences by noting,

Income, Wealth, and Race in America 175

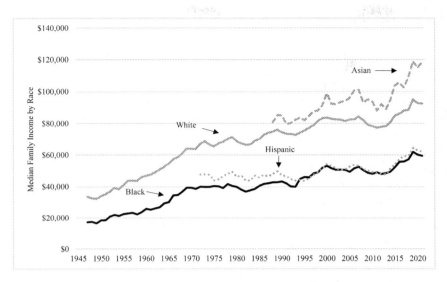

FIGURE 6.2 Median Income of Families by Race and Ethnicity, 1947–2021 (in 2021 dollars)

Source: Bureau of the Census, Current Population Survey, Annual Social and Economic Supplements, Table F-5, "Race and Hispanic Origin . . . —Families by Median and Mean Income: 1947–2021," https://www.census.gov/data/tables/time-series/demo/income-poverty/historical-income-families.html.

"A large and growing literature links the still-yawning racial gap in income, employment and wealth to the segregated communities, racial violence and unequal investment that have been a feature of American society for so long."[58] Nonetheless, those historic gaps did narrow noticeably in the third quarter of the twentieth century before widening again after 1980.

In this section and the next we look closely at the second half of the twentieth century and the early twenty-first century. Blessedly, it is during these years that consistent, high-quality data on employment, income, wealth, and poverty, often by race, becomes available. Figure 6.2 communicates two clear messages. One message is that Americans of all races and ethnicities got wealthier in the decades after World War II. Black median family income more than doubled, from $17,173 to $39,304, between 1947 and 1969, and then went flat, standing at $39,885 in 1993. It then rose steadily to $53,131 by 2000, then flattened, not breaking $53,000 again until 2016. Black median family income increased by an inflation adjusted 247 percent between 1947 and 2021. Hispanic median family income, first measured in 1972, ran slightly above Black median family income from 1972 through

1994, then closely tracked Black median family income thereafter. Even more remarkably, Hispanic income remained almost perfectly flat between 1972, when it registered $47,526, and 1997, when it registered $47,519. Hispanic median family income stood at $62,301 in 2021. White median family income stood at $33,590 in 1947, almost twice Black income, more than doubled to $71,349 in 1979 before stagnating into the mid-1990s. White median family income stood at $77,363 in 2011 before beginning a smart upward march that reached $92,427 in 2021, up 175 percent since 1947. The second message very clearly communicated in Figure 6.2 is that America has long had and continues to have a two-tier economy; Black and Hispanic Americans struggle in the lower tier while White and Asian Americans dominate the upper tier. Over seven decades, 1947 to 2021, Black families made modest but important gains against White median family income.

Economists have worked hard to pin down the timing and extent of Black income gains against White income since World War II. A general,

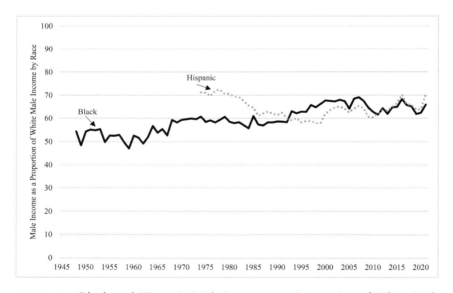

FIGURE 6.3 Black and Hispanic Male Income as a Proportion of White Male Income, 1948–2021 (in 2021 dollars)

Source: Bureau of the Census, Current Population Survey, Annual Social and Economic Supplements, Table P-2, "Race and Hispanic Origin of People by Median Income and Sex: 1947–2021," https://www.census.gov/data/tables/time-series/demo/income-poverty/historical-income-people.html. 1972–2021: White, Non-Hispanic; 1948–1971: White only, which includes Hispanics, but their number during this period were too small to affect results (1.5% in 1950, 4.4% in 1970).

if somewhat blurry, picture has emerged. Goldin and Margo, writing in 1991, described what they call "the great compression," or reduction of general income inequality, with "inequality falling during the 1940s, rising slightly in the 1950s and 1960s, and finally increasing sharply since the 1970s."[59] Leah Platt Boustan, writing two decades later, described mid-twentieth century income convergence similarly, but not identically, writing, "African Americans experienced two major episodes of wage convergence in the twentieth century, one during the 1940s and the other during the late 1960s and early 1970s."[60] Collins and Wanamaker in 2017 described Black income gains at mid-century like Boustan, writing: "World War II and the 1940s brought significant gains in income for black men relative to whites, . . . Yet it is the decade following the 1964 Civil Rights Act that stands out in retrospect. . . . The momentum did not continue into the post-1980 period."[61]

Figure 6.3 clarifies the relationship between the upper and lower tiers of the economy by presenting Black and Hispanic male income as a percentage of White male income. It shows that in the third quarter of the twentieth century, income inequality narrowed slightly as Black men made 54 percent of White income in 1950 and 61 percent in 1974. And then in the last quarter of the century gains ceased and Black and Hispanic income stayed flat into the early 1990s. Black income rose from 63 percent of White income in 1993 to 69 percent in 2007 before settling back to 66 percent in 2021, near where it had been more than a quarter century earlier. Hispanic male income as a proportion of White male income started above Black male income in 1974, settled slowly until it broke below Black income in the early 1990s, then rose to again be modestly above Black income after 2011.

The stark numbers laid out graphically in Figures 6.2 and 6.3 are presented by many scholars as clear evidence that racial income and wealth gaps are deeply rooted in the nation's history. The sociologist Joe Feagin, always uncompromising, has declared that, "This country's large-scale resource and wealth gap has long been the result of societal processes involving unjust enrichment for white Americans and unjust impoverishment for African Americans and many other Americans of color."[62] The Economic Policy Institute's Richard Rothstein, exploring how government policy empowered racial exclusions in the more recent past, observed that: "we cannot understand the income . . . gap that persists between African Americans and whites without examining government policies that purposely kept black incomes low throughout most of the twentieth century."[63] And Anthony Carnevale and his colleagues at Georgetown University's Center on Education and the Workforce concluded that, "Throughout the nation's history, Black Americans and Latino Americans have faced barriers to full . . . economic participation."[64]

An important, if somewhat technical, article by the economists Patrick Bayer and Kerwin Kofi Charles provides additional insights into earnings differences between Black and White men since 1940. Bayer and Charles distinguish between what they call the level gap and the rank gap in Black and White incomes. Each highlights an aspect of what Du Bois, in the headnote to this chapter, described as "a complete separation of classes by race, cutting square across the economic layers" of society. The level gap is a dollar amount while the rank gap is a percentage amount. Bayer and Charles describe the level gap, often measured at the median, as "the difference in earnings between black and white men at the same percentile of their respective earnings distribution." For example, in a given year, the White median income might be $50,000 and the Black median income $30,000, for a level earnings gap of $20,000 – and that gap might increase or decrease over time. The "rank gap measures how far below his percentile in the black distribution a black man's earnings would rank in the white distribution." Again, for example, a Black man's earnings might rank at the 50th percentile of the Black earnings distribution, but might rank at the 25th percentile if those earnings were placed within the White distribution.[65]

Bayer and Charles

find that after narrowing consistently from 1940 to 1970, the black-white difference in median annual earnings among all men has since widened substantially, growing by the end of the Great Recession [around 2010] to its size in 1950. . . . Among all men, the median black man's earnings would have placed him at the 24th percentile of the white earnings distribution in 1940. Years after the end of the Great Recession, his position had scarcely budged, rising to only the 27th percentile.[66]

Remarkably, Black income has risen and fallen with broad economic forces, leaving Black Americans no better off in relation to White Americans in 2010 than they had been shortly after World War II.

Nonetheless, some Black men have done better than other Black men. Men at the 90th percentile of the Black income distribution enjoyed gains from the 1940s through the 1970s and have done better at retaining those gains in recent decades. Higher earning Black men experienced positional earning gains in relation to their White counterparts. While the income of the median Black worker languished, "the earnings rank of the black man at the 90th percentile has steadily improved, rising from about the median to the 75th percentile of the white earnings distribution."[67] Remarkably, Bayer and Charles provide impressive empirical support for a point long understood within the Black community. The prominent Black psychologist, Kenneth B. Clark said in 1967 that, "The masses of Negroes are now starkly aware of the fact that recent civil rights victories benefited a very small number of middle-class Negroes while their predicament remained the same or worsened."[68] Clark's observation endures to this day.

Part of what allowed high-earning Black people to continue making gains after 1970 was that the professions were not fully open to them until at least the 1970s. For decades after the Civil War, Howard University (1867) and Nashville's Meharry Medical College (1876) were the only institutions training Black doctors. As late as "1964 eighteen of the nation's eight-five medical schools enrolled no Black students." In that same year, "schools certified by the American Bar Association graduated only 200 Black students out of more than 10,000 graduates nationwide."[69] These and other professions opened slowly and only partially to Black people, but they did open and that helped buoy the Black professional class but did little for the average Black worker.[70]

The Long Stagnation: Black Income and Wealth, 1970 to 2020

As the 1960s came to a close, Black Americans had just achieved what promised to be formal legal equality after 250 years of slavery (1619–1865) and nearly a century of Jim Crow segregation (1866–1954/1965). *Brown v. Board* (1954) slowly pried open the public schools and the Civil Rights Acts (1957, 1964, 1965), the Voting Rights Act (1965), and the Fair Housing Act (1968) promised broader social and political opportunities. Economic progress since the end of World War II had seen the income of Black men rise from 50 percent of White male income to 60 percent. And then, as Darity and Mullen wrote, "Astoundingly, the ratio of income the average black person receives relative to the average white person has remained largely unchanged for the past fifty years, at about 60 percent."[71]

Several changes in modern U.S. labor markets, and the economy more generally, have helped produce stagnation in income and wealth not just for Black Americans but for other minorities and many White Americans. When the New Deal/Great Society Democrat majority wheezed its last in the late 1960s, Richard Nixon was there to prescribe social conservatism and law and order.[72] But a group of European economists and their American apostles, led by Milton Friedman, James Buchanan, and Alan Greenspan, had a stronger prescription in mind. Once Ronald Reagan adopted their prescription of small government, low taxes, deregulation, and free markets – a policy package known as neoliberalism – getting government out of the way so capitalism and free markets could address society's needs seemed the new order of the day. Markets were said to be class- and color-blind.[73] Nonetheless, most minorities did not do well under the neoliberal order. Since the 1980s, most economic gains have gone to a narrow band of the wealthy, the overwhelming share of whom are White, though the Black middle and professional class has expanded somewhat. First we look at changes by race in labor force participation, unemployment, and poverty, and then we look at median family wealth by race.

For most Americans most of the time, a job, hopefully a stable job with good benefits, provides the foundation for income and wealth building. Historically, White Americans have had more consistent access to good jobs than Black and Hispanic Americans, but work is required of most, particularly in those decades between school, whenever that ends, and retirement, when and if that arrives. The Bureau of Labor Statistics, through its Current Population Survey, has long measured the labor force participation rate: the number of people in the labor force as a percentage of the civilian non-institutional population. The labor force includes the employed and the unemployed, those working or actively looking for work, but does

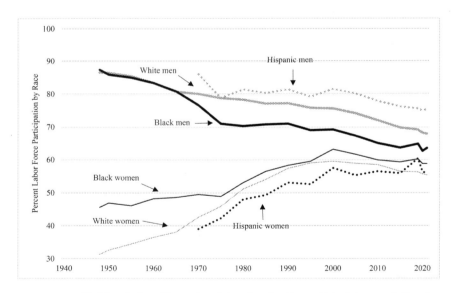

FIGURE 6.4 Civilian Labor Force Participation by Race, Ethnicity, and Gender, 1948–2021

Sources: ProQuest, *Statistical Abstract of the United States*, 2023 Online Edition, Table 621, "Civilian Labor Force Participation Rates and Projections: 2021–2031." Similar tables back to 1970. Data for 1948–1970 comes from "Manpower Report to the President," Department of Labor, March 1973, Table A-4, 131–132, files.eric.ed.gov/fulltext/ED075581.pdf; race divisions are White and Black and Other Races.

not include the military or those institutionalized in prisons, mental institutions, or similar facilities.

However, even among the civilian non-institutionalized population, not all adults, not even all healthy adults, actually work for pay. Some are sick or disabled, some are caregivers for the young or the old, some have few marketable skills, some simply choose not to work, and some are retired. Yet, the health and vibrancy of the U.S. economy has depended historically upon most adult men, and increasingly adult women too, working for income. Fortunately, we have excellent data on labor force participation rates since 1960 by race, ethnicity, and gender.

Figure 6.4 highlights a series of fascinating developments in who makes up the American workforce. The overall labor force participation rate (not shown in the figure) suggests glacial stability since 1960. From a labor force participation rate just under 60 percent in 1960, there was a slow steady rise through 2000 to 67.1 percent and then an equally slow and steady decline to 61.7 percent in 2021. Beneath this apparent stability has been broad, even tumultuous change – some for the good, some not.

First, labor force participation among men and women, irrespective of race (also not shown in Figure 6.4), has moved in broadly understandable ways. Labor force participation among men declined from 83.3 percent to 67.6 percent between 1960 and 2021. The participation rate slowly fell through the upper 70s between the mid-1960s and the mid-1990s, dipping below 70 percent in 2013 and settling at 67.6 percent in 2021. Countering the decline in male labor force participation was a somewhat larger rise in female participation. In 1960, just 37.7 percent of American women worked for wages. By 1978, 50 percent of women did, and the female participation rate peaked at 61.4 percent by 1998, and then began a two decade slow decline to 56.1 percent in 2021. Between 1960 and 2021, the male rate slipped 15.7 points, from 83.3 percent to 67.6 percent; the female rate over that same period rose 18.6 percent, from 37.7 percent to 56.1 percent. While these figures highlight gains to women's independence and equality, it is also true that women make less than men do, only about 60 percent of male wages in 1960 and 82 percent in 2020.[74] If women's pay continues to move towards men's pay, the U.S. economy will be more resilient and more equitable due to this broad realignment of the American workforce.

Other changes, quite evident in Figure 6.4, have also occurred. In 1960, 83.4 percent of White men and 83.4 percent of Black men were in the labor force. Black men made less, just 52.6 percent of what White men made in 1960, but by 1974 Black pay had broken 60 percent, crested at 69.1 in 2007, and then fell back to 61.8 percent in 2020. Adding to Black travails is that Black labor force participation fell below White participation by six percentage points in 1971, 79.2 percent to 73.2 percent, and has essentially stayed four to eight points behind White rates ever since. In 2021, the White male participation rate was 67.9 percent, the Black rate 63.5 percent. Hispanic male labor force participation, first reported in 1970 has run steadily ahead of White and Black male rates throughout – usually about five points ahead of White men and ten or twelve points ahead of Black men. In 2021, the Hispanic male labor participation rate was 75.4 percent.

In 1960, Black women were about 12 points more likely to be in the labor force than White women, 48.2 percent to 36.5 percent. White women made up much of that ground by 1980, 51.2 percent to Black women's 53.1 percent and Hispanic women's 48 percent. Black women have always run a few points ahead of White and Hispanic women in terms of presence in the labor force, though more narrowly in recent years. In 2021, 58.8 percent of Black women, 55.8 percent of Hispanic women, and 55.4 percent of White women were in the labor force. The decline in male labor force participation rates is unfortunate, for reasons that we will explore in more detail below, but the increase in female participation so evident in Figure 6.4 recovered part of that decline and enhanced economic equality in our society.

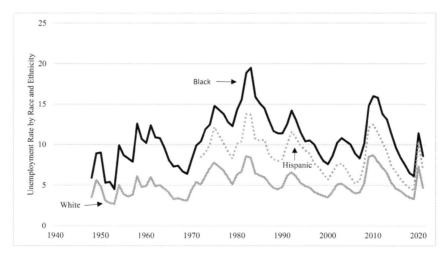

FIGURE 6.5 Unemployment Rate by Race and Ethnicity, 1948–2021

Sources: U.S. Census, *Statistical Abstract of the United States,* 2023 Online Edition, Table 657, "Unemployed Workers—Summary 1990–2021." Data for 1948–1971 comes from "Manpower Report to the President," Department of Labor, March 1973, Table A-14, 145, files.eric.ed.gov/fulltext/ED075581.pdf; race divisions are White and Black and Other Races.

Income, Wealth, and Race in America **183**

Still, Black and Hispanic incomes lag White incomes. Low wages and a limited financial cushion make periods of unemployment hard to endure, and yet, in our stratified economy, Black and Hispanic Americans suffer higher rates of unemployment than White Americans. Remarkably, as shown so clearly in Figure 6.5, while Hispanic unemployment rates run about 50 percent higher than White rates, Black rates run two to two and a half times higher than White rates – yes, two to two and a half times higher. The average unemployment rate for White Americans since 1972, when good data became available, has been 5.6 percent and never higher than the 8.7 percent reached in 2010. The average Hispanic unemployment rate since 1972 was 8.8 percent and went as high as 13.8 percent in 1982. Black unemployment, a true scourge over the past half century, has averaged 11.9, with a high of 19.5 percent in 1983.[75] While the White unemployment rate never breached 8.7 for a full year, the Black unemployment rate was above 10 percent in 37 of the 49 years after 1972, including every year in the quarter century between 1972 and 1997 and in all but two years between 2002 and 2014. Obviously, periods of unemployment interrupt income and inhibit wealth accumulation as people and families are forced to draw down savings.

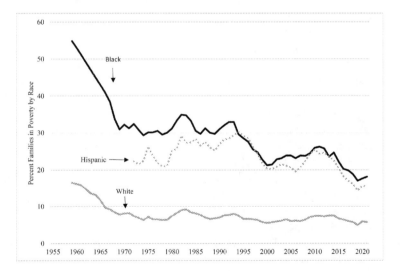

FIGURE 6.6 Poverty Status of People in Families by Race and Ethnicity, 1959–2021

Source: U.S. Census, Historical Poverty Tables, Table 2, "Poverty Status of People by Family Relationship, Race, and Hispanic Origin, 1959–2021," https://www.census.gov/data/tables/time-series/demo/income-poverty/historical-poverty-people.html.

Like unemployment, poverty has always been a major burden on minority life in the United States. In the nineteenth century, Black people were the poorest people in the poorest part of the country and Hispanics, then largely limited to the Southwest, were not far behind. Poverty was normal, if not quite universal, for Hispanic and Black Americans well into the twentieth century.[76]

In 1960, White families experienced poverty at a rate of 16.2 percent, but after President Johnson's Great Society programs, several of which explicitly were anti-poverty programs, took effect, White family poverty fell to 8.1 percent in 1970 and 6.3 percent in 1974. It bounced back up to 9.2 percent in 1983, before settling into a 4 to 8 percent range more recently. Minority poverty rates, while they have come down too, have remained two to three times White family poverty rates. Black and Hispanic family poverty rates have tracked each other closely since the early 1990s, well above White rates, clearly indicating a two-tier economic system.

Black family poverty rates remained over half, 53 percent, in 1960. They dipped below 40 percent for the first time in 1967, below 30 percent in 1974, and below 20 percent for the first time in 2017 and stood at the all-time low of 17 percent in 2019 before edging back up to 18.1 percent in 2021. Hispanic family poverty rates were measured for the first time in 1972 at 22.3 percent, ten points below the Black family poverty rate that year. Hispanic rates rose into the mid- and upper 20s through the 1980s and 1990s before settling back into the low 20s. Only once before 2017, in 2006, did Hispanic family poverty fall below 20 percent. In 2019, before the COVID-19 pandemic hit, the Hispanic family poverty rate hit 14.4 percent, an all-time low, before increasing to 15.5 percent in 2021. Clearly, family poverty rates have come down since 1960 but minority family rates almost always run two to three times the White family rate.

Low wages and high unemployment and poverty rates explain a lot, but there is a bigger picture. Perhaps the most powerful cause, certainly the most persistent cause, of Black economic stagnation, even during what seemed like the good times, is that the American dream of intergenerational progress has not and does not work for Black people, especially poor Black people. Collins and Wanamaker identify starkly limited intergenerational mobility for Black people as one of the most important factors holding Black Americans in the lower reaches of the income scale. Chillingly, they write that, "from the end of Reconstruction, . . . to the beginning of the twenty-first century. . . . our results show a sharp disadvantage for black men relative to white men in the likelihood of escaping the bottom ranks of the income distribution . . ."[77] But some have escaped and Black income has closed the gap from about half to almost 70 percent of White income, before slipping back to 66 percent in 2021.

Margo paints a similarly broad picture as follows: "between 1900 and 1940 the black-to-white earning ratio for adult men showed an improvement of just 3 percentage points," or a glacial 0.7 percent per decade, "while in the subsequent forty years the ratio increased by a dramatic 13 percentage points," or 3.25 percent per decade. "Thus, in 1940, the average annual earnings of black men were about 48 percent of those of white men, but in 1980 the earnings ratio had risen to 61 percent."[78] Even if the earnings gap had continued to close at the rate of 3.25 percent per decade, it would have taken a century to close completely – but the closing slowed. Collins and Wanamaker note that, "By 2010, the black/white income ratio had risen to 64 percent," or an increase of about 1 percent per decade since 1980.[79]

More recently Raj Chetty and his Harvard research team have been the most prominent and insightful analysts of racial economic prospects and accomplishments. Chetty is the William A. Ackman Professor of Economics and Founding Director of the Opportunity Insights project at Harvard. Chetty reported that "Among children who grew up in the bottom fifth of the [income] distribution, 10.6 percent of whites make it into the top fifth of household incomes themselves, . . . By contrast, only 7.1 percent of Hispanic children born in the bottom fifth make it to the top fifth, along with . . . a tiny 2.5 percent of black children." And at the top end of the income scale, "White children whose parents are in the top fifth of the income distribution have a 41.1 percent chance of staying there as adults; for Hispanic children, the rate is 30.6 percent, . . . But for black children, it's only 18 percent."[80]

Chetty's research is part of what Eduardo Bonilla-Silva has called, "A substantial body of literature on white-black employment differences [that] has documented the influence of labor market discrimination, wage differentials, occupational segmentation, as well as income and wealth inequalities, in explaining racially differentiated economic outcomes."[81] This work occurs throughout the social sciences, including in history, sociology, and political science. In economics it is often called "stratification economics." Stratification economics treats dual labor markets and outcomes, one for White people, another for minorities, as a long-standing, though perhaps not permanent, feature of the U.S. economy.

The Harvard philosopher Michael Sandel and others see a devaluing of work and working people;[82] while the sociologist Mark Robert Rank observed that, "One of the economic trends over the past 40 years [now 50] has been the declining percentage of good jobs that can adequately support a family. . . . jobs that pay a livable wage, have benefits, are relatively stable, and possess good working conditions. . . . approximately one-third of all jobs today are low paying."[83] At this point, it should come as no surprise that "whites have a disproportionate share of good jobs relative to their share of employment, and Blacks and Latinos are disproportionately underrepresented in good jobs. . . . [I]n 2016, 58 percent of whites, 41 percent of Blacks, and 37 percent of Latinos held good jobs."[84] A 2020 study of high-paying professional jobs, most requiring a college degree, declared that, "Structural racism is evident everywhere in America, but especially in the makeup of the country's highest paying professions. From law to finance to software development, data show wide gaps between white and Black workers, not only in salary but in racial representation in each field."[85] Minority representation and pay have been a general problem in the STEM fields and a particularly visible problem in high tech. As late as 2020, Google, as a particularly striking but not an isolated example,

> reported that 5.9% of its employees and contractors are Latino and 3.7% are Black. . . . The number of Black people in leadership or highly compensated roles is lower still. For instance, at Google, only 2.6 percent of leadership and 2.4 percent of technical workers are Black. At Facebook, Black people make up only 3.1% of those in leadership roles and 1.5% of those in technical roles.[86]

The wealth gap, usually measured as Black and/or Hispanic median net worth as a fraction or percentage of White median net worth, was the focus of an important study mentioned earlier in this chapter. Princeton economist Ellora Derenoncourt and her colleagues built a new data set measuring the Black/White wealth gap back to 1860. In 1860, with nine in ten Black people still enslaved, White people had 56 times the net wealth of Black citizens. By 1870, after emancipation, the White advantage had fallen to 26 to 1, 10 to 1 in 1920, and 7 to 1 by 1950, where it essentially remained stuck.[87] This paper will receive close scrutiny because its data are path-breaking.

The modern wealth gap, which we explore in Figure 6.7, has traditionally been studied using data from the Federal Reserve Bank of the United States. The Fed has conducted the Survey of Consumer Finances since 1948. The surveys, conducted every three years, were standardized in 1983 and the surveys from 1983 through 2019 are available on the Fed website. Between 1983 and 2019, Black and Hispanic families have steadily had one-sixth to one-eighth of White families' net worth, and sometimes one-tenth or less. Figure 6.7 again shows us a two-tier economy, not in terms of annual income, but in terms of net worth accumulated over lifetimes. The 1980s were difficult for minority families and net worth slumped. In 1995, Black families had $18,200 in net worth, Hispanic families had $20,300,

Income, Wealth, and Race in America   187

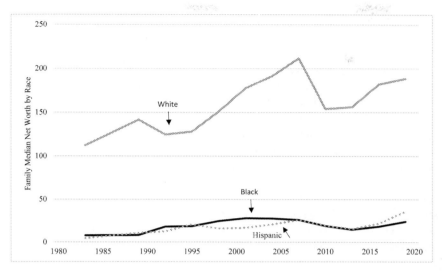

FIGURE 6.7   Family Median Net Worth by Race and Ethnicity, 1983–2019 (in thousands of 2019 dollars)

Source: Federal Reserve Bank of the United States, Survey of Consumer Finances, Table 4, "Family Net Worth, by Selected Characteristics of Families," 1989–2019 surveys, https://www.federalreserve.gov/econres/scfindex.htm.

and White families had $127,900. As late as 2013, both Black and Hispanic families had $14–15,000 in net worth while White family wealth was $155,900. 2019 was better for minority families, Black families had $24,100, Hispanic families had $36,200 while White family net worth was $188,200. But then the COVID-19 pandemic hit families, especially minority families, hard.[88] Not surprisingly, a recent study by the Federal Reserve Bank of Minneapolis, found that, "The racial wealth gap is . . . still as large as it was in the 1950s and 1960s. The median black household persistently has less than 15% of the wealth of the median white household."[89]

Moreover, among the wealthiest Americans, Black Americans are barely present. In late 2020, *The Economist* magazine reported that, "By one federal reserve measure, around 2% of black families have assets worth over $1 million; over 15% of white ones do."[90] A similar report from the Brookings Institution reported that, "Among the richest 10% of households, only 1.9% of these households are Black. . . . Within the top 1% of households, less than 1% identify as Black."[91]

Throughout this chapter we have presented evidence that Black Americans, and minority Americans more generally, enjoy fewer good jobs, less income and wealth, and suffer more unemployment, poverty, and inequality than White Americans. Scholars and analysts argue that these results are the product of an historical, deep-seated racism traced to the nation's early roots. This is undoubtedly true, at least in large measure, but many White Americans do not know it, do not believe it, and, perhaps more importantly, will not be convinced of it. Most White "Americans vastly underestimate racial economic inequality, especially the racial wealth gap."[92] A recent study in *Psychology Today* of 1,000 Americans reported that "the majority believed that black families . . . in 2016 were about nine-tenths as wealthy as white families. In fact, . . . black families had less than one-tenth the wealth of white families. . . ."[93] Drawing on these and similar insights, the political scientist John Sides and his colleagues have sought to explain at least some of Donald Trump's support in his 2016 presidential election victory in these terms, writing that, "There was a powerful idea that 'my group' – in this case, white Americans – was suffering because other groups, such as immigrants or minorities, were getting benefits they did not deserve."[94] If White Americans believe most minorities are doing just as well as they are in income and wealth, why would they support special compensatory programs for minorities – they wouldn't and they don't.[95]

We close this chapter with a tragi-comic example of White identity politics rallying to deny a benefit to Black Americans and preserve White advantage. The Biden administration proposed to acknowledge the negative impacts on Black farmers of decades of financial discrimination by paying off $4 billion of their debt. First, White farmers, declaring that they were victims of reverse discrimination, demanded debt forgiveness too, apparently undisturbed by the fact that they and their White farming ancestors had received loans denied to Black farmers. Second, three financial industry advocacy groups, including the powerful American Bankers Association, came out in opposition to the program arguing that the government paying the loans early would deny them the interest and fees they had expected to collect on those loans in the years ahead. The banks, wait for it, argued that if the struggling Black farmers were to benefit by loan forgiveness, they, the non-struggling banks, wanted their anticipated future interest and fees to be paid to them. To highlight the narrow selfishness of the banks' position, Alan Rappeport of *The New York Times* understatedly observed that, "While America's banks have flourished in the last century, the number of Black-owned farms has declined sharply since 1920, to less than 40,000 today from about a million."[96]

Typically, Black farmers pointed to historical discrimination and White farmers pointed to reverse discrimination in the current policy. John Boyd, a Black farmer lamented that, "Anytime . . . there's money for Blacks, those [White] groups speak up and say how unfair it is. But it's not unfair when they're spitting on you, when they're calling you racial epithets, when they're tearing up your application." Jon Stevens, a White farmer simply rejected the Black loan forgiveness program, saying "It's anti-white. . . . Since when does Agriculture get into this kind of racial politics."[97] Since forever, Jon. Remarkably, but not surprisingly, America First Legal, an advocacy group started by Trump senior advisor Stephen Miller, joined the fray on the side of the White farmers claiming discrimination.[98] The loan forgiveness program languished in the courts, until White farmers were made eligible as well.

In Chapter 5, we saw that Black people were denied access to education and under Jim Crow access was limited and remains limited today. Nonetheless, Black educational attainment has risen very near White levels in high school graduation rates, though they still lag in college and professional graduation rates. Yet, as we saw in this chapter, Black and Hispanic income as a proportion of White income, just under 50 percent for Black Americans in the late nineteenth century, rose into the mid- and upper 60s in the 2000s before dropping back to the mid-60s in 2021. This painfully slow economic progress was also reflected in the fact that Black and Hispanic Americans have between 10 and 15 percent of White net worth. Not surprisingly, Hispanic unemployment and poverty rates are half again as high as White rates while Black rates are two to three times higher. It is hard to get ahead when burdened by high unemployment and poverty and low pay and net worth. Now we turn to the myriad impacts of social and financial deprivation on Black health.

Notes

1 Peter H. Lindert and Jeffrey G. Williamson, *Unequal Gains: American Growth and Inequality since 1700* (Princeton, NJ: Princeton University Press, 2016), 14, 43–44.
2 Ian Morris, *Why the West Rules—For Now: The Patterns of History, and What They Reveal About the Future* (New York: Farrar, Straus, and Giroux, 2010), 40, 500. See also David Hackett Fischer, *African Founders: How Enslaved People Expanded American Ideals* (New York: Simon & Schuster, 2022), 390.
3 Lindert and Williamson, *Unequal Gains*, 37, 43, 95.
4 Woodrow Wilson, *A History of the American People*, 5 vols. (New York: Harper & Brothers Publishers, 1901–1902), 2:104. See also Richard F. Bensel, *Yankee Leviathan: The Origins of Central State Authority in America, 1859–1877* (New York: Cambridge University Press, 1990), 12.
5 Joe R. Feagin, *The White Racial Frame: Centuries of Racial Framing and Counter-Framing*, 3rd ed. (New York: Routledge, 2020), 40–41. See also Khalil Gibran Muhammad, "Sugar," in *The 1619 Project*, ed. Nikole Hannah-Jones, Caitlin Roper, Ilena Silverman, and Jake Silverstein (New York: The New York Times Co., 2021), 75; Heather McGhee, *The Sum of Us: What Racism Costs Everyone and How We Can Prosper Together* (New York: OneWorld, 2021), 7; see also "Race and Liberal Philosophy," *The Economist*, July 11, 2020, 47.

6 Lindert and Williamson, *Unequal Gains*, 77, 84–85.
7 W.E.B. Du Bois, *Black Reconstruction: An Essay Toward a History of the Part Which Black Folk Played in the Attempt to Reconstruct Democracy in America* (New York: Harcourt Brace and Company, 1935), 5. See also William J. Bernstein, *A Splendid Exchange: How Trade Shaped the World* (New York: Grove Press, 2008), 275; Edward L. Larson, *American Inheritance: Liberty and Slavery in the Birth of a Nation, 1765–1795* (New York: Norton, 2023), 193.
8 William A. Darity and A. Kirsten Mullen, *From Here to Equality: Reparations for Black Americans in the Twenty-First Century* (Chapel Hill, NC: University of North Carolina Press, 2020), 52, 54.
9 Robert William Fogel and Stanley L. Engerman, *Time on the Cross: The Economics of American Negro Slavery* (New York: W.W. Norton, 1974), 38.
10 Michael C. Dawson, *Behind the Mule: Race and Class in African-American Politics* (Princeton, NJ: Princeton University Press, 1994). See also Ismail K. White and Chryl N. Laird, *Steadfast Democrats: How Social Forces Shape Black Political Behavior* (Princeton, NJ: Princeton University Press, 2020), 197.
11 Frederick Douglass, "An Address to the Colored People of the United States," in *Frederick Douglass: Selected Speeches and Writings*, ed. Philip S. Foner (Chicago, IL: Lawrence Hill Books, 1999), 145. See also Rogan Kersh, *Dreams of a More Perfect Union* (Ithaca, NY: Cornell University Press, 2001), 155–162, 251.
12 Lindert and Williamson, *Unequal Gains*, 109. See also Bensel, *Yankee Leviathan*, 7, 42–43, 379, 416–419; Richard F. Bensel, *The Political Economy of American Industrialization, 1877–1900* (New York: Cambridge University Press, 2000), xxi, 2, 8, 12, 201, 218, 350, 488, 521.
13 Matthew Desmond, "Capitalism," in *The 1619 Project*, ed. Nikole Hannah-Jones, Caitlin Roper, Ilena Silverman, and Jake Silverstein (New York: The New York Times Co., 2021), 167, 184. See also Martin Wolf, *The Crisis of Democratic Capitalism* (New York: Penguin Press, 2023), 202.
14 Lerone Bennett, Jr., *Before the Mayflower: A History of the Negro in America, 1619–1962* (Chicago, IL: Johnson Publishing Company, 1962; Eastford, CT: Martino Fine Books, 2016), 73. See also Leon F. Litwack, *Trouble in Mind: Black Southerners in the Age of Jim Crow* (New York: Vintage Books, 1998), 65.
15 David W. Blight, *Frederick Douglass: Prophet of Freedom* (New York: Simon & Schuster, 2018), 77–78, 91. For comparison see the story of Lincoln's wages as a young White man in David Herbert Donald, *Lincoln* (New York: Simon & Schuster, 1995), 32–37.
16 Van Gosse, *The First Reconstruction: Black Politics in America from the Revolution to the Civil War* (Chapel Hill, NC: University of North Carolina Press, 2021), 24–25, 63–64, 384.
17 Ellora Derenoncourt, Chi Hyun Kim, Moritz Kuhn, and Moritz Schularick, "Wealth of Two Nations: The U.S. Racial Wealth Gap, 1860–2020," National Bureau of Economic Research, Working Paper 30101, June 2022, section 3.1, https://www.nber.org/papers/w30101.
18 Leon F. Litwack, *Been in the Storm So Long: The Aftermath of Slavery* (New York: Vintage Books, 1980), 81, 84.
19 Josiah Quincy, *Memoir of the Life of John Quincy Adams* (Boston, MA: Phillips, Sampson and Company, 1856), 400, 411. See also Gosse, *The First Reconstruction*, 157.
20 Steven Mintz and John Stauffer, *The Problem of Evil: Slavery, Freedom, and the Ambiguities of American Reform* (Amherst: University of Massachusetts Press, 2007), 287–297.

21 Lindert and Williamson, *Unequal Gains*, 151, 165; Bensel, *The Political Economy of American Industrialization*, 19.
22 Roger L. Ransom and Richard Sutch, *One Kind of Freedom: The Economic Consequences of Emancipation*, 2nd ed. (New York: Cambridge University Press, 2001), 176–177.
23 Litwack, *Trouble in Mind*, 34, 124–125.
24 Bennett, *Before the Mayflower*, 192; Bensel, *The Political Economy of American Industrialization*, 14.
25 Henry Louis Gates, Jr., *Stony the Road: Reconstruction, White Supremacy, and the Rise of Jim Crow* (New York: Penguin Books, 2020), 16.
26 Gavin Wright, *Old South, New South: Revolutions in the Southern Economy Since the Civil War* (Baton Rouge, LA: Louisiana State University Press, 1997), 30, 36, 87. See also Ransom and Sutch, *One Kind of Freedom*, 46.
27 Ransom and Sutch, *One Kind of Freedom*, 9.
28 Derenoncourt, et al., "Wealth of Two Nations," section 3.1.
29 Joe Martin Richardson, *The Negro in the Reconstruction of Florida*, Dissertation, Florida State University, 1963, University Microfilms, 6403611, 86.
30 Herbert G. Gutman, *Slavery and the Numbers Game: A Critique of Time on the Cross* (Chicago, IL: University of Illinois Press, 1975), 58.
31 Litwack, *Been in the Storm So Long*, 58.
32 Ransom and Sutch, *One Kind of Freedom*, 19, 198. See also Dawson, *Behind the Mule*, 53.
33 John R. McKivigan, Julie Husband, and Heather L. Kaufman, eds., *The Speeches of Frederick Douglass* (New Haven: Yale University Press, 2018), 414–453.
34 Fogel and Engerman, *Time on the Cross*, 261.
35 John W. Blassingame, ed., *Slave Testimony: Two Centuries of Letters, Speeches, Interviews, and Autobiographies* (Baton Rouge, LA: Louisiana State University, 1977), 492.
36 David Levering Lewis, *W.E.B. Du Bois: A Biography, 1868–1963* (New York: Henry Holt and Company, 2009), 159. See also Herbert Aptheker, ed., *Pamphlets and Leaflets by W.E.B. Du Bois* (White Plains, NY: Kraus-Thomson Organization Limited, 1986), 96.
37 Wright, *Old South, New South*, 12, 50, 75–76, 87. See also Richard F. Bensel, *Sectionalism and American Political Development, 1880–1980* (Madison: The University of Wisconsin Press, 1984), 62–63.
38 C. Vann Woodward, *The Burden of Southern History* (Baton Rouge, LA: Louisiana State University, 1960), 17.
39 William J. Collins and Robert A. Margo, "Historical Perspectives on Racial Differences in Schooling in the United States," National Bureau of Economic Research, Working Paper 9770, 21.
40 Ransom and Sutch, *One Kind of Freedom*, 3–4. See also Lindert and Williamson, *Unequal Gains*, 163.
41 Eduardo Bonilla-Silva, *Racism Without Racists: Color-Blind Racism and the Persistence of Racial Inequality in America*, 5th ed. (Lanham, MD: Rowman and Littlefield, 2018), 19. See also Isabel Wilkerson, "America's Enduring Caste System," *The New York Times Magazine*, July 5, 2020, 50.
42 Charles A. Roberts, "Interregional Per Capita Income Differentials and Convergence: 1880 to 1950," *The Journal of Economic History* 39, no. 1 (March 1979): 101, 111.
43 Kris James Mitchener and Ian W. McLean, "U.S. Regional Growth and Convergence, 1880–1980," *The Journal of Economic History* 59, no. 4 (December 1999): 1017, see also 1022, 1033.

44 William J. Collins and Marianne H. Wanamaker, "The Great Migration in Black and White: New Evidence on the Selection and Sorting of Southern Migrants," *The Journal of Economic History* 75, no. 4 (December 2015): 947.
45 Wright, *Old South, New South*, 55–57; see also Lindert and Williamson, *Unequal Gains*, 168.
46 Lindert and Williamson, *Unequal Gains*, 191–192.
47 Stephen Steinberg, *The Ethnic Myth: Race, Ethnicity, and Class in America* (Boston, MA: Beacon Press, 2001), 206–207. See also Isabel Wilkerson, *Caste: The Origins of Our Discontents* (New York: Random House, 2020), 135.
48 Neil Fligstein, *Going North: Migration of Blacks and Whites from the South, 1900–1950* (New York: Academic Press, 1981), 14.
49 Robert A. Margo, *Race and Schooling in the South, 1880–1950: An Economic History* (Chicago, IL: University of Chicago Press, 1990), 1, 129.
50 William J. Collins and Marianne H. Wanamaker, "Selection and Economic Gains in the Great Migration of African Americans: New Evidence from Linked Census Data," *American Economic Journal: Applied Economics* 6, no. 1 (January 2014): 220.
51 Darlene Clark Hine, *Black Victory: The Rise and Fall of the White Primary in Texas* (Columbia, MO: University of Missouri Press, 2003), 178.
52 Dorothy A. Brown, *The Whiteness of Wealth: How the Tax System Impoverishes Black Americans—And How We Can Fix It* (New York: Crown Books, 2021), 14.
53 Ira Katznelson, *Fear Itself: The New Deal and the Origins of Our Time* (New York: Liveright, 2014), 177.
54 "Report to the President on the Economic Condition of the South," Washington, D.C.: July 4, 1938, 21.
55 Michael Lind, *Land of Promise: An Economic History of the United States* (New York: HarperCollins, 2012), 343.
56 Rodney A. Brooks, *Fixing the Racial Wealth Gap* (Suffolk, VA: August Press, 2021), 8.
57 William J. Collins and Marianne H. Wanamaker, "Up from Slavery: African-American Intergenerational Mobility Since 1880," National Bureau of Economic Research, May 2017, 4.
58 Free Exchange, "Stony the Road," *The Economist*, June 13, 2020, 62.
59 Claudia Goldin and Robert A. Margo, "The Great Compression: The Wage Structure of the United States at Mid-Century," National Bureau of Economic Research, Working Paper 3817, August 1991, 1.
60 Leah Platt Boustan, "Competition in the Promised Land: Black Migration and Racial Wage Convergence in the North, 1940–1970," *The Journal of Economic History* 69, no. 3 (September 2009): 758.
61 Collins and Wanamaker, "Up from Slavery," 5.
62 Feagin, *The White Racial Frame*, 173.
63 Richard Rothstein, *The Color of Law: A Forgotten History of How Our Government Segregated America* (New York: Liveright, 2017), 153.
64 Anthony P. Carnevale, et al., "The Unequal Race for Good Jobs," Georgetown University Center on Education and the Workforce, 2019, 4.
65 Patrick Bayer and Kerwin Kofi Charles, "Divergent Paths: New Perspectives on Earnings Differences Between Black and White Men Since 1940," *Quarterly Journal of Economics* 133, no. 3 (2018): 1460–1461.
66 Bayer and Charles, "Divergent Paths," 1461.
67 Bayer and Charles, "Divergent Paths," 1461.

68 William Julius Wilson, *The Truly Disadvantaged: The Inner City, the Underclass, and Public Policy* (Chicago, IL: University Press of Chicago, 1987), 125.
69 Ellen Messer-Davidow, *The Making of Reverse Discrimination: How DeFunis and Bakke Bleached Racism from Equal Protection* (Lawrence, KS: University Press of Kansas, 2021), 211, 117.
70 Linda Villarosa, *Under the Skin: The Hidden Toll of Racism on American Lives and on the Health of Our Nation* (New York: Doubleday, 2022), 186.
71 Darity and Mullen, *From Here to Equality*, 38; see also Lindert and Williamson, *Unequal Gains*, 222–223.
72 Gary Gerstle, *American Crucible: Race and Nation in the Twentieth Century* (Princeton, NJ: Princeton University Press, 2001, rev. ed. 2017), 9–10.
73 Gary Gerstle, *The Rise and Fall of the Neoliberal Order: America and the World in the Free Market Era* (New York: Oxford University Press, 2022).
74 Gerstle, *The Rise and Fall of the Neoliberal Order*, 147.
75 Michelle Alexander, *The New Jim Crow: Mass Incarceration in the Age of Colorblindness* (New York: The New Press, 2010; 10th anniversary ed., 2020), 270–271.
76 Reuel Rogers and Jae Yeon Kim, "Rewiring Linked Fate: Bringing Back History, Agency, and Power," *Perspectives on Politics* 21, no. 1 (March 2023): 290–294.
77 Collins and Wanamaker, "Up from Slavery," 1–2.
78 Margo, *Race and Schooling*, 1, see also 129.
79 Collins and Wanamaker, "Up from Slavery," 1. See also Richard Haass, *The Bill of Obligations: Ten Habits of Good Citizens* (New York: Penguin Press, 2023), 29, 116–117.
80 Darity and Mullen, *From Here to Equality*, 34. See also Raj Chetty, Nathaniel Hendren, Maggie R. Jones, and Sonya R. Porter, "Race and Economic Opportunity in the United States: An Intergenerational Perspective," *Quarterly Journal of Economics* 135, no. 2 (May 2020): 711–783; David J. Erickson, *The Fifth Freedom: Guaranteeing an Opportunity Rich Childhood for All* (Washington, D.C.: Brookings, 2023), 5, 15–17.
81 Bonilla-Silva, *Racism Without Racists*, 44.
82 Michael J. Sandel, *The Tyranny of Merit: What's Become of the Common Good?* (New York: Farrar, Straus, and Giroux, 2020), 19.
83 Mark Robert Rank, Thomas A. Hirschl, and Kirk A. Foster, *Chasing the American Dream: Understanding What Shapes Our Fortunes* (New York: Oxford University Press, 2014), 70. See also Ashley Jardina, *White Identity Politics* (New York: Cambridge University Press, 2019), 93–94.
84 Carnevale, et al., "The Unequal Race for Good Jobs," 1–2.
85 Dan Kopf and Ana Campoy, "America's Highest- Paying Jobs Have the Worst Black-White Salary Gap," *Quartz*, August 3, 2020, https://qz.com/1882178.
86 Sam Dean and Johana Bhuiyan, "Why Are Black and Latino People Still Kept Out of Tech Industry," *Los Angeles Times*, June 24, 2020.
87 Derenoncourt, et al., "Wealth of Two Nations."
88 Patricia Cohen and Ben Casselman, "For Laid Off Minorities, Recovery Looks Distant," *New York Times*, June 6, 2020, B1, B4.
89 Moritz Kuhn, Moritz Schularick, and Ulrike I. Steins, "Income and Wealth Inequality in America, 1949–2016," Opportunity and Inclusive Growth Institute, Federal Reserve Bank of Minneapolis, Institute Working Paper 9, June 2018, 40. See also Derenoncourt, et al., "Wealth of Two Nations," Introduction and section 3.1.

90 "America's Black Elite," *The Economist*, August 22, 2020, 24–25.
91 Vanessa Williamson, "Closing the Racial Wealth Gap Requires Heavy, Progressive Taxation of Wealth," Brookings Institution, December 9, 2020, 8–9. See also Brooks, *Fixing the Racial Wealth Gap*, 56.
92 Michael W. Kraus, et al., "The Misperception of Racial Economic Inequality," *Perspectives on Psychological Science* 14, no. 6 (2019): Abstract. https://doi.org/10.1177/1745691619863049.
93 Brown, *The Whiteness of Wealth*, 215; see also Kraus, et al., "The Misperception of Racial Economic Inequality," 899–921.
94 John Sides, Michael Tesler, and Lynn Vavreck, *Identity Crisis: The 2016 Presidential Campaign and the Battle for the Meaning of America* (Princeton, NJ: Princeton University Press, 2018), 71. See also Thomas Bryne Edsall, *The Point of No Return: American Democracy at the Crossroads* (Princeton, NJ: Princeton University Press, 2023), 24.
95 George Packer, *Last Best Hope: America in Crisis and Renewal* (New York: Farrar, Straus, and Giroux, 2021), 138.
96 Alan Rappeport, "Banks Fight Biden's $4 Billion Plan to Ease Black Farmers' Debt," *New York Times*, May 20, 2021, A1, A17. See also Alan Rappeport, "Debt Relief Blocked, Black Farmers Fear Ruin," *New York Times*, February 22, 2022, A1, A16.
97 Jack Healy, "Windfall for Black Farmers Roils Rural America," *New York Times*, May 23, 2021, A1, A19.
98 Erik Larson, "Sue the Left," *BusinessWeek*, October 18, 2021. See also Ximena Bustillo, "Black Farmers Call for Justice from the USDA," *NPR*, February 12, 2023.

7
RACE AND HEALTH IN AMERICA

"Of all the forms of inequality, injustice in health is the most shocking and the most inhuman."

Martin Luther King, Jr., 1966,
Where Do We Go from Here

Human life for much of history was tenuous at best. Before modern medicine, which by any reasonable measure is no more than 150 years old, almost any injury or illness raised the harrowing prospect of debility and death. Treatment was rendered by family and friends and perhaps some keeper of the community's wisdom. Some treatments were effective, but many were not and some did additional harm. The weaker and more vulnerable the afflicted, the less likely their full recovery. Nature commonly took its course. These facts pertained over many millennia and, to some extent, their imprints remain visible today. Only recently, in the historical blink of an eye, did improvements in nutrition, security, and knowledge, disrupt the traditional structural sources of human vulnerability – though, as always, for some sooner and more thoroughly than for others.

In the U.S., both before and after care became particularly efficacious, the White and wealthy got what was accounted the best care, and those further down the hierarchies of race, gender, and wealth, got what care their station required or they could find. As medical advances slowly arrived and accumulated, their benefits remained overwhelmingly private, for those who knew of them, had access to them, and could afford them. Local governments made modest and grudging provision for indigent health care throughout colonial and early national history, but state and federal governments did not become active until the twentieth century. There was a brief and narrow federal initiative, through the medical division of the Freedmen's Bureau after the Civil War, but passage of Medicare and Medicaid in the 1960s and of Obamacare and its expansions after 2010 were the two great attempts to expand access and improve quality of care to those long excluded from the nation's medical services.

Health and Longevity

Archaeologists studying human fossils going back tens of thousands of years have found consistent human life-spans of thirty to thirty-five years and infant mortality rates averaging about 30 percent.[1] Plentiful sources of sustenance might improve those averages a bit and hard times certainly might limit life expectancy and increase child mortality, but the averages were remarkably consistent across time, space, and cultures.[2] Diseases, of course, affected man throughout time and all over the globe, but oftentimes broad civilizational communities would build some degree of immunity so that people and pathogens existed in an unhealthy balance. But since most death came mysteriously, from unknown air or waterborne pathogens, infection of small scratches and cuts, and sometimes from great injuries or wounds, it struck the meek and the mighty equally.

Counter-intuitively, as explained in Chapter 2, the Americas offered less natural support to daily sustenance and social development than did the Old World civilizational cores in the Mediterranean, Mesopotamia, India, and China. We think of the Americas, especially North America, as a rich and bountiful landscape, "amber waves of grain" and all that, but before and for centuries after first European contact the Americas were a hard place to be a human. Both plant and animal species and varieties were unevenly spread across the globe and could not be domesticated where their natural bases were not present. For example, of the five great civilizational grains, only the base of corn, called teosinte, existed in the Americas pre-contact. Similarly, of the great mammals most useful to man, none existed in the Americas pre-contact. Beyond the llama and alpaca in the Andean highlands, both too small to be ridden and capable of carrying only modest loads, the indigenous peoples of the Americas had only dogs.[3] And yes, the buffalo was present in North America, but he is an angry creature generally unwilling to do man's work. Moreover, the isolation of the Americas promoted a local balance of people and pathogens, but left the population acutely vulnerable to foreign pathogens should they ever appear.[4]

The American ecology made the always difficult transition from hunter-gatherer to agricultural society particularly challenging. Sometimes, changes, whether forced or chosen, brought wholesale death.[5] Excavation of the Dickson Mounds, Native American burial mounds in the Illinois River Valley, show the devastating impact of a twelfth century transition from a hunter-gatherer culture to a farming culture based on maize. Life expectancy dropped from 26 to 19, infant mortality rose from 30 to 50 percent, and the proportion of adults reaching 50 years of age dropped from 14 percent to 5 percent.[6]

Even more dramatically, "widespread dissemination of European-borne illnesses such as smallpox, measles, and influenza, fueled the decimation of tens of millions of Native Americans who lacked immunological protection against foreign germs."[7] The indigenous peoples of the Americas "died in droves of diseases the Europeans, Africans, and Asians had accommodated themselves to long, long ago."[8] In Mexico, Panama, and the Andean highlands European-borne diseases helped bring down the great Aztec and Inca empires, while in North America the more scattered indigenous populations also suffered greatly.

Disease as Mystery in Colonial America

It was common throughout the Americas for European diseases to outrun European soldiers and settlers so the invaders arrived in new territories to find the native population already ravaged. Thomas Hariot of the Roanoke Colony, established in 1587 at the entrance to Albemarle Sound off what would become the North Carolina coast, marveled that every native village they visited, "within a few days after our departure from everies such townes, that people began to die very fast, and many in short space." The early days of the Massachusetts Bay Colony saw similar pestilence; "A European who lived in that area in 1622 wrote that Indians had 'died on heapes, as they lay in their houses; and the living, that were able to shift for themselves, would runne away and let them dy. . . .'"[9] In running away, the survivors, if infected, spread the disease to others who had no direct contact themselves with Europeans.

The demise of the Native American population awed and strangely gratified the White settler populations. They concluded that God was clearing the continent for their more fruitful use, wielding disease to weaken and even remove their enemies. During the revolutionary and early national periods, both Crèvecoeur and Tocqueville authorized the settler view that, in Crèvecoeur's words, the natives had been "hastening toward a total annihilation" since the first colonists arrived and Tocqueville marveled at "an ancient people . . . melting away daily like snow in the sunshine and disappearing before our eyes from the face of the earth."[10] Few tears were shed; most settlers spent little time trying to figure out what was happening, much less how to stop it.

Though the native peoples were especially vulnerable, even among Europeans at home and in colonial America, these pathogens took a grave toll into the twentieth century. Progress against them came slowly, unevenly, and often unexpectedly. Smallpox was a particularly efficient, highly communicable killer of both Europeans and of Native Americans. Death rates averaged 30 percent among Europeans and much higher among Native Americans. While "variation . . ., a technique whereby healthy children were deliberately exposed" to smallpox was known in parts of Africa as well as "throughout China, India, and Persia by the 1600s," it was unknown in England and the colonies. Mary Montagu, wife of an English diplomat in Turkey, had her son exposed in 1718 and reported the treatment upon her return to London. By 1721 knowledge of this treatment was in Boston, likely arriving by various routes, including "via slaves who had a long history employing the procedure in their African homeland. . . . [A] slave named Onesimus. . . . informed his master that he was not vulnerable to the smallpox. 'People take juice of smallpox, cut skin, and put in a drop,' he explained. The master happened to be Cotton Mather," Boston's preeminent cleric.[11] Mather, and his doctor, Zabdiel Boylston, advocated inoculation during the 1721 plague in which 844 died. Mather, for his trouble, had a small bomb hurled through the window of his home. The bomb did not detonate, so the attached note survived; it read, "Cotton Mather, you dog, dam you! I'll inoculate you with this; with a pox to you." Anti-vaccination zealotry has a long history.

Fifty years later, as the American Revolution raged, smallpox tore through General George Washington's army. Sickness in the ranks was blamed for battlefield losses at Boston and Quebec. On February 5, 1777, Washington ordered mass inoculation to check the virus. Despite the fact that the procedure carried a 2 to 3 percent death rate, there was little reluctance among the troops. They understood, as Washington did, that: "Necessity . . . seems to require the measure, for should the disorder infect the army in the natural way . . . we should have more to dread from it than from the sword of the enemy." The inoculation campaign was successful – in fact, Cornwallis had his British troops inoculated as well – and by the 1790s vaccination replaced variation, making the procedure much safer for the recipient.[12]

Even natural processes like childbearing, which the vast majority of women have always experienced during the early adult years, carried risk for many. Robert "King" Carter, one of the wealthiest planters and slaveowners in early eighteenth-century Virginia, had sixteen children by two wives; six of the children died in infancy or childhood. Thomas Jefferson's wife, Martha Wayles Skelton, lost her first husband, Bathurst Skelton, and son, John, after a brief marriage. In ten years of marriage to Jefferson,

Martha bore six more children, only two of whom survived childhood.[13] Martha died of complications of childbirth in September 1782. Her last child, Lucy Elizabeth Jefferson, died at two and a half. The White and wealthy faced regular tragedy, but the Black and poor faced these tragedies alone. As Dayna Bowen Matthew, a health law and policy expert and Dean of the George Washington University Law School, has written, in colonial America and in America today, "health and illness for all racial and ethnic groups follow a social gradient so that minority populations, which disproportionately occupy low socioeconomic strata, also predictably suffer worse health outcomes than whites do."[14]

Although national life expectancy and infant mortality data did not become available until the late nineteenth century, one remarkable study reported sobering results for slave longevity on the Ball family's deadly South Carolina rice plantations between 1800 and 1860. During the early nineteenth century, male slaves lived an average of 20 years and female slaves 21.5 years. Child mortality averaged 21 percent before rising to 25 percent in the 1840s and 30 percent in the 1850s.[15]

Health and Health Care in the Early National Period

Despite occasional important advances, like smallpox inoculation, the states of medical knowledge and treatment in the late eighteenth and early nineteenth centuries were almost unimaginably primitive. The last days of former President George Washington, one of America's most prominent and wealthy citizens, involved multiple bleedings, in which 60 percent of his blood was drained, enemas, purges, and the application of exotic pastes and gargles.[16] None of it, presumably the best medical treatment available, worked. When Washington died on December 14, 1799, he likely welcomed it. Then as now, not everyone had such "good" care readily available to them. The treatment offered to Washington's slaves and other slaves throughout the nation would have been strictly at their master's discretion. Masters, of course, would have made an economic calculation about the amount and kind of medical care, as well as food, shelter, and leisure, required to maintain their human chattel as productive assets.

Even among White people, especially poor White people and immigrants, the rise of cities and manufacturing in the early decades of the nineteenth century, together with still limited knowledge of public health remediation, put health and longevity under increasing pressure. Remarkably, "overall life expectancy in the United States declined by *thirteen* years between 1800 and 1850. . . . Meaningful improvements in overall mortality would not arrive until the last decades of the nineteenth century."[17] The importance of hygiene, both personal and communal, remained a mystery until the arrival of germ theory late in the century.

That high and low, rich and poor, remained vulnerable, if not quite equally vulnerable, deep into the nineteenth century was highlighted by the experiences of Abraham Lincoln, Theodore Roosevelt, and many others. By his twenties, Lincoln had lost his brother Thomas, his sister Sarah, and his mother. Then his betrothed, Ann Rutledge, died. At forty-one he lost a son, Edward Parker Lincoln, just short of his fourth birthday. But the most stunning blow came on February 20, 1862, when Lincoln's eleven-year-old son Willie died of typhoid fever. Willie's younger brother Tad was stricken as well, but recovered. Both parents were grief-stricken and Mary Todd Lincoln was for a time debilitated. Just five months later, Secretary of War Edwin Stanton's son, James, a little less than one-year-old, died of a "botched smallpox vaccination."[18] Two decades later, Alice Lee, nineteen, married twenty-two-year-old Theodore Roosevelt. The Lees were wealthy and the Roosevelts were very wealthy. As T.R. served his first term in the New York Assembly, Alice remained in the city and prepared to deliver their first child. The child, Alice Lee Roosevelt was born on February 12, 1884. The next day in Albany, T.R. received a telegram saying his wife was not well. Presumably, everything that could be done was done, but soon after T.R. reached home, Alice died from complications following childbirth. Youth and wealth were no protection against the limits of late nineteenth-century medical knowledge and treatment. Every parent understood that if the sons and daughters of great men could be carried off against the best care available, then so certainly could their sons and daughters. The seeming randomness of it all added to the terror and the grief.

Not surprisingly, given the racial hierarchy so starkly embedded in American law and culture, when demographic information on Black citizens was first collected in the census of 1850, life expectancy and infant mortality figures differed dramatically by race; "While whites enjoyed an average life expectancy of 39.5 years," somewhat above the millennia-old average of thirty to thirty-five years, Black life expectancy was just 23 years. The high Black child mortality rate, 57 percent higher than for White children, drove down Black life expectancy."[19] Fully 90 percent of Black people were, of course, enslaved in 1850.

In twelve of the fourteen states that had appreciable slave populations in 1850, slave mothers lost more babies before their first birthday than did free mothers. Table 7.1 compares the percent enslaved in the state to the percentage of babies lost in the first year of life by slave mothers. The right-hand column presents the difference between the percent of slaves in the state population and the percent of babies lost by slave mothers. For

TABLE 7.1 Infant Deaths Among Enslaved Women as a Percent of Total Population and Deaths, 1850

State	% Enslaved of Total Population	Infant Enslaved Deaths as % of Total Infant Deaths	% Difference between Population and Infant Deaths
Maryland	15	18	+3
Virginia	33	50	+17
North Carolina	33	55	+22
South Carolina	58	75	+17
Georgia	42	61	+19
Florida	45	58	+13
Alabama	44	59	+15
Mississippi	51	50	-1
Louisiana	47	43	-4
Texas	27	34	+7
Arkansas	22	26	+4
Tennessee	24	40	+16
Kentucky	21	31	+10
Missouri	13	14	+1

Source: U.S. Census for 1850, section entitled, "Births, Marriages, and Deaths," "Deaths of Persons Under One Year of Age," and Tables XXI through XXIII.

example, slaves accounted for 33 percent of Virginia's population, but babies born to enslaved women accounted for 50 percent of all young child deaths – for a +17. North Carolina had a +22, Georgia a +19, and South Carolina, like Virginia, had a +17. Alabama and Tennessee were not far behind at +15 and +16 respectively. Somewhat surprisingly, two states, Louisiana and Mississippi, saw free and slave mothers equally vulnerable to child deaths.[20]

The broader ramifications of slavery for Black health, especially for Black children, were also clear. Robert W. Fogel, the Nobel Prize winning economist, received the prize in part for his path-breaking work on the historical connection between nutrition and labor productivity in Europe and in the American South. His 1994 Nobel Prize acceptance speech was entitled, "Economic Growth, Population Theory, and Physiology."[21] Its goal was to demonstrate that limited food consumption among the European poor and American slaves, particularly slave children too young to work, commonly produced malnutrition, which led to "childhood stunting and wasting . . . predicting chronic disease rates at young-adult and later ages."[22] While it seems almost self-evident today, Fogel and his collaborators were among the first to show empirically that limited nutrition in childhood reduced adult productivity.

A remarkable study by the economist Richard H. Steckel, a student of Robert Fogel, highlighted the extent to which limited nutrition for Black children was ingrained in the culture of slavery. Plantation life, in the main house and the slave cabins, was shot through with economic calculation, so workers ate first and best, and non-workers, the young, and the old ate what was left. Adult slaves, men and women, were well-advised to eat all they needed to survive long days of unremitting work, for failure to meet production standards, let alone collapse, brought punishment and no benefit to those, like children, who could not work anyway. Steckel analyzed data on slave height by year from 4.5 years of age to 21.5 for men and women. Young slaves were among the slowest growing populations ever studied, but adolescent and young adult slaves experienced some catch-up growth once they entered the workforce, at ten to twelve and sometimes earlier. As workers, they got adult rations, sometimes including meat. Steckel reported that, "On average slaves were roughly 5 to 5.5 inches below modern standards as children. The gap exceeded 6 inches during the years of growth spurt . . . and then gradually declined by adulthood to 1.6 inches for males and 1.35 inches for females." Both male and female slaves ended up at the 27th or 28th percentile of modern height standards.[23]

A similar study by the economist Scott Alan Carson highlighted the fact that both White and Black Americans were seriously impacted in terms of health, growth, and thriving by the Civil War and its aftermath. Texas' main state prison at Huntsville, built and occupied in the late 1840s and known as "the Walls," collected demographic data, including height, on 42,000 prisoners between 1873 and 1919. These inmates had been born between about 1830 and 1900, a period spanning the last several decades of slavery, the Reconstruction era, and the rise of Jim Crow segregation. Carson reported that for those born before and after the war, "At every age, the statures of black youths were lower than for white youths."[24]

Though Black people often were smaller than White people, both races suffered mightily during the Civil War from the limits of medical knowledge and practice, particularly ignorance of infection control. The historian Leon Litwack noted that, "For both white and black soldiers, the overwhelming majority of deaths resulted from disease rather than military action." And again, not surprisingly, "the death rate from disease was nearly three times as great for black soldiers as for whites." Of the 68,178 Black soldiers lost in the Civil War, just 2,751 died in combat, far more died of wounds, sickness, and disease.[25] Once the war was over, doctors and hospitals throughout the South simply refused to see, admit, and treat Black patients.

Health and Health Care from Reconstruction to 1900

The American Studies scholar Robert Perkinson insightfully observed that, "Out of the cauldron of slavery, with its endemic violence and dehumanization, emerged a political culture that . . . fought vigorously against intrusive government and all types of humanitarian initiatives."[26] While Perkinson wrote specifically about prisons, his point was much broader, applying in obvious and direct ways to health and health care in the South and the nation at large in the late nineteenth century. Social Darwinism provided the intellectual backdrop to American social theory, lauding competitive individualism and arguing that survival of the fittest identified superior individuals, groups, and races. White social and economic dominance was taken as scientific proof of racial superiority, while Black ignorance and poverty were taken as equally unequivocal signs of racial inferiority. Social Darwinism was the natural métier of White Southerners, but equally compelling to Northern elites.

Before the Civil War, most Black Americans were slaves and received whatever health care their owners and masters chose to provide, but their masters were motivated to keep their slaves healthy enough to work. After the war, former owners, even if now employers, had fewer incentives to see to Black health care and no public health care initially was available.[27] The first federal health care system was launched by General O.O. Howard, head of the Freedmen's Bureau, on June 1, 1865, as the Medical Division of the Bureau. It was at best a patchwork, short-lived, underfunded, understaffed, and undercut at every turn by the staunch opposition of President Andrew Johnson and his administration. Its fate was sealed from the beginning by the anomalous view of hospitals common throughout the nation, by fear that government benefits might discourage work and cause dependency among the former slaves, and by racism.[28]

First, health care in the nineteenth century was generally delivered by family in the home, to which a doctor might be called in lingering or difficult cases. Even for the wealthy, illness and injury, as well as childbearing for women, were dangerously uncertain. Sick persons without home or family, such as orphans, the single elderly, and prostitutes, sought public charity in asylums that offered shelter, clean clothes, food, moral instruction, and medical treatment as needed. Jim Downs' study of Freedmen's hospitals noted that "throughout the nineteenth century, there was minimal variation between institutions that provided shelter to the poor and . . . those that attempted to offer medical care." Like Northern asylums, "Freedmen's Hospitals . . . provided temporary care – namely shelter, clothing, food, and basic medical treatment – to freed slaves so that they could join the labor force."[29] Basic medical care was not the focus, just a part of the services designed to get the indigent on their feet, out the door, and into private employment and, it was hoped, self-sufficiency.

Second, White Americans in the nineteenth century were obsessed with the danger that government services, thin and scarce as they were, fostered dependence. White Southerners were convinced that Black people would not work without compulsion and White Northerners feared that public asylum care "jeopardized the prospect of a free labor economy, . . . and contradicted the widely embraced American notion of 'individualism.'"[30] As a result, to avoid dependency, the Medical Division was envisioned as sparse, limited, and, most important, temporary. "In the fall of 1865, there were roughly eighty doctors and only a dozen hospitals in operation to treat well over four million slaves."[31] Steady opposition led Congress in July 1868 to limit Freedmen's Bureau activities to education and employment claims. Always temporary in its aims, the federal government's first foray into medical care came to an end a little more than three years after it began. Moreover, Southern White doctors and hospitals operating outside the Freedmen's system generally refused to treat Black patients.[32]

The Civil War and Reconstruction were devastating to the South in every imaginable way, including the public's health. Again, studies of change in southern Black and White height after the war show that "height actually *declined* substantially for blacks and whites in the Reconstruction era." Moreover, Black people were most severely impacted, such that "the effects of slavery on subsequent African American health and economic outcomes may have taken several generations to run their course."[33] Many White Southerners took Black ill-health as confirmation of racial inferiority; "Dr. Eugene R. Corson of Savannah, Georgia, in an article in the *New York Medical Times* of 1887" opined that "Thrown into 'the struggle for existence' with a civilization 'of which he is not the product,' the Negro 'must suffer physically, a result that forbids any undue increase of the race, as well as the preservation of the race characteristics.'"[34] White Americans, particularly in the Southern medical community, confidently, and even hopefully, assumed that an uncompetitive Black race would decline and ultimately disappear from the American scene.

Perhaps the most eloquent and certainly the most poignant description of the consequences of inadequate and oftentimes non-existent health care for Black people comes from W.E.B. Du Bois. In 1896, Du Bois, with his Harvard Ph.D. in Sociology and his new wife Nina, accepted a one-year position as assistant in Sociology at the University of Pennsylvania. His assignment, in almost so many words, was to analyze what made the Black section of Philadelphia, the Seventh Ward, so burdened by crime, poverty, poor health, and immorality. His employers assumed the answer would have to do with moral, cultural, and physical deficiencies in the

Black community. Living on the fringe of the Black neighborhoods he was to study, Du Bois designed a sophisticated survey instrument and then administered it personally by visiting more than 2,400 households. One can only imagine what the householders thought of Du Bois, well-placed Homberg on his head, white gloves, and cane, but the product of his labors, published as *The Philadelphia Negro* (1899), became an early classic of empirical sociology. Du Bois concluded that racism, not inherent weaknesses of Black character and culture, squeezed Philadelphia's Black community into a crowded and unhealthy environment conducive to disease and death. Du Bois reported that, "the Negroes as a class dwell in the most unhealthful parts of the city and in the worst houses in those parts. . . . Of the 2,441 families of the Seventh Ward only 14 percent had water closets and baths."[35] Black isolation in the poorest and most unhealthy quarters of the city was of course aggravated by limits, often denial, of medical services.

While in Philadelphia, Will, as he was known to his intimates, sent the pregnant Nina north to his family in Great Barrington, Massachusetts, to prepare for the birth. Nina delivered a son – Burghardt Gomer Du Bois – on October 2, 1897. In December 1897, the family relocated to Georgia for Will to take up a professorship at Clark Atlanta University. He was exultant in his new, more secure academic position and in his expanded family. At just twenty months old, Burghardt contracted diphtheria and after a ten-day illness, died. Far worse, the racism of the deep South meant that the boy received no care beyond that provided by his distraught mother. As Burghardt weakened, Du Bois sent for one of the few Black doctors in the city but received no response. No White doctor or hospital would deign to treat this Black child. Antitoxins to treat diphtheria had become available earlier in the decade but whether they were available in Atlanta remains unclear. Nina, always uncomfortable in the South, was outraged, Du Bois himself was heartbroken. His eulogy to his son, published as "Of the Passing of the First-Born" in *The Souls of Black Folk* (1903), was and remains extraordinarily moving. The tragedy was clear, but the benefit of early death was the escape from compromises demanded by racism; Du Bois wrote, "Well sped, my boy, before their world had dubbed your ambition insolence, had held your ideals unattainable, had taught you to cringe and bow."[36]

Generally, life expectancy at birth for Black people stagnated between 1850 and 1900 at thirty-five or thirty-six years and did not begin rising until about 1910. Douglas Ewbank reviewed the existing literature and conducted his own studies to conclude that "there was little change between 1850 and 1880 and no change during the period of 1880 to 1900" in Black life expectancy.[37] He also noted, as Du Bois well knew, that Black child mortality rates between 1890 and 1940 were 50 to 70 percent higher than for White children.[38]

Early Twentieth Century: The Slow Emergence (for Some) of Modern Health Care

Over the first half of the twentieth century, health care and health care outcomes, as measured by key indicators like life expectancy and infant and maternal mortality, improved dramatically, though more rapidly for some than for others. Improvements came as a result both of better health science and better institutional organization and administration of health services. The U.S. led in health science discoveries but lagged in institutional organization, administration, and coverage. The late nineteenth century's greatest health care discovery, germ theory, taught that many diseases, as well as infections of accidental and surgical wounds, derived from microorganisms called germs or pathogens. More health science discoveries and advances resulted from developing knowledge of the importance of hygiene, simple washing of hands and medical instruments, clean water, antibiotics for infectious disease control, and better nutrition.[39] During the late nineteenth and early twentieth centuries, most Western nations adopted national health care programs and systems to insure widespread access to improved health care. The U.S. moved much more slowly, leaving health care access to be determined by income and, as we shall see, race.

Though it is hard to imagine today, large numbers of people, especially children, died of communicable diseases well into the twentieth century. In 1900, 72 people per 100,000 of the population died accidentally, while 202 died of the flu, 194 died of tuberculosis, and 143 died of gastrointestinal disorders like diarrhea. Typhoid (31), diphtheria (40), whooping cough (12), and measles (13) killed smaller numbers but still brought tragedy. The great flu of 1917–1918 raised deaths by flu from 164 in 1917 to 589 per 100,000 in 1918. By 1935, most of these killers were on the wane; the flu killed just over 100 per 100,000, tuberculosis just 55, and gastrointestinal disorders, 14. Typhoid, diphtheria, whooping cough, and measles were virtually gone, killing between 2.8 and 3.7 persons each per 100,000 of the population in 1935.[40]

Moreover, national health statistics and records became more reliable and consistent. Accurate registration of death in the United States began in 1900 with ten Northern states and D.C. providing data to the national Death Registration Area (DRA). Birth registrations began to be recorded in 1915 and by 1933 all forty-eight states were recording both births and deaths. Good data makes for better analysis and as Douglas Ewbank noted, "the study of racial differences in mortality provides one of the best approaches to measuring historical trends in relative standards of living of blacks and whites."[41]

Life expectancy had been steady, around thirty to thirty-five years for millennia, across continents and cultures. Recall that in 1850 White life expectancy in the U.S. was just under forty years while Black life expectancy was well under thirty years. By 1900, White life expectancy had risen to forty-eight years; Black life expectancy had risen too, but just to thirty-three years, still a fifteen-year gap.[42] Infant mortality, averaging 20 to 30 percent in many societies over millennia, began a rapid decline. Between 1900 and 1930 improved sanitation and medical treatment reduced infant mortality by more than 60 percent, but it remained higher for Black people than for White people.

Institutionally, health care in the U.S. remained an overwhelmingly private sector activity, lightly administered by state and local authorities, according to regional cultural precepts. Especially in the South, where 90 percent of Black Americans still lived in 1900, doctors rarely treated patients across racial lines, and hospitals, where they existed, were segregated by ward and often by entire institution. As late as 1928, one study estimated that there was one hospital bed for every 139 White Americans and one bed for every 1,941 Black Americans.[43] The federal government played a very limited role through the Department of Agriculture in U.S. health care before the Food and Drug Administration (FDA) was formed in 1906. Remarkably though, the early FDA was responsible only to confirm that ingredients claimed to be in drugs were actually there; it had no mandate to test for the health impact or efficacy of drugs brought to the U.S. market. The safety and efficacy of drugs did not become the legal and regulatory concern of the FDA until Congress passed and President Franklin D. Roosevelt signed the Food, Drug, and Cosmetic Act in 1938.

The overall U.S. life expectancy rate rose from 47.3 years in 1900 to 68.2 years in 1950; a total increase of 20.9 years. During the first half of the twentieth century, life expectancy, while trending up, remained volatile, subject to health and mortality shocks from traditional killers like diphtheria, the flu, depression, and war. As so clearly evident in Figure 7.1, the great influenza epidemic of 1917–1918 dropped the life expectancy rate from over 50 years, where it had been for a decade, to 39.1 years in 1918, before moving back over 50 in 1919. Smaller drops of three points in a single year occurred both during the depression and World War II. After the war, steady, incremental increases in life expectancy reached 78 years between 2007 and 2019, with a high of 78.9 in 2014, before dropping to a COVID-19 pandemic-produced 76.1 in 2021, a low not seen since 1996.

Of course, not all Americans began the twentieth century advance in life expectancy from the same level, advanced at the same rate, or ended at the same level. White Americans started well ahead of Black Americans, by 14.6 years, but gains in Black life expectancy over the last century and more had closed the gap to five years by 2019 before the pandemic pushed it back up to seven years in 2021. As we shall see in more detail later in this chapter, COVID-19 hit minority communities harder than White communities, especially early in the pandemic. Minority vulnerability to health challenges and limited treatment options when sick are old stories in U.S. health and medical history.

Figure 7.1 gives us a closer look at life expectancy rates for White and Black Americans and for both genders separately. The overwhelming impression from the figure is of choppy increases turning to steady increases for both races and genders with White advantage initially clear. However, the greater life expectancy of women saw Black women rise slightly above White men after 1965.

In 1900, life expectancy for White Americans was 46.6 years for men and 48.7 years for women, a 2.1 year advantage for women. By 2021, White men were living an average of 73.7 years, while White women were living an average of 79.2 years, a 5.5 year advantage. A five to six year life

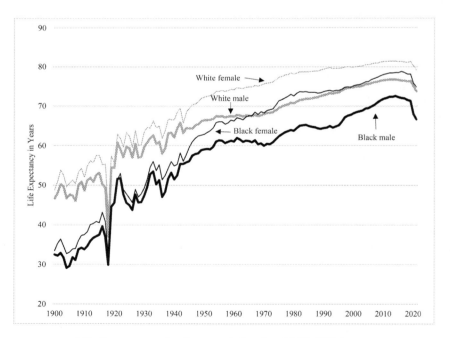

FIGURE 7.1 Life Expectancy by Race and Gender, 1900–2021

Sources: 1900–2019: https://www.cdc.gov/nchs/data-visualization/mortality-trends/index.htm. 2020–2021: NVSS, Personal Life Expectancy Estimates.

expectancy advantage for White women over White men has been in place since 2000 and was even a couple of years higher in the 1970s and 1980s. Over the decades, White men and women have experienced similar shocks to life expectancy from the flu pandemic of 1917–1918, a drop of about twelve years, the depression, a three-year drop between 1935 and 1936, and surprisingly, women experienced a somewhat greater shock to life expectancy, 2.7 years for men, 3.7 years for women, from World War II. Both dropped less than a year between 2019 and 2020.

Black men and women had nearly the same sad life expectancy rates in 1900, 32.5 years for men and 33.5 years for women, a one-year advantage for women. Within just a year or two, Black women's life expectancy advantage had increased to three or four years, where it held into the 1950s. In an interesting and unprecedented variation on women's longer lives, during and just after the flu pandemic of 1917–1918, Black women's life expectancy dropped slightly below Black men's life expectancy rates from 1918 through 1920. During the depths of the depression, 1935–1936, Black men's and women's life expectancy dropped four years, compared to three for White men and women. Since the 1960s, Black women's life expectancy rates have run seven to almost nine years ahead of Black men's life expectancy rates, slightly greater than White women's advantage over White men. In 2021, Black women had a life expectancy of 74.8 years, compared to Black men's life expectancy of 66.7 years, a Black women's advantage over Black men of 8.1 years.

Finally, we must note two other gaps, one closed, one not. In 1900, White men enjoyed a 13.1 year life expectancy advantage (46.6 to 33.5) over Black women. By 1950, the advantage had fallen to 3.6 years (66.5 to 62.9) and by 1965 it had disappeared completely; both White men and Black women were expected to live 67.6 years. On the other hand, the advantage that White women had over Black men in 1900 (48.7 years to 32.5 years), a remarkable 16.2 years, has edged down, but just barely. In 1950, the gap was still 13.1 years and in 1970 it was back up to 15.6 years. In 2021, the life expectancy gap between White women and Black men, the longest and shortest-lived race/gender combinations, was 12.5 years of life.

These general statistics, striking as they are, mask even more dramatic differences in life expectancy between wealthy White people and poor Black people. Steven Johnson, author of *Extra Life*, who is White, wrote that, "Where I live in Brooklyn, the average life expectancy is eighty-two, . . . But just twenty blocks away, in the poorer, largely African-American neighborhood of Brownsville, the average is seventy-three years. That," Johnson observed, "is the most fundamental form of inequality you can imagine."[44] Even more strikingly, Linda Villarosa, author of *Under the Skin*, who is

Black, wrote that, "Chicago has the country's widest racial disparity in life expectancy – a gap of thirty years between Streeterville . . ., where people expect to live to ninety, and my mom's old neighborhood, Englewood, where people live to only sixty."[45] It is notable, even remarkable, that even the experts write about these gaping longevity gaps in tones of disbelief.

Maternal and Infant Mortality

Poor health outcomes for Black people begin before birth and continue throughout the life cycle. Black mothers often get limited prenatal care, give birth to low-weight babies, and experience more stillbirths and maternal complications from childbirth. Black people at later life stages report poor health more frequently than White people and more health limitations than White people. Black people also report more chronic illness than White people, including hypertension, diabetes, and arthritis limiting normal activities. Health experts argue that generations of racism, poverty, and limited access to health care reach out of the past and extend into the future because "The effects of maternal nutrition and health may extend across generations. Mother's birth weight predicts children's birth weight."[46] These health differentials by race are evident in the fact that over the course of the twentieth century and into the twenty-first century, U.S. maternal and infant death rates have run two to three times those in other wealthy nations, and Black maternal and infant mortality rates in the U.S. have run about double those of White people.[47]

Maternal deaths directly related to childbirth have always been a hazard, though much less so over the last century. In 1915, when consistently good data initially became available, six White women died in childbirth for every thousand live births, while 10.6 Black women died. In 1935, 5.3 White women, compared to 9.5 Black women died in childbirth for every thousand live births. By 1950, medical and treatment advances had pushed the White maternal death rate below one per thousand, while the Black maternal death rate had fallen too, but just to 2.2 deaths per thousand live births. In 2021, just 0.19 percent of White women died in childbirth compared to 0.55 percent of Black women – small numbers to be sure, but mostly preventable tragedies and mostly befalling Black women and their families.[48]

Data recording infant mortality rates, defined as the number of children per 1,000 births that die before their first birthday, show the same downward trajectory as maternal death rates. In 2020, *The Economist* magazine reported that, "In 1899 infant mortality was almost twice as high among blacks as among whites; now it is 2.2 times higher."[49] As evident in Figure 7.2, census data beginning in 1915 and running through 2020 confirm both

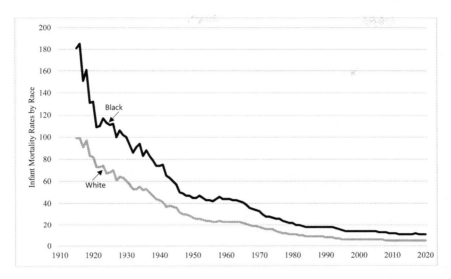

FIGURE 7.2 U.S. Infant Mortality Per 1,000 Live Births by Race, 1915–2020

Sources: U.S. Census, *Historical Statistics of the United States, Colonial Times to 1970, Vital Statistics*, Series B, 101–112, Fetal Death Ratio, etc. See also *Statistical Abstract of the United States, 1971* (#73), *1981* (#111), *1991* (#111), *2020* (#119), "Infant, Maternal, Fetal and Neonatal Death Rates by Race."

the remarkable decline in infant mortality over the past century and the continuing vulnerability of Black children to early death.

As reported earlier in this chapter, historical and even prehistorical infant death rates had averaged 20 to 30 percent and sometimes more. By 1915, U.S. infant deaths for White families were about 10 percent (99 per 1,000), while for Black families they were 18 percent (181 per 1,000). During the first half of the twentieth century, major medical advances served to preserve young life. Nonetheless, from that day to this, though the rates have dropped steadily for White and Black families, Black rates have remained nearly and sometimes literally twice White rates. By 1930, White families lost 60 children per 1,000, while Black families lost 100. By 1965, White families lost 22 children to Black families 41 children lost. In 1980, White families lost 11 to Black families' 22, and in 2020 White families lost 5 to Black families' 11.[50]

Late Twentieth Century Advances in Adult Care and Longevity

U.S. longevity rates rose in the twentieth century due to advances in medical care for children and adults. During the first half of the twentieth century, infant mortality rates fell by three-quarters; during the second half of the century, death rates for adults, especially the middle-aged and elderly, dropped in response to pharmaceutical and medical advances like Lipitor and heart bypass operations.[51] Heart disease, stroke, and cancer, all health risks for older adults, were reduced by new drugs and treatments.[52] Institutional and policy changes, including the expansion of private health insurance, the enhancement of the FDA, and the passage of Medicare and Medicaid as part of LBJ's Great Society program, improved health care access, delivery, and results. For example, in 1962 in the wake of the thalidomide scandal, Congress passed and President Kennedy signed the Kefauver-Harris Drug Amendments giving the FDA new powers. Prior to these amendments, drug companies had no legal obligation to show proof of the efficacy of their drugs. After the amendments, the FDA got new staff, more time to evaluate applications for new drugs, and the companies had to prove both safety and efficacy.[53]

As we have seen, life expectancy for both White and Black people rose steadily over the twentieth century, more than doubling for Black Americans, and maternal and infant mortality rates fell by 95 percent for White Americans and 94 for Black Americans, but Black rates remained higher than White rates. Black and White age-adjusted death rates put health status by race in the broadest context. Recent work by Emory University medical anthropologist Robert A. Hahn provided the basis for Figure 7.3.

Health statisticians use a number of standardization processes to facilitate meaningful comparisons because populations of interest differ by size, age distribution, and in many other ways. Population size, for example there are more White people than Black people in the U.S., is easily standardized by reporting events per 1,000 of the population. Similarly, if one population, say White people, skews older than another, say Black people, a statistical age-adjustment may be made to make the populations more directly comparable.[54] Table 7.3 shows quite clearly that Black age-adjusted death rates have almost always been higher than White rates for both men and women. While the racial gaps have narrowed, they remain clear.

Expanded access to health care facilities helped to improve health and longevity, especially among Black people, and especially in the South where more than half of Black Americans live even today. In the quarter century after World War II, the Hill-Burton Hospital Survey and Construction Act spread hospital care throughout the South and in rural and underserved areas throughout the nation. Since the South was still the nation's poorest region and because racism had limited social welfare programs, including health programs, more Southern states were eligible for Hill-Burton funds because they had fewer than 4.5 beds per thousand people. Jill Quadagno reported that, "Half of all southern hospitals were constructed in the program's first decade," though many were segregated by ward and often by

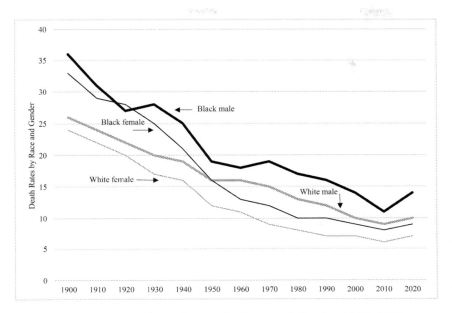

FIGURE 7.3 Age-Adjusted Death Rates by Race and Gender, 1900–2020

Sources: Robert A. Hahn, "Survival in Adversity: Trends in Mortality Among Blacks in the United States, 1900–2010," *International Journal of Health Services* 50, no. 4 (May 2020), Table 1. Data for 2020 is from NCHS Data Brief No. 427, December 2021, Figure 2. Data converted from per 100,000 to per 1,000 for comparability with other tables and figures in this chapter.

entire facility and Black doctors were regularly denied admitting and staff privileges at White hospitals.[55]

Access to medical care and hospitals was further expanded in the 1960s. In 1963, the U.S. Fourth Circuit Court of Appeals ruled, in the case of *Simkins v. Moses H. Cone Memorial Hospital*, a Greensboro, North Carolina facility, that institutions, even private hospitals, that accepted federal funds had to operate on a racially non-discriminatory basis. Just two years later, passage of the huge Medicare and Medicaid programs put even more federal money into health care and gave the federal government even more financial leverage over state and local health and health care institutions and programs.[56] Southern states complied reluctantly and often only partially, but Black and minority access to health care did improve.

Finally, the extension of health insurance coverage, especially to underserved minority populations, has been crucial to improved health. Private job-related health insurance became more common after World War II and public health insurance became more common after the passage of Medicare and Medicaid in 1965. Nonetheless, good data on the proportion of the population that is uninsured by race did not become available until 1987 and that data for children by race did not become available until 2002. Health insurance allows people to secure regular preventative care and to seek diagnosis and care early in an illness when intervention is most beneficial. Lack of health insurance means sporadic care, often in hospital emergency rooms, once illness has become acute. Not surprisingly, Figure 7.4 shows that lack of health insurance and, hence, timely health care has always been more common among minorities than among White Americans.

The share of the population without health insurance rose through the late 1990s, plateaued at 15 percent before Obamacare took hold in about 2013, and then declined to 8.3 percent in 2021. Figure 7.4 highlights lack of health insurance by race. Non-Hispanic White rates were the lowest throughout, usually half the rate of uninsurance suffered by Black people and one-third that suffered by Hispanics. Asian rates have fallen from near Black rates to near White rates by 2021. In fact, the uninsured rate for each racial and ethnic group in Figure 7.4 has fallen by nearly half since 1987,

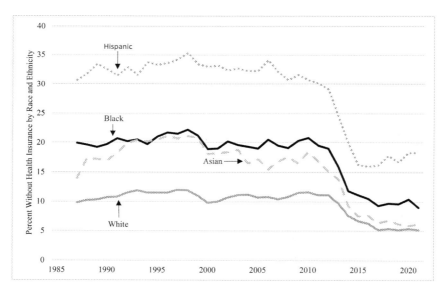

FIGURE 7.4 Percent of Americans Without Health Insurance by Race and Ethnicity, 1987–2021

Sources: U.S. Census, Historical Health Insurance Tables, 1987–2005. See also U.S. Census, Current Population Survey, Annual Social and Economic Supplements, "Percentage of People by Health Insurance Coverage and Type by Selected Demographic Characteristics" (i.e., race), Table H-01.

with most of the decline achieved after the implementation of Obamacare in the early 2010s. As late as 2023, seven of the ten states still declining Obamacare funds were in the South.

Uninsured rates for children under eighteen have also fallen since 2002 by nearly half, from 10.3 percent to 5.6 percent in 2020. Minority rates, two to three times higher than White rates in 2002, have fallen furthest. In 2002, 6.6 percent of White people under eighteen were uninsured, compared to 12 percent of Black people, 20.8 percent of Hispanics, and 11.6 percent of Asians. By 2020, just 3.8 percent of White children were uninsured, compared to 6.0 percent of Black children, 9.5 percent of Hispanic children, and 2.8 percent of Asian children. Insured children obviously have a better chance for a strong and healthy start in life than do uninsured children. As a result, academic studies report that "many programs – especially those focused on children and young adults – made money for taxpayers when all costs and benefits were factored in. That's because they improved the health and education of enrollees and their families, who eventually earned more income, paid more taxes and needed less government assistance over all."[57]

The Long History of Mistrust Between Black People and the Medical Community

For most of American history the medical community disdained treating Black people and Black people mistrusted the people and institutions that delivered what little care they received. Not only were Blacks and other minorities denied some or all medical treatment, they often were treated as the "filthy carriers of diseases" likely to be transmitted to White people. Paula D. McClain, a recent President of the American Political Science Association (APSA) and one of the nation's leading authorities on race and public policy, offered an APSA Presidential Address (2021) entitled, "Crises, Race, Acknowledgement: The Centrality of Race, Ethnicity, and Politics to the Future of Political Science."

McClain argued that: "Racial and ethnic minorities – Blacks, Latinos, Asians, and American Indians – have been convenient scapegoats for many – dare I say most – of the crises that the United States has experienced."[58] As early as 1793, Black people were blamed, or scapegoated, for profiting from a yellow fever outbreak in Philadelphia when actually free Black people had volunteered to treat sick White people.[59] At least 242 Black people died as a result of their efforts. The historian and American Studies scholar Natalia Molina has written that, "The use of disease as a basis for exclusion has been an explicit aspect of U.S. immigration policy since the nineteenth-century. . . . Used as an accusation . . ., disease intensifies the rhetoric of hatred, fear, and blame utilized against undesirable populations."[60] Chinese immigrants in the West were accused of carrying malaria, smallpox, and leprosy, while during the Great Depression, Mexicans and Mexican-Americans were accused of carrying disease and deported in large numbers. During the nineteenth century, minorities and immigrants were treated with wary disdain. Many were seen as intellectually and physically deficient and as posing an obvious threat to the broader community. More recently, President Trump and many others relished calling COVID-19 the "China virus" and many Asians were stigmatized and even assaulted in 2020 and thereafter.

Two medical atrocities, one perpetrated against women, the other against men, made deep historical impressions on Black Americans. During the middle decades of the nineteenth century, Dr. James Marion Sims entered medicine before modern training expectations were in place. Sims relocated from Lancaster County, South Carolina, to Montgomery, Alabama after the deaths of his first two patients. Around 1845 Sims began experimenting on enslaved Black women with new gynecological instruments and procedures. Sims performed his surgeries without anesthesia and only once his procedures were improved did he begin using them on White women. Once refined, his surgical techniques did provide relief from a painful and humiliating condition called vesicovaginal fistula, for repair of tears in childbirth between the uterus and the bladder. Sims rose to be President of the American Medical Association (1876) and the American Gynecological Association (1880), but the early experiments on enslaved Black bodies has made him a leading example of medical disdain for Black people, especially Black women.[61] Similarly, between 100,000 and 150,000 forced sterilizations of prisoners, the mentally disabled, and the poor, mostly of Black women, including the civil rights icon Fannie Lou Hamer, took place in the late nineteenth and twentieth centuries.[62]

Similar disdain for the medical health and welfare of Black men is not hard to find. One stunning abuse of medical ethics and governmental irresponsibility was the U.S. Public Health Service's "Study of Untreated Syphilis in the Negro Male."[63] In 1932, the Public Health Service, with some role played by the venerable Tuskegee Institute, founded in 1881 by Booker T. Washington, initiated a study of the disease course of syphilis, a then incurable venereal disease, among 600 Black men, most poor sharecroppers in Macon County, Alabama. Three hundred and ninety-nine of the men had syphilis and the other 201 served as an uninfected control group. The men were promised remedial treatment, though real treatment was withheld so the course of the disease could be studied at every stage, including death, after which autopsies were performed. Even when penicillin, a cure for syphilis, was discovered in 1947, no treatment was offered. The experiment did not end until 1972 when a disgusted health service investigator leaked information about the study to journalists. The stunning inhumanity of White doctors watching, waiting, and recording their medical observations as unwitting Black men slowly died became a watchword for medical disdain of Black people that has lasted to this day.[64]

The modern medical community is, of course, wrestling with this deeply troubling legacy and with the resulting Black mistrust. Many minority and some White doctors and other medical practitioners are convinced that structural racism pervades Black health outcomes. By structural racism, of course, is meant the cumulative impact of low pay, public-facing jobs, poor housing, lack of consistent medical care and insurance, and the general immune-reducing stress of everyday racism. Others believe that socioeconomic backgrounds, rather than race or racism, express themselves in higher rates of malady among Black people.[65] Dayna Bowen Matthew has written that whatever the etiology of Black health issues and concerns, "a vast body of social science research describes hundreds of experiments, in scores of medical journals, across virtually every major medical specialty that confirm that a patient's race and ethnicity continue to influence physician's medical conduct and decision-making."[66] Part of the issue certainly is structural racism, as we will see next, but part of it is also a fundamental dispute about whether or to what extent race itself is medically relevant or even cognizable.

There is no question that structural racism continues to impact medical research, training, practice, and outcomes. First, it was not until 1993 that federal guidelines required that women and minorities be included in clinical trials. Prior to 1993 they sometimes were, but not systematically.[67] Second, only recently have medical students and others began to complain that "almost all the images and data used in teaching were based on studies of White patients. But medical symptoms can present very differently on Black and brown skin, leading to misdiagnosis."[68] This point, once made, occasions no dispute, though change to expensive medical texts and images has been slow. Less obvious, and more insidious, is that White baselines are built into myriad medical tests and devices. Again, it would seem almost self-evident that "if you design a device which shines light through someone's fingertip to measure the oxygen level of their blood, then the color of the skin through which that light is shining should be a factor when the device is calibrated" – but it is not, or at least not always.[69] Failure to do so leads to oxygen levels in blood being overestimated for Black people three times more frequently than for White people.

More broadly, "race is incorporated into numerous medical decision-making tools and formulas that doctors consult to decide treatment for a range of conditions and services, including heart disease, cancer and maternity care."[70] Online calculators for kidney and lung function as well as for osteoporosis risk make adjustments for race that might result in earlier or better care for White than for Black patients.[71] So, many call for treating each patient, irrespective of race, as an individual and prescribing best care to that person. Failing to recommend kidney treatment to a Black man with a kidney score that would suggest treatment for a White man with the same score, might ill-serve this Black man, while a closer analysis of his particular situation, unburdened by the broader assumptions regarding kidney function in his "race," might suggest preventative care or treatment.

On the other hand, four of the nation's leading Black doctors and senior medical administrators at Howard, Meharry, Drew, and Morehouse, argue that Black people should play a larger role in medical testing, including COVID-19 vaccine testing, because "limited testing could have unanticipated effects on Black bodies. The impact of medication can differ significantly depending on a group's genetic makeup."[72] Given the modern conviction that "race" is a social construct, the extent to which "a group's genetic makeup" differs from that of other groups, and what that implies for health, health care, and beyond is, of course, fraught ground. The distinction between biology and genetics on the one hand and race on the other is not immediately obvious to many medical practitioners let alone common citizens.

Difficulties, not surprisingly, reach into the upper policymaking and scientific levels of the AMA. In November 2020 the AMA's House of Delegates adopted two resolutions decrying "racial essentialism" – the idea that there are medically relevant differences between Black people as a race and White people as a race – in the study and practice of medicine. The resolutions declared that race is "a socially-constructed category different from ethnicity, genetic ancestry, or biology, and aim to end the misinterpretation of race as a biological category defined by genetic traits or biological differences." A key goal of the resolutions was to end "the practice of using race as a proxy for biology in medical education, research and clinical practice."[73] Easier said than done. Less than a year after the AMA adopted its race as a social construct resolutions, Dr. Howard Bauchner, the Editor-in-Chief of the AMA's prestigious *Journal of the American Medical Association (JAMA)*, was forced to step down over comments by Dr. Edward Livingston, an editor working under Bauchner's oversight. In a podcast, Livingston said "Structural racism is an unfortunate term. . . . Personally, I think taking racism out of the conversation will help. Many people like myself are offended by the implication that we are somehow racist." Reverberations shook the AMA and its leading journal. Dr. Mary Bassett, Director of the Center for Health and Human Rights at Harvard, said "Medical journals have helped build the racist idea that races have intrinsic differences that have a bearing on health." She called on journals to "embrace, not only accept, racism as a health issue."[74] Clearly, even highly trained professionals operating within their areas of expertise have trouble talking about race, which they generally want to disclaim, and racism, which they generally want to combat.

Race, Ethnicity, and the Disparate Impact of COVID-19

In late February 2020, the first death from the coronavirus commonly referred to as COVID-19 occurred in a nursing home near Seattle. The virus had likely been circulating on the West Coast and in New England for months, but these first nursing home deaths brought the deadly virus much broader attention. Within just a few months, one troubling aspect of the COVID-19 infection, hospitalization, and death numbers became clear – Black people and other minorities were losing the fight in larger numbers than White people.

By summer 2020, it was clear that Black Americans were coming down with COVID at three times the rate of White Americans, were six times as likely to need hospital care, and twice as likely to die. Debate over the causes of these racial disparities also began early and followed traditional lines. Jay Pearson, a Duke University health policy expert, remarked with some clear exasperation that, "Usually what people will say is, 'Oh, clearly it's genetics, clearly it's socioeconomics, clearly it's individual behavior. . . . Well, it's not genetics at all. . . . What we're really talking about is structural racism."[75] Others noted that these same factors had produced elevated Black and minority sickness and death rates for tuberculosis in the 1900s, flu in the 1910s, polio at mid-century, AIDS late in the century, and a long list of maladies today, including heart disease and cancer. Black Americans enter every health crisis less healthy than White Americans and often are affected disproportionately.[76]

Not surprisingly, National Institutes of Health (NIH) data show that Black people and other minorities were exposed to COVID at greater rates than White people and, once vaccines became available, received them at lower rates than White people. An NIH study of blood samples nationally, conducted in mid-2020, found antibodies indicating prior COVID exposure in 14.2 percent of Black people, 6.1 percent of Hispanic people, and 2.5 percent of White people. NIH immunologist Dr. Kaitlyn Sadtler attributed these racial and ethnic disparities to "inequalities that prevent equal access to diagnostics, care, and treatment."[77] When vaccines appeared in 2021, some Black people and other minorities were skeptical for the historical reasons discussed above, while others lacked dependable online connections to sign up or transportation to get to inoculation sites. As a result, "Communities of color, which have borne the brunt of the

COVID-19 pandemic in the United States, have also received a smaller share of available vaccines. The vaccination rate for Black Americans is half that of White people, and the gap for Hispanics is even larger."[78] By late 2021 vaccination rates had equalized across racial and ethnic groups, but much time had been lost.[79]

By summer 2020, it was also clear that minority Americans were dying of COVID at younger ages and in larger numbers in proportion to their share of the overall population. One CDC study showed that the average White victim was nine years older than the average Black victim and ten years older than the average Hispanic victim.[80] Another showed that during the first half of 2020, Black, Hispanic, and Asian death rates were up at least 30 percent over an average of the previous five years, while the death rate among White people was up 9 percent. Again, experts blamed "structural racism."[81] As a very direct result, "the life expectancy gap between Black and white Americans, which had been narrowing, is now at six years, the widest it has been since 1998."[82]

Most analysts have concluded that the disparate racial and ethnic effects of COVID are not biological, but structural, built into the long-standing racial hierarchy of the nation. Therefore, Dr. Marcella Nunez-Smith, tapped by President Biden to lead a task force on structural racism in health care access and delivery, declared "what's needed to ensure equity in the recovery is not limited to health and health care. We have to have conversations about housing stability and food security and educational equity, and pathways to economic opportunities and promise."[83] Similarly, Dr. Sandro Galea, Dean of the Boston University School of Public Health, urged "attention to the underlying social structures that determine our health," including "whether you have a livable wage, whether you're living in a safe house, whether you're breathing clean air, have drinkable water, nutritious food, whether you have the opportunity to exercise."[84]

Surely, Drs. Nunez-Smith and Galea are correct that structural racism, the historic and pervasive disadvantaging of Black and other minority members of our society, leads to health disparities. And, as Dr. Galea concluded a speech in Dallas, "It comes down to politics, doesn't it, that we need to make sure that we are addressing all of these disparities."[85] Yes, it does, but it also raises a vexing question in regard to public policymaking and implementation. Do we need to resolve structural racism in order to treat health disparities, or income or wealth disparities, housing disparities, or can we work on them separately and incrementally? The answer had better be the latter because resolving systemic racism, healing our society of the consequences of its historic sins, is a tall order. Would incremental progress on these disparities in income, housing, and health constitute progress on institutional racism? It would, but incremental progress on multiple fronts is slow and patience has long since waned. Moreover, White resistance to policies designed specifically to uplift minorities remains determined.[86] These issues of political and policy strategy will be addressed in more detail in Chapter 10.

Both Drs. Nunez-Smith and Galea, along with W.E.B. Du Bois more than a century ago and many others since, have linked minority health outcomes to inadequate housing. We now turn for a close look at Black housing over the course of American history. For most of that history White people demanded and enforced residential racial segregation. The result was the Black ghetto in which not just poor health, but all those other elements of structural racism Drs. Nunez-Smith and Galea decried – poor schools, limited job opportunities, crime, and other maladies – were concentrated.

Notes

1 Angus Deaton, *The Great Escape: Health, Wealth, and the Origins of Inequality* (Princeton, NJ: Princeton University Press, 2013), 75–77. See also Thomas Piketty, *A Brief History of Equality* (Cambridge, MA: Harvard University Press, 2022), 16; Francis Fukuyama, *The Origins of Political Order: From Prehistoric Times to the French Revolution* (New York: Farrar, Straus, and Giroux, 2011), 238.
2 Steven Johnson, *Extra Life: A Short History of Living Longer* (New York: Riverhead Books, 2021), 18, 22.
3 Ian Morris, *Why the West Rules—For Now: The Patterns of History, and What They Reveal About the Future* (New York: Farrar, Straus, and Giroux, 2010), 114–118.
4 Charles C. Mann, *1491: New Revelations of the Americas Before Columbus* (New York: Alfred A. Knopf, 2005), 55, 90–94. See also Jared Diamond, *Guns, Germs, and Steel: The Fates of Human Societies*, 20th anniversary ed. (New York: W.W. Norton, 2017), 202, 358.
5 Deaton, *The Great Escape*, 78.
6 Johnson, *Extra Life*, 247–249. See also Bridget Alex, "Human Remains from the Chilean Desert Reveal Its First Farmers Fought to the Death," *Smithsonian*, August 25, 2021.
7 Dayna Bowen Matthew, *Just Medicine: A Cure for Racial Inequality in American Health Care* (New York: New York University Press, 2015), 13. See also Diamond, *Guns, Germs, and Steel*, 87, 188; Caroline Dodds Pennock, *On Savage Shores: How Indigenous Americans Discovered Europe* (New York: Alfred A. Knopf, 2023), 20–21, 40, 77–79.
8 Alfred W. Crosby, *The Columbian Exchange: Biological and Cultural Consequences of First Contact*, 30th anniversary ed. (Westport, CT: Praeger, 2003, 1st published 1972), 21. See also Morris, *Why the West Rules—For Now*, 430, 464.
9 Crosby, *The Columbian Exchange*, 40–42.
10 Adam Dahl, *Empire of the People: Settler Colonialism and the Foundations of Modern Democratic Thought* (Lawrence, KS: University Press of Kansas, 2018), 3, 83.

11 Johnson, *Extra Life*, 35, 50. See also Deaton, *The Great Escape*, 85; Thomas E. Ricks, *First Principles: What the Founders Learned from the Greeks and Romans and How that Shaped Our Country* (New York: HarperCollins, 2020), 43.
12 David Leonhardt, "The Revolution and the Right to Health," *New York Times*, October 1, 2021, A13. See also Mann, *1491*, 108; Simon Schama, *Foreign Bodies: Pandemics, Vaccines, and the Health of Nations* (New York: HarperCollins, 2023). Cornwallis' British forces also suffered greatly from smallpox, typhoid, and malaria; see Edward J. Larson, *American Inheritance: Liberty and Slavery in the Birth of a Nation* (New York: Norton, 2023), 146.
13 Dumas Malone, *Jefferson the Virginian* (Boston, MA: Little, Brown and Company, 1948), 211–214. See also Jon Meacham, *American Gospel: God, the Founding Fathers, and the making of a Nation* (New York: Random House, 2006), 70.
14 Matthew, *Just Medicine*, 1; Leo Lopez III, Louis H. Hart III, and Michael H. Katz, "Racial and Ethnic Health Disparities Related to COVID-19," *JAMANetwork*, January 22, 2021, https://jamanetwork.com/journals/jama/fullarticle/2775687.
15 Cheryll Ann Cody, "Slave Demography and Family Formation: A Community Study of the Ball Family Plantation," Dissertation, University of Minnesota, 1982, 410–411. See also David Hackett Fischer, *African Founders: How Enslaved People Expanded American Ideals* (New York: Simon & Schuster, 2022), 417.
16 Johnson, *Extra Life*, 28–29.
17 Johnson, *Extra Life*, 68.
18 James Matteson, *A Worse Place Than Hell: How the Civil War Battle of Fredericksburg Changed a Nation* (New York: W.W. Norton, 2021), 92, 94, 96. See also David Herbert Donald, *Lincoln* (New York: Simon & Schuster, 1995), 57; Noah Feldman, *The Broken Constitution: Lincoln, Slavery, and the Refounding of America* (New York: Farrar, Straus, and Giroux, 2021), 214.
19 Matthew, *Just Medicine*, 20. See also Michael Haines, "Fertility and Mortality in the United States," *EH.Net Encyclopedia*, edited by Robert Whaples, March 19, 2008.
20 More broadly, see Robert Wuthnow, *Rough Country: How Texas Became America's Most Powerful Bible-Belt State* (Princeton, NJ: Princeton University Press, 2014), 20.
21 Robert W. Fogel, "Economic Growth, Population Theory, and Physiology," *The American Economic Review* 84, no. 3 (June 1994): 371.
22 Fogel, "Economic Growth, Population Theory, and Physiology," 383; see also Deaton, *The Great Escape*, 92, 157–158. See also Leon F. Litwack, *Trouble in Mind: Black Southerners in the Age of Jim Crow* (New York: Vintage Books, 1998), 19.
23 Richard H. Steckel, "A Peculiar Population: The Nutrition, Health, and Mortality of American Slaves from Childhood to Maturity," *The Journal of Economic History* 46, no. 3 (September 1986): 726, 740.
24 Scott Alan Carson, "African-American and White Inequality in the Nineteenth Century American South: A Biological Comparison," *Journal of Population Economics* 22, no. 3 (July 2009): 147–149.
25 Leon F. Litwack, *Been in the Storm So Long: The Aftermath of Slavery* (New York: Vintage Books, 1980), 98.
26 Robert Perkinson, *Texas Tough: The Rise of American's Prison Empire* (New York: Metropolitan Books, 2010), 71. See also Rogan Kersh, *Dreams of a More Perfect Union* (Ithaca, NY: Cornell University Press, 2001), 131.

27 George C. Benjamin, MD, "Health Inequality from the Founding of the Freedmen's Bureau to COVID-19," *AMA Journal of Ethics* 23, no. 2 (February 2021): 189–195.
28 Paul M. Rego, *Lyman Trumbull and the Second Founding of the United States* (Lawrence, KS: University Press of Kansas, 2022), 142–143.
29 Jim Downs, *Sick from Freedom: African-American Illness and Suffering During the Civil War and Reconstruction* (New York: Oxford University Press, 2012), 66, 72.
30 Downs, *Sick from Freedom*, 67, see also 71.
31 Downs, *Sick from Freedom*, 75. See also Jeneen Interlandi, "Healthcare," in *The 1619 Project*, ed. Nikole Hannah-Jones, Caitlin Roper, Ilena Silverman, and Jake Silverstein (New York: The New York Times Co., 2021), 390–391.
32 Downs, *Sick from Freedom*, 68. See also Litwack, *Trouble in Mind*, 25.
33 Trevon D. Logan, "Health, Human Capital, and African American Migration Before 1910," National Bureau of Economic Research, Working Paper 14037, May 2008, 1, 26–27. See also Carson, "Biological Comparison," 750.
34 John S. Haller, Jr., *Outcasts from Evolution: Scientific Attitudes of Racial Inferiority* (Carbondale, IL: Southern Illinois University Press, 1971, 1995), 48.
35 W.E.B. Du Bois, *The Philadelphia Negro: A Social Study* (published for the University of Pennsylvania; Boston: Ginn, 1899), 148, 161.
36 David Levering Lewis, *W.E.B. Du Bois: A Biography, 1868–1963* (New York: Henry Holt and Company, 2009), 163–164.
37 Douglas C. Ewbank, "History of Black Mortality and Health Before 1940," *The Milbank Quarterly*, 65 (1987): 101, 106, 125.
38 Ewbank, "History of Black Mortality and Health Before 1940," 108, 116. See also Litwack, *Trouble in Mind*, 337.
39 Deaton, *The Great Escape*, 94, 99.
40 U.S. Census, *Historical Statistics of the United States, Colonial Times to 1970*, Series B, 114–128, "Death Rate, for Selected Causes, 1900 to 1956." See also Ewbank, "History of Black Mortality and Health Before 1940," 101, 107, 115–119, 122.
41 Ewbank, "History of Black Mortality and Health Before 1940," 100.
42 "Special Report: Race in America," *The Economist*, May 22, 2021, 6. See also Johnson, *Extra Life*, 215–216.
43 William A. Darity and A. Kirsten Mullen, *From Here to Equality: Reparations for Black Americans in the Twenty-First Century* (Chapel Hill, NC: University of North Carolina Press, 2020), 220.
44 Johnson, *Extra Life*, 219.
45 Linda Villarosa, *Under the Skin: The Hidden Toll of Racism on American Lives and on the Health of Our Nation* (New York: Doubleday, 2022), 92. See also Marin Wolf, "Expert Warns of Future Pandemics," *Dallas Morning News*, November 30, 2021, 8A.
46 Dora L. Costa, "Race and Pregnancy Outcomes in the Twentieth Century: Long-Term Comparison," *The Journal of Economic History* 64, no. 4 (December 2004): 1056–1057.
47 Isabel Wilkerson, *Caste: The Origins of Our Discontents* (New York: Random House, 2020), 355. See also Kate Kennedy-Moulton, et al., "Maternal and Infant Health Inequality: New Evidence from Linked Administrative Data," National Bureau of Economic Research, Working Paper 30693, November 2022.
48 Roni Caryn Rabin, "Despite Efforts to Improve Access to Care, a Racial Health Gap Exists," *New York Times*, August 18, 2021, A16. See also Roni Caryn

Rabin, "Maternal Deaths Rose During the First Year of the Pandemic," *New York Times*, February 23, 2022, A15.
49 Lexington, "Black America in Peril," *The Economist*, May 30, 2020, 25.
50 Austin Frakt, "U.S. Could Prevent Two-Thirds of Deaths Related to Pregnancy," *New York Times*, July 14, 2020, B2. See also "Mortal Danger to Mothers," *The Economist*, July 23, 2022, 25.
51 Robert D. Putnam, *The Upswing: How America Came Together a Century Ago and How We Can Do It Again*, with Shaylyn Romney Garrett (New York: Simon & Schuster, 2020), 27.
52 Deaton, *The Great Escape*, 127–128.
53 Johnson, *Extra Life*, 133–137. See also Christina Jewett, "F.D.A. Relies on Funding from the Drug Companies It Oversees," *New York Times*, September 16, 2022, A1, A15.
54 Lester R. Curtin and Richard J. Klein, "Direct Standardization (Age-Adjusted Death Rates)," CDC, National Center for Health Statistics, Statistical Notes, no. 6, revised March 1995, cdc.gov/nchs/data/statnt/statnt06rv.pdf.
55 Jill Quadagno, *One Nation Uninsured: Why the U.S. Has No National Health Insurance* (New York: Oxford University Press, 2006), 79.
56 Quadagno, *One Nation Uninsured*, 83–84, 204.
57 Seema Jayachandran, "Extending a Helping Hand Can Be Profitable," Economic View, *New York Times*, July 12, 2020, Bu3.
58 Paula D. McClain, "Crises, Race, Acknowledgement: The Centrality of Race, Ethnicity, and Politics to the Future of Political Science," *Perspectives on Politics* 19, no. 1 (March 2021): 7–18.
59 Van Gosse, *The First Reconstruction: Black Politics in America from the Revolution to the Civil War* (Chapel Hill, NC: University of North Carolina Press, 2021), 64–65.
60 Natalia Molina, *How Race Is Made in America: Immigration, Citizenship, and the Historical Power of Racial Scripts* (Berkeley, CA: University of California Press, 2014), 91–92.
61 Charles M. Blow, "How Black People Learned Not to Trust," *New York Times*, December 7, 2020, A18. See also Sydney Page, "New Clinic Planned Where Enslaved Women Were Tortured in Medical Experiments," *Washington Post*, November 30, 2022.
62 Linda Villarosa, "The Long Shadow of Eugenics in America," *New York Times Magazine*, June 12, 2022, 29–35, 46. See also Villarosa, *Under the Skin*, 22, 34–39, 42.
63 Susan M. Reverby, *Examining Tuskegee: The Infamous Syphilis Study and Its Legacy* (Chapel Hill, NC: University of North Carolina Press, 2009).
64 Ibram X. Kendi, *Stamped from the Beginning: The Definitive History of Racist Ideas in America* (New York: Bold Type Books, 2017), 333.
65 Rodney A. Brooks, *Fixing the Racial Wealth Gap* (Suffolk, VA: August Press, 2021), 77, 119, 123.
66 Matthew, *Just Medicine*, 35.
67 Lola Fadulu, "Experts Say Studies Fail to Include Black People," *New York Times*, March 30, 2022, A21.
68 Angelina Jolie, "A New Way to Fight Racial Disparities in Health Care," *Time*, July 5–12, 2021, 26.
69 "Design Bias: Working in the Dark," *The Economist*, April 10, 2021, 16. See also Maddie Burakoff, AP, "Common Medical Tool Not the Same for Everyone," *Dallas Morning News*, November 6, 2022, A5.

70 Gina Kolata, "Race Factors into Medical Decision-Making," *New York Times*, June 18, 2020, A4.
71 Joseph Goldstein, "Race-Based Medical Formula Is Keeping Some Black Inmates in Prison," *New York Times*, April 23, 2022, A18.
72 Wayne A.I. Frederick, Valerie Montgomery Rice, David M. Carlisle, and James E.K. Hildreth, "More Black Americans Should Be in Drug Tests," *New York Times*, September 14, 2020, A23. See also Meredith A. Anderson, Atul Malhotra, and Amy L. Non, "Could Routine Race-Adjustment of Spirometers Exacerbate Racial Disparities in Covid-19 Recovery?" *The Lancet 9*, no. 2 (February 1, 2021): 124–125; Yascha Mounk, *The Great Experiment: Why Diverse Democracies Fall Apart and How They Can Endure* (New York: Penguin Press, 2022), 37.
73 AMA, "New AMA Policies Recognize Race as a Social, not Biological, Construct," November 16, 2020. On March 14, 2023, the National Academies of Sciences, Engineering, and Medicine issued a study entitled "Using Population Descriptors in Genetics and Genomics Research" offering similar recommendations.
74 Apoorva Mandavilli, "Top Editor at JAMA to Step Down Amid Racial Reckoning Over a Podcast," *New York Times*, June 2, 2021, A15.
75 Gus Wezerek, "Racism's Hidden Toll," *New York Times*, August 16, 2020, SR3.
76 Villarosa, *Under the Skin*, 1–2.
77 Amina Khan, "Study: Most Cases Went Undetected Early On," *Los Angeles Times*, in *Dallas Morning News*, June 27, 2021, 14A.
78 Amy Schoenfeld, et al., "Racial Disparities Persist in Vaccinations," *New York Times*, March 12, 2021, A6.
79 David Leonhardt, "An Overlooked Covid Success Story," *New York Times*, October 5, 2022, A18.
80 Karen Kaplan, "CDC: Virus's Black, Latino Victims Younger," *Los Angeles Times*, in *Dallas Morning News*, July 11, 2020, A4.
81 Wire Reports, "Virus Taking Outsized Toll on People of Color," *Dallas Morning News*, August 22, 2020, A5.
82 Sabrina Tavernise and Abby Goodnough, "Covid Effect: Life Expectancy in U.S. Shows Stress," *New York Times*, February 18, 2021, A4.
83 Roni Caryn Rabin, "Leading New Task Force, Yale Doctor Takes Aim at Racial Gap in Care," *New York Times*, January 12, 2021, A5.
84 Wolf, "Expert Warns of Future Pandemics," 8A. See also Villarosa, *Under the Skin*, 2–3, 214.
85 Wolf, "Expert Warns of Future Pandemics," 8A.
86 Ilyana Kuziemko, Taly Reich, Ryan W. Buell, and Michael I. Norton, "Last Place Aversion: Evidence and Redistributive Implications," *The Quarterly Journal of Economics* 129, no.1 (2014): 105–149, see especially 140–145 on attitudes toward minimum wage.

8

HOUSING, NEIGHBORHOODS, AND OPPORTUNITY'S ENVIRONMENTAL CONTEXT

> "The Negro knocks at America's door and cries, 'Let me come in and sit by the fire. I helped build the house.'"
> George L. Vaughn in *Shelley v. Kraemer* (1948)

Hearth, home, family, and neighborhood are the climate and soil within which people grow. Home has the potential to be a place of solace and safety, a place to plan and prepare to engage the broader world in search of education, employment, security, and the blessings of life. Black people during most of American history were denied and then grudgingly permitted limited access to these protections and benefits. As a result, it has long been understood and recently noted again that, "It is residential segregation, by sorting people into particular neighborhoods or communities on the basis of race, that connects (or fails to connect) residents to good schools, nutritious foods, healthy environments, good paying jobs, and access to health care."[1]

Most Americans know their own neighborhoods well, but they tend to know distant neighborhoods, whether the distance is physical, social, or psychological, much less well. Nonetheless, they know that neighborhoods vary dramatically, some are rich and attractive while others are poor and run-down. Attractive neighborhoods are not just clean and safe, they are interesting and vibrant, offering good schools, rewarding jobs, and all the amenities that add up to a good quality of life. They are places you want to be. The least attractive neighborhoods are decaying and dangerous, bleak and depressing, with poor schools, few good jobs, and fewer amenities.

Attractive neighborhoods and communities seek to stay that way, directly or indirectly, at the expense of poor and downtrodden communities.[2] Social scientists have sought to describe the tools community leaders, especially the leaders of wealthy communities, use to shape and craft their cities.[3]

Cities are municipal corporations and, in some ways, they act more like private sector corporations than one might think. Municipalities compete with each other on service delivery and, like private corporations, they compete to offer the most attractive mix of quality and price. Community leaders know that potential residents assess the cost of living in a given community and the mix of tangible and intangible benefits that derive from living there. Elected and appointed officials design their communities to attract certain kinds of residents. Harvard political scientist Paul Peterson described how they do this in his path-breaking book, *City Limits*. Soothingly, Peterson began by assuming that "cities select those policies which are in the interest of the city, taken as a whole."[4] But he soon made clear that what most city leaders thought was in the city's best interest was to have a uniformly prosperous and accomplished citizenry. Peterson explained that, "cities develop a set of policies that will attract the more skilled and white collar workers without at the same time attracting unemployables.... They can provide parks, recreation areas, and good quality schools in areas where the most economically productive live. They can keep the cost of social services, little utilized by the middle class, to a minimum, thereby keeping local taxes relatively low."[5]

Municipalities shape themselves by pursuing a distinctive approach to aligning taxes paid with services received at the individual level. In larger, more diverse, cities, the same approach is applied in terms of neighborhoods. Everyone has noticed that some neighborhoods have smooth sidewalks and bricked medians while others have crumbling sidewalks and potholed roads. Peterson explained these neighborhood differences with what he called the "benefits received principle; ... A city concerned about its economic interests does not consider each taxpayers' benefit/tax ratio equally but in proportion to his contributions to the local coffers." The benefits received principle "specifies that individuals should be taxed in accordance with the level of services they receive. In this way, each individual consumes no more services than he pays for...."[6] But it also means that those who pay few taxes – the poor – have few claims on services.

These economic incentives seem clear, wealthy neighborhoods demand that their tax dollars be spent within the neighborhood while poor neighborhoods plead that all neighborhoods should receive an equal share of tax dollars. Acknowledging that rich neighborhoods, particularly rich urban and suburban neighborhoods, often are White, and poor neighborhoods, especially poor urban neighborhoods, often are Black and brown, raises the moral and political stakes on these municipal battles over resources. Atlanta, the leading city of the American South, is a case in point. Atlanta today has a majority Black population, has had mostly Black mayors since Maynard Jackson was first elected in 1973, and has a thriving Black middle class. In recent decades, many Black Americans returning to the South from other parts of the country have headed straight for Atlanta. But Atlanta, like many major American cities, also has some devastatingly poor Black and brown neighborhoods with all of the attendant concerns about education, employment, and crime.

Atlanta's northern sector, called Buckhead, is 82 percent White, 79 percent college graduate, and has a median household income two and a half times the rest of the city. Buckhead has appealed to the Georgia legislature to allow a deannexation referendum. The referendum was blocked in 2022 and again in 2023 but proponents have vowed to try again. Should the deannexation referendum ultimately succeed, Atlanta would lose 20 percent of its population, the 90,000 citizens that would form the new Buckhead, and 38 percent of its tax revenue. Buckhead would be a wealthy, White, inner suburb of Atlanta, with excellent schools and hospitals, and one of the nation's top private universities – Emory. But Atlanta would be left not half Black, but closer to two-thirds, poorer, with reduced tax revenues, and metastasizing public service concerns.[7] White wealth withdrawing out of sight of Black poverty is, as we shall see, an old American story as new as Buckhead's wish to be separate from those people.[8]

Black Home and Family in Slavery and Freedom

Frederick Douglass wrote extensively about the agony of family, mainly the absence of family, in slavery. Douglass declared that, "There is not beneath the sky an enemy to filial affection so destructive as slavery. It had made my brothers and sisters strangers to me; it converted my mother who bore me into a myth; it shrouded my father in mystery, and left me without an intelligible beginning in the world."[9] Of his mother, Douglass lamented, "It has been a life-long, standing grief to me, that I knew so little of my mother; . . . I have no striking words of her's treasured up. . . . My poor mother, like many other slave women, had *many children*, but NO FAMILY."[10] And of his father, Douglass wrote, "I say nothing of *father*. . . . Slavery does away with fathers as it does away with families. . . ."[11] Black or White, few could escape thoughts of broken families when considering the human dimensions of slavery. Some of Abraham Lincoln's first recorded thoughts on slavery, found in an 1841 letter from Lincoln to his friend Joshua Speed's half-sister, described seeing "twelve negroes . . . chained six and six together. . . . In this condition, they were being separated forever from the scenes of their childhood, their friends, their fathers and mothers, their brothers and sisters, and many of them from their wives and children, and going into perpetual slavery."[12] After the war, families destroyed in slavery made freedom charmless for many. One young woman accepted freedom passively, declaring "But that don't give me back my children. . . . that have been torn from my breast, and sold from me; and when I cried for them was tied up and had my back cut to pieces."[13]

When slave families or similar groupings were together, their surroundings were bleak. In the early nineteenth century, slave quarters across the South varied from large barracks to single and double style slave cabins averaging between 150 and 220 square feet per family or living group. Only the meanest frontier cabin inhabited by White people was of a similar size. Most White housing was twice this size or more.[14] Free Black Americans in the North fared only somewhat better as they squeezed into "shacks, cellars, and alleys of segregated 'Nigger Hill' in Boston, 'Little Africa' in Cincinnati, or 'Five Points' in New York."[15] Philadelphia's "Cedar Ward" and Pittsburgh's "Hayti" were similarly segregated Black neighborhoods.[16] Very few Black people controlled, let alone owned, the quarters in which they lived, North or South, during the first half of the nineteenth century.

Some analysts describe race relations for urban Blacks in the North before the Civil War and for most urban Blacks in the North and South after the war in humane terms, but most recognize a harsher reality. The sociologists Douglas Massey and Nancy Denton, who we will lean heavily on in parts of this chapter, asserted that, "There was a time, before 1900, when blacks and whites lived side by side in American cities. In the north, a small native black population was scattered widely throughout white neighborhoods. . . . In southern cities . . . black servants and laborers lived on alleys and side streets near the mansions of their white employers." This much is true, but it is misleading then to declare that, "The two racial groups moved in a common social world, spoke a common language, shared a common culture, and interacted personally on a regular basis."[17] They did share, to the extent they were allowed, a common culture and language, but not a common social world and their interactions were always tinged with uncertainty and often fear. This idyll of shared social space is principally a foil that Massey and Denton use to explain that Black residential segregation got much worse after 1900, but it elides an uglier reality.

Cincinnati was the nation's sixth largest city in the censuses of 1840 and 1850, four times the size of Chicago in 1850. By the late 1820s, Cincinnati had a 10 percent Black population, and White residents petitioned the city council to limit the Black presence in the city. When the city council moved too slowly, White residents rioted and chased half the Black residents, 1,100 people, from the city. White citizens rioted again in 1836, destroying Black businesses and homes, and in 1841, in an even more concerted onslaught, White residents fired a cannon three times "among the negroes" to drive them from the city.[18] While Black insecurity and vulnerability was different in the North than in the South during the first half of the nineteenth century, it was very real throughout the country. Black numbers in the North were small before the Civil War, but no one, Black or White, doubted that Black people were unwelcome.

Despite the presence of distinct Black enclaves in the cities, most Americans lived in small towns and villages or in the vast countryside. During the colonial and early national periods free or cheap land in the West was America's greatest untapped and undeveloped asset. It drew Easterners and immigrants from Europe into the Old Northwest and then beyond to settle the land and bring it into production. The Northwest Ordinance of 1787, the Land Act of 1800, and the Land Act of 1820 made progressively easier and cheaper purchase terms available to White men and their families. Since almost 90 percent of Black people were enslaved in the South and free Blacks in the North generally had half or less the income of White people, vanishingly few Black people got free or cheap land early in the nation's history. Even as the Civil War raged on, "The Homestead Act of 1862 offered 160 acres of . . . land west of the Mississippi to any citizen. . . . Fewer than six thousand Black families were able to become part of the 1.6 million landowners who gained deeds through the Homestead Act and its 1866 southern counterpart."[19] Six thousand, by the way, is just over one-third of 1 percent of 1.6 million.

After the Civil War, former slaves did gain control, though often tenuously, of farmland, mostly in the South. But as Black farm ownership increased through the late decades of the nineteenth century, traditional Southern elites were fastening Jim Crow segregation ever more tightly on the land. Black farmers, overmatched by White sheriffs, tax collectors, and judges, often lost their land.[20] Others were run off or simply killed if their land was good enough to attract White attention. Black-owned businesses, becoming too visibly prosperous, often were burned or seized and their owners warned to flee if they were lucky. As Richard Rothstein of the Economic Policy Institute described the process, "the former slaveholding aristocracy renewed African Americans' subjugation. Supported by a campaign of violence against the newly emancipated slaves, . . . African Americans in the South were reduced again to lower-caste status. Plantation owners redefined their former slaves as sharecroppers to maintain harsh and exploitative conditions."[21]

Under these pressures, Black Southerners began moving off the land and into the cities and, though in small numbers at first, out of the South entirely. The North offered some relief, but also a new set of problems.

Migrants moving North put ever-increasing pressure on the limited, segregated housing stock available to Black people. Black neighborhoods filled to overcrowding rather than expanded. As we shall see quite clearly later in the chapter, racial residential segregation, North and South, increased steadily from 1880 into the mid-twentieth century.[22] The economist Robert Margo noted that during the early years of the Great Migration, "Chicago's black population increased 248 percent between 1910 and 1920; Detroit's, by a factor of seven." Nonetheless, the newcomers soon found that "Stories of a promised land were exaggerated. . . . Housing conditions in migrant neighborhoods were deplorable. High rents sapped some of the higher pay."[23]

Measuring the Consolidation of the Modern Ghetto

Segregation always envisioned racial separation in public places, like buses, restaurants, hospitals, and schools, but also in residential spaces, Nob Hill versus the other side of the tracks. Two measures have been developed to describe levels of residential racial segregation and how they change over time. The principal measure, called the "dissimilarity index," ranges from zero to one hundred. At zero the races would be evenly spread throughout a city's neighborhoods, while at 100 complete segregation would exist between all-Black and all-White neighborhoods. The dissimilarity index is often described as the percentage of Black people that would have to move from segregated neighborhoods to create an even balance of the races across all neighborhoods. A dissimilarity index value below thirty is usually thought low, thirty to sixty moderate, and above sixty high. The "isolation index," which also varies from zero to 100, is a measure of a Black resident's likelihood of having Black or White neighbors. A Black resident in the unlikely circumstance of having more White than Black neighbors might rank twenty-five, an evenly mixed neighborhood would measure fifty, and all Black neighbors would produce an isolation index of 100. The dissimilarity index and the isolation index are highly correlated whether census tract, broader SMSA, or surface density data are used.[24]

The broadly similar trajectories of the dissimilarity index and isolation index in Figure 8.1 confirm that they are measuring steadily rising racial residential segregation from the late nineteenth century through 1970. After 1970, both lines suggest the beginnings of a slow and only very partial unwinding of housing segregation. Despite the downturn in recent decades, racial residential segregation over the past century and more has increased and held at remarkably high rates. The American ghetto shows few signs of breaking up, though upper- and middle-income Black Americans have increasingly found paths out.

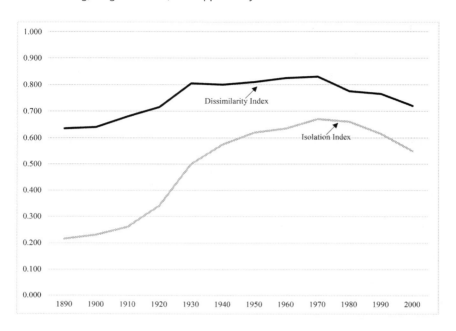

FIGURE 8.1 Dissimilarity Index and Isolation Index, 1890–2000

Source: Data derived from Allison Shertzer and Randall P. Walsh, "Racial Sorting and the Emergence of Segregation in American Cities," National Bureau of Economic Research, Working Paper 22077, March 2016, 37. Replotted by the author.

The classic book on racial residential segregation is by sociologists Douglas Massey and Nancy Denton, entitled *American Apartheid: Segregation and the Making of the Underclass* (1993). Most subsequent research extends, elaborates, or challenges *American Apartheid*. Massey and Denton argue that nineteenth-century American cities were less segregated than they would later become, with Black workers and servants living on side streets and alleys, interspersed among more affluent White citizens. Around the turn of the century, as Black migration to Northern cities increased, "racial views hardened and the relatively fluid and open period of race relations drew to a close."[25]

Residential segregation did increase rapidly as the twentieth century got underway, but characterizing the earlier period as a "relatively fluid and open period of race relations" is inaccurate. Instead, the violence so often used to control the Black presence in the nineteenth century was increasingly, though never completely, replaced by legal and regulatory restrictions in the early twentieth century. Recent research by economic historians Trevon Logan and John Parman has confirmed "sharp increases in segregation levels" between 1900 and 1940.[26] Similarly, the historian David Roediger, drawing on work by the sociologist Stanley Lieberson, also noted rapid increases in racial residential segregation after 1910. Black migrants out of the South were forced into existing Black neighborhoods, aggravating overcrowding and driving up rents. The consequences were inevitable. "Unable to build or expand, 'ghetto' residents paid exorbitant rents for substandard housing."[27] By 1940, "63 percent of all black families lived on a block that was more than 90 percent black and more than four out of every five black families lived on a block that was at least 75 percent black. Conversely, only 4 percent of black families lived on blocks that were greater than 75 percent white."[28]

Table 8.1, drawn from Massey and Denton's *American Apartheid* and from the Diversity and Disparities project at Brown University, provides scattered data, mostly for Northern cities, for 1860 and 1910, and then more complete data for both Northern and Southern cities for 1940 through 2020. The average racial dissimilarity index score for the sixteen Northern cities shown was 48.6 in 1860 and 59.2 in 1910. That slow increase over half a century preceded the dramatic increase to 88.0 in both 1940 and 1950 before a very slow decline from 85.2 in 1960 to 77.8 in 1990, and 65.6 in 2020.

The little data that exists for Southern cities, just Baltimore and New Orleans in 1860, does suggest a modest urban Black population scattered throughout the cities, probably housed near where they worked, whether slaves or free. Fuller data for eleven Southern cities beginning in 1940 show slightly higher dissimilarity indexes averaging 87.4, then 90.2 in 1950, peaking at 91.8 in 1960. As with the Northern cities, racial residential segregation began to decline in 1970, sinking to 88.9, then dropping to 72.8 in 1980, below the Northern average of 80.5, and then to 63.6 in 2000 and 57.2 in 2020.

In sum, Table 8.1 shows urban racial residential segregation increasing through the late nineteenth and early twentieth centuries, cresting at extraordinarily high rates in the mid-twentieth century, and then beginning a slow decline in the North and a somewhat quicker decline in the South. Of course, racial residential segregation proceeded differently in different cities, but it is sobering to note that few of the nation's major cities have made notable progress. Norfolk and Tampa might be the most obvious positive exceptions, going from the 90s in 1940 to below 50 in 2020. Evident laggards include Chicago, Detroit, and Newark.[29]

A recent study by Richard Sander of the UCLA School of Law and his colleagues, intriguing enough to have been picked up in *The Economist* magazine, showed that "the percentage of blacks that would have to move

TABLE 8.1 Indices of Racial Dissimilarity in Selected Northern and Southern Cities, 1860–2020

	1860	1910	1940	1950	1960	1970	1980	1990	2000	2010	2020
Northern Cities											
Boston	61.3	64.1	86.3	86.5	83.9	79.9	79.9	73.7	71.3	67.8	64.2
Buffalo			87.9	89.5	86.5	84.2	80.1	80.1	76.7	71.0	65.3
Chicago	50.0	66.8	95.0	92.1	92.6	88.8	89.1	85.2	81.5	77.1	73.8
Cincinnati	47.9	47.3	90.6	91.2	89.0	83.1	78.2	76.0	72.6	66.9	60.6
Cleveland	49.0	69.0	92.0	91.5	91.3	89.0	85.7	82.8	77.2	72.6	70.0
Detroit			89.9	88.8	84.5	80.9	83.0	85.6	85.9	79.6	74.5
Indianapolis	57.2		90.4	91.4	91.6	88.3	78.8	74.7	70.6	64.2	59.8
Kansas City			88.0	91.3	90.8	88.0	77.6	72.8	69.2	58.6	51.6
Los Angeles			84.2	84.6	81.8	78.4	81.1	73.0	67.3	65.0	59.7
Milwaukee	59.6	66.7	92.9	91.6	88.1	83.7	83.9	82.8	82.2	79.6	75.1
Newark			77.4	76.9	71.6	74.9	82.9	82.7	80.3	78.0	76.6
New York	40.6		86.8	87.3	79.3	73.0	81.7	82.0	81.2	79.1	74.3
Philadelphia	47.1	46.0	88.8	89.0	87.1	83.2	84.2	83.3	77.8	74.3	70.2
Pittsburgh			82.0	84.0	84.6	83.9	73.3	70.8	67.4	63.1	59.4
St. Louis	39.1	54.3	92.6	92.9	90.5	89.3	81.6	77.3	73.4	70.6	67.4
San Francisco	34.6		82.9	79.8	69.3	55.5	65.9	62.1	59.3	53.4	47.7
Average	48.6	59.2	88.0	88.0	85.2	81.5	80.5	77.8	74.6	70.1	65.6
Southern Cities											
Atlanta			87.4	91.5	93.6	91.5	76.9	66.1	63.8	58.2	58.5
Baltimore	22.1		90.1	91.3	89.6	88.3	74.4	71.4	67.6	64.3	59.9
Dallas			80.2	88.4	94.6	92.7	78.1	62.9	59.1	55.1	50.9
Greensboro			93.1	93.5	93.3	91.4	59.1	54.7	53.8	54.1	52.0

Houston			84.5	91.5	93.7	90.0	74.2	65.9	65.3	60.7	57.2
Memphis			79.9	86.4	92.0	91.8	68.8	65.3	65.7	62.2	58.9
Miami			97.9	97.8	97.9	89.4	79.4	71.8	74.2	73.0	72.1
New Orleans	35.7		81.0	84.9	86.3	83.1	70.1	68.1	68.6	62.9	60.2
Norfolk			96.0	95.0	94.6	90.8	70.1	57.3	52.8	50.8	49.0
Tampa			90.2	92.5	94.5	90.7	78.2	69.6	63.4	54.3	49.6
Washington			81.0	80.1	79.7	77.7	71.2	67.8	65.5	63.9	61.2
Average	28.9		**87.4**	**90.2**	**91.8**	**88.9**	**72.8**	**65.5**	**63.6**	**60.0**	**57.2**

Sources: For 1860–1970: Douglas S. Massey and Nancy A. Denton, *American Apartheid: Segregation and the Making of the Underclass* (Cambridge, MA: Harvard University Press, 1993), 21 (Table 2.1), 47 (Table 2.3), 64 (Table 3.1), 71 (Table 3.3), and 222 (Table 8.1). For 1980–2020: John Logan, ed., "Diversity and Disparities: America Enters a New Century," https://s4.ad.brown.edu/projects/diversity/index.htm.

to ensure equal distribution across a city," often called the "dissimilarity index," had risen between 1960 and 1970 and then trended steadily downward to 2010. Their data show a dissimilarity index of 93 percent in 1970, "By 2010, the dissimilarity index had declined to 70% – an improvement, but far from . . . [an] integrated society."[30] There is simply no question that urban racial residential segregation remains a major impediment to social progress in this country.

Public and Private Resistance to Black Visibility in America

Knowing that racial residential segregation increased during the late nineteenth century and most of the twentieth century is important, but so are how and why it happened. We now turn to those questions. As the trickle of Black Americans out of the South in the late nineteenth century turned into a broad, flowing stream in the first half of the twentieth century, public and private White authority sought to channel, direct, and locate them in their new segregated neighborhoods. As the great Black sociologist Kenneth B. Clark, associate of Gunnar Myrdal and Thurgood Marshall, wrote in *Dark Ghetto* (1965), "invisible walls have been erected by the white society, by those who have power, both to confine those who have *no* power and to perpetuate their powerlessness. The dark ghettos are social, political, educational, and – above all – economic colonies. Their inhabitants are subject peoples, victims of greed, cruelty, insensitivity, guilt, and fear of their masters."[31] The political scientists Desmond King and Rogers Smith have observed that, "these patterns became entrenched during the era of Jim Crow segregation, when residential racial segregation was broadly embraced as both public and private policy."[32]

In the private sector, national associations like the American Bankers Association (1875), the United States Building and Loan League (1893), the National Association of Realtors (1908), the National Association of Real Estate Boards (1909), and later the National Association of Home Builders (1942) arose to set and enforce standards and policies for the housing industry.[33] These and many other private sector institutions during the Jim Crow era "used overtly discriminatory practices such as real estate agents employing outright refusal or subterfuge to avoid renting or selling to black customers, . . . overtly discriminatory insurance and lending practices, and racially restrictive covenants on housing deeds in order to maintain segregated communities."[34] Private sector discrimination was backstopped and buttressed by explicit government authority and policy at every level and across the country. Richard Rothstein described in detail how "state and local governments supplemented federal efforts to maintain the status of African Americans as a lower caste, with housing segregation preserving the badges and incidents of slavery."[35] We shall trace in some detail, how, as King and Smith contend, "racial residential segregation was a foundational system of the 'separate but equal' Jim Crow America created in the 1880s, judicially legitimated in the 1890s, and sustained de jure until 1954, with consequences that, to some disputed degree, endure."[36]

White property-owners' responses to the arrival in Northern cities of migrants from the South, especially of Black Southerners seeking purchase or rental property outside segregated Black neighborhoods, were usually a mix of private blocking actions and public policies. White property-owners could draw on legally enforceable racial zoning ordinances and restrictive covenants. Racial zoning laws were general prohibitions against Black people in broad districts of a city while restrictive covenants were usually provisions of individual property deeds prohibiting sale of the property to Black buyers.

The United States Supreme Court established through a series of rulings in the last quarter of the nineteenth century, including most famously the *Civil Rights Cases* (1883) and *Plessy v. Ferguson* (1896), that while state-based racial discrimination might violate the Fourteenth Amendment, individual acts of racial discrimination, as in selling or renting property, were a private matter outside the purview of state and federal constitutions and laws. Therefore, White public officials and home-owners were stunned when the High Court, in *Buchanan v. Warley* (1917), sided with the NAACP in finding Louisville's residential racial segregation ordinance to be an unconstitutional violation of the Fourteenth Amendment.[37] The Court struck down racial zoning in the *Buchanan* case, arguing not that it limited the rights of potential Black purchasers, but that it limited the rights of White homeowners to sell to whom they pleased. White people were not pleased to have their rights acknowledged in this manner; Black people were not surprised that their rights went unacknowledged by the Court.

But White officials and homeowners had more arrows in their quiver. In 1921, President Warren G. Harding and Secretary of Commerce Herbert Hoover established an Advisory Committee on Zoning to assist municipalities in using economic zoning to guide and control racial dispersion within their cities. Local officials were advised that zoning rules that did not explicitly mention race, but that defined lot size, building codes, single family versus multifamily, strictly residential versus mixed versus industrial, and placement of dumps and other disposal sites, would likely pass judicial muster and they did.[38] Restrictive covenants, most of which applied only to Black people, remained a favored tool, especially after the 1926 Supreme Court decision in *Corrigan v. Buckley* that such covenants were voluntary private contracts, not state actions, and, hence, legally binding documents whose violation would void a sale.[39]

Real estate markets, which remained largely the sum of individual choices made by the majority White population, left Black Americans with just a few bad choices. White violence against perceived Black intrusion continued to be a common form of market maintenance. In Chicago alone, dozens of Black homes, often newly purchased or rented in White neighborhoods, were bombed between 1917 and 1921. When violence and other dissuasion failed to keep Black buyers or renters at bay, White homeowners often withdrew. A series of articles by the economists Allison Shertzer, Randall Walsh, and their colleagues concerning property markets in Northern cities between 1900 and 1930 highlighted both what later came to be called "white flight" and changes in property values that White residents often anticipated and the Black residents had to accept. They show that between a third and half of the increase in racial segregation in Northern cities between 1900 and 1930 resulted from "white flight from blacks," in fact, "black arrivals caused an increasing number of white departures in each decade: by the 1920s, one black arrival was associated with the loss of more than three white individuals."[40]

Moreover, homeowners and landlords anticipated the impact that Black migration and subsequent White flight would have on real estate values and rents. A 2019 study by Akbar, Li, Shertzer, and Walsh found that "over the course of a single decade [the 1930s] rental prices soared by roughly 50 percent on city blocks that transitioned from all white to majority black. Meanwhile, pioneering black families paid a 28 percent premium to buy a home on a majority white block. These homes then lost 10 percent of their original [pre-premium] value as the block became majority black."[41] These simple market movements, based on White property-owners' desire to compensate for declining property values in integrating neighborhoods and Black homebuyers' willingness to pay a premium to encourage white sellers to sell to them, had a devastating effect on the ability of Black families to accumulate wealth over time. The implications of these findings are truly remarkable. For most Americans, their home is their largest asset; the equity built up over the years in a home is greater than any cash, saving, or investment amounts they might accumulate. But Black families in the early twentieth century were forced to pay a premium to buy a depreciating asset. The authors estimated that the higher rents and purchase prices drained as much as 40 percent of the wage gains Black Americans enjoyed by moving North and cut deeply into the equity gains the Black homebuyers might otherwise have realized.[42]

The Great Depression of the 1930s and the Roosevelt administration's response to it brought the federal government into the real estate, housing, and mortgage markets in much bigger and more direct ways than before. When the Roosevelt administration came into office in early 1933, unemployment was near 25 percent, banks were buckling, and millions of mostly White homeowners faced default. During the famous first hundred days, FDR and the Congress created the Home Owners' Loan Corporation (HOLC). HOLC was empowered to take financial pressure off the banks by buying the defaulted mortgages the banks held and to offer struggling homeowners new mortgages with more favorable terms. The National Housing Act of 1934 established the Federal Housing Administration (FHA) to set national mortgage standards. Prior to the implementation of FHA standards, mortgages had been negotiated between the prospective buyer and the bank or other lender. Terms often required a 30 to 50 percent down payment, a two to seven year term of interest and expense payments, with the lump sum balance due at the end of the term.[43] FHA standards required economically sound loans, but on much more favorable terms to the buyer. The new terms included smaller down payments, fixed interest rates, longer terms, monthly payments of principal and interest, and, hopefully, a home owned free and clear at the end of the process.[44]

But, as always, not all potential homeowners were treated equally; some were favored, others disfavored or excluded. As the historian Ibram X. Kendi has remarked, "The Roosevelt administration's new Home Owners Loan Corporation (HOLC) and the Federal Housing Administration (FHA) handed Black residents the Old Deal when these agencies drew 'color-coded' maps, coloring Black neighborhoods in red as undesirable."[45] The HOLC ranked neighborhoods from most desirable and stable, "green," through "blue" and "yellow," to "red," the least desirable and most unstable neighborhoods. Black and other minority neighborhoods, or neighborhoods experiencing or threatened with increased diversity were invariably ranked "red," meaning economically unsound and so not good prospects for federally guaranteed loans. FHA soon adopted the HOLC color-coded maps, dramatically restricting federally secured home loans to Black people and other minorities.

Even in the wake of World War II, Black veterans continued to experience official discrimination. In 1944, Congress passed and President Franklin D. Roosevelt signed the G.I. Bill, more formally known as the Servicemen's Readjustment Act, to assist those who served in the military in reintegrating back into civilian life and in catching up with those who had not served. An important part of the G.I. Bill was the Veterans Administration (VA) home loan program. The VA home loan program did not make home loans directly to veterans, rather it insured loans against default so that banks and S & Ls would feel more confident in making loans to veterans. Because the VA program guaranteed loans made through the existing real estate industry and government regulators like the FHA, VA-backed mortgages went disproportionately to White veterans.

Soon though the big boat of U.S. housing policy began slowly to turn. The positive impacts of Myrdal's *The American Dilemma* (1944) and the new multiracial international presence of the U.N., as well as the negative impacts of Hitler's treatment of the Jews of Europe and Ku Klux Klan attacks on returning Black G.I.s, made overt racial discrimination more embarrassing and costly. President Harry S. Truman and his Attorney General, Tom Clark, decided it was time to move against racial residential segregation. Clark's Justice Department filed *amicus curiae* briefs in two cases before the Supreme Court, *Shelley v. Kraemer* (1948) and *McGhee v. Sipes* (1948), seeking to overturn racially restrictive covenants. Thurgood Marshall and the NAACP represented the Black plaintiffs before the Court.

The most famous of the two cases, *Shelley v. Kraemer*, began in 1945 when J.D. Shelley, a Black man, bought a house in St. Louis that, though he was unaware of it at the time, had a "restrictive covenant" prohibiting sale of the property to "people of the Negro or Mongolian race." The Missouri Supreme Court upheld the restrictive covenant and voided the sale. Shelley appealed to the U.S. Supreme Court on the argument that such racially discriminatory covenants violated his Fourteenth Amendment promise of equal protection of the laws. The Court held, somewhat unsatisfactorily, but quite effectively, that while private parties, a buyer and seller, might make such racially discriminatory agreements, the agreements could not be enforced by the courts because that would be "state action" to enforce discrimination and that would be a violation of the Fourteenth Amendment.[46]

The Supreme Court's decision came in an unusual 6–0 vote because three Justices found their own deeds contained restrictive covenants and so they were forced to recuse themselves.[47] Though the Court had ruled unanimously that restrictive covenants were legally unenforceable, lenders and real estate agents continued to honor White sellers' wishes only to sell to White buyers. Moreover, unscrupulous agents and investors, really speculators, sought to stampede White homeowners in neighborhoods rumored to be targets of Black buyers into low-ball sales before property values fell. If successful they might then turn around and demand premium prices of Black buyers, thereby pocketing a nice profit out of the racial fears of White people and hopes of Black people.[48]

Just months after the Supreme Court handed down its landmark decision in *Shelley v. Kraemer*, President Truman issued Executive Order 9981 integrating the United States military, though it took into the mid-1950s to overcome resistance within the Navy and Marines. Truman also expanded the Civil Rights Division of the Justice Department, appointed the first Black federal appeals court judge, William H. Hastie, and made a number of other high profile Black appointments to demonstrate his own and the administration's seriousness about desegregation. Nonetheless, the forces of racial inertia were great. King and Smith note that long after *Shelley*, "the pattern of entrenched segregated residential housing endured through a combination of private realtors' selling practices, white householders' preferences, and the modified but persisting federal mortgage A-D [green to red] grading schema."[49]

As always, Black access to the broad residential housing market was limited and changed slowly: "The Veterans administration along with the Federal Housing Agency (FHA) funded one-third of all mortgage loans in the 1950s. Together these two agencies underwrote 3 percent of Black mortgage loans and 42 percent of white loans."[50] Almost three decades would pass between the decision in *Shelley v. Kraemer* and the 1973 declaration by the U.S. Commission on Civil Rights, created by the Civil Rights Act of 1957, that the "housing industry, aided and abetted by Government, must bear the primary responsibility for the legacy of segregated housing.... Government and private industry came together to create a system of residential segregation."[51] Still, little of note was done to help Black would-be homeowners make up lost ground.

Race and Home Ownership

So, what have been the practical consequences of private and public collaboration in discriminating against Black and minority persons in the U.S. housing and rental markets? We now turn to the issue of home ownership – who gets to buy and own a home, where, and with what economic consequences. For most Americans, physical property and its improvement has been the principal way to build wealth and to pass it down within families from one generation to the next. Denial of access to property, whether complete denial of access to property ownership or access only to undesirable property of limited present or future value, is denial of the main wealth building opportunity provided by our society.

Dependable data on home ownership does not exist prior to 1870 and they do not become regular and systematic until the early twentieth century (see Figure 8.2). The overall U.S. home ownership rate in 1870 stood at just over 50 percent. From there it drifted slowly down to 45 in both 1910 and 1920, before bouncing up to 47 by the end of the Roaring '20s. The Great Depression of the 1930s took the home ownership rate down to a multi-decade low of 43 percent in 1940. The post-World War II boom in home ownership reached 57 percent in 1950, 66 percent in 1980, and 69 percent in 2004. In 2006, the U.S. home ownership rate began a slow, grinding slide of 5 percent, reaching 64 percent in 2017 before rebounding slightly to 66 in 2021. But how do U.S. home ownership rates look by race?

The economists William Collins and Robert Margo report that home ownership by race stood at 57 percent for White people in 1870 and at just

8 percent for Black people. It is important to remember that most Black Americans, just out of slavery in the late nineteenth century, rented or sharecropped, while many White homeowners and often their neighbors built most if not all of their own homes. People bought homes from each other, of course, from the colonial period through the nineteenth century, but home finance, professional builders, and real estate agents do not appear as standard until the twentieth century. Between 1870 and 1900, the 49 point gap between White and Black home ownership rates declined to 26 points as White homeowner rates declined somewhat to 50 percent and Black homeowner rates rose to 24 percent. The 7 point decline in White home ownership rates was likely a consequence of rising immigration and of the movement of native-born White people from rural to more expensive urban settings. The increase in Black home ownership rates between 1870 and 1900, from 8 to 24 percent, still only half the White rate, was a natural consequence of some Black Americans getting their financial balance as the slavery years receded. Between 1900 and 1940, both White and Black household rates of home ownership stagnated within a narrow three or four point range.[52]

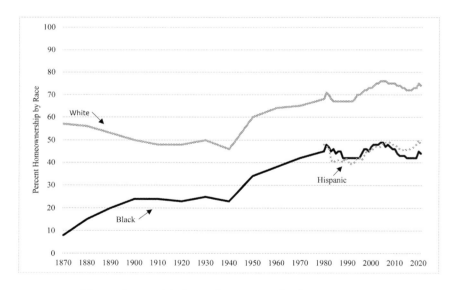

FIGURE 8.2 Home Ownership Rates by Race and Ethnicity, 1870–2021

Sources: U.S. Census, Table 1, "United States: Race and Hispanic Origin, 1790–1990;" William J. Collins and Robert A. Margo, "Figure 1: Race and Home Ownership from the End of the Civil War to the Present," *American Economic Review* 101, no. 3 (May 2011): 356; Chloe N. Thurston, *At the Boundaries of Home Ownership* (New York: Cambridge University Press, 2018), 85, Table 3.1; U.S. Census, Current Population Survey, Table HH-5, "Households by Tenure, Race, and Hispanic Origins of Householder, 1970–2016." See also Table 22, "Home Ownership Rates by Race and Ethnicity of Householder, 1994–2021."

Between 1940 and 1980, both White and Black home ownership rates rose substantially and very much in tandem.[53] Nonetheless, the steady rise in home ownership rates masked a great deal of movement below the surface. The economists Leah Boustan and Robert Margo report that in 1940 19 percent of urban Black citizens owned their own home, while by 1980 the rate had increased to 46 percent. Boustan and Margo describe a racial two-step in which urban White people, some feeling minority pressure on their neighborhoods, others just wanting newer homes and more space, decamped to the booming suburbs. At least some of the older housing stock the White sellers left behind was available to Black buyers. As neighborhoods turned from White to Black, prices rose initially then fell as the neighborhood became populated mainly by Black people, but in the process some Black renters became homeowners.[54]

Since 1980, White home ownership rates have increased slightly within a tight band from the upper 60s to the mid-70s; 74 percent of White people were homeowners in 2021. Black home ownership rates have drifted up and down, always within the 40s, beginning at 45 percent in 1980 and ending at 44 in 2021.[55] This apparent calm masks a roller-coaster ride during the two decades after 1990. Federal policy spurred home ownership rates to new highs for White people and minorities during the 1990s and early 2000s. When the housing market collapsed after 2006, leading to the Great Recession, minority families were hard hit. Black home ownership fell from 49 percent in 2005, the all-time high, to 41 percent in 2019.[56] Remarkably, as Georgetown Law's Sheryll Cashin observed in *White Space, Black Hood*, "By 2020, the Black-white home ownership gap had widened to a chasm not seen *since* 1890."[57]

The gap between White and Black home ownership represents generations of opportunity to build wealth denied to Black families. As mentioned in Chapter 6, among the most highly respected ongoing studies of U.S. income and wealth has been the Federal Reserve Board's Survey of Consumer Finances (SCF). Conducted every third year between 1983 and 2019, the SCF reports data on income, wealth, and debt by age, education, race, and, critically, homeowner and renter status (see especially Tables 1 and 2 in each survey). In every survey, except the first in 1983, homeowners have enjoyed incomes at least twice as high as renters. In 2019, the before tax median family income of homeowners was $77,400, while for renters it was $35,600. This is not terribly surprising as most people choose to move from renting to owning when their income permits. More surprising, even stunning, is that the median family net worth, which is assets minus debts, of homeowners is dozens of times greater than that of renters. For example, in 1983, the net worth of owners was $50,100 and of renters was 0 dollars. In 1989, owners' net worth was $97,300 and that of renters was $2,200. In 2019, the median net worth of homeowners was $255,000 and that of renters was $6,300.

Now, to be clear, renters are generally younger than homeowners and many renters will ultimately become homeowners, but there is no gainsaying the fact that home ownership is among the surest paths to growing net worth and to at least opening the possibility of passing family wealth from one generation to the next. Unfortunately, few will be surprised to learn that a greater proportion of Black people than of White people rent their shelter. For example, in 1970, 65 percent of White people owned their homes, compared to 42 percent of Black people. Over the last half century, Black home ownership has never reached 50 percent, while White home ownership has generally held in the 70s since the mid-90s.

So, again, if home ownership is such an obvious way to build wealth, why has Black home ownership always lagged White home ownership? The answer, of course, is that homes are expensive, the largest purchase that the vast majority of families will ever make, and median Black income has ranged between 50 and 70 percent of median White income since the early 1960s. Figure 8.3 displays the median price of houses in the U.S. from 1963 through 2021 as a multiple of median family income by race. The question answered in Figure 8.3 is how many years of income it costs the average White family to buy the average home compared to the number of years it costs the average Black, Hispanic, or Asian family to buy that home.

In 1963, the first year for which we have good U.S. census data on both median house prices and median family income by race, it cost the average White family 2.75 times annual income to buy the median priced home while it cost the average Black family 5.19 times median income. By 1970, because incomes had risen faster than house prices since 1963, the average White family paid 2.29 times annual income to buy the median priced home while it cost the average Black family 3.73 times family income. Coming off that 1970 low, home prices have risen somewhat faster than incomes for the past half century. By 1990 data on Hispanic (1972) and Asian (1988) family income had also become available. In 1990, the average White family could buy the median priced home with 3.21 years of income while the average Black family had to spend 5.74 years of income. The average Hispanic family required 5.25 years of income while the average Asian family required only 2.91 years of income.

Even as home prices rose and fell in relation to median family income, the average White family never had to commit more than 3.81 (in 2005) times annual income to purchase an average home. In 2005, Black families had to commit 6.79 years of income to buy the average home, while Hispanic families had to commit 6.36 years and Asian families 3.49 years.

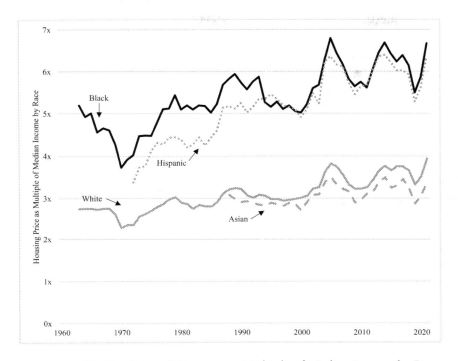

FIGURE 8.3 Median Price of Houses as a Multiple of Median Income by Race, 1963–2021

Sources: "Median and Average Sale Prices of Houses by Region," https://www.census.gov/construction/nrs/historical_data/index.html; Table F.5, "Race and Hispanic Origin of Householder—Families by Median and Mean Income, 1947–2021," current dollars, https://www.census.gov/data/tables/time-series/demo/income-poverty/historical-income-families.html.

Finally, in 2021, before home prices plateaued in the second half of 2022, White families had to commit an all-time high of 3.93 years' average income, Black families 6.67 years, Hispanic families 6.37 years, and Asian families 3.35 years' average income to buy a home.

Clearly, Black and Hispanic families face a difficult decision when considering buying a home because, with lower incomes on average than White and Asian families, down payments will be harder to put together and the monthly note will be harder to carry. Some Black and Hispanic families will, of course, simply give up the desire to own while others will look down market, often well below the median priced home, for affordability. Hence, Michelle Singletary, the *Washington Post* financial columnist, pointed out that in 2019, "45% of Black families own their homes, with a median home value of $150,000. That compares to a 73.7% home ownership rate for white families, with a median home value of $230,000."[58]

As is commonly the case, racial and ethnic discrimination is both structural and personal. At the structural level, social, economic, and political processes operate to limit, channel, and often exclude minorities from opportunities open to White people. Moreover, circumstances, conditions, and facts at the structural level often shape those at the individual level. At the individual level, incomes may be adequate to aspirations or not, loans are approved or not, homes are shown or not, and offers are accepted or not. One utterly remarkable but not totally surprising fact at the structural level was highlighted in a 2023 report prepared by Harvard University's "Initiative for a Competitive Inner City" for Grove Impact and the Siegel Family Endowment. The report, entitled "Breaking the Glass Bottleneck: The Economic Potential of Black and Hispanic Real Estate Developers and the Constraints They Face," found that White people owned more than 99 percent of U.S. real estate investment companies and of the top 383 real estate investment companies by income, one was Hispanic and none were Black.[59] When it comes to what housing gets built, where, with who in mind, and at what price point, it is very much an all-White decision structure. And as we see in the final sections of this chapter, it remains so as individuals enter the housing market.

Continuing Discrimination in Housing Markets

Until the last third of the twentieth century, federal, state, and local laws and regulations, condoning and abetting private actions within the real estate industry, determined where White, Black, Hispanic, and other Americans might live. Redlining channeled people into certain neighborhoods based on their race and the placement of public housing in already densely populated minority urban neighborhoods helped to create and then harden racial boundaries. Many hoped that passage of the Fair Housing Act of 1968 would provide a legal framework for breaking down racially distinct neighborhood boundaries by providing equal access to the nation's housing stock. While racial residential segregation has declined somewhat since 1970, it remains robust. A 2015 study found that "the city of Houston *concentrated more than 71 percent of all government-subsidized housing in only five of its 88 neighborhoods, all of which were very poor and nonwhite.*"[60]

Most analyses of discrimination in housing markets over the past half century find less overt discrimination, like hard-edged redlining, but little change in housing inequality itself.[61] If overt discrimination has declined, though not disappeared, why have housing inequalities by race not closed more since the Fair Housing Act was passed? One obvious but powerful explanation, as we saw in Figure 8.3 above, was that "most Black and brown families can't afford to rent or buy in the places where white families are, and when white families bring their wealth into Black and brown neighborhoods, it more often leads to gentrification and displacement than enduring integration."[62] So, in the housing market, as in high end department stores, minorities may now window shop, though they may be viewed with suspicion, and likely will not be able to afford the merchandise.

Nonetheless, continuing racial discrimination in the mortgage and housing markets, combined with deficits in minority income and wealth, make these communities particularly vulnerable. The subprime home mortgage crisis of the late 2000s nearly collapsed the U.S. economy and struck a particularly heavy blow to minority homebuyers and homeowners. The sociologists Michael Omi and Howard Winant observe that, "People of color were more than three times as likely as whites to have subprime and high-cost loans. Such loans accounted at one point for more than 55 percent of all black and Latino mortgages."[63] The consequences were both harsh and at least partially unnecessary. A *Wall Street Journal* report showed that in 2006 fully 60 percent of subprime loans went to people who could have qualified for less expensive prime loans. Tony Pugh of the McClatchy Newspapers reported that, "nearly 8 percent of blacks and Latinos who got home loans or refinanced between 2005 and 2008 ultimately lost their homes to foreclosure between 2007 and 2009, compared with only 4.5 percent of non-Hispanic whites."[64]

So redlining is gone, at least in its classic form, but minority Americans still struggle to get home loans on the same terms as White people; minority borrowers are still seen as risky bets. A study conducted by the Center for Investigative Reporting in 2018 of 31 million records mandated by the Home Mortgage Disclosure Act showed continuing widespread discrimination by lenders against minority applicants. The records included every application made in 2015 and 2016 for a conventional home loan. Those conducting the study controlled for nine social and economic variables, including applicants' income, amount of the loan, as well as racial makeup and average income in the neighborhood where the home was located. The study found that in 48 of 61 major metropolitan areas analyzed, Black people were denied traditional home loans at significantly higher rates than White people. Lenders claimed that non-public information, like the applicants' credit history and credit score, help explain the racial difference in approved loans, not discrimination, but the long history of racial residential discrimination made many wonder.[65] Another recent study of racial discrimination in U.S. housing and home loan markets concluded that, "Black and Hispanic home seekers continue to be rejected at higher rates than whites with similar characteristics and are also more likely to receive high-cost mortgage products."[66] Moreover, when Black and minority buyers do purchase a home, it is likely to be in a minority neighborhood and the broader environment may be unfavorable.

Neighborhoods, Communities, and Their Environments

Neighborhoods, communities, towns, cities, and major metropolitan areas are contexts and environments within which people and families live their lives and make their futures. Some neighborhoods and communities help people to do that successfully and some neighborhoods and communities hinder people, even preclude them, from making a livable future.[67] Many studies, some explored in this and previous chapters, describe the social, economic, and political vulnerability of Black homeowners and the neighborhoods in which they live.

Poverty and exclusion make Black people and their communities vulnerable to environmental racism; vulnerable to White officials' choices and decisions concerning zoning, highway location, factory siting and regulation, as well as where to put garbage dumps, private landfills, and toxic and industrial waste disposal sites.[68] Imagine again the most attractive community you know and then think about whether any of the issues just mentioned, dumps, waste disposal, etc. bother those communities – you can stop thinking now, they do not. Now think about minority communities on the "other side of the tracks" – you'll have trouble counting the dumps, smelters, mills, and plants. Vulnerable communities have few ways and fewer means to fight adverse environmental targeting. When they do fight, they find the courts largely unreceptive. Richard Rothstein has reminded us that, "For the most part, courts have refused to reject toxic siting decisions without proof of explicit, stated intent to harm African Americans because of their race."[69] Public officials, of course, know this, so few have been clumsy enough to admit Black animus as the reason for locating a noxious site in or near Black communities.

Government, often local government, zoning decisions have served to concentrate Black people geographically where their communities are then vulnerable to adverse siting decisions. Robert Bullard, a long-time professor of urban planning and environmental policy at Texas Southern University, a historically Black university near Houston, has written extensively on these issues. One of his early research projects on Houston, begun in 1978, found that, "all five municipal dumps, six of eight city-operated garbage incinerators and three of four private landfills were located in Black communities – though African-Americans made up only 25 percent of the population at the time. What the data showed was a pattern of racist decisions over years and years by city officials."[70]

Housing, Neighborhoods, and Opportunity's Environmental Context **249**

Poverty and exclusion invite social and political disregard. Chandra Taylor of the Southern Environmental Law Center explained that, "Whenever there's a question of where to site a polluting facility, there's a calculus to that decision. . . . Part of that calculus involves zoning decisions. Part of that calculus involves the price of land. And part of the calculus involves the political power of the communities that are near that property."[71] Justin Onwenu of Sierra Club observed that, "Communities of color, especially Black communities, have been concentrated in areas adjacent to industrial facilities and industrial zones, and that goes back decades and decades, to redlining."[72] Finally, a study by Christopher Tessum, an environmental engineer at the University of Illinois at Urbana-Champaign, found that the result of long-standing environmental racism was that, "Black Americans are exposed to more pollution from every type of source, including industry, agriculture, all manner of vehicles, construction, residential sources and even emissions from restaurants. . . . while white people were exposed to lower-than-average concentrations from almost all categories."[73]

Black Americans have never had housing options, let alone a housing market, that even resembled the housing options, markets, and benefits that White Americans enjoyed. In slavery, most Black people were property and so were housed at their owner's discretion, while fewer than one in ten Black people who were nominally free lived in the generally substandard housing that was all they could afford. As late as the end of the nineteenth century, decades after the end of slavery, W.E.B. Du Bois reported in an article drawn from his classic study, *The Philadelphia Negro* (1899), that "the Negro problem" as White people described the presence of Black residents in their city, was "not one problem, but rather a plexus of social problems."[74] Racial residential segregation forced urban Black citizens into defined ghettos in which poverty, crime, and disease were aggravated by poor but expensive housing. As Black people moved into a particular street or part of town, White people left and property values fell, so landlords raised rents in order to keep their return on investment stable. Black Americans in a position to buy homes found that a premium was demanded over what White people were charged and then property values fell as the block or section transitioned from a majority White population to a majority Black population. The result over generations was that the wealth accumulation through property appreciation that so many White families enjoyed was deeply undercut for Black families.

Racial residential segregation, as intended, cut Black people off from the broader White society and economy. In these segregated communities, public facilities were poor, jobs were scarce, wages low, unemployment common, and wealth accumulation limited. Under those inauspicious circumstances, crime festered and White authorities responded with more police, more arrests, and more incarceration. The direct result was more limited and blunted Black lives. In Chapter 9 we turn to the fraught relations between the nation's criminal justice system and its minority communities.

Notes

1 Stephen Menendian, Arthur Gailes, and Samir Gambhir, "The Roots of Structural Racism: Twenty-First Century Racial Residential Segregation in the United States," Othering and Belonging Institute, University of California, Berkeley, June 21, 2021, 1.
2 Linda Villarosa, *Under the Skin: The Hidden Toll of Racism on American Lives and on the Health of Our Nation* (New York: Doubleday, 2022), 91. See also Robert Wuthnow, *The Left Behind: Decline and Rage in Small-Town America* (Princeton, NJ: Princeton University Press, 2018), 13–43; Michael C. Steiner, *Horace Kallen in the Heartland: The Midwestern Roots of American Pluralism* (Lawrence, KS: University Press of Kansas, 2020), 16.
3 Robert J. Sampson, *Great American City: Chicago and the Enduring Neighborhood Effect* (Chicago, IL: University of Chicago Press, 2012), 356.
4 Paul Peterson, *City Limits* (Chicago, IL: University of Chicago Press, 1981), 4.
5 Peterson, *City Limits*, 27.
6 Peterson, *City Limits*, 36, 71.
7 Valencia Jones, CW69, "A New Push to Turn Buckhead into Its Own City," *CBS News*, February 9, 2023.
8 Sheryll Cashin, *White Space, Black Hood: Opportunity Hoarding and Segregation in the Age of Inequality* (Boston, MA: Beacon Press, 2021), 110–111. See also Mara Gay, "To Cut New York Housing Costs, Ease Suburbs' Zoning Laws," *New York Times*, February 23, 2023, A22.
9 Frederick Douglass, *My Bondage, My Freedom* (New Haven, CT: Yale University Press, 2014; 1855 reprint), 47.
10 Douglass, *My Bondage, My Freedom*, 39–40, 45–46.
11 Douglass, *My Bondage, My Freedom*, 41, 61–63.
12 Abraham Lincoln, "Letter from Lincoln to Mary Speed," September 27, 1841, in Roy P. Basler, ed., *The Collected Works of Abraham Lincoln*, 9 vols. (New Brunswick, NJ: Rutgers University Press, 1953), 1:260. See also "Graphic Detail: Slavery in America," *The Economist*, June 18, 2022, 77.
13 Charles Carleton Coffin, *Four Years of Fighting* (Boston, MA: Tickner and Fields, 1866), 416.
14 Lee Soltow, "Egalitarian America and Its Inegalitarian Housing in the Federal Period," *Social Science History* 9, no. 2 (Spring 1985): 199–213. See also David Herbert Donald, *Lincoln* (New York: Simon & Schuster, 1995), 22; Leon F. Litwack, *Trouble in Mind: Black Southerners in the Age of Jim Crow* (New York: Vintage Books, 1998), 137.
15 Ibram X. Kendi, *Stamped from the Beginning: The Definitive History of Racist Ideas in America* (New York: Bold Type Books, 2017), 170. See also David Hackett Fischer, *African Founders: How Enslaved People Expanded American Ideals* (New York: Simon & Schuster, 2022), 93, 186, 228.
16 Van Gosse, *The First Reconstruction: Black Politics in America from the Revolution to the Civil War* (Chapel Hill, NC: University of North Carolina Press, 2021), 120.
17 Douglas S. Massey and Nancy A. Denton, *American Apartheid: Segregation and the Making of the Underclass* (Cambridge, MA: Harvard University Press,

1993), 17–18. See also Cashin, *White Space, Black Hood*, 42–43; and even the hard-headed W.E.B. Du Bois, *The Souls of Black Folks, with an Introduction by Arnold Rampersad* (New York: Alfred A. Knopf, 1993, first published 1903), 145. For a more negative view, see Litwack, *Trouble in Mind*, xvi, 20; Eugene D. Genovese, *Roll, Jordan, Roll: The World the Slaves Made* (New York: Pantheon Books, 1974), 74.

18 Kate Masur, *Until Justice Be Done: America's First Civil Rights Movement, from the Revolution to Reconstruction* (New York: W.W. Norton, 2021), 83–84, 102, 190–191. See also Fischer, *African Founders*, 198.

19 Heather McGhee, *The Sum of Us: What Racism Costs Everyone and How We Can Prosper Together* (New York: OneWorld, 2021), 21. See also Richard Edwards, "The Homestead Act and the Struggle for African American Rights," *Great Plains Quarterly* 41, no. 3 (2021): 176; Benjamin T. Lynerd, "Emancipation, the *Ager Publicus*, and Black Political Thought," *American Political Thought* 12, no. 1 (Winter 2023): 27–49.

20 Rodney A. Brooks, *Fixing the Racial Wealth Gap* (Suffolk, VA: August Press, 2021), 18.

21 Richard Rothstein, *The Color of Law: A Forgotten History of How Our Government Segregated America* (New York: Liveright, 2018), 40.

22 Rothstein, *The Color of Law*, 39. See also Valerie Sweeney Prince, *Burnin' Down the House: Home in African American Literature* (New York: Columbia University Press, 2004), 15.

23 Robert A. Margo, *Race and Schooling in the South, 1880–1950: An Economic History* (Chicago: University of Chicago Press, 1990), 114–115.

24 Michael R. Kramer, et al., "Do Measures Matter: Comparing Surface-Density-Derived and Census-Tract-Derived Measures of Racial Residential Segregation," *International Journal of Health Geographies* 9, no. 29 (2010): 9–29.

25 Massey and Denton, *American Apartheid*, 30.

26 Trevon D. Logan and John M. Parman, "Segregation and Home Ownership in the Early Twentieth Century," *American Economic Review* 107, no. 5 (May 2017): 411.

27 David R. Roediger, *Working Toward Whiteness: How America's Immigrants Became White* (New York: Basic Books, 2005), 176–177.

28 Prottoy Akbar, Sijie Li, Allison Shertzer, and Randall P. Walsh, "Racial Segregation in Housing Markets and the Erosion of Black Wealth," National Bureau of Economic Research, Working Paper 25805, May 2019, 11.

29 Eduardo Bonilla-Silva, *Racism Without Racists: Color-Blind Racism and the Persistence of Racial Inequality in America*, 5th ed. (Lanham, MD: Rowman and Littlefield, 2018), 24. See also Cashin, *White Space, Black Hood*, 55–56, 71.

30 "Briefing: Race in America," *The Economist*, July 11, 2020, 16. See also Richard Sander, Yana Kucheva, and Jonathan Zasloff, *Moving Toward Integration: The Past and Future of Fair Housing* (Cambridge, MA: Harvard University Press, 2018), 414.

31 Kenneth B. Clark, *Dark Ghetto: Dilemmas of Social Power* (New York: Harper and Row, 1965), 11, 63.

32 Desmond King and Rogers M. Smith, *Still a House Divided: Race and Politics in Obama's America* (Princeton, NJ: Princeton University Press, 2011), 143.

33 Peter Robison and Noah Buhayar, "Realtors Are Sorry About All the Discrimination," *BusinessWeek*, December 27, 2021, 55–59.

34 Bonilla-Silva, *Racism Without Racists*, 24–25.

35 Rothstein, *The Color of Law*, 122; see also Massey and Denton, *American Apartheid*, 51.
36 King and Smith, *Still a House Divided*, 144.
37 Chloe N. Thurston, *At the Boundaries of Home Ownership: Credit, Discrimination, and the American State* (New York: Cambridge University Press, 2018), 103.
38 Rothstein, *The Color of Law*, 51–53. See also Richard D. Kahlenberg, "Zoning Is a Social Justice Matter," *New York Times*, op-ed, April 20, 2021, A25.
39 David R. Roediger, *Working Toward Whiteness*, 170; see also Thurston, *At the Boundaries of Home Ownership*, 104.
40 Allison Shertzer and Randall P. Walsh, "Racial Sorting and the Emergence of Segregation in American Cities," National Bureau of Economic Research, Working Paper 22077, March 2016, revised June 2018, Abstract, 4–5, 33.
41 Akbar, et al., "Racial Segregation in Housing Markets and the Erosion of Black Wealth," Abstract.
42 Akbar, et al., "Racial Segregation in Housing Markets and the Erosion of Black Wealth," 4, 6.
43 Rothstein, *The Color of Law*, 63.
44 Thurston, *At the Boundaries of Home Ownership*, 46–50, 73.
45 Kendi, *Stamped from the Beginning*, 337.
46 Rothstein, *The Color of Law*, 82, 85; David Levering Lewis, *W.E.B. Du Bois: A Biography, 1863–1963* (New York: Henry Holt and Company, 2009), 673.
47 Robert P. Jones, *White Too Long: The Legacy of White Supremacy in American Christianity* (New York: Simon & Schuster, 2020), 64.
48 Thurston, *At the Boundaries of Home Ownership*, 116; Kendi, *Stamped from the Beginning*, 357.
49 King and Smith, *Still a House Divided*, 147.
50 Michael K. Brown, "Divergent Fates: The Foundation of Durable Racial Inequality, 1940–2013," Demos, 2013, 15. See also Thurston, *At the Boundaries of Home Ownership*, 91.
51 U.S. Commission on Civil Rights, "Understanding Fair Housing," February 1973, 3, 5.
52 William J. Collins and Robert A. Margo, "Race and Home Ownership from the End of the Civil War to the Present," *American Economic Review* 101, no. 3 (May 2011): 355–359. See also Robert J. Shiller, *Irrational Exuberance*, revised and expanded, 3rd ed. (Princeton, NJ: Princeton University Press, 2016), especially Chapter 3.
53 Dorothy A. Brown, *The Whiteness of Wealth: How the Tax System Impoverishes Black Americans—And How We Can Fix It* (New York: Crown Books, 2021), 16.
54 Leah P. Boustan and Robert A. Margo, "A Silver Lining to White Flight: White Suburbanization and African-American Home Ownership, 1940–1980," *Journal of Urban Economics*, 78 (2013): 71–80.
55 Jonathan Spader, "Tenure Projections of Homeowner and Renter Households for 2018–2038," Joint Center for Housing Studies of Harvard University, March 2019, 5. See also Stefanos Chen, "No Shelter from the Ills of Racial Bias," *New York Times*, August 22, 2021, Bu8.
56 Gary Gerstle, *The Rise and Fall of the Neoliberal Order: America and the World in the Free Market Era* (New York: Oxford University Press, 2022), 211–218.
57 Cashin, *White Space, Black Hood*, 7.

Housing, Neighborhoods, and Opportunity's Environmental Context   **253**

58 Michelle Singletary, "Being Black Lowers Home Values: Legacy of 'Redlining,'" *Dallas Morning News*, November 8, 2020, D3. See also Chen, "No Shelter from the Ills of Racial Bias," Bu8.
59 Initiative for a Competitive Inner City, "Breaking the Glass Bottleneck: The Economic Potential of Black and Hispanic Real Estate Developers and the Constraints They Face," https://reports.groveimpact.org/breaking-the-glass-bottleneck/. See also Colette Coleman, "Black and Latino Developers Face Tall Hurdles," *New York Times*, March 5, 2023, BU9.
60 Cashin, *White Space, Black Hood*, 113. Emphasis in original.
61 Lincoln Quillian, John J. Lee, and Brandon Honore, "Racial Discrimination in the U.S. Housing and Mortgage Lending Markets: A Quantitative Review of Trends, 1976–2016," *Race and Social Problems* 12 (2020): 13–28, see 14. See also Hilary Hurd Anyaso, "Racial Discrimination in Mortgage Market Over Four Decades," *Northwestern Now*, January 23, 2020.
62 Rick Brooks and Ruth Simon, "Subprime Debacle Traps Even Very Credit-Worthy," *Wall Street Journal*, December 3, 2007. See also McGhee, *The Sum of Us*, 172, 177; Ezra Klein, "Why a Middle-Class Lifestyle Remains Out of Reach for So Many," *New York Times*, July 20, 2022, A23.
63 Michael Omi and Howard Winant, *Racial Formation in the United States*, 3rd ed. (New York: Routledge, 2015), 1–2. See also McGhee, *The Sum of Us*, 70.
64 Tony Pugh, "Blacks, Latinos Were Most Likely to Suffer Foreclosure," *McClatchy Newspapers*, June 21, 2010.
65 Aaron Glantz and Emmanuel Martinez, "For People of Color, Banks Are Shutting the Door to Homeownership," Reveal: Center for Investigative Reporting, February 15, 2018. See also Emily Flitter, *The White Wall: How Big Finance Bankrupts Black America* (New York: Simon & Schuster, Atria/One Signal, 2022).
66 Quillian, et al., "Racial Discrimination in the U.S. Housing and Mortgage Lending Markets," 23–24. See also Shawn Donnan, Ann Choi, Hannah Levitt, and Chris Cannon, with Jason Grotto, "A Racial Refinancing Gap at Wells Fargo," *BusinessWeek*, March 14, 2020.
67 Michelle Alexander, *The New Jim Crow: Mass Incarceration in the Age of Colorblindness* (New York: The New Press, 2010; 10th anniversary ed., 2020), xxxi.
68 Joe R. Feagin, *The White Racial Frame: Centuries of Racial Framing and Counter-Framing*, 3rd ed. (New York: Routledge, 2020), 10–11. See also Kevin P. Josey, et al., "Air Pollution and Mortality at the Intersection of Race and Social Class," *The New England Journal of Medicine*, March 24, 2023, 6–7.
69 Rothstein, *The Color of Law*, 56.
70 Linda Villarosa and Hannah Price, "The Refinery Next Door," *The New York Times Magazine*, August 2, 2020, 33–34. See also Robert D. Bullard, *Dumping in Dixie: Race, Class, and Environmental Quality*, 3rd ed. (New York: Routledge, 2018), 42–43; Glenn Thrush, "Justice Dept. Launches Environmental Racism Inquiry in Houston," *New York Times*, July 23, 2022, A9; Cara Buckley, "Father of Environmental Justice for Poor Meets the Moment," *New York Times*, September 13, 2022, A13.
71 Quoted in Margaret Renkl, "A Rare Victory Against Environmental Racism," *New York Times*, August 18, 2021, A19.
72 Quoted in Maria Virginia Olano, "Chart: Black Americans Hit Hardest by Deadly Air Pollution," *q*, January 14, 2022.

73 Quoted in Hiroko Tabuchi and Nadja Popovich, "A Stark Inequality More Harmful with Each Breath," *New York Times*, April 29, 2021, A21. See also Amudalat Ajasa, "Toxic Metal Pollution Is 10 Times Worse in Racially Segregated Communities," *Washington Post*, November 1, 2022.
74 W.E.B. Du Bois, "The Study of the Negro Problems," *Annals of the American Academy of Political and Social Science* 11 (January 1898): 3.

9
RACE, ETHNICITY, AND THE CRIMINAL JUSTICE SYSTEM

> "Yonder boy born in poverty and filth begotten in shame and trained in crime – who shall judge the depth of his guilt. . . . The question still remains . . . who manufactures such criminals?"
> W.E.B. Du Bois, 1899, "The Problem of Negro Crime"

The criminal justice system, including the lawmaking apparatus, police, courts, prisons and jails, and society's monitoring and surveillance systems are directed not only at defining and punishing crime, but at deploying, disciplining, and controlling those on the social margins, especially people of color. Scholars have long described the criminal justice system as a social control mechanism designed especially to monitor and discipline those whose presence, place, and role in society least reflect mainstream appearances and expectations. Instructive here is a literature that developed out of Michel Foucault's 1975 description of the criminal justice systems as the "carceral archipelago" – others have called it the carceral state. Ruby Tapia, Chair of Women and Gender Studies and Associate Professor of English at the University of Michigan, defined the carceral state as "logics, ideologies, practices, and structures, that invest in . . . punitive orientations to difference, to poverty, to . . . crossers of constructed borders of all kinds."[1]

In the study of race, justice, and incarceration, as in the study of race relations more generally, scholars have noted stability and change, cycles of systemic stability, disruption, and reconstitution. Systems of racialized social control have included slavery, Jim Crow segregation, and mass incarceration – all directed generally toward Black people and selectively toward other minorities. After long stretches of relative stability, systemic collapse – the Civil War's dismantling of slavery and the civil rights movement's dismantling of Jim Crow – brought the frantic search for new mechanisms of social control to serve the old purposes of racial hierarchy. Those systems – slavery, Jim Crow, and mass incarceration – did not arise in a moment; they grew over a period of decades as new strands intertwined and reinforced each other until a new and seemingly impregnable social control system was in place. Michelle Alexander, the legal scholar and author of the influential 2010 book *The New Jim Crow*, noted that "systems of racial and social control adapt, morph, rebound, and are reborn. . . . Like [slavery and] Jim Crow, mass incarceration operates as a tightly networked system of laws, policies, customs, and institutions that operate collectively to insure the subordinate status of a group defined largely by race."[2] Just as importantly, Bryan Stevenson in *The 1619 Project* declared that "Recognizing the unbroken links between slavery, Black Codes, lynching, and our current era of mass incarceration is essential."[3]

Slave Justice in Colonial and Early America

We have talked about Black chattel slavery, 1619–1865, throughout this book, so here only a few points related to the criminal justice system of the nation's formative period need to be made. First, the Pulitzer Prize-winning journalist Douglas Blackmon reminded us that "prior to the Civil War, all of government . . ., at every level, was unimaginably sparse by modern standards" and that "incarceration was an expensive and impractical outcome," particularly in regard to a working asset like an able-bodied slave.[4] Even taxing citizens to build jails and prisons to house and feed White prisoners, except the most heinous and violent, seemed extravagant when you could as easily pistol whip or hang them. Hence, private justice, vigilante and plantation justice, reigned for centuries.

Second, the semi-private criminal justice system in early America was defined and shaped by its primary purpose – controlling the poor and the enslaved. Police forces as we know them today did not exist until the mid-nineteenth century in the urban North and until after the Civil War in the urban South. Formal police forces were preceded by night watches and court constables while persons and businesses were largely responsible for their own day-to-day security.[5] New York City established its police force in 1845, Baltimore in 1853, and Boston and Philadelphia in 1854. In the South, "early police forces were slave patrols, made up of white volunteers empowered to use vigilante tactics to enforce laws supporting slavery."[6] More formal police forces were established in Houston in 1866, Atlanta in 1873, and Dallas in 1881. Their responsibilities remained focused on control of the freed slaves.

While almost all night watches, patrols, and constables before the Civil War were local and most police are still today, courts sometimes were foreign, federal, or part of other state judicial systems and that represented uncertainty and danger to American slaveholders. For example, "the freedom principle" acknowledged in international law and in the American colonies North and South, held that slavery could only exist and be enforced where law supported it. Where law did not support slavery, as was the case in Britain and increasingly in the Northern states, slavery could have no presence.[7] The freedom principle was dramatically reflected in the case of *Somerset v. Stewart*. In 1769 a Virginia merchant named Charles Stewart carried his family, including a slave named James Somerset, to London for an extended stay. Somerset, assisted by the anti-slavery activist Granville Sharp, sued for his freedom in the British courts before Lord Mansfield, Chief Justice of the King's Bench, claiming that he could not be held as a slave in a free country.[8] The court found for Somerset and set off a wave of similar findings in the Northern colonies, later states, during and immediately after the Revolution. Southern courts tightened their Slave Codes and the U.S. Congress and federal courts enforced slaveowner rights to control their property, but the South clearly understood the freedom principle as a major threat.

Black people, slave and free, were denied most rights of citizenship and due process, and slaves in particular were left to the not so tender mercies of plantation justice. The economic historians Robert Fogel and Stanley Engerman, authors of the path-breaking *Time on the Cross*, wrote: "Within fairly wide limits the state, in effect, turned the definition of the codes of legal behavior of slaves, and of the punishment for infractions of these codes, over to planters. . . . For most slaves it was the law of the plantation, not of the state, that was relevant."[9] Slaveowners were, of course, aware of and even reveled in their complete dominance over their slave property. The South Carolina planter-politician James Henry Hammond famously bragged that "on our estates we dispense with the whole machinery of public police and public courts of justice. Thus we try, decide, and execute the sentences, in thousands of cases, which in other countries would go into the courts."[10]

While there were laws seeming to forbid the egregious torture and killing of slaves, enforcement was uncommon because plantations operated as closed units where plantation justice displaced the formal justice system. In fact, the formal justice system had no place for Black claimants. Decrying the Fugitive Slave Act of 1850 in his famous Fourth of July, 1852, oration, Frederick Douglass reminded his audience that,

> The oath of any two villains is sufficient, under this hell-black enactment, to send the most pious and exemplary black man into the remorseless jaws of slavery! His own testimony is nothing. He can bring no witnesses for himself. The minister of American justice is bound by the law to hear but one side; and *that* side is the side of the oppressor.[11]

As late as March 1857, the slave Dred Scott sought to avail himself of the freedom principle, claiming that having been carried from the slave states of Virginia and Missouri into Wisconsin, a free state, he could no longer be treated as a slave. Chief Justice Roger B. Taney declared that in America, Black people, slave or free, were not citizens, had no standing to be in federal court, and as property could be taken by their owners wherever in the U.S. those owners pleased. Taney, writing for a 7–2 majority, declared that Black people were "beings of an inferior order, and altogether unfit to associate with the white race, either in social or political relations; and so far inferior that they had no rights which the white man was bound to respect."[12] Republicans led by Abraham Lincoln, as well as Senator Lyman Trumbull of Illinois, Governor Salmon P. Chase of Ohio, and many others responded in chorus with the freedom principle, but to no immediate avail.[13] While slavery and the place of "free" Black people before the Civil War were defined by a network of laws and restrictions enacted between the mid-seventeenth century and the Fugitive Slave Act noted above, Black people were the mere objects of these laws and little protected by them.

After the Civil War: From Slave Pens to Convict Leasing

In previous chapters, we have described the end of chattel slavery, brought by the Confederate defeat in the Civil War, and apparently locked down by the postwar Thirteenth, Fourteenth, and Fifteenth Amendments to the Constitution. The Thirteenth Amendment ended slavery, the Fourteenth conferred citizenship on the former slaves, and the Fifteenth gave Black men the right to vote. Well before the *Slaughterhouse Cases* (1873), the *Civil Rights Cases* (1883), and *Plessy v. Ferguson* (1896) trimmed back the import of these Amendments, the states of the former Confederacy exploited a major loophole in the Thirteenth Amendment to undercut Black freedom. Section I of the Thirteenth Amendment read: "Neither slavery nor involuntary servitude, except as a punishment for crime whereof the party shall have been duly convicted, shall exist within the United States, or any place subject to their jurisdiction."

The Thirteenth Amendment was passed in Congress on January 31, 1865, a little more than two months before General Lee's April 9 surrender at Appomattox Courthouse, and ratified by twenty-seven of the then thirty-six states by December 6, 1865. Within a matter of months, Southern state legislatures began using the Thirteenth Amendment's language: "except as a punishment for crime whereof the party shall have been duly convicted," as the constitutional and legal foundation for new and expanded "Black Codes." Those postwar social control statutes were designed to channel the freedmen back toward their traditional social and economic roles. They included provisions prohibiting loitering and requiring Black people to prove continuous employment and to sign annual labor contracts, as well as other new mandates and prohibitions, violations of which triggered burdensome fines and long jail terms.[14] Within ten years, "every southern state enacted an array of interlocking laws essentially intended to criminalize black life" and "By the end of Reconstruction in 1877, every formerly Confederate state except Virginia had adopted the practice of leasing black prisoners into commercial hands."[15]

Convict leasing was a particularly diabolical system. Recently freed slaves, often illiterate and penniless, might be arrested on a minor charge, say loitering, often trumped up, were jailed and, unable to pay fines and fees, leased for a term of "involuntary servitude" to a local plantation, mine, or lumber camp. Extended sentences for "misbehavior" were not uncommon. Not only did local officials, usually sheriffs, earn fees on the arrest and court processing, but the county saved money on the housing and feeding of prisoners and made money on the prisoner leases. Black labor as in the slavery days was captive and usable at discretion. Worse still, no one – not the sheriff or the leaser – had a long-term property interest in the health or even the life of the leased prisoner. Work one to death and lease another was efficient economics that tolerated, even promoted, a level of carnage that went on for decades.[16]

Political scientists Michael Dawson and Megan Francis wrote that, "After Reconstruction, the criminal justice system became the institution at the heart of southern efforts to strip African Americans of their citizenship rights."[17] Convict leasing served as a sturdy bridge between the collapse of the slave regime and the rise of Jim Crow segregation in the first decade of the new century. For example, in 1878 the state of Texas began leasing prisoners, mostly Black, to the Imperial Sugar plantations near Sugarland, Texas, about twenty miles southwest of Houston. In 1909, Texas opened the Imperial State Prison Farm, renamed the Central State Prison Farm in 1930, better to serve the Imperial Sugar plantations. Leased prisoners helped provide sugar to the nation for decades. The 2018 discovery of ninety-five bodies, all but one of them male, between the ages of fourteen and seventy, in an unmarked Sugarland, Texas cemetery momentarily focused national attention on the post-Civil War convict leasing system. CNN, the *Washington Post*, the *New York Times*, and all of the major Texas newspapers ran stories about the brutal history of the convict leasing system. Such unmarked graves of convict leasing victims, in ones and twos and dozens, undoubtedly are scattered across the South. Of course, "Black Codes" and convict leasing alone did not produce the kind of control over the Black population that White Southerners demanded.

Lynching as a Social Control Mechanism

In the wake of the Civil War, a battle for control of the defeated South took place between the freedmen and federal forces of occupation, scattered thinly throughout the region, and the region's native White population. During Reconstruction the native White population did not control the formal institutions of government, police, courts, jails, and prisons, so they used illegal violence and intimidation to preserve or restore White supremacy. Intimidation and violence took many forms, from social and economic pressure, to beatings, property destruction, and murder. Lynchings, generally defined as illegal killings by a mob of four or more, were among the most dramatic uses of violence, meant to cow and intimidate whole communities and regions. Lynching was used principally against Black men and principally in the South, but it befell others, like Mexicans in Texas, in smaller numbers and with less focused and systematic intent. Lynching a White cattle rustler or horse thief might be a warning to other miscreants, but lynching a Black man in the South during and after Reconstruction sent a much broader and more chilling message about racial hierarchy – about what had changed and what hadn't; White supremacy hadn't changed.

The NAACP and the Equal Justice Initiative, as well as others, have collected data on lynching; each differs from the others in minor ways, but the data presented in Tables 9.1 and 9.2 are broadly accepted.[18] Stunning as these numbers are, they do not begin until 1882, so they provide no insight into the very bloody Civil War and Reconstruction years between 1861 and 1881. Over those two decades Black people began abandoning plantations to run for Union lines, often with slave patrols in pursuit, and in the years 1865 through 1881 freedmen moved into the public square, experimenting with economic independence, voting, and standing for office while White people worked with every means at hand to restore the old order. For example, the Ku Klux Klan was established within months of Lee's surrender, had taken its White supremacist form by 1867, and had spread throughout

TABLE 9.1 Lynchings in the United States, 1882–1962

	Total	Black	% Black
1880s	1,203	534	44
1890s	1,540	1,111	72
1900s	895	791	89
1910s	621	568	91
1920s	315	281	89
1930s	130	119	92
1940s	33	31	94
1950s	8	6	75
1960s	1	1	100
Total	4,746	3,442	73

Source: Margaret Werner Cahalan, "Historical Corrections Statistics in the United States, 1850–1984," NCJ-102529, December 1986, Table 2–2.

TABLE 9.2 Lynchings by U.S. Region, 1882–1962

	Total	Black	% Black
Northeast	12	8	67
Midwest	425	152	36
West	378	18	5
South	3,921	3,264	83
Total	4,736	3,442	73

Source: Margaret Werner Cahalan, "Historical Corrections Statistics in the United States, 1850–1984," NCJ-102529, December 1986, Table 2–6.

the South by 1870. The bloody tolls of the Klan and other White supremist organizations, including the Knights of the White Camelia, established in Louisiana in 1867, are broadly known to history, but dependable data and records do not exist prior to 1882. Nor are racial killings after 1962, even the grisly 1998 East Texas murder of James Byrd, tied behind a truck by three White men and dragged until dead and dismembered, recorded in these databases. Oh, and remember, it takes four White men to be a mob, so James Byrd was not lynched – right!

Nonetheless, Tables 9.1 and 9.2 tell us a great deal. First, Table 9.1 shows that the two decades from 1882 to 1900, as Jim Crow was being fastened down, were the height of the lynching culture in America. More than 1,200 people were lynched between 1882 and 1890 and then 1,540, 72 percent of them Black, were lynched in the 1890s. Victim numbers began to decline by about 50 percent per decade after 1900, except for the deadly 1910s, but the focus on Black people intensified. Between 1900 and

1962, fully 90 percent of those lynched were Black. The political scientists Desmond King and Rogers Smith have observed that, "there were more than 100 recorded lynchings per year every year but one from 1882 . . . to 1901; and there were at least 60 per year throughout the Progressive Era and World War I."[19]

Second, while lynching was not exclusively a Southern phenomenon, it was overwhelmingly a Southern phenomenon – that is, after all, where Black people were in the period under consideration.[20] Table 9.2 shows that 83 percent of lynchings took place in the South and that 83 percent of people lynched in the South were Black. On the other hand, 95 percent (3,264 of 3,442) of Black people lynched in the U.S. were lynched in the South. Mississippi accounted for 578 lynchings (93 percent Black victims), Georgia accounted for 530 (also 93 percent Black victims), Texas accounted for 493 (71 percent Black victims), Louisiana accounted for 391 (86 percent Black victims), Florida had 282 lynchings (91 percent Black victims), and South Carolina lynched 160 (a stunning 98 percent Black victims).[21]

Third, while Black people were the main target of lynching, they were not its only target. Hispanics were "the second largest group (after African Americans) of American ethnic-racial victims, with a documented 605 individual cases occurring between 1848 and 1928."[22] Most of the violence against Hispanics occurred in the Southwest, especially Texas, and was supplemented by a heavy mix of semi-official violence perpetrated by the Texas Rangers and other law enforcement officials.[23] Finally, the historian David Roediger was at pains to make the point that lynching was not aimed at difference, as Russian Jews, Polish Catholics, and Latvian Orthodox Christians had little to fear – it was aimed at racial difference, mainly in the defeated and roiling South. Roediger asserted that, "In the United States, no European immigrant group suffered anything like the terror that afflicted people of color. . . . African American lynchings outstripped those of new immigrants by perhaps a factor of 75 to 1 or more."[24]

The easiest course for us today, but not the best and most truthful course, is to view lynching as unalloyed barbarism of little relevance to modern race relations. Taking this view is not the best course because we know that most White Southerners saw lynching as a post-Civil War social and cultural necessity, and so, sometimes a little more reluctantly, did many others. From 1868 until his death in 1906, Nathaniel Southgate Shaler was professor of paleontology and geology and eventually Dean of the Lawrence Scientific School at Harvard. Born into a slave-holding Kentucky family in 1841, Shaler studied under Louis Agassiz as an undergraduate at Harvard, spent two years as a Union army officer, then spent two years in Europe, before permanently settling in as a member of the Harvard science faculty. Southerner by birth, a leading member of the New England intellectual elite by training, Shaler spent decades, in the scientific journals and in popular magazines and the press, interpreting American post-Civil War race relations and how they might best be ameliorated in light of what he took to be the scientific insights of physical anthropology and evolutionary biology.

Shaler was an apologist for Black subordination and an advocate of Anglo-Saxon White supremacy, whose understanding of Christian love led him to advocate for Black improvement within what he thought science described as their natural limits. He argued that the freedmen of the postwar South needed the firm guiding hand of White Southerners who understood them best. Shaler believed that Black people had "in their African life, come to a state of arrest in their development; . . . beyond which they were not fitted to go. . . . [A]ny further progress must depend on an imitation of a mastering race."[25] So convinced was Shaler that former slaves were evolutionary laggards with much still to be learned from White Southerners that he rationalized lynching as an unfortunate, but unavoidable, necessity. He argued that Black people possessed a thin veneer of civilization stretched over ancestral passions that sometimes broke through. Lynching was not, he wrote in *The International Monthly* in 1901, "sign of low moral estate, but rather a rude though high conception of the measure of protection owed to the defenseless, and above all to women."[26] The defenseless needing protection were, of course, White women, not the much more literally defenseless Black subjects of the lynch mobs. In fact, Shaler rationalized lynching much as the insurrectionists of January 6, 2021, defended their actions, not as lawlessness, but as defense of the true law and Constitution overthrown by a new and illegitimate racial order. Shaler opined that "so far as I have been able to judge the state of mind of lynchers, it is useless to talk to them concerning the dignity of the law, for they really feel that they are its most effective agents."[27]

Twentieth-Century Criminal Justice and Social Control

Jim Crow segregation was largely in place by 1900 and was further tightened and elaborated in the early decades of the new century. Douglas Blackmon has recounted that, "By 1900, the South's judicial system had been wholly reconfigured to make one of its primary purposes the coercion of African Americans to comply with the social customs and labor demands of whites."[28] The criminal justice system, once reorganized to focus on a free Black population, fed on a perverse internal logic. As the historian Ibram X. Kendi has asserted, "higher Black arrest and prison rates substantiated the racist ideas of more Black crime. And these racist ideas

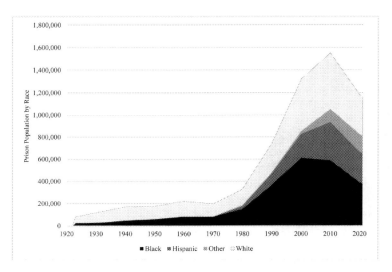

FIGURE 9.1 U.S. State and Federal Prison Population by Race and Ethnicity, 1923–2021

Sources: 1923–1970 calculated by the author from prisoner data by race; U.S. Department of Justice, Bureau of Justice Statistics, Margaret Werner Cahalan, "Historical Corrections Statistics of the United States, 1850–1984," Table 3–31. Data after 1980 from BJS, Prisoner Series, various years, Table 3.

spun the cycle of racial discrimination in the criminal justice system, more suspicions of Black people, more police in Black neighborhoods, more arrests and prison time for Black people, . . . and on and on."[29]

Over the course of the twentieth century, the non-Hispanic White population declined from about 88 percent of the total population to 59 percent in 2021. The Black population held very steady at about 13 percent, while the Hispanic population rose from 1 percent early in the century to about 19 percent in 2021. As clearly displayed in Figure 9.1, the U.S. federal and state prison populations grew throughout the twentieth century from a modest base; more than doubling between 1923 and 1950, growing by just 12 percent between 1950 and the mid-1970s, and then exploding from the late 1970s through 2010. In 1970, there were fewer than 200,000 state and federal prisoners, by 1980 there were just under 330,000, and from there it was straight up to 1.55 million prisoners by 2010. Since 2010, the number of inmates drifted down to 1.16 million in 2021, but, in many ways, the damage to American minority lives and communities, especially Black lives and communities, had already been done. Mass incarceration at its peak in the first decade of the twenty-first century saw 7 million persons in prisons or jails, on parole, or on probation – all under the surveillance and control of the criminal justice system and most of them minorities.[30]

Remarkably, as Figure 9.1 shows so clearly, throughout the twentieth century, Black people have been dramatically overrepresented in state and federal prisons, usually by a factor of 2.5 times, Hispanics have been in prisons at numbers somewhat greater than their rapidly rising share of the U.S. population, while non-Hispanic White people have been in prisons at rates well under their presence in the population. Figure 9.1 shows a prison system growing modestly through most of the twentieth century, increasingly focused on Black people, with a stunning 50 percent of the prison population being Black in 1990, before racial inequality began to abate over the last couple of decades.[31]

To better explain the focus of the criminal justice system on Black people, and Black men in particular, we turn to the famed twentieth century sociologist and criminologist, Johan Thorsten Sellin of the University of Pennsylvania. Sellin, born in Sweden in 1896, died just before his 98th birthday in 1994, and between those dates taught for forty-five years at Penn. Like Myrdal, Sellin brought fresh eyes to U.S. race relations. Almost seventy years before the political scientist Michael Dawson articulated the "linked fate" concept, Sellin observed that, "It is commonly believed that the Negro in our country is more criminal than the white. . . . In setting the hall-mark of his color upon him, his individuality is in a sense submerged, and instead of a mere thief, robber, or murderer, he becomes a representative of his race."[32] Sellin's point was that Black people, seen as members of a race disposed to crime, face a remorseless criminal justice system.

Another common way of discussing and visualizing differences in how the U.S. criminal justice system interacts with racial communities is through incarceration rates. Rather than assessing the raw number of White, Black, and Hispanic people in prison, incarceration rates register the number of White, Black, and Hispanic people in prison per 100,000 of each group's population. Incarceration rates allow comparison of the proclivity to incarcerate across nations, irrespective of their population size, or across the fifty states – despite the fact that California has a population of 39 million and Wyoming has a population of just 579,000 – or across racial and ethnic groups in this case.

The importance of incarceration rates is that they allow an apples to apples comparison of presence in state and federal prisons of populations of different sizes. For example, in 1923, the first year for which we have good data on prisoners in the U.S. by race, the overall U.S. population was 89 percent White and 10 percent Black. Not surprisingly, there were more White (55,036) than Black (25,090) prisoners being held. But when you ask how many White people per 100,000 of White population, and ask the same question for Black people and Hispanics, you get a more nuanced,

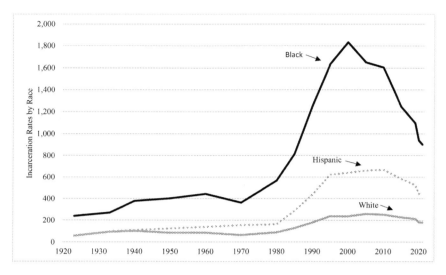

FIGURE 9.2 Incarceration Rates by Race and Ethnicity, 1923–2021

Sources: 1923–1970 calculated by the author from U.S. Census population and prisoner data by race. Prisoner by race data comes from U.S. Department of Justice, Bureau of Justice Statistics, Margaret Werner Cahalan, "Historical Corrections Statistics of the United States, 1850–1984," Table 3–31, December 1986. Data after 1980 from Bureau of Justice Statistics, Prisoner Series, various years, Table 5.

apples to apples comparison. As Figure 9.2 clearly shows, in 1923 there were far more Black prisoners per 100,000 of the Black population than there were White prisoners per 100,000 of the White population – 58 for White prisoners and 239 for Black prisoners.

The White incarceration rate remained remarkably low and stable between 1923 and 1970, beginning at 58 and ending at 65; it tripled by 1990 to 179, and then rose and fell moderately to end at 181 in 2021. The Black incarceration rate started from a base four times higher than the White rate, 239 compared to 58, and stayed three to four times higher, moving to five times higher by 1960, six times higher in 1980, 7.7 times higher by 2000, before it crested and started down. While both White and Black incarceration rates began to stabilize and then decline after 2000, a remarkable 5x gap remained in 2021. The Hispanic incarceration rate, not consistently available before 1970, has ranged between the White and Black rates, usually two to 2.7 times the White rate.

The Societal Implications of Mass Incarceration

For most White Americans, but few Black and other minority Americans, the claim that slavery, Jim Crow, and modern mass incarceration, even with liberal use of the death penalty, are equivalent, or at least similarly designed as systems of social control, is a stretch.[33] Most would see a difference in kind, not just degree, between slavery, Jim Crow, and imprisonment, even mass imprisonment disproportionately of minorities. And there are huge differences between buying and selling human beings, a strict apartheid separation of the races, and mass incarceration following modern legal processes. But if one thinks of the purposes of slavery, Jim Crow, and mass incarceration – social and political control of a suspect population, rather than the particular mechanisms of control – the role and purpose of all three merge and meld.[34]

Black people off the plantation during slavery, on the wrong side of town during Jim Crow, or in the streets during the modern civil rights movement, threatened the social order and, to many, demanded a response. The short decade between 1964 and 1973 saw a pattern of escalating confrontation between American authorities – governments broadly, as well as police, courts, and prisons – and Black Americans. Unlike during most of American history, Black people stayed in the streets and fought back and blood flowed on both sides. In *America on Fire*, Elizabeth Hinton, professor of history and law at Yale, recorded that: "Between 1964 and 1972, but especially between 1968 and 1972. . . . some 960 segregated Black communities across the United States witnessed 1,949 separate uprisings. . . . Over these four years, nearly 40,000 people were arrested, 10,000 were injured, and at least 200 people were killed."[35] Authorities responded to Black unrest by increasing police resources: "The federal allocation to local police forces went from nothing in 1964 to $10 million in 1965, $20.6 million in 1966, $63 million in 1968, $100 million in 1969, and $300 million in 1970."[36] Black people were eventually forced from the streets and the militarization of the nation's police continued apace.

Not surprisingly, the Black community has long had an ambivalent, even antagonistic, relationship with the police. Princeton race scholar Eddie Glaude, Jr., summarizing and then quoting Huey P. Newton, cofounder of the Black Panther Party, wrote "The police weren't in black communities to protect the people. 'Instead they act as the military arm of our oppressors and continually brutalize us.'"[37] Even Robert Kennedy, U.S. Attorney General in John F. Kennedy's administration and then U.S. Senator from New York, asked after the Watts riot in 1965, "How can you ask Negroes in Harlem and Bedford Stuyvesant to obey the law, when the law is used against them?"[38] So, from the perspective of many in the Black community, it is not more crime that draws more police who then make more arrests, it is more police in Black neighborhoods, justifying their presence by making more arrests, leading to the perception of more crime.[39] Robin DiAngelo, an English professor and corporate consultant on race, took a similar view, declaring that, "It has been well documented that blacks and Latinos are stopped by police more often than whites are for the same activities and that they receive harsher sentences than whites do for the same crimes."[40]

Naturally, scholars, criminal justice experts, and many others have asked what accounts for this step-level increase in the U.S. proclivity to arrest and imprison, whether that proclivity is viewed in terms of raw numbers or incarceration rates. The sociologists Michael Omi and Howard Winant have asserted that, "A massive increase in incarceration – unabashedly and disproportionately targeting black and brown men – began in the early 1980s."[41] By 1980, the Black arrest rate was three times that for Whites and "Eight to nine percent of all blacks ... [were] arrested every year."[42] These annual arrest rates meant that by 2010, "One out of every six African-American men has spent time in prison, one out of every thirteen Hispanics, ... [but] only one in thirty-nine white men has ever been to prison."[43] Even more strikingly *The Economist* magazine estimated in 2020 that, "One in three African-American men born in 2001 can expect to be imprisoned at some point in his life, compared to 1 in 17 white boys." The magazine understatedly concluded that, "The criminal-justice system is a baleful presence in black lives."[44]

While these numbers are extraordinary, they are just half the story. Two other questions will flesh out the story – first, who are we talking about here beyond Black people and other minorities, and second, what does involvement with the criminal justice system cost beyond imprisonment? The answer to the first question, who exactly are we talking about in regard to mass incarceration is, yes, Black people, but more narrowly, young, poor, poorly educated Black offenders and reoffenders. The sociologist Mark Robert Rank and his colleagues explained the rapidly rising incarceration rates by noting that, "only about 15 percent of Black male high school dropouts could expect to spend time in prison by their mid-30s at the beginning of the 1980s, but a remarkable 68 percent in recent years."[45] The legal scholar Michelle Alexander has confirmed that about 70 percent of the incarcerated are high school dropouts, about half are functionally illiterate, 70 to 80 percent are poor, and about 30 percent will be rearrested within six months and more than two-thirds within three years. And most are Black; "African American youth account for 16 percent of all youth, 28 percent of all juvenile arrests, 35 percent of the youth waived to adult criminal court, and 58 percent of youth admitted to state adult prison."[46]

The answer to the second question is that there is a great deal more at stake in arrest and conviction than time behind bars. As the journalist Matt Taibbi explained in *The Divide: American Injustice in the Age of the Wealth Gap*, the downward slide into second-class citizenship begins with poverty, perhaps illiteracy, and the inability to afford a lawyer from first contact with the criminal justice system. Taibbi explained that defense lawyers have a saying, "If you go in, you stay in. If you get out, you stay out;" and the best and often only way to stay out is bail – posting a money bond. "It's a resource game. . . . If they have the money to bail out, they fight it. If they don't, they plead;" but 80 percent of those charged are indigent, represented by over-worked public defenders, so they take a plea deal, often to a lesser charge, and less jail time, but it's a guilty plea and much follows from it.[47]

One of the most powerful aspects of Michelle Alexander's *The New Jim Crow* is the argument that, "our current system of mass incarceration. . . . is a set of structural arrangements that locks a racially distinct group into a subordinate political, social, and economic position, effectively creating a second-class citizenship."[48] Here, obviously, we begin to see how it might make sense to discuss mass incarceration in the same breath with slavery, lynching, and Jim Crow exclusion. As Omi and Winant note, "Perhaps the most important aspect of mass imprisonment . . . is its anti-democratic effects: Not only does it banish millions of felons and ex-felons from the electoral rolls, but it comprehensively disadvantages low-income people of color on a mass scale."[49] So a very great deal follows from arrest, trial, and imprisonment.

A Slow Decline in Mass Incarceration

Between the late 1970s and 2006 mass incarceration grew unabated. One of the most remarkable indicators of the impact of mass incarceration on White and Black men is the proportion of men not employed. The census reports three categories of non-working men: the incarcerated, those not incarcerated but not working, and those in the workforce but unemployed. Black and White unemployment rates rise and fall with the economy but Black rates, as we saw in Chapter 6, have remained about twice White rates for decades. Rates for incarceration and men not incarcerated but not in the labor force have increased ominously for both White and Black men, but more for Black men. An important study by Patrick Bayer, an economics professor at Duke, and Kerwin Kofi Charles, Dean of the Yale School of Management, reported that, "rates of institutionalization . . . increased sharply since 1980, more than doubling for both whites (0.7% to 1.5%) and black men (3.3% to 8.0%) by 2014." More important than the idea that both doubled, which they did, is the fact that the Black rate started at 4.7 times the White rate and finished at 5.3 times the White rate. Bayer and Charles also reported that, "While 7.3% of black men were out of the labor force (and not institutionalized) in 1960, this figure peaked at 19.4%

in 2000 and remains above 16% in the 2007–2014 sample."[50] It seems highly likely that Black men out of the labor force but not institutionalized had been institutionalized and were suffering the post-incarceration economic consequences described above.

Despite these remarkable numbers, there has been some relatively recent good news. The total number of persons in U.S. prisons and jails declined from 2.3 million in 2008 to just under 1.8 million in 2021, the fewest since 2003. Incarceration rates over that same timeframe dropped from 1,000 per 100,000 of population to 680 per 100,000, the lowest since 1995. Finally, the Black incarceration rate dropped by 28 percent since 2011 while the Hispanic rate dropped by 20 percent and the White rate dropped by 18 percent. Nonetheless, Black people remained dramatically overrepresented in prisons and jails compared to their presence in the population. Black people, 13 percent of the population, account for 33 percent of prisoners; White people, 59 percent of the population, account for 37 percent of prisoners; and Hispanics, 19 percent of the population, account for 20 percent of prisoners.[51]

Two key reasons for the modest stemming of mass incarceration are adverse comparisons with the rest of the world and cost. Most advanced industrial nations have much smaller prison populations than the U.S. Our 1.8 million looms over the U.K.'s 78,750, Germany's 58,004, Japan's 48,429. Others imprison large numbers of their citizens; China does not provide dependable numbers but they are understood to be large, Brazil holds 811,707, Russia 472,216, and Iran 189,000, but these are not comparisons the U.S. wants. If the incarceration rate is the measure, the U.S. again leads, followed by El Salvador, Turkmenistan, Rwanda, and Cuba, again, not comparisons the U.S. wants. As to costs, the Interrogating Justice think tank calculated the 2021 cost per prisoner at about $30,000, with a range by state between $14,000 and $70,000. Multiply $30,000 through 1.8 million prisoners and you get $54 billion – a big enough number to make state and federal budget hawks blink.

Though the numbers have been coming down slowly, the criminal justice system continues to focus on Black and other minority Americans.[52] From first to last contact with the criminal justice system, Black people receive inordinate attention. Neil Gross, a sociologist at Colby College, reported that among the 19 million vehicle stops each year, Black people are stopped on average 43 percent more than others and Black and Hispanic drivers and their cars are searched twice as often as White drivers.[53] Erwin Chemerinsky, Dean of the University of California, Berkeley School of Law declared that New York City's 4.4 million traffic stops snared Black drivers at a rate more than twice their presence in the population, Hispanic drivers at their presence in the population, and White drivers at less than one-third their presence in the population. In 2015, all the way across the country in San Francisco, Black drivers accounted for 15 percent of the population but 42 percent of persons searched during traffic stops.[54] Arrest records for 2013–2017 secured by the American Civil Liberties Union (ACLU) from the Metropolitan Police Department of Washington, D.C. showed that "Black people were arrested at *ten times the rate of whites*."[55] Similarly, "Fort Worth Police Department records show that since 2015, Black people have been targets of about 43 percent of police Taser deployments while making up 19 percent of the city's population."[56] Ian Haney López of the University of California, Berkeley School of Law also noted that "blacks are about 12 percent of the population but roughly 43 percent of those on death row."[57] Not surprisingly, many agree with the observation by political scientists Michael Dawson and Megan Francis, that "The state . . . the police, the courts, and the massive prison system . . . remains complicit in reproducing racial disparities and enforcing white supremacy."[58]

The Death Penalty in the United States

The U.S. incarcerates a great many people, more than any other country in the world, except perhaps China, and executes a great many people as well, again, more than any other country in the world for which we have good data. The "Espy File," constructed by M. Watt Espy and John Ortiz Smykla, maintained by the Death Penalty Information Center (DPIC), presents all the executions in what became and is now the United States from 1608 through 2022 (see Table 9.3). While we will look most closely at how and against whom the death penalty has been used in the U.S. in the twentieth and twenty-first centuries, we begin by presenting

TABLE 9.3 Persons Executed in the U.S. by Race and Ethnicity, 1608–2022

	Espy File 1608–1972		*DPIC* 1976–2022		*Executions* 1608–2022	
Race	Number	%	Number	%	Number	%
White	5,902	40.7	865	55.8	6,767	42.2
Black	7,084	48.9	529	34.1	7,613	47.5
Native American	353	2.4	18	1.2	371	2.3
Hispanic	295	2.0	130	8.4	425	2.6
Other	855	5.9	8	1.5	863	5.4
Total	14,489		1,550		16,039	

Source: Death Penalty Information Center, "Executions in the U.S., 1608–2022: The Espy File," December 16, 2022.

executions by race since 1608. Though Black people in America have averaged just 10 to 20 percent of the total population, throughout the nation's history, colonial and national, 47.5 percent of all executions have been of Black people, 42.2 percent have been of White people, and about 10 percent of others.

Two more tables will quickly show that heavy use of the death penalty during the Jim Crow era slowed after 1950 and again more recently, but the focus on Black people remained fairly relentless.[59] They will also show that the South, the region most committed to controlling its Black

TABLE 9.4 Executions Per Decade under Civil Authority, 1890–2020

	Executions	*% Non-White*
1890s	1,215	55
1900s	1,190	62
1910s	1,042	47
1920s	1,169	49
1930s	1,670	52
1940s	1,287	63
1950s	719	56
1960–67	192	52
1968–76	0	
1977–79	3	
1980s	117	42
1990s	478	34
2000s	590	34
2010s	341	32
Total	10,013	52

Sources: Margaret Werner Cahalan, "Historical Corrections Statistics in the United States, 1850–1984," NCJ-102529, December 1986, Table 2–1; *Statistical Abstract of the United States, 2022*, #401; Death Penalty Information Center, Executions Database.

TABLE 9.5 Executions by Region, 1976–2022

Region	*Total Executions*	*% of Total*
Northeast	4	0.3
Midwest	194	12.5
West	89	5.7
South	1,271	81.6
Total	1,558	100

Source: Death Penalty Information Center, "Executions by Region Since 1976," accessed December 16, 2022.

population, was by far the heaviest user of the death penalty in the modern era. Combining our earlier discussion of lynching, with its focus in the South, with the heavy use of the death penalty in the South, adds tragic weight to the idea that the criminal justice system, at base, is a social control mechanism. Since 1976, fully 81.6 percent of all executions in the U.S. have taken place in the South.

The same sensibilities, both in U.S. domestic and international politics, that brought on the civil rights movement also drew commitment to the death penalty into question. From the 1890s through the 1940s, as we see in Table 9.4, more than 1,000 people per decade, more than half of them Black, were executed. Executions dropped to 719 in the 1950s and then to 192 between 1960 and 1967. Inconsistency in how the death penalty was applied in the U.S. led the Supreme Court, in a series of decisions beginning with *Robinson v. California* (1962) and culminating in *Furman v. Georgia* (1972), to find the death penalty, as then applied, to be unconstitutional in light of the Eighth and Fourteenth Amendment provisions regarding "cruel and unusual punishment" and "equal protection of the laws." The Court noted racial disparities in the application of the death penalty but it did not cite them as the basis for unconstitutionality. Nonetheless, the Court's decision reflected the increasing discomfort of Americans with the death penalty. *Furman v. Georgia* required that states revise their death penalty statutes to make them more consistent across cases before they could resume executions. Most states proceeded very deliberately, delaying executions even prior to the *Furman* decision, revising their statutes, and then watching how the Court received the new statutes. No executions occurred in the U.S. between 1968 and 1976, when the Court in *Gregg v. Georgia* (1976) reestablished the death penalty. The 1980s continued to see limited use of the death penalty, it rebounded in the 1990s and 2000s, before beginning an ongoing decline in the 2010s.

The U.S. Supreme Court decided the landmark case *McCleskey v. Kemp* (1987), answering again whether the obvious imbalance by race in the administration of the death penalty proved violation of the Eighth and Fourteenth Amendments to the Constitution. The case centered on a statistical study by the law professor David Baldus of approximately 2,000 murders that had taken place in Georgia during the 1970s. McCleskey, a Black man, was charged, convicted, and sentenced to death for the killing of a White police officer during the commission of an armed robbery. The Baldus study showed that while the race of the defendant made no difference to the likelihood of being sentenced to death, the race of the victim made a big difference. Killers of White people were four times more likely to be sentenced to death than killers of Black people. The Court, by a narrow 5–4 majority, upheld McCleskey's death sentence, declaring that statistical evidence of racial imbalance in Georgia's judicial system in regard to the death penalty did not prove that McCleskey's case had been wrongly decided or that he had been denied his Eighth or Fourteenth Amendment rights.[60]

In the wake of the McCleskey trial, David Baldus, George Woodworth, and Charles Pulaski published *Equal Justice and the Death Penalty* (1990). This book extended the study of Georgia's death penalty system back to 1873 and broadened its focus to other states. Baldus' conclusion that killers of White victims were sentenced to death more frequently than killers of Black victims did not change. More recently, Scott Phillips and Justin Marceau, law school and sociology professors at the University of Denver, extended the Baldus study by asking whether racial discrimination and inequities were aggravated or alleviated during the post-conviction sentencing, appellate, and clemency processes. They found "that racial disparities persist and indeed are magnified during the appellate and clemency processes."[61]

The criminologist James M. Marquart and his colleagues provocatively titled their 1994 book on capital punishment in Texas and the South, *The Rope, the Chair, and the Needle*. They opened their analysis with a provocative declaration, saying "Any account of capital punishment must address this basic question: Why was there such a concentration of executions in a single region of the country? . . . the former Confederacy." They answered that, "The common denominator . . . is to be found in a cultural tradition of exclusion. . . . Such exclusion was a basic element of the legacy of slavery."[62] In 2020, the DPIC released *Enduring Injustice: The Persistence of Racial Discrimination in the U.S. Death Penalty*, calling the death penalty a "Descendant of Slavery, Lynching, and Segregation." The author, DPIC's Senior Director for Research, Ngozi Ndulue, wrote that, "The death penalty has been used to enforce racial hierarchies throughout United States history, beginning with the colonial period and continuing to this day."[63]

Police Violence and Black Vulnerability

Throughout American history, sheriffs, police, and other public officials have both facilitated and conducted violence against Black people and stepped aside when White mobs sought to do that work. Violence was both wholesale, as in the 1921 sacking and burning of the Greenwood district of Tulsa, known as the Black Wall Street, and retail as in the many lynching and killings of individual Black people across the South and the nation. One remarkable instance of police misconduct set right way too late played out in a New York City courtroom in late 2021. Malcolm X, the Black radical alternative to the more moderate Martin Luther King, Jr. during the 1950s and 1960s, was assassinated while giving a speech at Harlem's Audubon Ballroom in 1965. Malcolm X had split with the Nation of Islam about a year earlier and tensions were high. Despite contradictory evidence and testimony, three men with connections to the Nation of Islam were quickly arrested, convicted, and imprisoned in 1966. Two of the men, Muhammad A. Aziz and Khalil Islam, maintained their innocence from the beginning, while the third, Talmadge Hayer, admitted his guilt but declared that Aziz and Islam had not been involved. All three languished in prison for decades. Aziz was paroled in 1985, Islam was paroled in 1987 and died in 2009, while Hayer was paroled in 2010.

In early 2019, the Manhattan District Attorney, Cyrus R. Vance, the Innocence Project, and lawyers for Mr. Aziz and Mr. Islam's family launched an investigation into long-standing questions about Malcolm X's killing and the trials and convictions that followed. The investigation discovered that police organizations, including the F.B.I., withheld evidence indicating Aziz's and Islam's innocence. District Attorney Vance proposed and the court agreed, fifty-five years after their conviction, that Aziz and Islam should be exonerated on all charges. Mr. Aziz declared that the corrupt process that had taken more than twenty years of his adult life and hobbled decades more "is all too familiar to Black people, even in 2021." The Innocence Project's Vanessa Potkin agreed, saying "We still have a system that works to oppress some and protects others."[64]

Police violence continues to plague our society; between 2015 and 2020 police shot and killed 5,400 people, about 1,000 people a year. Of those killed, 45 percent were White, 23 percent were Black, 16 percent were Hispanic, and 9 percent were unidentified by race.[65] The murder of George Floyd by Minneapolis police officer Derek Chauvin in May 2020 once again brought police violence to national attention and sparked demonstrations that brought more White people into the streets than previous protests. Almost unprecedentedly, Chauvin was convicted of second degree intentional murder and other charges and sentenced to 22.5 years in prison. Ominously, deaths at the hands of police did not decline in the eighteen months following George Floyd's murder and the "national reckoning" that many hoped would result from it sputtered out.[66]

A recent study by scholars at the University of Washington's Institute for Health Metrics and Evaluation, published in the British health journal. *The Lancet*, paints an even bleaker picture of police violence. The study, which compared official statistics from the National Vital Statistics System (NVSS) with information from three organizations that track police violence, news reports, and open records requests, found that NVSS undercounted deaths by police violence by more than half. The key cause of the undercount was that medical examiners often listed official cause of death as something other than police violence, say underlying health conditions, drug use, or simply unknown causes. The study estimated that 31,000 deaths by police violence, rather than the 14,000 recorded in NVSS, occurred between 1980 and 2018. To no one's particular surprise, "Black Americans were 3.5 times as likely to be killed by the police as white Americans were. . . . Latinos and Native Americans also suffered higher rates of police violence than white people." The study also found that "racial disparities in police shootings have widened since 2000."[67]

Nonetheless, convictions of police for on-duty violence, even formal charges, are uncommon. Policing expert and Georgetown University law school professor Paul Butler has written that "throughout the history of policing roughly 150 officers have been charged with murder, but only ten have ever been convicted of murder."[68] Others have noted that only ten non-federal police officers in addition to Chauvin were convicted of murder for on-duty deaths since 2005.[69] Whether the timeframe is the history of policing or since 2005, ten murder convictions is a small number in light of the hundreds of Black deaths at police hands each year. But obviously, for a police officer to be convicted, he or she must be judged guilty of illegal and punishable conduct by a court.

Erwin Chemerinsky has described the limited police oversight provided by the courts during most of America's history, the Warren Court's important limits on police misconduct, and the subsequent chipping away or hollowing out of those citizen protections by subsequent courts. He declared that, "throughout American history, the Court has . . . consistently empowered police and legitimated the racialized policing that especially harms people of color."[70] Chemerinsky was skeptical that today's conservative Supreme Court would move to limit police violence and events after George Floyd's murder seem to have confirmed that view. Moreover, in September 2021, following many months of negotiations in Congress, Democrats and Republicans failed to agree on police reforms and the negotiations collapsed. Discussions sought to ban "chokeholds" and limit the militarization of the police, but perhaps the most difficult issues involved qualified immunity.

Qualified immunity is a legal concept established by the Supreme Court in the 1967 case *Pierson v. Ray*. The progressive Warren Court, at the height of the civil rights movement, sought to protect public officials, including police officers, from what were often called "frivolous lawsuits." Qualified immunity was initially intended to protect police officers against civil suits for actions that a reasonable person would not have seen as clear violations of "statutory or constitutional rights." Its original goal was to protect good faith actions taken by officers in legally ambiguous or murky circumstances. Later judicial rulings, in the view of many, made qualified immunity a shield against obvious police misconduct involving clear violations of legal or constitutional civil rights. Specifically, the 1983 case *City of Los Angeles v. Lyons* held that overcoming police claims of qualified immunity required citing a previous case with virtually identical facts in which a court ruling made the officer aware of its actionable illegality. Since very few cases arise in which facts are identical to an earlier case of police misconduct, officers rarely lose qualified immunity protections.[71]

The American Bar Association and many others point to the outcome in *Corbitt v. Vickers* (2019) to problematize qualified immunity. Deputy Sheriff Michael Vickers, pursuing a suspect with other officers, entered Amy Corbitt's yard where several small children and pets were playing. With the suspect unarmed and compliant and the children controlled, Officer Vickers fired two shots at the non-compliant but non-threatening family dog, "Bruce," but mistakenly hit a child. On appeal, Vickers prevailed because, while his actions violated law and common sense, says the ABA, "no prior judicial decision involved 'the unique facts of this case.'" In other words, since the Corbitt family could not point to a specific prior case in which facts very much like these, a police officer attempting to shoot the family dog accidentally hitting a child, had been litigated in the plaintiff's favor, qualified immunity pertained. Many see qualified immunity as fundamentally unlawful, but the broad pro-police sentiment in the nation motivates Republicans to protect it against reforms.

Seeing slavery, Jim Crow segregation, and racialized mass incarceration as integrated and purposeful mechanisms for monitoring and controlling marginal or non-normative populations is deeply sobering. But considering the data on both lynching and executions by region and race – both overwhelmingly deployed against Black people in the South – leaves little choice but to admit that the nation's history must be told as that of an evolving carceral state.

What remains then is to ask where we go from here. White supremacy and the various systems of racial discrimination that have sustained it have divided and weakened our country. Like the post-Reconstruction South, we spend so much of our energy on maintaining racial hierarchy that we have too little energy left for charting a way forward for all our citizens. Chapter 10 asks whether the shadow that has darkened the American dream for decades might be lifted and how that might be done. Do we as a people still share the values, purposes, and commitments that will allow us to move forward together? We must hope we do. We conclude with a discussion of the policies, reformist and revolutionary, that might restore the dream by opening and equalizing opportunity for education, jobs, income and wealth, health care, housing, and justice in America.

Notes

1. Carceral State Project, "What is the Carceral State?" May 2020, https://storymaps.arcgis.com/stories/7ab5f5c3fbca46c38f0b2496bcaa5ab0.
2. Michelle Alexander, *The New Jim Crow: Mass Incarceration in the Age of Colorblindness* (New York: The New Press, 2010; 10th anniversary ed., 2020), xviii, 16.
3. Bryan Stevenson, "Punishment," in *The 1619 Project*, ed. Nikole Hannah-Jones, Caitlin Roper, Ilena Silverman, and Jake Silverstein (New York: The New York Times Co., 2021), 279–280, 282. See also Thomas Piketty, *A Brief History of Equality* (Cambridge, MA: Harvard University Press, 2022), 86.
4. Douglas A. Blackmon, *Slavery by Another Name: The Re-Enslavement of Black Americans from the Civil War to World War II* (New York: Anchor Books, 2009), 61–62.
5. Maurice Chammah, *Let the Lord Sort Them: The Rise and Fall of the Death Penalty* (New York: Crown Books, 2021), 132.
6. Erwin Chemerinsky, *Presumed Guilty: How the Supreme Court Empowered the Police and Subverted Civil Rights* (New York: Liveright, 2021), 19.
7. Joseph T. Murphy, "The British Example: West Indian Emancipation, the Freedom Principle, and the Rise of Antislavery Politics in the United States, 1833–1843," *Journal of the Civil War Era* 8, no. 4 (December 2018): 621–646. See also Edward J. Larson, *American Inheritance: Liberty and Slavery in the Birth of a Nation, 1765–1795* (New York: Norton, 2023), 63–71.
8. Tyler Stovall, *White Freedom: The Racial History of an Idea* (Princeton, NJ: Princeton University Press, 2021), 117.
9. Robert William Fogel and Stanley L. Engerman, *Time on the Cross: The Economics of American Negro Slavery* (New York: W.W. Norton, 1974), 128–129.
10. Herbert G. Gutman, *Slavery and the Numbers Game: A Critique of Time on the Cross* (Chicago, IL: University of Illinois Press, 1975), 38.
11. Frederick Douglass, "What to the Slave is the Fourth of July," in *The Speeches of Frederick Douglass*, ed. John R. McKivigan, Julie Husband, and Heather L. Kaufman (New Haven: Yale University Press, 2018), 77.
12. *Dred Scott v. Sandford*, 60 U.S. 393.
13. Paul M. Rego, *Lyman Trumbull and the Second Founding of the United States* (Lawrence, KS: University Press of Kansas, 2022), 28–29.
14. Natalia Molina, *How Race Is Made in America: Immigration, Citizenship, and the Historical Power of Racial Scripts* (Berkeley, CA: University of California Press, 2014), 126.
15. Blackmon, *Slavery by Another Name*, 53, 56.
16. Richard F. Bensel, *The Political Economy of American Industrialization, 1877–1900* (New York: Cambridge University Press, 2000), 152–156.
17. Michael C. Dawson and Megan Ming Francis, "Black Politics and the Neoliberal Racial Order," *Public Choice* 28, no. 1 (2016): 34. See also Leon F. Litwack, *Trouble in Mind: Black Southerners in the Age of Jim Crow* (New York: Vintage Books, 1998), 248–249.
18. See also Michael Barnes, "Project Documents Over 700 Lynchings," *Austin American-Statesman*, January 15, 2021.

19 Desmond S. King and Rogers M. Smith, *Still a House Divided: Race and Politics in Obama's America* (Princeton, NJ: Princeton University Press, 2011), 69. See also Lerone Bennett, Jr., *Before the Mayflower: A History of the Negro in America, 1619–1962* (Chicago, IL: Johnson Publishing Company, 1962; Eastford, CT: Martino Fine Books, 2016), 280, 293–294; Jon Meacham, *The Soul of America: The Battle for Our Better Angels* (New York: Random House, 2018), 162.
20 Robert P. Jones, *White Too Long: The Legacy of White Supremacy in American Christianity* (New York: Simon & Schuster, 2020), 13, 196–197, 220.
21 Robert Wuthnow, *Rough Country: How Texas Became America's Most Powerful Bible-Belt State* (Princeton, NJ: Princeton University Press, 2014), 164.
22 F. Chris Garcia and Gabriel R. Sanchez, *Hispanics and the U.S. Political System: Moving into the Mainstream* (New York: Routledge, 2007), 26.
23 William D. Carrigan and Clive Webb, *Forgotten Dead: Mob Violence Against Mexicans in the United States, 1848–1928* (New York: Oxford University Press, 2013).
24 David R. Roediger, *Working Toward Whiteness: How America's Immigrants Became White* (New York: Basic Books, 2005), 106.
25 Nathaniel S. Shaler, *The Neighbor: The Natural History of Human Contacts* (New York: Houghton, Mifflin and Company, 1904), 134–135. See also David N. Livingstone, "Science and Society: Nathaniel S. Shaler and Racial Ideology," *Transactions of the Institute of British Geographers* 9, no. 2 (1984): 181–210; and John S. Haller, Jr., *Outcasts from Evolution: Scientific Attitudes of Racial Inferiority, 1859–1900* (Carbondale, IL: Southern Illinois University Press, 1971, 1995).
26 Nathaniel S. Shaler, "American Quality," *The International Monthly* 4 (1901): 62. Shaler was not alone in his assessment. Recall the Woodrow Wilson quote from Chapter 5 about "a host of dusky children untimely put out of school," meaning slaves released from bondage/tutelage too soon. Wilson, "The Reconstruction of the Southern States," *Atlantic Monthly*, January 1901, 6.
27 Shaler, "American Quality," 62.
28 Blackmon, *Slavery by Another Name*, 7.
29 Ibram X. Kendi, *Stamped from the Beginning: The Definitive History of Racist Ideas in America* (New York: Bold Type Books, 2017), 282.
30 Alexander, *The New Jim Crow*, 77.
31 Robert D. Putnam, *The Upswing: How America Came Together a Century Ago and How We Can Do It Again*, with Shaylyn Romney Garrett (New York: Simon & Schuster, 2020), 220.
32 Thorsten Sellin, "The Negro Criminal: A Statistical Note," in Donald Young, "Forward," *Annals of the American Academy of Political and Social Science* 140 (1928): 52. See also Litwack, *Trouble in Mind*, 249, 256; Michael C. Dawson, *Behind the Mule: Race and Class in African-American Politics* (Princeton, NJ: Princeton University Press, 1994), 76–80, 82–84; Linda Villarosa, *Under the Skin: The Hidden Toll of Racism on American Lives and on the Health of Our Nation* (New York: Doubleday, 2022), 135.
33 Peniel E. Joseph, *The Third Reconstruction: America's Struggle for Racial Justice in the Twenty-First Century* (New York: Basic Books, 2022), 96.
34 Eddie S. Glaude, Jr., *Begin Again: James Baldwin's America and Its Urgent Lessons for Our Own* (New York: Crown Books, 2020), 177. See also Ellen Messer-Davidow, *The Making of Reverse Discrimination: How DeFunis and Bakke Bleached Racism from Equal Protection* (Lawrence, KS: University Press of Kansas, 2021), 54.

35 Elizabeth Hinton, *America on Fire: The Untold History of Police Violence and Black Rebellion Since the 1960s* (New York: Liveright, 2021), 2, 10. See also Gary Gerstle, *American Crucible: Race and Nation in the Twentieth Century* (Princeton, NJ: Princeton University Press, 2001, rev. ed. 2017), 301.
36 Hinton, *America on Fire*, 22–23.
37 Glaude, *Begin Again*, 85.
38 Patricia Sullivan, *Justice Rising: Robert Kennedy's America in Black and White* (Cambridge, MA: Harvard University Press, 2021), xvii.
39 Nicholas Eubank and Adriane Fresh, "Enfranchisement and Incarceration After the 1965 Voting Rights Act," *American Political Science Review* 116, no. 3 (August 2022): 791–806.
40 Robin DiAngelo, *White Fragility: Why It's So Hard for White People to Talk About Racism* (Boston, MA: Beacon Press, 2018), 63.
41 Michael Omi and Howard Winant, *Racial Formation in the United States*, 3rd ed. (New York: Routledge, 2015), 216. See also Patrick A. Langan, "The Prevalence of Imprisonment," Bureau of Justice Statistics Special Report, July 1985.
42 Eduardo Bonilla-Silva, *Racism Without Racists: Color-Blind Racism and the Persistence of Racial Inequality in America*, 5th ed. (Lanham, MD: Rowman and Littlefield, 2018), 34.
43 Robert Perkinson, *Texas Tough: The Rise of America's Prison Empire* (New York: Picador, 2010), 2.
44 "Briefing: Race in America," *The Economist*, July 11, 2020, 14.
45 Mark Robert Rank, Lawrence M. Eppard, and Heather E. Bullock, *Poorly Understood: What America Gets Wrong About Poverty* (New York: Oxford University Press, 2021), 59.
46 Alexander, *The New Jim Crow*, 148, see also 107, 118, 187, 194.
47 Matt Taibbi, *The Divide: American Injustice in the Age of the Wealth Gap* (New York: Random House, 2018), 117–118.
48 Alexander, *The New Jim Crow*, 229.
49 Omi and Winant, *Racial Formation*, 216.
50 Patrick Bayer and Kerwin Kofi Charles, "Divergent Paths: New Perspectives on Earnings Differences Between Black and White Men Since 1940," *Quarterly Journal of Economics* 133, no.3 (2018): 469.
51 John Gramlich, "America's Incarceration Rate Falls to Lowest Level Since 1995," Pew Research Center, August 6, 2021, and "Black Imprisonment Rate in the U.S. Has Fallen by a Third Since 2006," Pew Research Center, May 6, 2020.
52 Heather McGhee, *The Sum of Us: What Racism Costs Everyone and How We Can Prosper Together* (New York: OneWorld, 2021), 237.
53 Neil Gross, "Still Guilty of Driving While Black," *New York Times*, op-ed, September 10, 2020, 423.
54 Chemerinsky, *Presumed Innocent*, 29–30, 18, see also 114.
55 Sheryll Cashin, *White Space, Black Hood: Opportunity Hoarding and Segregation in the Age of Inequality* (Boston, MA: Beacon Press, 2021), 172.
56 Mitch Mitchell, "Tasers Used Against Black People More Often," *Dallas Morning News*, September 15, 2020, B8.
57 Ian Haney López, *Dog Whistle Politics: How Coded Racial Appeals Have Reinvented Racism and Wrecked the Middle Class* (New York: Oxford University Press, 2014), 35–36.
58 Dawson and Francis, "Black Politics and the Neoliberal Racial Order," 45.
59 See Bonilla-Silva, *Racism Without Racists*, 37.

60 Adam Liptak, "Executions Less Likely When Victims are Black," *New York Times*, August 4, 2020, A16.
61 Scott Phillips and Justin F. Marceau, "Whom the State Kills," *Harvard Civil Rights and Civil Liberties Law Review* 55 (2020): 600–658. See also Litwack, *Trouble in Mind*, 252–253.
62 James M. Marquart, Sheldon Ekland-Olson, and Jonathan R. Sorensen, *The Rope, the Chair, and the Needle: Capital Punishment in Texas, 1923–1990* (Austin, TX: University of Texas Press, 1994), x–xi, see also 4.
63 Ngozi Ndulue, *Enduring Injustice*, Death Penalty Information Center, September 2020.
64 Jonah E. Bromwich, Ashley Southall, and Troy Closson, "Exonerations in Malcolm X's Death are Official but 'Bittersweet,'" *New York Times*, November 19, 2021, A1, A18.
65 "Nearly 1000 Fatally Shot by Police Each Year," *Washington Post* in *Dallas Morning News*, June 9, 2020, A9. See also David Nakamura, "In A Polarized America, Justice Department Police Reform Unfolds Slowly," *Washington Post*, May 24, 2022.
66 Tim Arango and Giulia Heyward, "Despite Protests, Number of Fatal Police Encounters is Unchanged," *New York Times*, December 25, 2021, A15.
67 Tim Arango and Shaila Dewan, "Study's Stark Findings: Over Half of Police Killings Go Uncounted," *New York Times*, October 1, 2021, A1, A19.
68 Adrienne A. Wallace, "Social Media for Social Good," in *Democracy in the Disinformation Age*, ed. Regina Luttrell, Lu Xiao, and Jon Glass (New York: Routledge, 2021), 15.
69 Tammy Webber, AP, "Impact on Policing Yet to be Seen," *Dallas Morning News*, June 27, 2021, A4.
70 Chemerinsky, *Presumed Guilty*, xi.
71 Chemerinsky, *Presumed Guilty*, 4, 8, 12, 199, 265–270.

10

SOCIAL JUSTICE AND THE MODERN AMERICAN PROMISE

The Way Forward

> "Can the white and colored people of this country be blended into a common nationality, and enjoy together, in the same Union, under the same flag, the inestimable blessings of life, liberty, and the pursuit of happiness, as neighborly citizens of a common country? I answer most unhesitatingly, I believe they can."
>
> Frederick Douglass, 1863, "The Present and Future of the Colored Race in America"

Americans remain ever hopeful, or at least they did until recently, that their founding principles and institutions will bring them once again to a brighter day.[1] Citizens of all social classes and partisan stripes praise the ideals of the Declaration of Independence and trust that, in the hands of good men and women, the nation's constitutional structures will produce peace, stability, and prosperity. But, as the Founders knew, even carefully constructed republican political institutions require well-intending citizens and public officials to make them work effectively. They knew and we know today that party politics and ideological polarization can threaten once robust ideals and institutions. That is why, as we noted early in this book, when asked what kind of government the Philadelphia Convention had given the new nation, Benjamin Franklin responded, "A republic, if you can keep it." Today, like those Philadelphians on September 17, 1787, we wonder whether we can keep our republic.[2] Still, we draw some confidence from the knowledge that our republic has already passed several severe tests.

DOI: 10.4324/9781003449188-10

The new republic passed its first test before it was even born. On December 23, 1783, George Washington, victorious commander-in-chief of the revolutionary army, won renown at home and abroad for voluntarily resigning his military commission in a congressional ceremony designed to highlight civil and political control of the military. Washington solidified the idea that political authority, even presidential authority, is limited and temporary public service when he declined in 1796 to stand for a third term as president, returning again to the pursuits of private life at Mount Vernon. Washington's respect, sometimes grudging, but unfailing, for the republican limits of the constitution and laws was a profound, but vulnerable, legacy.

A young Abraham Lincoln, just 28 on January 27, 1838, took republican vulnerability as his topic in one of his first published speeches, "The Perpetuation of Our Political Institutions."[3] With social and political tensions already building, but civil war not yet on the horizon, he asked what form danger to our institutions, laws, and norms might take and how those dangers might be averted. He quickly discounted foreign dangers to warn that "If destruction be our lot, we must ourselves be its authors. . . . As a nation of freemen, we must live through all time, or die by suicide." With ominous familiarity today, Lincoln pointed to a "disregard for law which pervades the country; the growing disposition to substitute the wild and furious passions, in lieu of the sober judgment of the Courts; and the worse than savage mobs, for the executive ministers of justice."

The broader threat of mobs and lawlessness was in Lincoln's day and remains in ours that over time good citizens, the patriotic and law-abiding, lose confidence in social and political norms and institutions intended to protect their persons, families, security, and property – thus opening the door to the usurper promising to quell the instability and restore order if not law. Lincoln warned that the political figure that "thirsts and burns for distinction. . . . coupled with ambition sufficient to push it to its utmost stretch. . . . would set boldly to the task of pulling down." Lincoln called these dominant figures – Alexander, Caesar, and Napoleon – "the family of the lion, or the tribe of the eagle."[4]

From our further vantage point and recent experience, it seems clear that the greatest threats to our republic have not come from our great military men, Washington, Grant, Eisenhower; they were too well trained in our constitution, laws, and doctrines of civil control of the military.[5] Greater threats have come from smaller men of lesser, but still dangerous, talents. Leaders of the mob, like Aaron Burr, Huey Long, Joseph McCarthy, and George Wallace, who sought to arouse, divide, and exclude. Our great good fortune, even most recently with Donald J. Trump, has been that these agitators were not of the "family of the lion, or the tribe of the eagle," but of the less consequential family and tribe of the jackal and the vulture. When the advocates of institutions and order finally did stand up, whether they were compelling figures like the now former Wyoming Congresswoman Liz Cheney, or unlikely figures like Brad Raffensperger, the Georgia Secretary of State, the interlopers have tended to doubt, quake, and deny. They have not, as Lincoln feared, pushed their efforts to the "utmost stretch." Nonetheless, the servants of chaos and disorder, like the Bannons, Giulianis, Eastmans, and Navarros, and the willing tools, like Ivanka and Jared, Mike Pompeo, Wilbur Ross, and Kayleigh McEnany, pose a danger. As we have seen, when social cohesion and support for our institutions, laws, and norms erode, even the jackals and vultures stand a chance of breaking through.[6]

So, in this concluding chapter we confront the fact that we as a people, generation after generation, have failed to live up to our founding promises of equality and opportunity. Not surprisingly, then, the deepest sources of the social tensions and dislocations that threaten our republic, that underlie the White supremacist march through Charlottesville, the many mass shootings, Donald Trump's rise to prominence, and the parading of the Confederate battle flag through the Capitol on January 6, 2021, are racial hierarchy, injustice, and exclusion. The vast racial disparities that we have highlighted throughout this book, in citizenship rights, education, income and wealth, housing, and access to health care and justice, have undercut our cherished national memories, promises, and claims. As Robert P. Jones warned in *White Too Long*, "[W]hite supremacy is . . . a source of life-threatening conflict in our communities. . . . Continued racial inequality, injustice, and unrest harm our ability to live together in a democratic society."[7] Of course Jones has not been alone in his assessment and warning; many others have made similar observations. But pointing to a problem, important as that is, does not resolve it.

Those who have offered thoughts on how to resolve our racial tensions have not always convinced. The physician Jonathan M. Metzl, in a book dealing with racial inequities in health care mentioned prominently in Chapter 7, argued "that the way forward requires a white America that strives to collaborate rather than dominate, with a mind-set of openness and inter-connectedness that we have all-too-frequently neglected."[8] Similarly, Michelle Alexander, whose important book on the criminal justice system we discussed in Chapter 9, declared that "A new social consensus must be forged about race. . . . to expand our sphere of moral concern so widely that none of us . . . can be viewed or treated as disposable."[9] Alas, one reads these lofty aspirations with doubt, even skepticism, given the polarization and deadlock we see in our Congress and on our streets. We are not reassured, but are perhaps steeled to the long battle, to know that some men and women in all previous stages of our national history have rejected racial inequalities and worked to overcome them. Sometimes they prevailed, often not, and never fully.

As a result, the broad history of race in America produces two quite different reactions, one of general futility and another of some specific hope. First, the idea that each generation of Americans must be summoned to herculean efforts to broaden the narrow range of social and political space allowed to Black people and other minorities is sad and dispiriting. So, at this late day, are declarations that progress still must await the arrival of an open-handed White public willing to share and collaborate with those still struggling for recognition, fairness, and a shot at the dream. Second, what gives some cautious hope is that a few pivotal historical battles – the American Revolution, the Civil War and Reconstruction, and the Civil Rights struggles of the mid-twentieth century – brought social, economic, and political progress, some lost to backlash each time, but some retained to be built upon the next time. It is important to remind ourselves of that progress and that each battle changed our society and left us in a better but still complex and unsatisfactory place.[10]

It also helps to recall that our great Founding documents have not been static but have been deepened and broadened through time. Library shelves groan under the weight of books describing how the meaning of the word "all" in the Declaration's phrase "all men are created equal" has developed and opened up since Jefferson, a slaveholder all his life, offered it as a standard toward which to strive. Similarly, the great Harvard historian Bernard Bailyn and many others have explained that the Constitution as originally written and understood "is simply a different instrument from the Constitution as we know it now. Hundreds of federal court decisions implementing clauses of the Constitution have given them new shape. The amendments that have been added to the Constitution – especially the Civil War amendments . . . – have fundamentally altered the scope and meaning of the Constitution."[11] One must also note that the critical legislation of the modern Civil Rights era – the Civil Rights Acts, the Voting Rights Act, and the Fair Housing Act – were built on this broadened constitutional foundation.

But backlash and retrenchment followed each reform period and gobbled up many of their gains. Van Gosse, whose fine history of the fight for Black citizenship and political rights in the revolutionary and early national periods we reviewed in Chapter 3, concluded that, "Black citizenship, full and absolute citizenship for *all* the people who do not fit into the category of 'White Men!,' has been and continues to be put on hold, and then actively suppressed and denied, despite our many Reconstructions."[12] White supremacy through slavery, Jim Crow segregation, and eyes-closed colorblindness, has always been and remains part of our national life and psyche. The excuses and denials that have swirled around White supremacy continue to limit and stall most social reform. The resulting political gridlock has robbed our national political institutions of the ability to address, let alone resolve, major issues like voting rights, immigration, or climate change.[13]

Despite widespread recognition of our growing political dysfunction, Harvard political scientists Steven Levitsky and Daniel Ziblatt created quite a stir with their 2019 book *How Democracies Die*. A nervous recognition that the nation's democratic institutions were in disarray and even some level of decay became a much deeper fear in the wake of the January 6, 2021 storming of the Capitol by a pro-Trump mob. With Lincoln nodding in the historical background, Levitsky and Ziblatt wrote that, "Democracies . . . survive longest, in countries where written constitutions are reinforced by their own unwritten rules of the game. These rules and norms serve as soft guardrails of democracy, preventing day-to-day political competition from devolving into a no-holds-barred conflict." The two norms that they pointed to as most critical were "mutual toleration and institutional forbearance."[14] Few honest observers failed to see Donald Trump's efforts to overturn his 2020 presidential election defeat as a failure of mutual toleration and institutional forbearance and, consequently, of the American democracy.

And so, our American promise that "all" people will have an equal chance to strive and succeed remains an unmet charge on our national responsibility. The fact that this commitment has gone unfulfilled for so long raises a dangerously fundamental question: do we or do we not, as a people, believe in our founding values of freedom, equality, and opportunity? Historically, the honest answer has been no, not for everyone; but what is our answer today and for the future? We stand where every previous generation of Americans have stood – asking whether we still believe – ever believed – our founding ideals.[15] In answering, it is daunting but also liberating to realize that we cannot, should not, look to the Founders for answers; we must interrogate ourselves about our character, our values, and how we believe we ought to live.[16] The Founders have done their work; we should let them rest. Now it is our turn.

Promises and Broken Dreams

Our goal must be to throw open the traditional American dream of equality and opportunity to all of our citizens. The American dream expects, even demands, both that individuals prepare themselves through education and training for productive work and that society and the economy be designed as open and receptive to the potential and effort of everyone. But when we think of the dream in light of our racial history, both in regard to individual preparation and effort and social openness, we find that: "Individual-level factors are simply not the explanation for the differences in the economic fortunes of Black and white people. . . . Instead," says Vanessa Williamson of the Brookings Institution, racial inequality "should be recognized as the consequence of discrimination, public and private, through American history and continuing to this day."[17]

To chart a new course, we must recognize that the principal story we have told ourselves about America, that we are a society in which good preparation and hard work can lift anyone to success and security, has never been true for everyone. Many Americans have grown up under circumstances that left them unprepared and so far out of the competition to come that success, however defined, was not plausible. It is particularly critical today that White Americans recognize that society and its benefits have never been equally open to all and that Black people and other minorities have never enjoyed equality with, much less advantages over, White people in schooling, jobs, income, housing, health care, and other opportunities and benefits. Painful as it is for most White Americans to admit, racial prejudice and racial domination by White people of Black people and other minorities have been deeply embedded in our national history and psychology and they remain there, somewhat degraded but still virulent.

Social, economic, and political inequalities, built up literally over centuries, are extraordinarily complex and hard to unravel. This intertwined complexity has been well understood by scholars and policy analysts. Anthony P. Carnevale and his colleagues at the Georgetown University Center on Education and the Workforce concluded that, "The persistent racial divide . . . reflects a variety of factors, including differential access to high-quality, well-resourced K-12 schools and selective colleges and universities; employment discrimination; segregated social and professional networks; and other forms of systemic privilege and discrimination based on race and ethnicity."[18] Kevin Long, an economics professor at Brown University, explained that the several dimensions of racial inequality are not independent, they are interdependent and intertwined because: "Disparities build on each other, income disparities lead to neighborhood disparities, which produce education disparities, which produce labor market disparities."[19]

While the compounded social consequences of racial inequity are well understood, more puzzling has been what this complexity means for policy intervention. Harvard government professor Robert Putnam and the Brookings Institution's Shaylyn Romney Garrett, in discussing their important book, *Upswing*, asked and answered a critical question about periods of profound change – the Revolution, the Civil War, and, to a lesser extent, the modern civil rights movement – and their limits: "Why, then, when the dam of legal exclusion finally broke, didn't those trends accelerate toward full equality?" Why indeed! Their answer was "white backlash," that "when push came to shove, many white Americans were reluctant to live up to these principles."[20]

Willful White denial of racism and its consequences continues, as it has from the nation's earliest days, to limit, crimp, and distort the American dream of equality, opportunity, competition, and the right to enjoy the benefits of honest effort. Worse still, it seems clear that denying access to the dream to Black people and other minorities has compromised it for everyone. The American working and middle classes, irrespective of race, have long felt opportunity, let alone security, slipping beyond their grasp. The sociologist Mark Robert Rank and his colleagues argued that the promise of American life was compromised by a debilitating paradox; "As long as we believe that everyone has a fair shot . . ., then if you do not succeed, it must be your fault. . . . It provides a justification for the status quo . . . [and] a rationale for inaction among those who are privileged enough to have achieved the American Dream, and whose affluence may seem threatened if policies were enacted to truly make the Dream accessible to all."[21] So long as there are identifiable groups subject to discrimination, and there always have been in our society, there is the ever-present likelihood that others will be pushed toward and perhaps into that disadvantaged group. Moreover, our frayed social bonds have made it ever harder to react collectively, politically, to the pain and dismay of others, especially those not like ourselves in terms of race, class, or lifestyle.

Prominent think tanks on the left and the right have been warning of increasing economic inequality and social stratification for decades. On the think tank left, Amy Traub and Heather McGhee of Demos observed that, "Over recent decades, many political leaders have failed to reckon with a basic fact of the new economic era – for millions of Americans, no amount of individual effort . . . can guarantee a secure middle-class life. The American social contract . . . is fundamentally broken."[22] Upping the ante from millions to tens of millions, Donald Barlett and James Steele announced "The dismal fact . . . that for tens of millions of middle-class Americans, as well as for the working poor who hope to achieve that status, the American dream is over."[23] The same concern has been voiced on the right. Tim Carney, commentary editor at the *Washington Examiner*, a visiting fellow at the American Enterprise Institute, speaking at the Heritage Foundation – all respected conservative institutions – declared that "The suffering of America's working class is real. Immobility, inequality, a retreat from marriage, and deaths of despair are the symptoms. In short, for much of the country, the American Dream is dead."[24] Critically, none of these critiques even mentioned race. Instead, they all say, whether looking at the problem from the left or the right, that the bottom half of our society, in all its multicolored diversity, is struggling and in danger of losing hope.

Respected and highly accomplished scholars have reached remarkably similar conclusions regarding the health and future prospects of the American promise and of those who depend upon it. The well-known sociologist Arne Kalleberg and the even better known economist Joseph Stiglitz are representative. Kalleberg has asserted that "people are now, more than ever, 'on their own.'. . . This situation is analogous to the ideology of social Darwinism, . . . which applied Darwin's idea of survival of the fittest to the human economic and social realm."[25] Stiglitz, Chair of the Council of Economic Advisers under Bill Clinton and former President of the World Bank, concluded that "There's no use pretending. In spite of the enduring belief that Americans enjoy greater social mobility than their European counterparts, America is no longer the land of opportunity . . . today's reality is that for a large segment of the population that dream has now vanished."[26] How might the dream be restored and what Lincoln called "the paths of laudable pursuit" be reopened? How can we assure that each of our citizens arrives at adulthood with the tools to compete and succeed in American life and that our society provides opportunities worth competing for?[27]

What Is To Be Done?

This famous phrase, "What is to be done?", is particularly apt to the broad question of how America might effectively address its racial inequalities and animosities. As we have seen above, many prominent analysts say, go big or go home; confront structural racism in its full breadth and range or accept the grinding impact of racial tensions on the nation's prospects and promise. Others point to polarization and gridlock and ask how revolution, or even reform, is possible. They call for ameliorative reforms if they call for reforms at all. First, we will look at a series of sectoral policy reforms to improve equity in political participation, education, income, health, housing, and criminal justice. We will argue that some reforms, perhaps many, are best seen through a class lens rather than, or at least in addition to, a race lens. These sectoral policy reforms can and should be pursued incrementally, but, if the political door to broader reforms should swing open, together they might constitute a *New* New Deal or a New Great Society. Second, we must look through the race lens at the revolution option – usually called reparations – designed to compensate Black America, even if only partially, for the effects of slavery, Jim Crow, and racial discrimination more generally.

The political scientists Desmond King and Rogers Smith have given sage counsel concerning how to think about and pursue ameliorative social reform in contemporary American politics. They advised that "American leaders all along the nation's ideological spectrum ought to focus attention on questions about the public *policies* that can offer hope of improving racially unequal material conditions . . . in education, income and wealth, health, housing, crime and incarceration rates, political representation, and more, in ways that are both materially effective and politically sustainable."[28] Ian Haney López of the Berkeley School of Law has offered equally shrewd but somewhat different counsel. He argued that support for progressive policies on education and jobs, access to health care and good housing, as well as justice reform benefit when it is mentioned that all races, "white, Black, and brown" will benefit. Race-based policies set White teeth on edge, so where possible class-based rather than race-based policy designs might be more successful. Balancing politics and policies highlighting racial equity and broad transracial benefits will be even more difficult now that the Supreme Court has struck down race-based affirmative action in college admissions and registered doubt about it in other settings.[29] Whether our political system is capable of setting aside partisan and ideological divisions to focus on problem-solving remains very much an open question. Nevertheless, scholars, experts, and policymakers must proceed with the planting and fertilizing even though the harvest may seem far off.

We begin with a discussion of democracy, the right to be heard, to join with others in the public square, to vote and to have that vote counted. Throughout American history, socially and legally acknowledged access to the public square and to the ballot have been among the most meaningful markers of full citizenship. As such, it has always been challenged as it relates to marginalized groups; but limits on suffrage pose broader threats to democracy itself. In a paper delivered before the American Academy of Political and Social Science in 1928, W.E.B. Du Bois warned that, "On account of the 'Negro problem' we are making democratic government increasingly impossible in the United States."[30] Almost a century on we still find that laws and policies aimed at excluding Black people have tended to limit other minorities, young people, and the poor generally.

These concerns reverberate powerfully today. Especially over the last decade, managing the electorate and the conduct of elections for partisan advantage has been nearly continuous. But since Donald Trump's loss in the 2020 presidential election, Republican state officials have launched a concerted push to tighten voter rules and control election results.[31] Despite a complete lack of evidence of widespread election fraud, scores of bills have been introduced in state legislatures and dozens have passed, most notably in Georgia and Texas, to limit early voting, voting by mail, drive through voting, ballot drop boxes, and to empower partisan poll watchers and election officials.[32] Limits on early voting, especially pews to the polls early voting on Sundays, and empowered partisan election officials often target minority and young voters. Alternatively, Democrats have charted the better course; seeking to highlight the importance of voting, increase access to voting, and ease the process of voting.

Seventy percent of voters in 2020 cast ballots early or by mail, so those popular voting options should be expanded. Voters should be allowed to "cure" their ballots, or correct flaws and mistakes on their ballots, so that those ballots can be counted. More states should follow those who have eased laws severely limiting or prohibiting voting by former felons. Broad suffrage is critical to a healthy democracy, so its supporters should continue to push on all these fronts. One might wish that voting rights could be secured at the national level, but partisan divisions and claims that election laws and voting rules are matters of state responsibility have blocked national voter protection legislation. Finally, the federal courts' *laissez-faire* approach to gerrymandering should be set aside in favor of a more active defense of one-man-one-vote to assure that Black urban votes and White rural votes are equally weighed.[33]

An informed citizenry has long been seen as the foundation of democratic politics. Education at least through some degree of literacy was the basis for full citizenship in the North from first settlement, though it did not permeate the South until after the Civil War. Denial of access to education, or access only to a degraded and underfunded education, marked Black people and other minorities as legally and functionally excluded from the ranks of citizens. Though full exclusion receded after the Civil War, the impact of unequal funding and quality continues to have widespread impacts. Therefore, most discussions of policy reforms intended to improve racial material outcomes begin with education.

A good educational foundation improves future prospects for income, wealth-building, housing, health, and much more. Systematically higher funding for White schools than for Black and minority schools has long been a load-bearing wall in the structure of institutional racism. Most public schools are funded through local property taxes, so wealthy neighborhoods with expensive homes generate more revenue for schools than do poorer neighborhoods with less expensive homes. State and federal funds help to make up some of the funding gap, but research shows a remaining $23 billion gap between White versus non-White school districts.[34] Few reforms promise a more important impact than addressing the funding gap between White and minority school districts.

What would school administrators and teachers do, particularly in poorer schools, if they had more resources? Education experts favor universal, full-day pre-school for three- and four-year-olds to insure that all children reach primary school ready to learn. Limited class sizes and well-trained teachers, classroom aides, resource officers, and librarians all make for effective learning environments. Outside the classroom, culturally sophisticated support and guidance, particularly for at-risk students, will be necessary. No early failure, unaddressed, should be allowed to define a child.

Improved public education would give all students more equal access to higher education and to improved labor skills, job prospects, and economic stability. Now that the Supreme Court has struck down affirmative action at the nation's elite colleges and universities, it is all the more important that governments and philanthropies focus aid and support on mid-level public universities, HBCUs, and community colleges, where most minority students actually attend. Increasing federal Pell Grants so they cover tuition, fees, and some living expenses, as they did when they were first introduced half a century ago, would help vulnerable poor and minority students navigate the financial challenges of college. Federal policy should encourage counseling to keep first time students on track and reward colleges and universities for admitting and graduating poor and minority students. And federal policy should regulate both for-profit colleges and public and private universities so that increased federal spending aids students and is not simply sopped-up by rising tuition and fees.

Limited education chilled the economic prospects of minorities and women through most of American history. Black Americans in slavery and in freedom well into the twentieth century made half or less or what White Americans made. As late as 1962, Black men made just 49.2 percent of what White men made and in 2021 Black men made just 65.9 percent and Hispanic men just 70.6 percent of what White men made. These are remarkably modest economic gains over more than six decades and they declare ongoing limits to minority options and opportunities for housing, health care, the accumulation of retirement assets, and much more.

In a market-based economy such as ours, having less income than most is a daily trial. We know that education often opens the path to better jobs and higher income, but we should not be mesmerized by that fact. Most young Americans still enter the workforce without a college degree. The Harvard social and legal theorist Michael Sandel has made the important point that personal, social, and economic prospects all are enhanced by finding the right socially-useful, productive work. Sandel says correctly that we need to "rethink the way we value different kinds of work. . . .

Learning to become a plumber or electrician or dental hygienist should be respected as a valuable contribution to the common good."[35]

Honoring work also means respecting and assisting those on the margins. Like Pell Grants, the federal minimum wage has been allowed to languish since the 1980s, meaning that many low-skill and entry level workers, disproportionately female and minority, work full-time and still cannot support themselves. A living minimum wage, automatically adjusted for inflation, would enhance the dignity of this work and these workers. Companies might also be given state and federal financial incentives to locate in low income areas, in order to bring jobs closer to those that need them most. Taxing the inheritance of the wealthy, say 5 million or greater, would provide a revenue stream to support social programs like those outlined above to buoy up the working poor, working class, and lower middle class of all races. As always, helping those who are struggling helps minorities disproportionately. As late as 2020, more than half of Black and Hispanic workers made less than $15 an hour.[36]

Federal and state law and policy has favored employers over employees since the 1950s and should be rebalanced. Wage transparency in the workplace is an important way to give employees the information needed to seek redress if they are being treated unfairly. Most such issues would be resolved within the company, but there should be an office within Human Resources to which people can take questions and complaints and, outside the company, state offices and the federal Equal Employment Opportunity Commission (EEOC) should be funded and empowered. Limiting, if not banning, mandatory arbitration and nondisclosure requirements would enhance the power of workers in relation to management. All workers should have the right to join a union.

It should also be noted that Black businesses often operate at a disadvantage. Most policymakers simply do not realize that, "Of all Black-owned businesses, only 5% have employees." Those few Black-owned businesses that do have employees have less than half as many on average than White-owned businesses.[37] Black-owned businesses are especially vulnerable, as we saw in the COVID-19 pandemic, and would benefit by easier access to credit, hiring subsidies, and clear pathways to compete for government sales and contracts. Finally, since most Black employees work for White-owned companies, encouraging a more diverse workforce, from entry-level employees to team leaders, and more diverse management teams and corporate boards are critical.

The wealth gap between White and Black and other minority families has also drawn a great deal of attention and we will have more to say about it presently. For now, the Duke University economist William Darity, Jr. has noted that "Twenty-five percent of white households have a net worth in excess of $1 million, in contrast to a mere 4 percent of Black households."[38] Many suggestions have been made for ameliorating the racial wealth gap and for enhancing wealth equity more generally. At the front-end of life baby bonds and child savings accounts produce resources for later key goals. Baby bonds, usually thought of as in the small thousands of dollars, awarded to every child at birth are intended to grow with the child and then to be used for some life-enhancing purpose like education, job training, or a down payment on a home.[39] In mid-life, automatic enrollment in employer-based retirement programs or encouragement to start an Individual Retirement Account (IRA), may provide the "nudge" many need to invest in low-cost mutual funds, as well as stocks and bonds. Saving is admirable, but it is investing that moves many into the middle class and above. At the back-end of life, social security is already a major source of income for retirees and even those still working past seventy. Low-income workers currently receive a larger share of their working income from social security than do high-income workers, though high-income workers receive a bigger monthly check. Reforms could make the social security system even more progressive to the benefit of low-income workers of all races.

Racial discrimination and social exclusion in our history showed themselves most dangerously in denial of health care and medical treatment. After slavery, White Americans had little interest in the quality of Black life. The death of W.E.B. Du Bois's young son and the Tuskegee experiments suggest the willfully callous view taken by White society toward Black health. Today, minorities lack health insurance and, hence, access to timely treatment more frequently than White people do. The veterans' health and hospital system, Medicare and Medicaid, Obamacare, and private, usually employer-sponsored, health insurance cover more than 90 percent of Americans. Democrats have promoted universal health care, advocating expanded access to Medicare as the surest path to covering the last 10 percent. As always, that last 10 percent is heavily minority.

Programs insuring access to health care, including mental health care, will allow people to engage steadily and consistently in the social and economic life of their community with the best chance of success and security. Nonetheless, the relationship between minorities and health care has long been fraught and involves issues both of access and trust. Issues of access undoubtedly will require continued expansion of the federal role. Expanding neighborhood clinics would aid the poor, and controlling, hopefully lowering, prescription drug prices would help the elderly. Expanding paid family and medical leave would help all Americans. Long-standing issues of trust can be addressed over time by monitoring racial differentials in clinical trials, diagnostic and treatment differentials by race, diversity in staff and administration, and cultural awareness.

Good housing provides a haven for individuals and families while poor housing poses real dangers to them. The Biden administration's economic stimulus and infrastructure programs included tens of billions of dollars to replace lead pipes in the nation's drinking water systems, which especially threaten children's health, and to treat superfund waste sites, disproportionately located in minority neighborhoods. The Biden administration also touted a universal housing voucher program to supplement or replace the existing Section 8 Housing Choice Voucher Program. These vouchers are intended to help families move from poor housing to better housing in better neighborhoods.[40] Unfortunately, some neighborhoods, even many, preclude subsidized housing out of a purported fear of inadequate upkeep and crime. Limiting exclusionary zoning and expanding assistance for first-time home buyers are both critical. Moreover, all levels of government should directly address the nation's housing shortage by encouraging affordable homes and apartments. Responsible promotion of homeownership is important because home equity is the largest source of middle-class wealth.[41]

Laws, police, courts, and prisons have borne down hard on Black people, other minorities, and the poor throughout American history. The vast criminal justice system will be slow to change, but change it must. First and foremost, while the prison population has come down a bit in recent years, a striking observation made a decade ago by Michelle Alexander still stuns: "If our nation were to return to the rates of incarceration we had in the 1970s, we would have to release 4 out of 5 people behind bars."[42] To continue unwinding modern mass incarceration, reforms should make fewer crimes subject to jail as punishment, make the sentences for jailable offenses shorter, and make petty theft and drug possession for personal use not subject to imprisonment. Similarly, abolishing cash bail would insure that the poor are not made to languish in jail or encouraged to plead guilty to lesser, though still often serious, charges to conclude the process, do their time, and get out. The resulting criminal record can nonetheless have crippling implications for voting, employment, and access to social services. Programs, staff, and professional expertise supporting probation, parole, and remediation should be expanded. It also seems critical to supplement police with social and psychological expertise for interactions with the homeless and people experiencing mental and psychological issues – especially when those issues result in disruptive but non-criminal behavior. Finally, recent events, including the George Floyd murder and Derek Chauvin conviction, make obvious the need for better tracking of police violence and misconduct, as well as legal and constitutional reviews of police liability. While many of the reforms outlined above would be beneficial if adopted incrementally, life-changing for some people, even if adopted as a package they would not produce equality for most Black people anytime soon.

Roll Up the Cannon: Wealth Taxes and Reparations

When the normal politics of partisanship and polarization stymie reform, revolution may seem the only path forward, but American history suggests that such paths open only rarely. Still, they do open on occasion. When considering racial inequality, especially wealth inequality, revolution has two faces: a revenue face and a spending face. On the revenue side, Vanessa Williamson of Brookings has written that "Any plan to eliminate the total racial wealth gap requires, . . . a program of heavy and highly progressive taxation aimed at the very wealthiest Americans." She also suggests the possibility of wealth and inheritance taxes. Only with these funds in hand can a willing administration consider "a transformative national investment in Black households and communities."[43] Daniel Markovits of the Yale Law School has also been clear that "Curing economic inequality requires redistribution, and redistribution means taxes. . . . Income taxes can help, but the best way to reduce inequality and honor shared citizenship is to tax wealth." While Markovits was not focused strictly on racial wealth inequality, the numbers he derived apply to that conversation as well. He noted that the year-long bull market between March 2020 and March 2021, "added $4.8 trillion of wealth to the richest 1% of American households" and over $7 trillion if one includes the appreciation of privately held companies and real estate.[44] Increased income taxes, wealth taxes, and inheritance taxes would pull down on wealth accumulation at the top and produce significant funds year-to-year to invest at the bottom of the income and wealth scales.

The best known advocates of a full-blown program of racial reparations are William A. Darity, Jr. and A. Kirsten Mullen, authors of *From Here to Equality: Reparations for Black Americans in the Twenty-First Century* (2020). The concept in play here is "loss and damages." The argument is that Black Americans through slavery, Jim Crow segregation, and ongoing discrimination suffered economic loss and damages that justice requires to be redressed through reparations. Darity and Mullen define reparations as "a program of acknowledgement, redress, and closure for a grievous injustice. . . . [R]estitution for African Americans would eliminate racial disparities in wealth, income, education, health, sentencing and incarceration, political participation, and subsequent opportunities to engage in American political and social life."[45] Darity and Mullen reviewed several "present-value calculations of unpaid wages, land value [for the promised 40-acres and a mule] not awarded . . . at compound interest . . . rates – 4, 5, 6 percent." Those calculations produced reparation cost totals in the $5 to $15 trillion range, and Darity's and Mullen's own calculations, based on the Fed's 2016 "Survey of Consumer Finances" showing differences between White and Black household wealth, came in at $7.95 trillion. In another place, an estimate of $11.2 trillion was reached.[46] Those are big numbers and many, most White Americans to be sure, reject them out of hand. Nevertheless, discussions are ongoing in a number of settings.

Initial steps, very tentative, have been taken to consider reparations in Congress. Former Michigan congressman John Conyers began introducing a bill to study reparations in 1989. When Conyers resigned from Congress in 2017, Texas congresswoman Sheila Jackson Lee and others continued to push the idea of a reparations commission. In April 2021, the House Judiciary Committee approved House Resolution 40 (HR 40) which would establish a commission "to study and consider a national apology and proposal for reparations for the institution of slavery, its subsequent de jure and de facto racial and economic discrimination against African-Americans, and the impact of these forces on living African-Americans, to make recommendations to the Congress on appropriate remedies, and for other purposes."[47] When HR 40 was adopted by the Judiciary Committee, Congresswoman Jackson Lee opined on behalf of the measure's sponsors that, "We think it will be cleansing for this nation and will be a step moving America forward to see us debate this issue on the floor of the House."[48] Senator Mitch McConnell of Kentucky, Republican Leader in the Senate, already feeling fairly cleansed, countered that Barack Obama's election as president largely had expunged the "sin of slavery" and besides, "it'd be pretty hard to figure out who to compensate."[49]

In addition to simple cash payments, a menu of reparations initiatives might include "programs to fund college education, forgive student loans, and promote homeownership and entrepreneurship in the Black community . . . [as well as] a system of baby bonds."[50] While an apology for slavery and Jim Crow seems possible, even likely, at least from a Democrat Congress and administration, and other programs, perhaps targeted at the poor rather than explicitly as reparations for slavery, also seem possible, a large cash reparations program seems unlikely and even its hardiest proponents know it. Darity and Mullen argue that for monetary reparations to be adopted, "New national leadership must be committed fully to black reparations . . . [and] not only would white animosity toward blacks need to decrease . . ., but such animosity actually would need to be converted into support. Only after this work has been done can reparations be achieved."[51] Assuming that this very high standard effectively takes reparations off the table, what paths remain open to those who see racial tensions as compromising our national health and vitality?

History tells us at least three things about the prospects for the kind of dramatic social change that would redress long-standing racial hierarchy in America. First, dramatic social reforms require the backdrop of great and tumultuous events – revolution, Civil War, depression, and roiling social turmoil – that challenge and loosen existing structures. Second, great and tumultuous events occur unpredictably; few realized when the colonists dumped tea in Boston Harbor that independence was nigh; or when the *Dred Scott* decision was handed down that slavery would soon be abolished; or when John F. Kennedy was assassinated that strong civil rights and voting rights bills would soon be signed into law. But tumult opens new possibilities. And third, work has to proceed in the dark because it is never clear when the dawn will come.

Many believed that the broad popular response, not just domestically but globally, to the killing of George Floyd in 2020 might usher in a racial reckoning, perhaps not on the scale of the Civil War, but maybe on the scale of the Great Society reforms of the 1960s. Thousands of interracial demonstrations occurred across the nation, opinion polls suggested White recognition of racial injustice, and politicians promised action. Several bills moved through Congress that supported poor families, clean water, and historically black colleges and universities, but a major police reform bill ultimately foundered for lack of Republican support. Attention strayed, emotion drained away, and the chance for deep and fundamental change was lost.

Almost simultaneously, pandemic relief policies and programs not explicitly directed at race and income inequality had a substantial impact on the bottom half of the income scale, where most Black people and other minorities find themselves. Trillions of dollars in COVID relief money, expanded unemployment compensation payments, enhanced child tax credits, and a strong post-pandemic job market allowed lower income Americans to accumulate a bigger share of the nation's wealth than they had enjoyed in decades. Along with a declining stock market, predominantly affecting the upper levels of the income scale, inequality in the U.S. declined significantly.[52] While unexpected gains in income and wealth equity are welcome, it is still sobering to think that actual plans to address inequities so often fall victim to polarization and gridlock.

Two approaches to racial justice beyond the occasional policy initiative are available, though one has already been delimited. One path would be a rejuvenation and broadening of affirmative action, a policy approach now limited to government contract awards and employment, that gives advantages today to members of groups, including minorities and women, systematically and often legally disadvantaged in the past. The Supreme Court has checked and limited important elements of affirmative action, most recently in striking it down in college admissions, so it will take a more liberal court to breathe new life into it, but that is at least possible as affirmative action itself has not, or at least not yet, been declared unconstitutional.

Second, an approach to policymaking that benefits the poor, rather than minorities more explicitly, would nonetheless benefit many minorities because minorities are disproportionately low income. Various programs, free school lunches, child tax credits, housing vouchers, and Medicaid to name just a few, already serve the poor and sometimes the not so poor of all races. A broad-based poverty alleviation approach might clash with the important role of individualism in our society, but it would not run head-on into the brick wall of White supremacy. Perhaps a class-based strategy until a rejuvenation of affirmative action is possible might be the best short- and medium-term approach to redressing racial differences and injustices in our society. The culture is set up to oppose even that, so progress will be difficult and almost certainly incremental.

Unfortunately, our polarized political system seems incapable of systematic, fact-based inquiry and sustained, consistent problem-solving. So, we can only assume that racial tensions will continue to build, social pressures to increase, and an explosion of some level of destruction will occur – perhaps not revolution or civil war, as in our distant past, but likely a long decade or two of turmoil, as between *Brown v. Board* in 1954 and Watergate and Richard Nixon's resignation in 1973. Years of turmoil, some significant racial progress, followed by White backlash, and a sullen return to some modified regime of White advantage if not supremacy is a dispiriting prospect. Failing to act, fighting off social change, has been our default option; still, it must be remembered that social disruption is costly and is best addressed before the bills come due. The fact that a new Civil Rights Revolution seems remote today must not dissuade from the routine tillage and cultivation that always precedes the harvest.

Notes

1 Yascha Mounk, *The Great Experiment: Why Diverse Democracies Fall Apart and How They Can Endure* (New York: Penguin Press, 2022), 15.
2 David W. Blight, "The Irrepressible Conflict: Was the Civil War Inevitable? As America Struggles Through Another Era of Deep Division, the Old Question Takes on New Urgency," *New York Times Magazine*, December 25, 2022, 28–33, 44–45.
3 George Packer, *Last Best Hope: America in Crisis and Renewal* (New York: Farrar, Straus, and Giroux, 2021), 5.

4 Roy P. Basler, ed., *The Collected Works of Abraham Lincoln*, 9 vols. (New Brunswick, NJ: Rutgers University Press, 1953), 1:109, 114.
5 Susan B. Glasser and Peter Baker, "Inside the War Between Trump and His Generals," *The New Yorker*, August 8, 2022, https://www.newyorker.com/magazine/2022/08/15/inside-the-war-between-trump-and-his-generals.
6 Gary Gerstle, *The Rise and Fall of the Neoliberal Order: America and the World in the Free Market Era* (New York: Oxford University Press, 2022), 289. See also Anne Applebaum, *Twilight of Democracy: The Seductive Lure of Authoritarianism* (New York: Doubleday, 2020); Steven Levitsky and Daniel Ziblatt, "Opinion: Trump Is Nothing Without Accomplices," *New York Times*, September 10, 2023, SR10; Michael Wayne Santos, *Rediscovering a Nation: Will the Real America Please Stand Up* (Lanham, MD: Rowman and Littlefield, 2022), 57–58, 61–65.
7 Robert P. Jones, *White Too Long: The Legacy of White Supremacy in American Christianity* (New York: Simon & Schuster, 2020), 232.
8 Jonathan M. Metzl, *Dying of Whiteness: How the Politics of Racial Resentment is Killing America's Heartland* (New York: Basic Books, 2020), 19.
9 Michelle Alexander, *The New Jim Crow: Mass Incarceration in the Age of Colorblindness* (New York: The New Press, 2010, 10th anniversary ed.; 2020), 19, xlii.
10 Thomas Piketty, *A Brief History of Equality* (Cambridge, MA: Harvard University Press, 2022), 226–227.
11 Bernard Bailyn, *To Begin the World Anew: The Genius and Ambiguities of the American Revolution* (New York: Vintage Books, 2004), 105. See also Bailyn's discussion of Supreme Court Justice Thurgood Marshall's bicentennial speech celebrating the 200th anniversary of the Constitution, *To Begin the World Anew*, 149.
12 Van Gosse, *The First Reconstruction: Black Politics in America from the Revolution to the Civil War* (Chapel Hill, NC: University of North Carolina Press, 2021), 550. See also Packer, *Last Best Hope*, 120.
13 David F. Damore, Robert E. Lang, and Karen A. Danielsen, *Blue Metros, Red States: The Shifting Urban-Rural Divide in America's Swing States* (Washington, D.C.: Brookings Institution Press, 2020), 50.
14 Steven Levitsky and Daniel Ziblatt, *How Democracies Die* (New York: Crown Books, 2019), 101–102, see also 150.
15 Woodrow Wilson, "The Ideals of America," *Atlantic Monthly*, December 1902, 726.
16 Bailyn, *To Begin the World Anew*, 149. See also Kermit Roosevelt III, *The Nation That Never Was: Reconstructing America's Story* (Chicago, IL: University of Chicago Press, 2022), 132.
17 Vanessa Williamson, "Closing the Racial Wealth Gap Requires Heavy, Progressive Taxation of Wealth," Brookings Institution, December 9, 2020, 4.
18 Anthony P. Carnevale, et al., "The Unequal Race for Good Jobs," Georgetown University Center on Education and the Workforce, 2019, 2. See also Douglas S. Massey and Nancy A. Denton, *American Apartheid: Segregation and the Making of the Underclass* (Cambridge, MA: Harvard University Press, 1993), 150.
19 Eduardo Porter, "Black People Narrowed Skills Gap, But Pay Gap Persists. Is It Racism?," *New York Times*, June 28, 2021, B1, B2.
20 Shaylyn Romney Garrett and Robert D. Putnam, "Why Did Racial Progress Stall in America," *New York Times*, December 6, 2020, SR10.

21 Mark Robert Rank, Thomas A. Hirschl, and Kirk A. Foster, *Chasing the American Dream: Understanding What Shapes Our Fortunes* (New York: Oxford University Press, 2016), 160–161. See also Mounk, *The Great Experiment*, 184.
22 Amy Traub and Heather C. McGhee, "State of the American Dream," Demos, June 6, 2013, 2.
23 Donald L. Barlett and James B. Steele, *The Betrayal of the American Dream* (New York: Public Affairs, 2013), xx.
24 Tim Carney, "The American Dream is Dying Where Civil Society is Eroding," Heritage Foundation, March 12, 2019.
25 Arne L. Kalleberg, *Good Jobs, Bad Jobs: The Rise of Polarized and Precarious Employment Systems in the United States, 1970s to 2000s* (New York: Russell Sage Foundation, 2013), 78.
26 Joseph E. Stiglitz, *The Price of Inequality: How Today's Divided Society Endangers Our Future* (New York: W.W. Norton, 2013), 265, 274. See also Joseph P. Ferrie, "History Lessons: The End of American Exceptionalism: Mobility in the United States Since 1850," *Journal of Economic Perspectives* 19, no. 3 (Summer 2005): 199–215; Timothy Noah, *The Great Divergence: America's Growing Inequality Crisis and What We Can Do About It* (New York: Bloomsbury Press, 2013), 37.
27 Martin Wolf, *The Crisis of Democratic Capitalism* (New York: Penguin Press, 2023), 35, 195, 218–219, 323.
28 Desmond S. King and Rogers M. Smith, *Still a House Divided: Race and Politics in Obama's America* (Princeton, NJ: Princeton University Press, 2011), 284–285, 12.
29 Ian Haney López, *Merge Left: Fusing Race and Class, Winning Elections, and Saving America* (New York: The New Press, 2019), 186. See also Theodore R. Johnson, *When the Stars Begin to Fall: Overcoming Racism and Renewing the Promise of America* (New York: Grove Press, 2021), 15; Thomas Bryne Edsall, *The Point of No Return: American Democracy at the Crossroads* (Princeton, NJ: Princeton University Press, 2023), 162; Piketty, *A Brief History of Equality*, 181, 194, 263–266.
30 W.E. Burghardt Du Bois, "Race Relations in the United States," *The Annals of the American Academy of Political and Social Science* 140 (November 1928): 7. See also Angela Y. Davis, *Abolition Democracy: Beyond Empire, Prison, and Torture* (New York: Seven Stories Press, 2005), 73; W.E.B. Du Bois, *Black Reconstruction: An Essay Toward a History of the Part Which Black Folk Played in the Attempt to Reconstruct Democracy in America* (New York: Harcourt, Brace and Company, 1935), 698–708.
31 Carroll Doherty, Jocelyn Kiley, and Calvin Jordan, "Republicans and Democrats Move Further Apart in Views of Voting Access," Pew Research Center, April 22, 2021.
32 Barton Gellman, "Trump's Next Coup Has Already Begun," *The Atlantic*, December 6, 2021.
33 Packer, *Last Best Hope*, 214.
34 Sheryll Cashin, *White Space, Black Hood: Opportunity Hoarding and Segregation in the Age of Inequality* (Boston, MA: Beacon Press, 2021), 213.
35 Michael J. Sandel, *The Tyranny of Merit: What's Become of the Common Good?* (New York: Farrar, Straus, and Giroux, 2020), 191. See also Wolf, *The Crisis of Democratic Capitalism*, 267.
36 Richard Haass, *The Bill of Obligations: The Ten Habits of Good Citizens* (New York: Penguin Press, 2023), 35.

37 Tynesia Boyea-Robinson, "Opinion: Jump Start Black-Owned Businesses," *Dallas Morning News*, March 24, 2021, 16A.
38 William Darity, Jr., "The True Cost of Closing the Racial Wealth Gap," *New York Times*, May 2, 2021, Wk3.
39 Ben Steverman, "The Intellectual Father of Baby Bonds," *BusinessWeek*, March 21, 2022, 44–51. See also Andrew Brown, "CT Political Leaders Cheer Start of State Baby Bonds Program," *Connecticut Mirror*, June 28, 2023.
40 Raj Chetty, Matthew O. Jackson, Theresa Kuchler, Johannes Stroebel, et al., "Social Capital II: Determinants of Economic Connectedness," *Nature*, published online, August 1, 2022, nature.com/articles/s41586-022-04997-3.pdf.
41 Debra Kamin, "Remote Appraisal of Homes Could Reduce Racial Bias," *New York Times*, March 22, 2022, B5.
42 Michelle Alexander, "Opinion: In Prison Reform, Money Trumps Civil Rights," *New York Times*, May 15, 2011, Wk9.
43 Vanessa Williamson, "Closing the Racial Wealth Gap Requires Heavy, Progressive Taxation of Wealth," Brookings Institution, December 9, 2020, 2, 12–13.
44 Daniel Markovits, "We Need to Tax Wealth," *Time*, May 10–17, 2021, 27–28.
45 Markovits, "We Need to Tax Wealth," 2–3.
46 Markovits, "We Need to Tax Wealth," 260–263. See also Darity, "The True Cost," Wk3; William Darity, A. Kirsten Mullen, and Lucas Hubbard, *The Black Reparations Project: Handbook for Racial Justice* (Oakland, CA: University of California Press, 2023).
47 See Eddie S. Glaude, Jr., *Begin Again: James Baldwin's America and Its Urgent Lessons for Our Own* (New York: Crown Books, 2020), 204.
48 Nicholas Fandos, "Committee Set to Advance Bill on Slavery Reparations," *New York Times*, April 15, 2021, A17.
49 Jones, *White Too Long*, 225.
50 Williamson, "Closing the Racial Wealth Gap," 5.
51 William A. Darity, Jr., and A. Kirsten Mullen, *From Here to Equality: Reparations for Black Americans in the Twenty-First Century* (Chapel Hill, NC: University of North Carolina Press, 2020), 27, 244.
52 Ben Steverman and Alex Tanzi, "A Less Unequal America," *BusinessWeek*, June 13, 2022, 26–29.

INDEX

The 1619 Project 35, 165, 256
Adams, John 67
Adams, John Quincy 67, 166
affirmative action programs xxi, 108, 113, 154–155, 157, 290, 292, 298–299
Afghanistan withdrawal xviii
Agassiz, Louis 76, 262
Age of Discovery 6
agriculture 30, 34, 137, 196–197; farm ownership 230; income and wealth 162–164, 168, 172, 188–189
Akbar, Prottoy 238
Alexander, Michelle 256, 268–269, 284, 295
Allwright, S. E. 79
American Anti-Slavery Society 70
American Bankers Association 188, 236
American Bar Association (ABA) 277
American Civil Liberties Union (ACLU) 271
American Community Survey 43
American First Legal 189
American Medical Association (AMA) 216, 218
American National Election Studies 108
American Political Science Association (APSA) 215
American Revolution 8, 11, 16, 67, 163, 198, 285

Anderson, Benedict 100–101
Anti-Defamation League's Center on Extremism 112
anti-lynching legislation 79
Asians xvi, 1, 19; Census 43, 46–47; in Congress 89; COVID 216, 220; education 152, 153; health insurance 214–215; home ownership 244–245; immigration 53–54; intermarriage 59; party preference 85; voter registration 81; voter turnout 82–83
asylum 53
Atlanta 228
Atwater, Lee 87
Austen, Ralph 3
Aziz, Muhammad A. 275
Azzimonti, Marina 88

baby bonds 294
Bailyn, Bernard 285
Baldus, David 273–274
Baldwin, James xv, xvi, xx, 104–105, 112
Banneker, Benjamin xix, 103
Barlett, Donald 288
Bartley, Numan V. 52
Bassett, Mary 218–219
Bauchner, Howard 218
Bayer, Patrick 178–179, 269–270
Bazile, Leon M. 106

Bell, Daniel 114
Bell, Derrick xx
beloved community 100–101
Bennett, Lerone Jr 4
Biden, Joe xviii–xix, 7, 88, 92, 124, 155, 188, 220, 295
birth rates *see* fertility rates
"Black Codes" 76, 168, 256, 259–260
Black Lives Matter (BLM) xix, 120–121
Black Wall Street xxi, 274
Blackmon, Douglas A. 18, 77, 118, 256
Blight, David W. 13–14, 70
Blumenbach, Johann Friedrich 9–10
Bonilla-Silva, Eduardo 20, 185
Boustan, Leah Platt 177, 243
Boyd, John 188–189
Boylston, Zabdiel 198
Bradley, Joseph P. 76, 87
Brookings Institution 187, 287, 296
Brooks, David xvii
Brown, Dorothy A. 173–174
Brown, John 166–167
Brown, Michael 108, 119, 120
Brown v. Board of Education 84, 107, 133, 143, 144–145, 299
Bruce, Blanche K. 74
Bruni, Frank 153
Bryan, Guy Morrison 15
Buchanan, James 71, 179
Buchanan v Warley 237
Buckhead 228
Buckley, William F. 84–85
Bullard, Robert 248
Bunche, Ralph 19
Bureau of Labor Statistics 154, 180
Burr, Aaron 283
Bush, George H. W. 87
Butler, Paul 276
Byrd, James 261

capitalism 5, 17, 179
Capitol storming xvii, xviii, 88, 112, 284, 286
Carnegie Corporation 19
Carnevale, Anthony 177, 287
Carney, Tim 288
Carson, Scott Alan 202
Carter, Robert "King" 198
Cashin, Sheryll 6–7, 23, 147, 152, 243
Census 41–48, 54, 58, 72, 138, 142

Center for Disease Control (CDC) 220
Center for Investigative Reporting 247
Charles, Kerwin Kofi 178–179, 269–270
Charlottesville march 48, 112, 284
Chase, Salmon P. 258
Chauvin, Derek 119, 275, 295
Chávez, Dennis 89
Chemerinsky, Erwin 270, 276
Cheney, Liz 284
Chetty, Raj 185
children: baby bonds 294; malnutrition 201–202; mortality 199, 200–201, 206, 207, 210–211
Chinese xix, 40, 216; Census 43; intermarriage 57
Chinese Exclusion Act 40
Cincinnati 229–230
citizenship 65–99, 259, 291
City of Los Angeles v. Lyons 277
Civil Rights Acts 53, 73–74, 285; 1875 16, 76; 1957 84, 241; 1964 20, 85, 107, 133, 177; 1965 20, 85, 107, 133; opinion polls 112
Civil Rights Cases of 1883 76, 87, 237
Civil Rights Era 85–87, 143–148
Civil Rights movement 8, 11, 19–20, 53, 267, 276, 285
Civil Rights Revolution 42, 52–53, 85, 109, 133
Civil War xxi, 8, 11–16, 38–39, 48, 133, 285; citizenship and suffrage 72–77; health 202, 204; income and wealth 164–165, 172; infection control 202; land 230, *see also* Reconstruction
Clark, Kenneth B. 179, 236
Clark, Tom 240
Clinton, Bill 90–91
Coates, Ta-Nehisi 122
colleges 132, 142, 148–152; graduation rates 153–154
Collins, Francis 21–22
Collins, William 140, 170, 172–173, 177, 184–185, 241–242
colonialism 5
colorblind society 21, 23
Colored National Convention xix–xx
Columbus, Christopher 30–33
Commission on Civil Rights 241

Commission on Higher Education for American Democracy 142
Confederation Congress 134
Constitution xvi–xvii, xxi, 12, 14, 38, 73, 285; Census 41; Eighth Amendment 273, 274; electoral rules 68; Thirteen to Fifteen Amendments 16, 73–76, 78–79, 106, 140, 145, 154, 237, 240, 258–259, 273–274
Constitutional Convention xvii, 67, 282
Conyers, John 121, 297
Corbitt, Amy 277
Corbitt v *Vickers* 277
Cornerstone Speech 12
Cornwallis, Charles 198
Corrigan v *Buckley* 237
Corson, Eugene R. 204
Cortés, Hernan 31, 34, 35
COVID-19 pandemic 148, 153, 187, 207–208, 216, 218, 219–220, 293, 298
Creighton, Brandon 156
Crèvecoeur, J. Hector St John de 197
Crick, Francis 21
criminal justice system 255–281, 284, 295–296, *see also* death penalty; lynching; police; prisons
critical race theory (CRT) xx, 156–157
Crosby, Alfred 30
Crowley, James 124
Cumming v. *Richmond County Board of Education* 139–140
Current Population Survey 180
Curry, Jabez 141
Curtis, Benjamin 71–72

da Gama, Vasco 31
Darity, William A. 122, 163–164, 179, 293–294, 296–297
Darwin, Charles 16, 76
Davis, Hugh 38
Davis, John W. 144–145
Dawson, Michael 17, 21, 164, 259, 265, 271
Dawson, William 89
deannexation referendum 228
death penalty 267, 271–274
Death Penalty Information Center (DPIC) 271, 274

Death Registration Area (DRA) 206
Deaton, Angus 30
Declaration of Independence 100, 282, 285
demographic stability 29–64
Denton, Nancy 229, 232, 233
DePriest, Oscar 89
Derenoncourt, Ellora 166, 186
Desmond, Matthew 165
DiAngelo, Robin 21, 22, 267–268
Dickson Mounds 197
Dies, Martin 174
disease 196–199, 206; Native Americans 30–31, 34, 35–36, *see also* health
dissimilarity index 231–236
DiTomaso, Nancy 114
Diversity and Disparities project 233
Douglas, Stephen A. 12, 13, 71–72
Douglass, Frederick xix–xx, 11, 13–14, 20, 29, 65, 70, 73, 79, 102–103, 104, 164, 165–166, 169–170, 228, 258, 282
Downs, Jim 203
Dred Scott v. *Sandford* 71–72
Driver, Justin 145
Du Bois, W. E. B. xx, 11, 49, 53, 58, 100, 102–103, 104–105, 149, 155, 161, 163–164, 170, 178, 204–205, 221, 249, 255, 290, 294

Easterlin, Richard 172
Economic Policy Institute 177, 230
education 132–160, 189, 291–292; graduation rates 143, 152, 153–154; opinion polls 117–118, 145, 147–148; salaries 141, 142; segregated schools 135, 144–145, 147–148
Egypt 2, 3, 30
Einstein, Albert 19
Eisenhower, Dwight D. 144–145
elected officials 89–94
electoral reform 290–291
Elementary and Secondary Education Act 1965 133, 146–147
Eltis, David 37
Emancipation Proclamation 13, 16, 39, 73
Emerson, Ralph Waldo 48–49
Enforcement Act 1870 75
Engerman, Stanley 3, 170, 257

environmental racism 248–249
Equal Employment Opportunity Commission (EEOC) 293
Equal Justice Initiative 260
"Espy File" 271
Espy, M. Watt 271
Ethridge, Robbie 36
eugenics 17, 18
Ewbank, Douglas 205–207

Fair Housing Act 1968 20, 85, 107, 246, 285
family 228–230
Feagin, Joe 5, 7, 35, 107, 163, 177
Federal Convention 1787 134
Federal Housing Administration (FHA) 239, 241
Federal Reserve Bank 88, 154, 186–187, 243
fertility rates 54–55
First Founding 8, 16, *see also* American Revolution
Fisher, Dana R. 120
Fitzgerald, F. Scott 18
Fligstein, Neil 173
Floyd, George 108, 112, 119, 120, 126–127, 275, 295, 298
flu 197, 206, 207, 209, 219
Fogel, Robert 3, 170, 201–202, 257
Foley, Neil 40, 42
Food and Drug Administration (FDA) 207, 212
Food, Drug, and Cosmetic Act 1938 207
Foucault, Michael 255
Fourth of July 111–112
Francis, Megan 17, 21, 259, 271
Franklin, Benjamin xvii, 54, 282
Frazier, E. Franklin 19, 58
Free Soil party 70
Freedmen's Bureau 137, 149, 196, 203–204
Freedmen's hospitals 203–204
freedom principle 257, 258
Friedman, Milton 179
Fugitive Slave Act 1850 258
Furman v *Georgia* 273

G. I. Bill 1944 149, 239
Galea, Sandro 220–221
Garcia, Chris 53
Garfield, James A. 75

Garner, Eric 120
Garrett, Shaylyn Romney 287–288
Gates, Henry Louis Jr 15, 74, 79, 124, 137
genetics 21–22
George III, King 36
germ theory 206
gerrymandering 87, 291
Gest, Justin 114
ghettos 221, 231–236, 246, 249
Glaude, Eddie S. Jr xxii, 7, 112, 267
Gold Rush 40, 43
Goldin, Claudia 150, 177
Goldwater, Barry 86
González, Henry B. 89
grade schools 132
Grant, Madison 18
Grant, Ulysses S. 66
great compression 177
Great Depression 18–19, 52, 84, 132, 173–174, 209, 216, 238–239, 241
Great Dying 31–36
Great Migration 50–52, 231
Great Recession 92
Great Society xxi, 20, 80, 85, 184, 212
Greeley, Horace 13
Greenspan, Alan 179
Greenwald, Anthony 114
Gregg v *Georgia* 273
Gross, Neil 270
Grove Impact 246
Grovey v. *Townsend* 78, 79
Gusfield, Joseph 114

Hahn, Robert A. 212
Hale, Edward Everett 168
Haller, John 11–12, 73
Hamer, Fannie Lou 216
Hammond, James Henry 257
Hammurabi, King 2
Harding, Warren G. 237
Hariot, Thomas 197
Harlan, John Marshall 76, 140
Harris, Kamala 91, 92
Harrison, William Henry 67
Hart-Celler Act *see* Immigration and Nationality Act of 1965
Hastie, William H. 78, 79, 240
Hayer, Talmadge 275
Hayes, Rutherford B. 15–16
health 195–225, 284, 294; infection control 202; insurance 214–215,

294–295; malnutrition 201–202; medical experiments 216–217; medicine mistrust 215–219, *see also* disease
Heaney, Michael T. 120
Heflin, Howell T. 139
Heflin, J. Thomas 'Cotton Tom' 139
Helper, Hinton Rowan 134
Hernandez, Joseph 74
Herndon, C. C. 78
Hersh, Ken xvi
high schools 132–133, 134, 137, 139–140; graduation rates 143, 152
Higher Education Act 1965 149
Hill-Burton Hospital Survey and Construction Act 212
Hine, Darlene Clark 74, 77, 173
Hinton, Elizabeth 267
Hispanics xvi, 1, 19, 32; affirmative action 113; Census 42–43, 46–47; in Congress 74, 89; COVID 220; education 152, 153, 154–155; elected officials 89; fertility rate 54; health insurance 214–215; home ownership 244–245, 247; immigration 53; income and wealth 161, 175–176, 177, 182–187, 189, 292; intermarriage 58–59; lynching 262; opinion polls 108–110, 116, 117–118, 119, 121, 126; party preference 85; police stops 270–271; police violence 275–276; prison 264, 265–266, 268, 270; voter registration 81; voter turnout 82–83
Holmes, Oliver Wendell 78
Home Mortgage Disclosure Act 247
Home Owners' Loan Corporation (HOLC) 239
Homestead Act 1862 230
Hoover, Herbert 237
housing 221, 226–254, 295; ghettos 221, 231–236, 246, 249; opinion polls 118; ownership 241–246, 295; restrictive covenants 236, 237, 240; VA loans 239; voucher program 295
Howard, O. O. 203
HR 40 121, 297
Hughes, Langston 1
Hume, David 9

Humphrey, William 135
Hurston, Zora Neale 59
Hutchinson, Anne 35

illiteracy 137–139, 141
imagined communities 100–101
immigration 38, 48–59
Immigration Act 20, 49
Immigration and Nationality Act 1952 38
Immigration and Nationality Act 1965 53
Imperial Sugar plantations 259–260
in-group favoritism 114–115
income and wealth 161–194, 292–294, 296–297; education level 154; home ownership 244–246; minimum wage 174, 293; unemployment rates 183, 189; wage transparency 293
Individual Retirement Account (IRA) 294
individualism 103, 203, 204
infanticide 3
"Initiative for a Competitive Inner City" 246
Innocence Project 275
institutionalization 269–270
insurance 214–215, 294–295
interracial marriage 57–59, 69, 72, 105–107
Irish Catholics 40
Islam, Khalil 275
isolation index 231–232

Jackson, Andrew 66
Jackson Lee, Sheila 121, 297
Jardina, Ashley 58, 112, 114–115
Jefferson, Thomas xix, 9, 10–11, 36, 66, 100, 101, 111, 139, 198–199, 285
Jeter, Mildred 105–106
Jim Crow segregation xx–xxi, 1, 7, 16–19, 20, 39, 77, 92, 141–142, 156–157, 263, 266–267; housing 236; income and wealth 161, 167–172, 173; reparations 289, 296–297; social control 255–256, 277
jobs: labor force participation 180–182; minimum wage 174, 293; opportunities 116–117; technology 186, *see also* income and wealth

Johnson, Andrew 203
Johnson, Lyndon B. xxi, 20, 80, 84, 85, 86, 146, 149, 169, 184, 212
Johnson, Steven 209
Johnston, Parke 170
Jones, Robert P. 284

Kaepernick, Colin 111
Kalleberg, Arne 289
Kant, Immanuel 9
Katz, Lawrence F. 150
Kazin, Michael 103
Kefauver-Harris Drug Amendments 212
Kendi, Ibram X. 4–5, 7, 239, 263–264
Kennedy, John F. 20, 85, 86, 145–146, 212
Kennedy, Robert 85, 267
King, Desmond 7, 21, 87, 236, 237, 241, 262, 290
King, Martin Luther xx, 20, 85, 100–101, 103, 104–105, 120, 195
Knights of the White Camelia 261
Know Nothing party 54, 70
Koch, Alexander 34–35
Kraus, Michael W. xxii
Ku Klux Klan 240, 260–261

Land Acts 230
Land Grant College Act 132
leasing convicts 259–260
Lee, Alice 200
Levitsky, Steven 286
Lewis, David Levering 16, 37, 51, 139, 141
Lewis, John 66
Li, Sijie 238
Lieberson, Stanley 233
life expectancy 199–201, 205–215, 220; children 199, 200–201, 206, 207, 210–211; slaves 199, 200–201
Lincoln, Abraham 12–13, 14, 71–72, 73, 75, 83, 101, 132, 167, 200, 228–229, 258, 283, 289
Lindert, Peter 162, 167, 173
"linked-fate" hypothesis 164, 265
Linnaeus, Carl 9
Lipset, Seymour Martin 114
Litwack, Leon 202
Livingston, Edward 218
loan forgiveness program 188–189

Logan, Trevon 232–233
Long, Heather 154
Long, Huey 283
Long, Kevin 287
López, Ian Haney 115, 271, 290
Lovejoy, Paul 3–4, 37
Loving, Richard 105–106
Loving v. *Virginia* 58, 106–107
lynching 79, 256, 260–263, 273, 274, 277

McAdam, Doug 120
McCarthy, Joseph 283
McClain, Paula D. 215
McCleskey v *Kemp* 273–274
McConnell, Mitch 297
McGhee, Heather 34, 150, 288
McGhee v *Sipes* 240
McGovern, George 86
McLean, Ian 172
Madison, James 66
Magellan, Ferdinand 6, 35
Malcolm X 274–275
malnutrition 201–202
Mansfield, Lord 257
Marceau, Justin 274
Margo, Robert 140, 142, 170, 177, 185, 231, 241–242
Markovits, Daniel 296
Marquart, James M. 274
marriage deficit 59
Marshall, Thurgood 78, 79, 144, 240
Martin, Trayvon 112, 120
Mason-Dixon line 52, 141
Mass Immigration 48–54
mass shootings xviii, 48, 284
Massachusetts Bay Colony 8, 197
Massey, Douglas 229, 232, 233
Masur, Kate 11
Mather, Cotton 198
Matthew, Dayna Bowen 199, 217
Mayer, Jeremy 114
Medicaid 196, 212, 213, 294, 299
medical schools 179
Medicare 196, 212, 213, 294
Meharry Medical College 179
Mettler, Suzanne 150, 151, 153
Metzl, Jonathan M. 284
Mexico 30–31, 34–35, 53, 197, 216; Mexican-American War 74;

Revolution 42; Texas 39–40, 260; wall 46, 54
Micheletti, Steven 57
migration 230–231; education correlation 139; Great Migration 50–52, 231, *see also* immigration
Miles, Tiya 35–36
military service 11, 13, 39, 52, 67, 69, 73, 240; education 141–142; G. I. Bill 1944 149, 239; infection control 202; pay 166
Miller, John Fulenwider 77
Miller, Stephen 189
Milliken v *Bradley* 147
minimum wage 174, 293
miscegenation 57, 72
Mississippi Plan 77
Mitchell, Arthur 89
Mitchener, Kris 172
Molina, Natalia 40, 215–216
Monroe, James 66
Montagu, Mary 198
Moore, Wes 93
Morgan, Hera 58
Morrill Land Grant College Act 1862 149
Morris, Ian 30
mortgages 239, 241, 247–248
Moynihan, Daniel Patrick 20
Mullen, A. Kirsten 122, 163–164, 179, 296–297
Myrdal, Gunnar 19, 145, 240

Nackenoff, Carol 40
Nation of Islam 275
National Association for the Advancement of Colored People (NAACP) 77–79, 80, 237, 240, 260
National Association of Home Builders 236
National Association of Real Estate Boards 236
National Association of Realtors 236
National Defense Education Act 1958 149
National Education Association (NEA) 141–142
National Housing Act 1934 239
national identity 112
National Institutes of Health (NIH) 219

National Vital Statistics System (NVSS) 275–276
Native Americans xvi, 1, 8, 19, 30–35, 197–198, 276
NATO xviii
natural rights 11
natural selection 16–17, 21, 22
Naturalization Act 38
Ndulue, Ngozi 274
Negro Academy xx
neoliberalism 22, 179–180
New Deal 66, 79, 85
Newsom, Gavin 122
Newton, Huey P. 267
Nixon, Lawrence A. 78
Nixon, Richard 80, 86, 179, 299
Nixon v. *Herndon* 78
Northwest Ordinance 134, 230
nostalgic deprivation 114
Novkov, Julie 40
Nunez-Smith, Marcella 220–221

Obama, Barack 80–81, 88, 91–93, 108, 119, 123–126, 297
Obamacare 196, 214–215, 294
Omi, Michael 5, 6, 7, 20, 247, 268, 269
"one drop" rule 42, 57
O'Neil, Robert M. 155
Onwenu, Justin 249
opinion polls 101–102, 106–111, 112–113; education 117–118, 145, 147–148; interracial marriage 105, 106–107; Obama's presidency 123–126; public policy 115–123; Trump's presidency 126–127

Packer, George 152
Parman, John 232–233
partisan conflict index 88
partisan polarization 87–89
Pearson, Jay 219
Pell Grants 149, 150–151, 292, 293
Pennock, Caroline Dodds 34
peonage 168
Perkinson, Robert 203
Peterson, Paul 227
Pettigrew, Thomas 114
Pew Research Center 43, 59, 89, 107, 116, 117, 120
Philadelphia Convention xvii, 282

Phillips, Kevin 86
Phillips, Scott 274
Pierson v *Ray* 276
pilgrims: landing 8
Pinchback, Pinckney 74
Pizarro, Francisco 35
Plessy v *Ferguson* 140, 144, 237
police 267–268, 270–271, 295; early 256–257; opinion polls 118–121; qualified immunity 276–277; violence 119, 274–277, 295–296, *see also* Floyd, George
Potkin, Vanessa 275
poverty 184, 203, 269, 299; environmental racism 248–249, *see also* income and wealth
Powell, Lewis 87
prisons 118–119, 202, 216, 263–264, 295; convict leasing 259–260; mass incarceration 118, 255–256, 264–271, 277, 295
private education 133, 134
public policy 115–123
Pugh, Tony 247
Pulaski, Charles 274
Putnam, Robert 74, 287–288

Quadagno, Jill 212–213
qualified immunity 276–277

race riots 20, 51–52, 229–230, 267
racial hierarchy 1, 6, 10, 11, 15, 17, 19, 43, 58–59, 67, 256, 260, 277, 284, 298; American mind 101, 105, 115; death penalty 274; education 153, 156; health 200, 220
Racial Integrity Act 1924 105
racial orders 1–28, 65, 112
racial regimes 7–8, 65–66
Raffensperger, Brad 284
Rank, Mark Robert 185–186, 268, 288
Ransom, Roger 134, 167, 169, 171
Rappeport, Alan 188
Reagan, Ronald 86, 108, 179
Reconstruction 8, 11, 14–16; health 204; income and wealth 167–172, 173, *see also* Civil War
redlining 246, 247, 249
Reed, Stanley F. 79
religion 9, 12
Reny, Tyler 114

replacement theory 48
"Report to the President on the Economic Condition of the South" 174
restrictive covenants 236, 237, 240
Revels, Hiram 74
Richardson, David 37
Roanoke Colony 162, 197
Roberts, Charles A. 172
Roberts, John 147
Roberts, Owen 78, 79
Robinson, Donald xv
Robinson v *California* 273
Robison, Clay 156
Roediger, David R. 19, 233, 262
Roman Empire xvi–xvii, 3
Roosevelt, Eleanor 79
Roosevelt, Franklin D. 79–80, 83, 85, 174, 207, 238–239
Roosevelt, Theodore 200
Roper polling organization 54
Rothstein, Richard 177, 230, 236–237, 248
Roybal, Edward R. 89
Russia: Ukraine invasion xviii

Sadtler, Kaitlyn 219
Sanchez, Gabriel 53
Sandel, Michael 151, 153, 185, 292–293
Sander, Richard 233
Scott, Dred 71, 258
Scott, Tim 94
Second Founding 8, 16, *see also* Civil War
sectoral policy reforms 289
Segregation Index 147
Sellin, Johan Thorsten 265
Servicemen's Readjustment Act *see* G. I. Bill 1944
Shaler, Nathaniel Southgate 262–263
Sharp, Granville 257
shatter zone 36
Shelley, J. D. 240
Shelley v *Kraemer* 240–241
Shertzer, Allison 238
shipyards 165
Sides, John 188
Siegel Family Endowment 246
Simkins v. *Moses H. Cone Memorial Hospital* 213
Sims, James Marion 216

Skelton, Martha Wayles 198–199
slavery xxi, 1, 2–5, 8–11, 12–15, 92, 94, 118, 266–267; abolition 8, 68; Census 41–42, 47; Cornerstone Speech 12; criminal justice system 256–258; education 134; families 228–229; health 203; income and wealth 162–169, 171–172; Lincoln 12–13; longevity 199, 200–201; malnutrition 201–202; medical experiments 216; New Nation 38–41; presidents' slaves 66–67; reparations 121–123, 289, 296–297; social control 255–256, 277; suffrage 70–72, 76–77; Thirteenth Amendment 76; three-fifths compromise 67; trade to Americas 36–38; variolation 198
smallpox 198, 200
Smith, Lonnie 79
Smith, Rogers 7, 21, 87, 236, 237, 241, 262, 290
Smith v. *Allwright* 78, 79, 80, 83, 94
Smykla, John Ortiz 271
social competition 132–160
social control 118, 255–256, 259–267, 273, 277; "Black Codes" 76, 168, 256, 259–260; lynching 79, 256, 260–263, 273, 274, 277, *see also* criminal justice system; Jim Crow segregation; slavery
social Darwinism 17–18, 21–22, 169, 203, 289
social justice 53, 282–302
social security 294
Somerset, James 257
Somerset v *Stewart* 257
Soto, Hernando de 35
Spear, Samuel T. 102
Spencer, Herbert 18, 22, 137
Stanton, Edwin 200
status politics 114
Steckel, Richard H. 202
Steele, James 288
Stephens, Alexander H. 12
Sterner, Richard 19
Stevens, Jon 189
Stevens, Thaddeus 14–15, 111, 169
Stevenson, Bryan 256
Stewart, Charles 257
Stiglitz, Joseph 289
Stoddard, Lothrop 18

Storey, Moorfield 78
Stovall, Tyler 53
stratification economics 185
strikes 52
structural racism 186, 217–221, 246, 289
suffrage xxi, 8, 16, 65–99; voter registration 80–81, 85, 87; voter turnout 82–85, 91
sugar plantations 259–260
Sumner, William Graham 18, 22, 137
Survey of Consumer Finances 186, 243, 297
Sutch, Richard 134, 167, 169, 171
syphilis 216–217

Taibbi, Matt 268–269
Taney, Roger B. 71–72, 258
Tapia, Ruby 255
taxation 41, 140, 296
Taylor, Chandra 249
Taylor, Zachary 66–67
technology jobs 186
Tessum, Christopher 249
Texas 39–40, 42, 78–79, 89, 156, 202, 259–261, 262
thalidomide scandal 212
Third Founding 8, 20, *see also* Civil Rights movement
three-fifths compromise 67
Tobriner, Mathew xxi–xxii
Tocqueville, Alexis de 36, 134, 197
Trans-Atlantic Slave Trade Database 37
transport segregation 140
Traub, Amy 288
Treaty of Guadalupe Hidalgo 40
Truman, Harry S. 80, 84, 85, 142, 240
Trumbull, Lyman 14, 71, 258
Trump, Donald 88–89, 119, 123, 126–127, 188, 216, 283–284, 286, 290
Turnbull, Malcolm xviii
Tuskegee Institute 216–217, 294
Twilight, Alexander 148

Ukraine: Russian invasion xviii
unemployment rates 183, 189, 269
United States Building and Loan League 236

United States v *Reece* 75
universities 133, 137, 148, 151, 153–156

vaccination 198, 200, 218, 219–220
Van Buren, Martin 66–67, 69
Van Dam, Andrew 154
Van Gosse 11, 165–166, 285
Vance, Cyrus R. 275
variolation 198
Vaughn, George L. 226
Venter, J. Craig 22
Veterans Administration (VA) 239, 241
Vickers, Michael 277
Villarosa, Linda 209–210
Virginia Company 36
Virginia General Assembly 38
Voltaire 9
voter registration 80–81, 85, 87
voter turnout 82–85, 91
Voting Rights Act 1965 20, 80, 85, 94, 285
voting-age population (VAP) 80

Waite, Morrison 75
Walker, Francis Amasa 48
Wallace, George Corley 86, 127, 283
Walsh, Randall 238
Wanamaker, Marianne 172–173, 177, 184–185
Warren Court 276
Warren, Earl 144–145
Warren, Robert Penn 104
Washington, Booker T. 103, 132, 136, 216
Washington, George 11, 66, 198, 199, 283
Watson, James 21
Watts, Edward J. xvii
Watts riot 267
Weber, Max 115–116

white flight 238
White, George Henry 89
White Lion 8–9, 37
white supremacy xv–xvi, xix, xx, 2, 6, 23, 39, 57, 77, 86, 260–261, 263, 277, 284–286; Census 43; Cornerstone Speech 12; Fourth of July 111–112; mass shootings xviii, 48, 284; social Darwinism 18; Southern Strategy 21
Whitman, Walt 75
Wilkerson, Isabel 22, 51, 57, 88
Williams, David R. 58
Williams, Roger 35
Williamson, Jeffrey 162, 167, 173
Williamson, Vanessa 287, 296
Wilson, Thomas Woodrow 135–136, 162–163
Winant, Howard 5, 6, 7, 20, 247, 268, 269
Winthrop, John 35
women: childbearing 54–55, 198–199; labor force participation 181–182; life expectancy 208–209; maternal deaths 210–211; medical experiments 216
Woodard, Colin 34
Woodard, David 74
Woodson, Carter G. 104
Woodward, C. Vann 15, 170
Woodworth, George 274
World War II 52, 141, 177, 209
Wright, Gavin 52, 170
Wright, Rev. Jeremiah 70–71, 92–93

Xi, Wang 66

Yeardley, George 37

Ziblatt, Daniel 286
Zimmerman, George 120
zoning laws 237, 248–249, 295

Printed in the United States
by Baker & Taylor Publisher Services